A Neighbor Among Neighbors:

Erie Neighborhood House
150 Years as a Home with No Borders

by Maureen Hellwig

A Neighbor Among Neighbors:

Erie Neighborhood House
150 Years as a Home with No Borders

by Maureen Hellwig

To all the friends of Erie Neighborhood House whose dedicated service
and gifts have brought new hope and a new way of life
to those we call neighbors.

To all who believe that "a fence at the edge of the abyss is
better than an ambulance at the foot."

- Rev. J.W.G. Ward, First Presbyterian Church of Oak Park,
Forward to *Neighbors* by Florence Towne

Acknowledgments

As a first-time author, I prepared myself to write my own "Acknowledgments" essay by reviewing what other authors I respected had written. In that process, a flood of awareness rolled over me as I came to realize just how many individuals and institutions I needed to thank. Because, to tell the true story, the good piece of writing that every author works toward is definitely influenced by many factors that happened long before the specific writing journey began.

Some authors thank their parents, and I must do the same. While neither Pat or Phil Hellwig were still alive when I started writing this book, I want to acknowledge that my earliest interest in history must be attributed to my father. While he was unable to finish high school at Lane Tech, due to the impact of the Great Depression on his family and his need to work, his love of reading took his education well beyond a college degree. His reading immersed him in histories of the Civil War, and the family on vacations trekking around Civil War battlefields. His personal life experience provided stories at the dinner table comparing the failure of Herbert Hoover to lead America out of the Depression with FDR's New Deal leadership. My mother preferred Agatha Christie mysteries, but the point is that reading was big at my house, for both knowledge and entertainment. And as any English teacher will tell you, good writing has its source in good reading.

Building on this example from my parents, I was blessed with a K-16 education by teachers who stressed both reading and writing, from elementary school through college. Most of these teachers were members of the School Sisters of St. Francis. From 5th grade on we wrote all the time--at St. Matthias Grade school and Alvernia High School in Chicago--so that my English 101 teacher in college commented on how fortunate I was that I already knew how to write. I also developed a further love of history, with the unusual opportunity in high school (1959-63) to take classes in Latin American history and 20th century US History, in an era when most US history classes ended with the close of World War II. But Alvernia High School did much more than sharpen my writing skills and expand my interest in history. Because it was an all-girls school, I was encouraged to find my voice as a woman, and I found a lifelong mentor in my sociology teacher, Ann Seng. She introduced me to issues of social justice then, and later in life, made me a fan of Jane Addams and the social settlement movement, encouraged my respect for the profession of community organizing, gave me my first settlement job at Uptown Center Hull House in the 1970s, and referred me to Rafael Ravelo for my first job at Erie Neighborhood House.

The School Sisters were there again, at Alverno College, where the chair of the history department was Sister Joel Read, one of the co-founders of the local chapter of NOW, who went on to serve as president of the college for many years. She made "Western Civ" come alive with such comments as "You realize, don't you, that 'the Greeks' did not know that they were 'THE GREEKS.'" Here at this Catholic women's college in 1966 I was able to take classes in Russian History and Marxist philosophy at the same time, followed by a class in 20th Century *avant-garde* thinking taught by the former Socialist Mayor of Milwaukee, Frank Zeidler.

Coming back to Chicago after college, my first teaching assignment was at Santa Maria Addolorata School. From there one could walk across Ohio Street, through a parking lot, and arrive at the back door of Erie Neighborhood House (ENH). You can read the story of the implications of that walk in this book. The principal, Sister Marian Dahlke, SSSF, did more than run the school. She was a role model for getting involved in the neighborhood and facilitated the beginning of my long association with Erie House, as a volunteer and an employee. This was the beginning of one

8

of those "beautiful friendships" Humphrey Bogart spoke of in the movie, *Casablanca.* And so, as Erie House was approaching its 150th year, and realizing I had been connected to this place for about 50 of those 150 years, I felt I was in as good a position as any to tell their story.

This brings me to all the gratitude I must express to those more directly involved in this labor of love. First, thanks to Ami Novoryta, previous Director of Development at ENH, who, with the assistance of Loyola intern, Rebecca Banks, rounded up all the boxes of paper from closets, under desks, and in the backs of file cabinets, that embodied the history of ENH, and donated them in 2004 to the Chicago History Museum. This wise move allowed me to spend a year of Fridays, when the Research Center was open all day, to work my way through the 14 manuscript boxes that held much of the content that made this book possible. A special thanks to the staff at the Research Center, especially Lesley Martin, who facilitated my work there and always had a word of encouragement to keep me going. My thanks to Erie staff members, Brian Paff and Rosalba Castrejon, who helped me find and organize five more boxes of material, accumulated since 2004, boxes that will soon be donated to CHM as well.

Next, I must acknowledge my good fortune in that six of the eight executive directors of Erie House are still alive and well, still feeling an attachment to Erie, and willing to share their Erie stories with me through in-person interviews, as well as reviewing chapters. Their leadership was such a key part of Erie's longevity and success that I structured the book around their administrations. After Florence Towne and Rev. Ross Lyman each spent 25 years at the head of the House, these leaders include: Merri Steinberg Ex, Rafael Ravelo, Esther Nieves, Ricardo Estrada, Celena Roldán, and Kirstin Chernawsky. I cannot thank them enough for their time and interest in this project, and for their contributions to the Erie House that shines in this text. And as noted many times throughout the book, Erie House would not have become "a legacy of excellence with a future of promise" if not for the dedicated Board members and church volunteers named in this book, with apologies to those whose names have slipped away over time. And let me specifically acknowledge the many church members, encouraged by the Mission Extension Board of the Presbytery of Chicago, who came to Erie Street because they heard the social gospel and took it seriously.

Finally, I want to acknowledge my editor, K. J. Wetherholt, who shepherded me through all of the final stages of polishing and publishing a book. I could not have done it without her.

But the very last word, must be a salute to the generations of immigrants, to their courage and determination to succeed. I thank them for their stories and the debt we owe to them for growing this country and this city.

Maureen Hellwig

Table of Contents

ABBREVIATIONS

ASM: After School Matters
ASN: Alternative Schools Network
BPI: Business & Professionals in the Public Interest
BRC: Bickerdike Redevelopment Corp.
CAAELII: Coalition of Asian, African, European and Latino Immigrants of Illinois
CABA: Chicago Ashland Business Association
CASA: Community Alliance for Strategic Action
CASL: Chinese American Service League
CATE: Community Action for Training and Education
CCAC: Chicago Central Area Committee
CCUA: The Chicago Council on Urban Affairs
CDBG: Community Development Block Grants
CDC: Community Development Corporation
CEB: Church Extension Board
CEPA: Center for Economic Policy Analysis
CHA: Chicago Housing Authority
CHM: Chicago History Museum
CIR: Comprehensive Immigration Reform
CJC: Chicago Jobs Council
CMA: Certified Medical Assistant
CMHN: Chicago Mutual Housing Network
CNA: Certified Nursing Assistant
CNC: Computerized Numerical Control
CNE: Chicago Neighborhood Experiment
CNLN: Chicago Neighborhood Learning Network
CNT: Center for Neighborhood Technology
COFI: Community Organizing for Family Issues
COPA: Conservation of Property Association
CPS: Chicago Public Schools
CRS: Community Renewal Society
CSPP: Chicago School of Professional Psychology
CURL: Center for Urban Research and Learning
DACA: Deferred Action for Childhood Arrivals
DAPA: Deferred Action for Parents of Americans
DCCA: Department of Commerce and Community Affairs (state)
DCEO: Department of Commerce and Economic Opportunity (new name for DCCA)
DCFH: Day Care Family Homes Network
DCFS: Department of Children & Family Services (state)
DCHO: Day Care Homes Online

DFSS: Department of Family Support Services (city)
DHS: Department of Human Services (state)
DOMA: Defense of Marriage Act
DREAM Act: Development, Relief and Education for Alien Minors
DUR: Department of Urban Renewal (City of Chicago)
ECI: Erie Chapel Institute
EECS: Erie Elementary Charter School
EFHC: Erie Family Health Center
EISJ: Erie Institute for Social Justice
ENH: Erie Neighborhood House
ESC: Executive Service Corps
ESL: English as a Second Language
ETC: Erie Technology Center
ETO: Efforts to Outcomes (software)
FHA: Federal Housing Administration
GED: General Educational Development (certificate)
HPVEC: Humboldt Park Vocational Education Center
IAFC: Illinois Action for Children
IAF: Industrial Areas Foundation
ICCB: Illinois Community College Board
ICIRR: Illinois Coalition for Immigrant and Refugee Rights
ICNC: Industrial Council of Northwest Chicago
IDHS: Illinois Department of Human Services
IDPL: Instituto del Progreso Latino
IFF: Illinois Facilities Fund
INS: Immigration & Naturalization Service (federal)
IQC: Illinois Quality Counts
ISBE: Illinois State Board of Education
KNLP: Kellogg National Leadership Program
KONC: Keep Our Neighborhood Clean
LDI: Leadership Development Institute
LSC: Local School Council
LV: Little Village
LVCDC: Little Village Community Development Corp.
LVIRC: Little Village Immigrant Resource Center
MALDEF: Mexican American Legal Defense & Education Fund
MCF: Marguerite Casey Foundation
MOW: Meal on Wheels
MVS: Mennonite Volunteer Service
NAEYC: National Association for the Education of the Young Child
NAI: New Americans Initiative
NCLR: National Council of La Raza
NCO: Northwest Community Organization

NCUEA: National Center for Urban Ethnic Affairs
NHS: Neighborhood Housing Services
NLEI: National Latino Education Institute
NNCC: Near Northwest Civic Committee
NNCS: Noble Network of Charter Schools
NPA: National Peoples Action
NUSH: Northwestern University Settlement House
OSC: Organization of Southwest Chicago
PASO: Proyecto de Acción de los Suburbios
PRAG: Policy Research Action Group
PSK: Project Smart Kid
PTP: Parent-to-Parent
PTS: Pathways to Success
RICI: Refugee & Immigrant Citizenship Initiative
ROI: Return on Investment
SDD: Senior Director of Development
SDP: Senior Director of Programs
SLIAG: State Legalization Impact Assistance Grants
SMA: Santa Maria Addolorata
SOS: Secretary of State-funded Literacy program
SSA: Social Service Administration (at the University of Chicago)
STEM: Science, Technology, Engineering, Math programs
SWOT: Strengths, Weaknesses, Opportunities, Threats analysis
TEAM: Tutoring to Educate for Aims and Motivation
TOP: Tenant Ownership Project
TWO: The Woodlawn Organization
UCC: United Church of Christ
UIC: University of Illinois Chicago
WIA: Workforce Investment Act
WTU: West Town United
YOU: Youth Options Unlimited
WIC: Women, Infants, Children (a government subsidized nutrition program)

Introduction

First, the story of Erie Neighborhood House (Erie House, or just Erie) is one that needs to be told, because few social service agencies in Chicago have survived 150 years; Erie reached that benchmark in 2020. This remarkable achievement raises the question: How is it that Erie and other settlement houses continue to be successful in the 21st century, based on a model rooted in the late 19th century?

Second, this study also needs to be written because Erie and other settlements have lived too long in the shadow of Hull House. There is no doubt that Jane Addams and Hull House had an enormous impact on Chicago and the nation, not only through the services it provided on Halsted Street, but also through its pioneering work in public policy, the field of the social sciences, and the profession of social work. In recognition of all of this there is even a hotel in Chicago today named the St. Jane, a nod to her huge and holy work. We know about all of this, partly, due to the genius of Jane Addams, the writer and publicist, and additionally, to the many scholars and practitioners that have analyzed and chronicled her life and work, over and over again. However, her work, and that of her contemporaries, like Graham Taylor, founder of Chicago Commons, inspired many more settlements to spring up in Chicago and cities throughout the US east of the Mississippi. Most of their stories exist only on agency websites. This book will correct that problem by telling one of their stories on a more prominent platform.

Third, to help in the creation of this narrative there is an extensive primary source record available in 14 manuscript boxes of Erie House materials archived at the Chicago History Museum, and other material in storage at Erie Neighborhood House. In addition, between volunteer work beginning in 1969, serving on the Board, and working there as an employee, the author writes from the perspective of about 50 years as a participant-observer.

Fourth, while much has been written about Chicago in the late 19th century, there are few in-depth histories that have shed light, in the form of a case study, on the long-term outcome of the efforts of a Protestant denomination that struggled to identify their mission in an emerging and rapidly changing urban environment. The Erie House story provides a lens for viewing this struggle that is connected to the Social Gospel movement and the later follow-up known as community organizing. It illustrates how one Protestant denomination, the Presbyterian Church in Chicago, through the work of its Mission Extension Board, addressed the challenge of supporting the needs of a growing inner-city immigrant population at the same time as its core membership was steadily locating outside the city and becoming increasingly more affluent. Furthermore, their affluence was often due to the contribution of the workforce that was now living where they used to live. The Erie House story introduces numerous small and large businessmen heroes and their heroine wives--people of faith--who dedicated themselves to helping Erie do the mission work that a sincere reading of the Gospel called for. Their names have not made the history books to date, but some of them should and will in this book.

The role of the Presbyterian Church in the Erie House story is especially pertinent due to the fact that the role of faith-based institutions in the settlement movement was controversial in some quarters. Some leaders in the settlement movement, such as Robert Woods in Boston, a co-founder of the National Federation of Settlements, banned church-affiliated neighborhood houses from membership in the National Federation, insisting that "pure" settlement work was humanitarian, but non-sectarian. In contrast, under the leadership of Addams, the Chicago Federation of Settlements had no such ban. The Erie House story is a case study of what Robert Woods missed by his definition of the movement.

Fifth, few other agencies provide observers a view of the ethnic "parade" of so many successive waves of different immigrant groups through the same neighborhood over such a long period of time. Erie traces its origins to the Holland Presbyterian Church and the Rev. Van Orden, ready to serve the Dutch immigrants, who touched down in Chicago in the earliest days of the city but quickly moved on. Research reveals how the Presbyterian church convention held in Chicago in the 1840s braced for the Norwegian onslaught that did not quite materialize on the grand scale anticipated. They moved fairly quickly past Erie Street to settle further west in Humboldt Park, leaving behind Norwegian American Hospital to remember them by. Then the Germans arrived and established St. Boniface Catholic Church just north of Erie House, and numerous Lutheran churches everywhere. The Poles, the Italians, the Puerto Ricans, and Mexicans followed – all Catholics. So, the Erie story is one of model ecumenism that evolved in Erie's neighborhood, as the Presbyterian church steadfastly continued to serve the mainly Catholic immigrants for these 150 years.

While much has been written about how it all began, much less has been offered about how the settlement houses have persevered, doing the impactful work – serving the poor and shaping public policy – that has continued for many years after Jane Addams's death in 1935, and even after the demise of Hull House in 2012. Addams's legacy is diminished by focusing only on Hull House and not the successor organizations that continue her work.

Since the "heyday" of the settlement movement in the Progressive Era leading up to World War I, settlement houses have continued to not only provide the kind of programs Hull House pioneered, but have also made unique contributions to help their urban neighbors.[1] For example, Erie House founded Erie Family Health Center in 1957, which has grown from a back room at 1347 W. Erie, to 13 clinics throughout the Chicagoland area.[2] In partnership with other community institutions, in 1967, Erie helped launch Bickerdike Redevelopment Corp.[3] that just marked its 50th anniversary, as one of the oldest, most successful developers of affordable housing in the country. In 1996, Erie opened one of the first community-based technology centers designed to serve low-income immigrants in Chicago, and in 2004, this settlement house launched the Erie Elementary Charter School in East Humboldt Park. This is just a brief sample of stories to be told. Indeed, there was and is life after Jane.

Finally, to really understand the longevity and success of Erie Neighborhood House, the contribution of its leaders, whether they are called "reverend," "head resident," or "executive director," must be told. There is not an extensive historical record to describe the work of the ministers and elders who envisioned service to immigrants as a Christian duty, the lay men and women who shared that vision and acted it out, or the dedicated professionals, from Florence Towne to Kirstin Chernawsky, who embraced the opportunity to lead Erie Neighborhood House, and contributed one astounding accomplishment after the other.

Therefore, it is the purpose of this book to tell the Erie story, not just due to its amazing longevity as an institution, but also, to provide insight into a living, breathing organization that has read the social gospel, understood its message, and effectively worked for social justice as its mission. Regardless of race or religion, the Erie House story holds a lesson for everyone on how to be of valuable service to humanity.

How the Story is Presented

Chapter One addresses the origins of Erie House, before there was such a thing as a "settlement house." This is the story of its earliest roots in the first Presbyterian churches in Chicago, and their efforts to define their mission

20

among the early immigrant groups to occupy the neighborhood that came to be the home of Erie Neighborhood House. The second chapter lays out the origins of what came to be known as a settlement house through the pioneering work of Jane Addams and Hull House in Chicago. The subsequent chapters, three through nine, are based on the leadership of each person who took the helm at Erie House during its long history.

These chapters follow the steps from church outreach to the installation of **Florence Towne** (1926-1951) as Head Resident in 1926. In Chapter Three, the rise of "Miss Florence," from kindergarten teacher to "Angel of the Alleys," marks the beginning of Erie's modern-day leadership.[4] While Florence was no Jane Addams in a public sector arena, there is no question that she held a revered position in the hearts of the residents of the neighborhood, personally touched by her over her 26 years as Head Resident.

Miss Towne was succeeded by a Presbyterian minister, the **Rev. Ross Lyman** (1952-1977) whose story unfolds in Chapter Four. While there were always ministers around Miss Florence, they focused on providing church services for the congregation of Erie Chapel. Certainly, many good men served in this role. Nevertheless, as one Erie participant from the 1930s and 40s put it, "On Sunday, after church services, two lines formed at the door. One line led to the minister and the other to Miss Florence. Her line was always longer." [5]

But Rev. Lyman brought a different tone to Erie House in 1952. He came from the East Coast, generally wore a 3-piece suit, and had a wife and two children. His very persona led to the change from "head resident" to "executive director." But his demeanor could be misleading. This was the man that brought Erie House to the world of Saul Alinsky,[6] and brought professional social workers and clinicians to Erie House, while continuing to be the presider at church services on Sundays. His collaboration with the Sisters at the Catholic school, just behind Erie House, in the 1960s, is a story worth telling as well.

After 25 years, Rev. Lyman, who later shared that he might have stayed too long, groomed a young protégée to take his place. Her name was Merri Steinberg, a Jewish woman in her 20's who spoke fluent Spanish, had come to Erie as a community organizer and left as an executive director and a married woman, now called **Merri Ex** (1977-1985) She presided at Erie from 1977 until 1985, as told in Chapter Five. Her Spanish language skills were important as those of European ethnicity were gradually being replaced, first by Puerto Ricans, and then Mexicans, in the Erie neighborhood, throughout West Town[7] and Humboldt Park.[8] (See Community Areas map. The park lies just between the West Town and Humboldt Park community areas.)

Merri was followed by Erie's first Latino director, **Rafael Ravelo** (1985-1997). This is Chapter Six. He was himself an immigrant, one of the "Peter Pan" children brought out of Cuba at the time of the Castro-led revolution. Under his leadership, Erie House expanded in size through the acquisition of a new building, and by growing its child care program from 40 to 185 children. He opened the Technology Center and collaborated with the Chicago Council on Urban Affairs in a research study and strategic plan called "The Chicago Neighborhood Experiment." Under his administration the sources of Erie's financial support moved beyond the Presbyterian churches to expanded United Way support, to foundation grant-writing, and larger and larger government contracts.

He was followed by **Esther Nieves** (1997-2003) a Puerto Rican woman who grew up in Humboldt Park as what she liked to call a "PK" or preacher's kid. Her leadership story is told in Chapter Seven. Before coming to Erie, she was active in promoting the contribution of women to Chicago, worked in philanthropy, and served as Executive

Director of Mayor Harold Washington's Commission on Latino Affairs. She worked with Ravelo as Erie's Associate Director, and then succeeded him in 1997 when he became ill.

In 2003, Nieves's Associate Director, **Ricardo Estrada** (2003-2010), succeeded her. Estrada, a Mexican immigrant, grew up in the Little Village area of Chicago. In many ways, his is the ultimate success story of an undocumented individual who gained citizenship through his US-born sister, in the 1990s, a path to citizenship that has since been cut off. He eventually earned advanced degrees from the University of Chicago and University of Illinois Chicago. He led the launch of Erie Elementary Charter School, led Erie to participate in many immigration reform marches, positioned Erie to influence the campaign for Dreamers, and took the work of Erie to the predominantly Mexican Little Village area of Chicago in 2004. His story is the narrative for Chapter Eight.

In Chapter Nine, we learn that in 2010, Estrada was succeeded by another Puerto Rican, Erie's Child Care Director, **Celena Roldán** (2010-2015). A second-generation Puerto Rican in the US, she came from a distinguished Chicago family – the daughter of Paul Roldán, founder of the highly regarded Hispanic Housing organization, and Dr. Ida Roldán, a successful clinical social worker and therapist with her own practice. Roldán was Executive Director until 2015, where this narrative will draw to a close, covering all but the last 5 years prior to its 150th anniversary in 2020.

As these chapters unfold, Chicago as context is another "character" in the story and is key to understanding the emergence of church-supported, immigrant-focused services, and the birth and growth of the settlement movement in the US. Immigrants + social gospel movement + settlement movement are the intertwining elements of the Erie story amidst the evolving metropolis of Chicago. For

150 years, Erie Neighborhood House and Chicago grew up together.

Chapter One: The Earliest Days: Just Before and Just After the Fire, 1870-1914

The Erie Mission Phase, 1870-1914

The origins of Erie Neighborhood House begin with the Holland Presbyterian Church, founded in 1870, 5 years after the Civil War ended, one year after the 207-acre Humboldt Park was established, and one year before the Great Chicago Fire of 1871. Ulysses S. Grant was president. Chicago was just 33 years old, having been declared a city in 1837. The church's existence was noted in Alfred T. Andreas's extensive history of Chicago.[9] The church opened its doors at the corner of Erie (650 north) and Noble (1400 west) --just a half block from the Erie House of today—on December 4, 1870. For those not familiar with the Chicago street numbering system, all addresses stand in relation to the intersection of State Street (that great street) and Madison Avenue (not as great as New York's of the same name). This intersection is far from being a central crossroads in the Chicago of today. In fact, it is in Chicago's downtown, just a few blocks west of Lake Michigan. So that means that the geographic origins of Erie House were just 6.5 blocks north (3/4 of a mile) and 14 blocks west (1 and 3/4 miles), or an easy walk, from what became the heart of downtown Chicago. Years later, when the Chicago Community Areas map was drawn, it became known as West Town. It was in the first ring of residential communities that grew up around the "Loop," a nickname based on the image of river and elevated transit tracks that encircled the central business district.

In 1870, Roswell B. Mason was mayor of Chicago, elected on the Citizens Party ticket in the 1869 election, where just over 31,000 people voted, the largest number to date in the city's young life.[10] Mayor Mason would witness the opening of the first Palmer House Hotel in 1870, which burned to the ground the following year, and the opening of St. Ignatius College that eventually became Loyola University. Lincoln Park Zoo was just two years old, and the team that would become the Chicago Cubs started playing baseball for Chicago. And on a more serious note, the 15th Amendment to the Constitution passed, giving all MEN, including black men, the right to vote.

The city was prospering as a railroad, meat-packing, and manufacturing center. Such prosperity creates demand for a labor force. Plus, as a result of the fire, the need to rebuild drew individuals who became known as some of the best architects in the world, and more laborers to work in the construction trades. That the supply responded to the demand is evidenced in the rapid growth of Chicago over the next 20 years. In 1870 the population of the city was 298,977; by 1880 it had increased 68% to 503,185. In the next 10 years it doubled to 1,099,850. By 1900, Chicago was home to the following ethnic groups: Irish, Germans, Poles, Dutch, Czechs, Slovaks, Danes, Norwegians, Swedes, Croatians, Lithuanians, Greeks, and African Americans. Chinese and Japanese also lived in the city by then, albeit in much smaller numbers.

The Dutch

Given the name, Holland Presbyterian Church and its founding minister, Rev. Emanuel Van Orden, the origins of this faith community were clearly Dutch. In fact, the Dutch were among the first immigrants to settle in Chicago or its vicinity, as early as 1839. Of three early Dutch settlements identified, two would have been agricultural areas outside the city limits. One is still outside, and is known as the suburb of South Holland; a second was the area that is today called Roseland, a neighborhood inside the city, not that far north of South Holland. The third was in the city at the time, sometimes referred to as the Graningen quarter (named after the Graningen province in The Netherlands), and was just west of downtown.[11]

Since most Dutch who identified with an institutional church belonged to the Dutch Reformed Church, or as it became known in North America, the Christian Reformed Church, one wonders what they were doing at Holland Presbyterian. The answer to that may lie in the fact that, theologically, both Presbyterians and Reformed Christians followed some version of a Calvinist tradition. On the other hand, as the congregation struggled to gain members, it benefited from the support of larger, more established Presbyterian congregations such as Second Presbyterian at 1936 S. Michigan Ave. The historical record proudly notes that Mrs. William Blair of that church donated a communion set to the fledgling church.[12]

After just two years, Rev. Van Orden moved on and was replaced by Rev. Jacob Post from Milwaukee. He stayed on until 1884. During his tenure, services in English were added, but the membership had only grown to 100 when John Vanderhook arrived from Kalamazoo, Michigan to serve as pastor. In fact, a likely indication of the church's struggle to survive was documented in an Erie House 75th anniversary publication, "Notes of Encouragement: 1870-1945." According to this publication, Holland Presbyterian passed their Noble Street Mission, also known as Erie Chapel, at Erie and Noble, to Third Presbyterian Church in 1882. The Noble Street Mission utilized space in a former Temperance Hall at Noble and Ohio Streets.

Under the stewardship of Third Presbyterian, the Erie Chapel was built in 1886 at what was then 312 W. Erie Street, now 1347 W. Erie, the address of the building that replaced the chapel in 1935 with the current structure. At the time, Third Pres was located at the corner of Washington and Carpenter Streets, just a little more than one mile from what began as Holland Presbyterian Church, but later came to be referred to as the Noble Street Mission, or simply, Erie

Chapel. With their beginning in 1847, Third Pres was founded just one year after Old St. Patrick's Catholic Church, just a few blocks away. The war with Mexico was just ending and the US was issuing its first postage stamp. Chicago had a population of 17,000, with 20 churches, 3 colleges, 3 libraries, and 4 public schools. (New York City had no public schools.) The oldest and largest school stood at the corner of State and Madison. It was subsequently replaced by Boston Store, still there in 1947, but was eventually the location of the Carson, Pirie, Scott department store, replaced by Target in 2012. So, Third Pres was about 40 years old when it stepped up to take responsibility for the Noble Street Mission and provided funds for Erie Chapel Institute's first building at 1347 W. Erie, that would eventually evolve into Erie Neighborhood House. While Third Pres was originally built at Washington and Carpenter, it was later re-located at the intersection of Ogden and Madison.[13] By 1947, Third Pres had moved to Ashland and Ogden. A snapshot of activities at Erie Chapel during the Third Presbyterian era, appears in a church report for a one-year period ending March 27, 1897.[14] It describes staff, programming, and budget that suggest Third Pres helped Erie Chapel become a growing concern. The Templetons, Thomas and Hannah, important benefactors of Erie, were members of Third Presbyterian.

The Norwegians

The fact that "Holland" was dropped as part of the name for the Erie Street church presence, was logical in light of the fact that the Dutch had moved on and the Norwegians had moved in. Like the Dutch, Norwegians arrived early in Chicago.[15] This immigrant group had its beginnings in the city in 1836, and evolved into the third Norwegian settlement in America, after an earlier Norwegian settlement in western New York state, and the one closer by, in the Fox

River area of Illinois. The first Norwegian settler in Chicago was a sailor named David Johnson. This is not surprising as many Norwegians came to the region via their work on the Great Lakes as seamen, shipbuilders, and eventually shipping industry owners and managers. Side by side with the Irish, they helped build the Illinois & Michigan Canal that opened in 1848. Eventually, Norwegian men found a niche in the building trades and as tailors; the women worked in domestic service. As compared to other immigrant groups, the gender balance in their community suggests they left their homeland as family units.

The Presbyterian Church of Chicago exhibited its awareness of a growing Norwegian community in Chicago, and had that group on its agenda at the Presbyterian/ Congregational Convention of 1847. Clergy from the Midwest assembled at Second Presbyterian Church in Chicago on June 17. From research carried out by Elizabeth Tjoelker, a graduate student at Loyola University Chicago in 2004,[16] resolutions were passed "that would ultimately come to shape the contours of pastoral ministry in Chicago and other urban and industrial areas in the latter half of the 19th century. . . that anticipated the needs of European immigrants who would soon arrive in neighborhoods, and at the doors, of countless churches."[17] One of these resolutions addressed the "constantly increasing immigration from Norway." [18] The convention described these new arrivals as appearing to be open to opportunities for improvement, and who would undoubtedly exert wide influence upon our country, at least in Illinois and Wisconsin. While Norwegian influence may not have materialized to the extent imagined in comparison with the Irish, the Germans, and much larger influxes of Poles and Mexicans, for example, they made their mark.

By 1850, it appears that more than 500 Norwegians lived in Chicago. However, the unsavory conditions of "the Sands," their first settlement, just north of the Chicago river, compelled them to move north and west of the river's north branch, settling along Milwaukee Avenue near what is now Grand Avenue (about 500 north and 800 west). By 1860, more than 60 % of Chicago's 1,300 Norwegians lived in this area. They brought with them their connection with the Lutheran religion, establishing churches all around their Grand and Milwaukee neighborhood: Bethania at Grand & Carpenter, Bethany Norwegian Lutheran at Ancona and Sangamon, and at Huron and Racine, all within a mile of the future Erie House.[19] While this was predominantly a working-class community, their more prosperous compatriots moved further north along Milwaukee Avenue, into an area that came to be known as Wicker Park, near the intersection of Milwaukee and North Avenue (1600 North and 2000 west).

As the Norwegian community in Chicago continued to grow, it also continued to move – north and west -- into Logan Square and Humboldt Park, as other immigrant groups arrived and took their places in the smoky, industrial "river wards" they vacated. From their second generation came Victor Lawson, famed journalist and editor of *The Chicago Daily News,* and the founders of Norwegian-American Hospital, still a major health care provider in Humboldt Park. And college football fans would want it noted that, in 1893, at the age of five, Knute Rockne arrived in Chicago, later to become famed football coach at Notre Dame.

But the significance of the 1847 convention is not diminished by special attention given to Norwegians. Rather, the significant point was that a commitment to future immigrants was articulated by this gathering of clergy that underpinned their future ministry as missionaries to emerging urban areas and their immigrant arrivals.

The Germans

While arriving on the scene later than the Dutch and Norwegians, the Irish and the Germans would constitute the next wave of immigrant arrivals in Chicago. Each departed for America to escape crises in their homelands that were both economic and political. In Ireland, the failure of the potato crop in the late 1840s resulted in widespread hardship, and aggravated by British policies, brought many Irish families to the brink of starvation. In Germany, and central Europe in general, the "revolution of 1848" brought political unrest, while the economic impact of the Industrial Revolution put many German craftsmen out of work. Ironically, the later development of that Industrial Revolution in America meant there was still demand for these craftsmen and an opportunity to fill a void.

But as far as the neighborhood around Erie House was concerned, the German immigration was much more significant. The early Irish arrivals tended to settle on the near west side, building the parishes of St. Patrick (now "Old St. Patrick's in the West Loop), St. Malachy, and Holy Family on Roosevelt Road, and which now sits next to St. Ignatius High School, formerly St. Ignatius College, the forerunner of Loyola University. And of course, they settled in Bridgeport, close to their jobs building the I &M canal. Two churches in West Town did have Irish roots – St. Columbkille, near Grand and Ashland, and St. Mark's at Thomas and Campbell. The first was torn down in 1975, long after the Irish had moved on. St. Mark's gradually transitioned to serving the Hispanic community, especially the Puerto Ricans, as they arrived in West Town in the 1950s.

The Germans, on the other hand, headed to the north side, and in 1865, organized St. Boniface parish at Chestnut (900 north) and Noble (1400 west), just 3 blocks north of what would become Holland Presbyterian Church and, eventually, Erie House. In the parish's 115th anniversary booklet, they noted that members stood on the church's steps and watched the city burn down in 1871. There were also Lutheran German immigrants, and on a walk through the neighborhood, one can still find those churches/*kirchen* with their name inscribed in German. Two locations noted on the Newberry Library's "Chicago Ancestors" website[20] included Cortez and Oakley and Chicago and Noble, lying just between St. Boniface and Holland Presbyterian. The church at Walton and Hoyne was being transformed into condominiums in 2019; the one at Chicago and Noble was torn down long ago. By 1889, the same year Hull House opened, there were 35 wards in Chicago <u>and 60 convents</u>. Organized religion, both Protestant and Catholic, was alive and well in the latter half of the 19th century Chicago.

In his book, *Ethnic Chicago,* Melvin Holli says,

> *No continental foreign-born group has been so widely and favorably received in the United States as the Germans or won such high marks from their hosts. . . before World War I.[21]*

He cites figures from the 1980 census that indicated 28% of the American population traced ancestral roots of one or more parent to German immigration, making it the largest ethnic group in the US, ahead of the Irish and English. By 2013, the percent of Americans with German ancestry had dropped to 15%, but still leading all groups, with Mexicans close behind. However, after two world wars in which Germany was the aggressor and enemy of the US, it has been evident that public expression of German ethnicity is nowhere proportionate to its numbers in the US, then or now.[22]

But for the time period, 1870-1914, the German community in Chicago was thriving and in the early days of that period, living in the Erie House neighborhood. Those who arrived in the 1850s, as noted above, were predominantly skilled craftsman who had been protected for centuries by the guild system in Europe. The mechanization of production undermined that system and put those in the handicraft trades out of work. In the US, and especially in Chicago, their skills were in demand. After the Great Fire of 1871, contrary to doomsday thinkers, the population of Chicago doubled by 1890. German carpenters and other building trades craftsmen contributed to and benefited from Chicago's rebirth.

Along with their skills they brought to Chicago their guild experience. Flavored with Marxist socialist thinking, they sat in the driver's seat of the American Labor movement, especially in terms of the AF of L that began as a union of craftsmen – the butchers and bakers, (no candlestick-makers), but printers, carpenters, and brewers. And from Haymarket (1886) to the present day, Chicago has been home to the labor movement. In fact, a reading of the list of those arrested who were associated with the Haymarket affair, reveals a disproportionately large share of German names. It was the German carpenters that pulled together the other nationalities into a single union that won the 8-hour day and higher wages.

By 1900, those higher wages had evidently paid off, and reporters for what had been left-wing German language newspapers wrote that many Germans "have turned bourgeois." [23] Prosperity seemed to have undercut the need for radical socialism. That same prosperity had the Germans of West Town moving away from the St. Boniface area, proceeding northwest up Milwaukee Avenue, as did their Norwegian predecessors, and set about building many of the mansions that have survived in Wicker Park to this day – for the most part, the houses that beer built.

And among these businessmen, German Jews joined the Catholics and Lutherans and synagogues mingled with the Christian churches to fill out the West Town landscape.

The Harts, Schaffners and Marxes exemplified the craft of tailoring, the Florsheims took care of the shoes, the Mandels opened department stores, and Julian Rosenwald master-minded the transformation of a watch company, called Sears & Roebuck, into a multi-million-dollar mail-order house. And besides their success in the business world, it was a German-born immigrant, Theodor Thomas, who founded one of Chicago's greatest treasures, the Chicago Symphony Orchestra, in 1891. Not bad for a "bunch of immigrants." Sadly, the Germans' most favored nationality status was virtually erased by the animosity toward them as the guns of August placed the fatherland in as negative a scenario as warfare can conjure.[24]

So, from this short ethnic history, we find the answer as to why the Germans, who were certainly present at the time of Holland Presbyterian Church and its successors, the Noble Street Mission, and Erie Chapel Institute, were not found in great numbers among Erie participants. Their financial success moved them away geographically and put them more into the role of benefactor than recipient of services. As this story moves forward into the days of Florence Towne and the Erie Chapel Institute in subsequent chapters, this role will become more evident.

The Noble Street Mission, 1897-1914

Before addressing the next wave of immigrants, Erie's organizational evolution can be updated as follows. By 1897, four years after the World's Fair in Chicago proclaimed to the world that the city was back and booming, the Rev. J.M. Wallace was ministering at the Noble Street Mission/Erie Chapel; James Creighton is identified as "Superintendent." That title evolved over the years to Head Resident and then, Executive Director. Mr. Creighton was also listed as Colonel of the Boys' Brigade. This may be an honorary title or evidence of the fact he served in the Civil

War 30+ years earlier. In addition to the Boys' Brigade, other activities included: The Industrial School where women sewed clothing, the Intermediate, Junior, and Young People's versions of "The Society of Christian Endeavor," a choir, Sunday School, and the Woman's Foreign Missionary Society.

A twelve-month finance report indicated receipts of $2,663 and expenses of $1,146.[25] Membership for all activities for the previous year was reported as 2,126 (duplicated). So, this was more of an attendance count than "membership" since, if Johnnie attended Boys' Brigade once a week, he was counted 52 times. But women-- those who came to sew, and those who provided the sewing machines—were also engaged. It was also noted that 1,364 of their count represented Sunday School attendance, suggesting that at this very early date, children were a big part of the Erie House story. It also suggests that programs that became associated with settlement work were also under way, side by side with church services. This was all happening in the building known as Erie Chapel, a 2-room edifice built in 1886, and was going on for 19 years, just 2.5 miles to the north and west, before Jane Addams moved to the house on Halsted Street in 1889. By 1895, a third room was added to the building on Erie Street, mainly to accommodate church services and Sunday School that boasted an enrollment of 1500, the largest in Chicago at that time.[26]

Historical Context, 1870-1900

To keep in mind the context, both local and national, for the evolution of Erie Neighborhood House, it should be noted that the 1880's marked the beginning of the first father/son mayoral dynasty in Chicago. Carter Harrison I and II are generally forgotten in the shadow of the dominance of Richard J. and Richard M. Daley in the 20th century. But Carter Henry Harrison, Sr., first elected in 1879 on the Democratic ticket, was re-elected 3 more times, keeping him in office until 1887. The mayor's term of office at that time was only two years; if it had been four, his time in office would have rivaled Richard J's 20+ years.

Given that Chicago was home to labor unrest, and what was referred to as "anarchy," in connection with the Haymarket Affair, it is interesting to note that beginning with Harrison's first election in 1879, candidates of the Socialist Labor Party are frequently on the ticket in mayoral elections. They appear on the ballot five times before the beginning of his fifth term in 1893, having been elected just in time to preside over the 1893 World's Fair in Chicago. He died shortly thereafter at the hands of an assassin. Four years later, in 1897, his son, Carter Harrison II, picked up where he left off, and like his dad, was re-elected three more times, replaced by Edward Dunne in 1905. Between the two Harrisons, the office of mayor was occupied by Republican John Roche, Democrat, DeWitt Clinton Cregier, who was mayor when Jane Addams arrived on Halsted Street, and Hempstead Washburne, who ran on the Reform ticket in 1891, and left his name to Chicago's Washburne Trade School.

The decades after the fire in Chicago, as noted earlier, were a time of tremendous growth. But this was not just in population. There were numerous events and institutions that emerged during this era that made Chicago the city it is today. Certainly, the beginning of what became the settlement house movement in the US was key among them, with the roots of Erie Neighborhood House and Onward House already planted, and with Northwestern University Settlement, Chicago Commons, and Association House not far behind Hull House.

But this was also the time when the Field & Leiter store evolved into Marshall Field & Co., the town of Pullman was built, and US Steel opened South Works. Sears moved to Chicago, Schwinn Bicycles started production, and Nabisco opened a plant in the city. Peoples Gas and Illinois Bell telephone came on the scene. The American labor movement took shape in the cauldron of Haymarket (1886) and the Pullman Strike (1894), side by side with the opening of museums, parks and the Art Institute. In 1892, Ellis Island opened as the gateway to later immigrant groups that followed the Dutch, Norwegian, Irish, and Germans already in Chicago, pre-dating that experience. And, of course, Chicago stood proud as, just 22 years or one generation after the Great Fire, they hosted the world at the Columbian Exposition in 1893. A year later, in 1894, the first public bath opened in Chicago, an early victory for the settlement workers. A year after that, Hull House published its Maps and Papers, a result of the kind of investigative work that came to be the underpinning of the fields of sociology and urban planning. By 1898, the Polish Women's Alliance had been formed, and St. Vincent College/DePaul University joined St. Ignatius College/Loyola University, that had opened 28 years earlier, to provide more opportunities for higher education.

So, this was the context for Erie's early mission years, the history that Hull House was born into, and where the settlement movement flourished. It was Sandburg's "hog butcher, tool maker, stacker of wheat, player with railroads, nation's freight handler–City of the Big Shoulders."[27] It was an immigrant refuge, where immigrants got the job done of re-building the city. It was a city full of churches, but becoming more and more Catholic, and less and less Protestant. It was home to a symphony orchestra and a cacophony of labor unrest.

As the century was coming to a close, the 1890s could be characterized as a transitional decade for the Erie neighborhood. This was true organizationally and in terms of the people Erie would serve next, as Erie witnessed the shift in migration from Western to Eastern and Southern

Europe and the earlier immigrant groups described above were gradually replaced by Poles and Italians.

The Italians

As early as 1850, there were a small number of "Italians" in Chicago. However, that is somewhat of a misnomer, as there was no such place as Italy at that time. There were fruit sellers, restaurateurs, and assorted shopkeepers from Genoa, and plaster workers from Lucchese, all in the north of the country we know as Italy today. From about 1815 to 1871, the regions of Italy pursued unification, also known as the *Risorgiamento*. This first group of immigrants clustered in the Near North area, broadly speaking, north of Grand Avenue to North Avenue, and east of Halsted. As conditions here were grim, it was identified as a slum in Zorbaugh's classic work, *The Gold Coast and the Slum*, published in 1929. In homage to probably the most famous Italian immigrant in Chicago (except for Al Capone), Mother Frances Cabrini, the public housing that later replaced her *pisani* was named Cabrini, and then linked to another cluster of public housing nearby, known as the Green buildings. Thus, Cabrini-Green, that, unfortunately, evolved into yet another "slum," as the high-rise, high concentration plan for public housing proved to be an unsuccessful strategy.

But most Chicagoans of Italian descent trace their ancestry to the much larger number of immigrants arriving from 1880-1914, this time from central and southern Italy, among mostly unskilled peasants. They started chains of migration that brought people from their hometowns in the mother country to re-establish themselves as "colonies" in US cities. The top three destinations were New York, Philadelphia, and Chicago, in that order. Dominic Candeloro, in his chapter in *Ethnic Chicago,* describes them as agrarian, Christian, and family-oriented. He outlines the growth of the Italian population in Chicago as follows:

1880	1,357
1890	5,685
1900	16,000
1910	45,169
1920	59,215[28]

So, clearly, 1890-1910 was the major growth period, with the population tripling every ten years. Nevertheless, in terms of numbers and general impact, Italian immigrants were much more evident in New York. In Chicago they were overshadowed by the German, Irish, and eventually, the Polish and Mexican immigration. However, in the neighborhood around Erie House, Italian immigrants were an important group of neighbors that used the settlement extensively.

Throughout the city, Italian communities tended to be anchored by a Catholic Church. This reality was both cultural and conflictual. Because the Vatican had stood in opposition to the unification of Italy for many years, the resentment of this fact was the source of a pervasive anti-clericalism in Chicago's Italian communities. While this kept some Italians, men in particular, out of Church on Sunday, it did not keep them from celebrating with religious festivals and processions or forming clubs and mutual benefit societies named after saints.

The earliest group that lived Near North established the oldest Italian Catholic church in Chicago, Assumption, which now sits in the shadow of the Merchandise Mart, and was started by an order of priests called the Servites, in 1881. But the church that most Italians coming to Erie House attended was Santa Maria Addolorata, built at Grand (500 north) and Peoria, just west of Halsted, in 1903, and staffed by the Scalabrini Fathers. They were headquartered in

Northern Italy but followed their countrymen to the US to minister to their spiritual needs. This church was later re-built just one block from Erie, in the 1960s, after becoming a casualty of the construction of the Kennedy Expressway. Santa Maria Addolorata was known for its San Rocco di Madugno fest in August. The San Rocco Club had its meetings in a storefront at the corner of Ohio and Noble, one block from the new church built at Ada and Ohio. Holy Rosary was built in 1904, at 612 N. Western Avenue (2400 west). Many of these parishioners would have gone to another nearby settlement, Onward House, at Ohio & Leavitt, just one mile west of Erie.

When asked why they left Italy to come to America, a common answer was *pane e lavoro,* bread and work.[29] One of the better-known Italian names in the Erie House area was Gonnella, a family who started baking bread in 1886, and still does so very successfully to this day. Alessandro Gonnella began with a small bakery on DeKoven Street, on the Near West Side. In 1896, he re-located to a larger facility on the Near Northwest Side at Ohio and Sangamon (just north of Grand Avenue and just west of Halsted). There his wife, Maria Marcucci and her brothers joined him in the business. They moved to a new plant on Erie Street, just west of Damen, in 1915. From there, bread was delivered to 200 homes, daily, by horse-drawn wagons, until deliveries to grocery stores and restaurants became more efficient and more profitable. But, eventually, they succumbed to an offer from residential developers, sold the Erie property, and re-located production to Aurora, Illinois in the western suburbs, Schaumburg and two other locations. Amidst all of this growth, it remains a family-owned and run business.

Where Gonnella started his business was possibly the most renowned Italian district in the city. It was on the Near West Side, in the area served by Hull House, Holy Guardian Angel Church established in 1899, and Our Lady of Pompei, built in 1910. This area was sometimes referred to as "Little

Italy"; today it might be referred to as the Taylor Street area, but still home to a number of Italian restaurants and shops. Much of this district, including the square block of Hull House buildings, was wiped off the map when Mayor Richard J. Daley decided to locate the University of Illinois Chicago campus there, in spite of the heroic fight to save the neighborhood led by Florence Scala. This was another example of an unfortunate pattern that seemed to plague Italian communities in Chicago--displacement by public policy via public housing, highway construction, and a university campus.

No doubt, too much has been written about Al Capone, the Mafia, and the violence they initiated that became indelibly attached to the name and image of Chicago of the 1920s. And as late as the 1960s, the Nitti family name, with a connection to Frank Nitti of the Capone gang, could be seen on stores in the Erie neighborhood. This had nothing to do with the majority of Italians living in Chicago who spent generations trying to eradicate this defamation. Especially active in this endeavor was the Joint Civic Committee of Italian Americans (JCCIA) who worked diligently with members of the media to stop using words like "Mafia" and "Cosa Nostra" and shift to the more ethnic-neutral "organized crime." They also engaged in more positive publicity through sponsorship of the annual Columbus Day parade. Finally, in the 1990s, the rise of a Chicago sports legend had American tourists from Chicago being greeted abroad with a smile and the connection of Chicago with Michael Jordan instead of Al.

The connection between Erie House and the Italians will become evident in Chapter 3, a narrative of the leadership years of Miss Florence Towne, from 1926 to 1951.

The Poles

Like the Italians, the Polish immigration to America
was driven by economic and structural changes in Poland.
As noted earlier, the Italians described their motivation as
pan e lavoro, bread and work; the Poles called it *Za
Chlebem,* simply, for bread.[30] And, while Italians came from
a place that was not yet a nation, Poles came from a nation
divided, partitioned into three sections – one taken by
Germany, one by Russia, and one by the Austrian Empire.
While some Poles came as early as the 1850s, their arrival in
the US, and in Chicago, accelerated after 1890. According
to Kantowicz's research, there were 40,000 Poles in Chicago
in 1890. [31] That number increased 5-fold, to 210,000 in
1910, and doubled to 401,316 by 1930. He argues that he is
including only Catholic Poles in this number, as the majority
of Poles in Chicago at this time were Catholic, and that the
Polish Catholics built their community separately and
differently from Jewish Poles. Clearly, without this
distinction the number of Polish immigrants would be even
larger. The 400,000 in the US by 1930 made up 12% of
Chicago's population of 3,376,438. By 1970, they made up
20% of Chicagoans, and had become the largest white ethnic
group in the city.

For the most part, the Polish peasants who came here
headed for cities like Buffalo and Chicago where industry
was crying for manpower and skills were not required.
Then, within the cities they clustered in areas where
manufacturing jobs were readily available. In Chicago, this
took them to West Town on the northwest side, living just
west of the Goose Island manufacturing district, to
Bridgeport and Back-of-the-Yards on the near southwest
side, to work in the meatpacking industry, and to the far
south side to work in the mills of Wisconsin and US Steel.

But what came to be known as "Polish Downtown,"
in the vicinity of Division, Ashland and Milwaukee,

represented an overwhelmingly Polish population of 86.3% Poles in 1898, including one precinct that was 99.9% Polish. As a map of Polish Downtown, circa 1900 shows,[32] this area stretched from North Avenue (1600 north) to Grand Avenue (500 north) on the south, and from the Chicago River on the east to Oakley Blvd. at 2300 west. Erie House was located in its southeast quadrant.

Initially, these very Catholic Poles attended churches that had been founded by the Irish and German Catholics that had preceded them. In the Erie House area, for example, they went to St. Boniface, a German parish that was not very welcoming to the new ethnic arrivals. So, it did not take long for the Poles to begin to dream and plan for their own church. Anthony Smarzewski-Schermann immigrated from Poland to work as a carpenter in the US. Eventually he opened a grocery store at Noble (1400 west) and Bradley Street (1300 north, called Potomac Avenue, further west). He became a leader in that Polish community, where they founded the first Polish Catholic parish in Chicago, St. Stanislaus Kostka, on Noble Street, in 1867, 3 years before Holland Presbyterian/ Erie House began its mission just 7 blocks to the south. The number of parishes that identified as Polish grew to 60.

> *In Chicago, the creation of ethnic Catholic parishes provided both a stable institutional base for community and a status symbol that announced the importance of the new immigrant colony.[33]*

In 1870, Bishop Thomas Foley invited the Resurrectionist Fathers, from Poland, to minister to Chicago's Polish Catholics, just as the Scalabrini Fathers came from Italy to minister to Italian immigrants in Chicago. Over time, both of these orders played an important role, beyond the parish, in the development of their ethnic community's identity as hyphenated Americans in the city. The Resurrection Fathers established what became Weber

High School and Gordon Tech, but it was the Holy Cross Brothers from Notre Dame that founded Holy Trinity High School on Division Street. The Felician Sisters and the Sisters of the Holy Family of Nazareth staffed many of the parish schools and high schools for girls, such as Holy Family on Division Street, across from Holy Trinity. They also staffed St. Mary of Nazareth Hospital in the 2200 block of West Division.

According to Kantowicz: "Demographic mixing, where it took place, did not generally lead to social mixing."[34] Or, as Pacyga put it:

> *Like other European ethnic groups at the time, Poles lived in diverse neighborhoods that were residentially integrated (by ethnicity, if not by race), but tended to be socially segregated.*[35]

In other words, they developed their own churches, schools, clubs, newspapers, and commercial areas so as to be practically self-sufficient, with few reasons to interact with the host society. Kantowicz notes that by 1919 there were 74 parish societies at St. Stanislaus Kostka alone.[36] If this sounds like a ghetto, to a certain extent it is. There is definitely a pejorative connotation to that term, with the limitations imposed by cultural isolation. However, there are pluses that emerge from a closely-knit collaborative milieu that supports immigrants in their struggle for survival and success in their earliest days in a foreign environment. This included supporting Polish-owned local businesses. *"Swoj do Swego,"* "support your own" resonates today with the campaigns to "Buy Local" being used by companies like Jewel Foods and Walgreens pharmacies that have their origin in Chicago. It was also a motto in Bronzeville, where African Americans were encouraged to do the same. They added, "Don't shop where you can't work."

Besides the parish church, the Poles of Chicago built a stronger community through the development of mutual benefit societies. Two of the largest and most successful of these are the Polish Roman Catholic Union (PRCU, 1873) and the Polish National Alliance (PNA, 1880) both of which still exist today. The PNA followed the Polish migration up Milwaukee Avenue, "Polish Broadway," to the suburb of Niles. But the PRCU is still located in Polish Downtown at Augusta Blvd. and Milwaukee Ave, just 4 blocks from Erie House. Their sign, painted on the side of the building, is easily visible from the Kennedy Expressway. Their building there also houses the Polish Museum of Chicago, home to Paderewski's piano and the story of Maria Sklowdowska (Madame Curie), who discovered polonium and radium and was the first woman to win the Nobel Prize. Through the PNA and PRCU, American Poles kept alive hope for the re-unification of an independent Polish state. This hope was realized at the end of World War I.

Another form of mutual aid organization was the building and loan association. The Polish peasants' dream of owning land, someday, translated into the goal of owning one's home in Chicago. By making payments of 50 cents or a dollar a week, the Poles saved up their down payment and the building and loan made up the rest with a low interest loan for the purchase. "By 1900, Polish building and loan societies held assets approaching one million dollars."[37] Home ownership expanded to ownership of multi-family buildings that provided a good supplementary income, a significant resource for movement of second generations to the middle class. Ownership of property also proved to be an anchor, making Poles the last of European ethnics to move to the suburbs in substantial numbers.

A facsimile of an ad for *Bank Polski* pictures its location in a building at 1201 N. Milwaukee in the heart of Polish Downtown.[38] This building is still there and served as the offices of the *Polish Daily Zgoda* newspaper as late as the 1960s. Eventually, a new building just to the west, housed the Security Federal Savings & Loan, where you could find one of the Kovac Brothers, who owned it in the 1970s, in their office just off the lobby, and wave to them; they always waved back. That building is now occupied by Fifth Third Bank; waving is no longer a common practice.

Two areas where Poles did collaborate with "outsiders" was in the labor movement and in community-based organizations (CBOs). They forged crucial alliances with other immigrant groups through union activities. This kind of collaboration was crucial in taking control of their future economic success, the fight for *Za Chlebem* – bread. In fact, the largest local in the Amalgamated Meat Cutters' Union was led by John Kikulski. And when the stockyards workers went on strike in 1921, their own ethnic solidarity was an asset, when the pastor of St. John of God, Packingtown's largest parish, openly supported the strike. Over the years, Polish workers joined the industrial unions, not only in the meatpacking industry, but also in steel, adding to the ultimate success of the Congress of Industrial Organizations (CIO), just as the German craftsmen before them helped build the AF of L. Polish workers in Chicago definitely got the message: "Workers of the World Unite."

No doubt, when Saul Alinsky set out to organize Back-of-the-Yards almost 20 years later, he was familiar with the role of the Poles in the meatpacking industrial unions, and the actions of the St. John of God pastor. He brought unions and Catholic pastors together, from the Polish and other ethnic parishes, a coalition that brought the meatpacking companies to the negotiating table to improve the plight of their workers. Ultimately, this same coalition, through the Back-of-the-Yards Council, reversed the community's slide toward slum conditions, and transformed it into a respectable working-class community. This same pattern would repeat itself in the 1960s in West Town, where Fr. Tony Janiak, pastor of Holy Innocents, two blocks from

Erie House, would work with Alinsky's successor organizers to build the Northwest Community Organization (NCO), founded in 1962. [More on this in chapter 4, the story of Ross Lyman's leadership of Erie House.]

Before closing this foundational story of Poles in the Erie House neighborhood, it is important to note that, while Kantowicz chose to exclude Polish Jews in his narrative of the Polish community, they were there, and they were major contributors to the economy, not only of the Polish Downtown but to the economy of Chicago. This is acknowledged by Dominic Pacyga in his article on the Poles of Chicago in the *Encyclopedia of Chicago*. Most significantly for the Polish community in West Town, was the opening of the first Goldblatt's Department Store on Chicago Avenue, just west of Ashland. East European Jews were also the founders of the Meyers Department Store on Chicago Avenue, just east of Ashland and Polk Bros. Furniture stores. By the early 1900s, about 25% of Chicago's Jewish population lived in the area just east of Humboldt Park. The population of West Town peaked around 1910, but there were still 212,000 people living there in 1920, 44% being foreign-born. By 1930, 49% of West Town residents were Poles.[39]

Having laid out the ethnic and economic context for Erie House in its earliest days, 1870-1914, in order to understand how Holland Presbyterian Church became Erie Chapel Institute, and then became Erie Neighborhood House, there are two components of that context that need to be introduced. Both have roots in the 19th century: the Social Gospel Movement and the Settlement House movement sparked by Jane Addams. The Social Gospel will be addressed first due to its influence on both Jane Addams's Hull House and the evolution of Erie Neighborhood House.

Chapter Two: The Emergence of Hull House and the Settlement House Model, 1889-1924

In reviewing the origins of the settlement movement in Chicago, there needs to be an understanding of how it distinguished itself from church dogma, but not necessarily from churches all together, and how Addams's approach to challenging the impact of industrialization on workers spread to many more urban areas throughout the Midwestern and Northeastern United States, in the period from 1889 to 1920. This work has depended heavily on three sources to understand the context for Erie's origins :

1. Jane Addams herself, in her work *Twenty Years at Hull House, 1909;*
2. Allen Davis's 1985 edition of S*pearheads for Reform: The Social Settlements and the Progressive Movement, 1890-1914;*
3. Eleanor Stebner's *The Women of Hull House: A Study in Spirituality, Vocation, and Friendship, 1997.*[40]

The Social Gospel Movement

The Social Gospel Movement traces its origins to the late 19th century and is often identified with the writings of Washington Gladden (1836-1918), an American Congregational minister, who suggested that Christians who claimed to be followers of Jesus ought to pattern their lives after his. As Christ preached: "Blessed are the poor," he also spent most of his ministry among them. He did not call upon the rich and famous to be his disciples; instead he went to fishermen and women who were poor, working class people. With this reading of the Gospel, Gladden's preaching and writing was laced with calls for social justice, applying Christian ethics to social problems like economic inequality, child labor, slums, poor schools, racial tensions, and the danger of war, and arguing that the purpose of wealth was not to hoard it but to share it with those less fortunate. Other Protestant ministers picked up on his perspective and began to connect salvation with good works, theology with sociology, as Allen Davis suggested.[41]

The Social Gospel movement also rejected the concept of Social Darwinism, which suggested the poor were weak, or unfit, a condition of their "nature," not due to their environment. Advocates of the Social Gospel challenged that idea with the argument that the causes of poverty were primarily systemic, that the system most at fault was unbridled capitalism, evident in the latter half of the 19th century. This was a period also associated with the era of "Robber Barons," like Cornelius Vanderbilt, whose extreme wealth was flaunted in "summer homes," like "The Breakers" in Newport, valued at $150 million in today's dollars. Clinton Stockwell points out that:

> *Most of the models of urban presence by*
> *Protestants prior to 1890, except the abolitionist*
> *movement, were really concerned more about*
> *elevating the morality or saving the souls of*
> *individuals. Only abolitionism was concerned*
> *about the structural conditions that accompanied*
> *slavery.*[42]

Until the settlement movement, as he notes in the same article,

> *. . .that settlement workers knew the urban*
> *immigrant poor, not as "clients," but as neighbors*
> *and friends. A more structural critique of urban*
> *society emerged that challenged the paternalistic*
> *approach of victimizing the individual for*
> *circumstances often beyond one's control.*[43]

On the one hand, Davis suggests that one of the most important outcomes of the Social Gospel Movement was the emergence of settlement houses. Given the numerous Congregational and Presbyterian founders of settlements, one can see the ready connection. But Davis also suggests that Addams, for one, may have been as much a creator of the movement as an outcome of it. As with most movements. The seeds of it are germinating in many individuals before it fully blossoms into a "movement." As Jane herself attests, throughout the pages of *Twenty Years at Hull House,*[44] she saw settlement work as an expression of "Christian humanitarianism." This is a belief in the Gospel version of religion, that could only be "social," versus the various dogmatic interpretations that institutional church clergy had devised, that had people turned in upon themselves to find salvation, rather than reaching out to others. She states that the essential elements of religion are not based on doctrine, but on the faith typical of the early Christian community, rooted in the teachings of the gospels and manifest in expressions of fellowship. Addams regarded this early Christian community as a church of the poor, as the one that should be presented to the poor of her day. After all, she reflected, it was those simple people who took the message to the more prosperous Romans.[45]

Stebner underscores the views of Addams regarding a faith rooted in the Gospel teachings, pointing to the social settlement movement as adding a fuller dimension to conventional religion. She states that the faith of the settlement was made evident by its works.[46] She then cites Dean George Hodges' description of a settlement:

> *For beneath its roof the blind begin to see and the lame begin to walk, and they who have been palsied take on strength, and the poor hear the good newsof the gospel of the love of God which is interpreted by the service of man.*[47]

She also cites David Barry's Chicago Theological Seminary dissertation from 1941, arguing that for settlement workers, "Religion was a *way of life,* not a creed, a belief, a book, a ritual, or a form of church organization."[48]

So, when Holland Presbyterian Church/Erie House began in 1870, and Jane Addams, without the benefit or obligation of ordination, followed in 1889, and Graham Taylor, a minister with roots in the Dutch Reformed Church, founded Chicago Commons in 1894 on that set of beliefs, who is to say which was more influential? Was it the Social Gospel movement, or the settlement house movement that demonstrated what it meant? The answer may call forth another adage: One picture (demonstration) is worth 1,000 words.

The Settlement Movement and the Progressive Era

What is without dispute, is that the Settlement Movement carried the Social Gospel into the 20th century and used it to support what American historians call the Progressive Movement in US history. This is a key argument of Allen Davis's book, *Spearheads of Reform.* Over a span of close to 30 years, settlement workers led the charge in passing city, state, and federal legislation that led to the abolition of child labor, the establishment of a juvenile court system, the growth of labor unions to win the eight-hour day, the right of women to vote and yes, the temporary prohibition of alcohol consumption. And as the commitment to reform was renewed during the administration of Franklin Delano Roosevelt, the fingerprints of settlement workers and former settlement participants were all over the New Deal.

Furthermore, they reformed what were described as charity organizations that had been motivated by religious beliefs that were more influenced by Darwin and Calvin than by Jesus. Before the settlements modeled a different approach, charity was synonymous with *noblesse oblige,* given by the superior inhabitants of an affluent society, that looked down upon the inferior inhabitants of the slums of the burgeoning industrial cities with pity. Even more disturbing, they often attempted to sort out the "worthy poor," i.e., workers, struggling to make it with poverty wages, from the unworthy sinners, usually excluded from employment due to race, ethnicity or gender.

Ultimately, what began as a critique of traditional charity organizations evolved into a collaboration, as the two groups began to hold joint annual conferences. Certainly, Jane Addams and her colleagues at Hull House, and Lillian Wald at Henry Street Settlement in New York, or Robert Woods in Boston, did not neglect to feed the poor, but at the same time they insisted that the *cause* of hunger be studied and challenged. Indeed, study of social problems, investigation and gathering of facts, were hallmarks of early settlement work. It was the maps and papers that described what they witnessed in their neighborhood, published by the women of Hull House, that set the example of how to bring about systemic change. Their work became the foundation for the discipline of sociology as well as the profession of social work. In *Modern American Religion,*[49] Martin Marty suggests that "The word 'social' acquired a new power at the turn of the century (19th-20th). Sociology, social settlement, social service, social gospel, social philosophy, were all invented."[50]

The Holland Presbyterian Church of 1870, and its successor formulations as the Noble Street Mission (1886) or Erie Chapel Institute (1915), may not have understood and embraced all of these aspects of the Settlement Movement. But, what eventually emerged as Erie Neighborhood House in 1935, was a product of all of these elements. The recipe for the Erie settlement was cooked in the cauldron of church and charity reform. And while the 1935 cornerstone of the new building celebrates with the words "To the Glory of

God," evidence, reflected through its work in subsequent years, suggests this was Jane's God and her "church" that were to be celebrated. Throughout Erie's history, the church people that recognized and supported the settlement's good work, understood and subscribed to G.K. Chesterton's belief that "Your religion is not the church you belong to, but the cosmos you live inside of."[51] Their experience when they came to Erie House, broadened the boundaries of that cosmos.

Hull House and Jane Lead the Way

From 1889 forward, Addams worked to actualize the principles of the social gospel through the evolution of the settlement model. Whether intentionally part of the "Social Gospel movement" or not, Addams made clear in many of her writings that the "Settlement Movement" did intend to bring to life the teachings of Jesus on the streets of Chicago and all of the emerging industrial cities of the US in her time. Beginning with Florence Towne, the first modern day lay leader of Erie Neighborhood House, this model became the guide as to how to combine respectful charity with social justice for the working poor immigrant, and to keep in mind all members of the family, from pre-school to adult learners

A careful reading of Jane, herself, reveals certain intertwined themes that explain the values that have contributed to endurance, that have kept Erie House and many other settlements successful for 100+ years. While there have been many modifications of the work in response to changing times, the essence of the wisdom and practical applications of the early years are still evident in the most successful present-day versions of settlement work. The themes that follow will be referenced often throughout the subsequent chapters of this book that address the work of Erie House from 1915-2015.

These essentials include commitments to:

- *preserve* humanistic and spiritual values–not dogma -- in a world dominated by materialism, the world of the 19th,20th, and 21st centuries;
- *believe* that the most valuable learning about people and places you are meeting for the first time comes from practice/experience, or what Samuel Barnett of Toynbee Hall described as "education by permeation";
- *conduct* investigations, gathering data at the neighborhood level, rooted in this "permeation" and critical in strengthening advocacy and winning reforms;
- *replace* the Darwinistic notion held by many "charity workers" of the 19th century (and subsequent centuries) that people were poor because they were ignorant and lazy, or "colored", with their recognition of the cause of poverty as environmental and systemic in a capitalistic society--what Davis referred to as "the poverty of opportunity v. the poverty of clothes";
- *understand* that while working for systemic change in the long run, their neighbors needed to be fed, educated, housed, and their health care and employment needs addressed in the short run; and
- *recognize* that this was most effectively done by working with the whole family, but beginning with the children.

In summary, Jane Addams defined a settlement this way:

The Settlement then, is an experimental effort to aid in the solution of the social and industrial problems which are engendered by the modern conditions of life in a great city. ... The one thing to be dreaded is that it lose its flexibility, its power of quick

*adaptation, its readiness to change its methods as
its environment may demand. . .have a deep and
abiding sense of tolerance. . .It must be grounded in
a philosophy whose foundation is on the solidarity
of the human race. . .ready to arouse and interpret
the public opinion of their neighborhood.[52]*

By being good neighbors on a daily basis, settlement
workers could learn how to be effective advocates for the
changes needed and, most importantly of all, the best way to
deliver or implement the changes required. Shaping legal
decisions into practical applications, settlement workers
were often the only ones who really understood the maxim
that "the devil is in the details," and they were the devil's
most effective opponent.

A further characteristic that continues to contribute
to the success of the settlement house comes from a
willingness to not just *serve* their neighbors, but to *embrace*
them and underscore the value of who they are, and who they
might become. The concept of neighbor v. client, or in more
technical parlance, a participant v. a client, gives the
immigrants status as collaborators in their own success v.
victims of circumstances they cannot change. To the extent
that settlement workers over the centuries, whether they live
nearby or not, understand and embrace this strategy, they can
carry forward the success of their foremothers and
forefathers, and have done so.

In 1998, almost 90 years after Addams's definition
of settlement work cited above, John McDowell, former
executive director of the National Federation of Settlements
and Neighborhood Centers, described the settlement house
as follows:

*Settlement houses or neighborhood centers are
staffed by trained and sympathetic workers who
study the needs of a particular local community by*

participating in its life and by enlisting the assistance of local people. They devise and carry out a program of services to individuals, families and organizations that supplements and reinforces those of existing institutions. From the beginning settlements have sought to reform the social order (to address)injustice or uncalled for hardships on disadvantaged members of society. . . Settlements are firmly committed to democratic methods in bringing about social changes; methods that include education, discussion and citizens' activity. . .[53]

McDowell goes on to cite these key characteristics of settlement work:

- Emphasizing social reform rather than social work (Which did not even exist as a profession at the time of Jane Addams);
- Desiring to live as neighbors to those living around them;
- Emphasizing education, both as a means and an end, in assisting people to achieve greater economic independence and greater civic awareness;
- Pioneering in early childhood education;
- Programming for adolescents to keep them off the streets, in school, and on to college;
- Committing to eradicate slums;
- Taking stands on local, state, and national issues that affect their neighbors;
- Working toward inter-ethnic and interracial harmony.[54]

While Allen Davis argues that the "golden age" of the settlement house movement happened from 1890 to 1914, Erie Neighborhood House, Chicago Commons,

Association House, Onward House, Northwestern University Settlement House, Gads Hill, Christopher House, in Chicago, Henry Street Settlement in New York, and Birmingham Settlement in England, are living proof that settlement work lives on and is strong when it stays committed to Jane's vision, re-stated by McDowell 90 years later.

What Addams Learned the First 20 Years

To further set the scene for the Erie Neighborhood House story, a look at those first 20 years at Hull House that Jane reflected on in 1909, is essential. From Jane's own words,

> *Hull-House was soberly opened on the theory that the dependence of classes on each other is reciprocal; and that as the social relationship is essentially a reciprocal relation, it gives a form of expression that is of peculiar value.*[55]

In other words, settlement workers and their neighbors would need to learn from each other. She often brought one of her Hull House neighbors with her when she went to give a talk about Hull House, so as to begin the process of disabusing her ignorant audience of any preconceived notions they had about people they never met. No doubt, she wanted to illustrate a point made by Canon Barnett of Toynbee Hall as she quotes him as saying, "The things which make men alike are finer and better than the things that keep them apart."[56]

Addams observed that the Jews and Italians around Hull House worked for local clothing manufacturers doing jobs formerly done by "Americans," that is, Norwegians, Germans and Irish, who would no longer submit to the very low wages paid under the sweating system. Erie House observed the same phenomenon over and over as each new ethnic group took over the unpleasant jobs their predecessor ethnic groups had left behind.

Miss Addams commented on the dilapidated, over-crowded housing; Miss Towne found the same, even a generation older. Addams acidly commented: "The theory that wealth brings responsibility . . .in these cases fails utterly."[57]

When Ellen Gate Starr, co-founder of Hull House, hosted "reading parties," the women of Hull House learned that "a combination of social atmosphere and serious study was best practice"–a lesson Erie House followed, especially in their adult education program.

Jane noted that kindergarten and programs for children were the first to be undertaken, as was also the case at Erie. But, she went on, "we were very insistent that the Settlement should not be primarily for children, and that it was absurd to suppose that grown people would not respond to opportunities for education and social life."[58] Miss Towne came to Erie as a Kindergarten teacher, but also realized that mothers followed their children, first, because that is what mothers do, and then because, as women, they sought social contacts and skills training, for their own self-esteem and for the social and economic well-being of their children. The fathers and brothers followed.

And, of course, those pre-schoolers headed for elementary school. With both parents working, Hull House and Erie House stepped up to offer after-school care. From early days, recruiting and working with the boys (and men) was the greater challenge. Miss Addams said that the secret to working with older children was two-fold (at least): 1) a resourceful and devoted leader; 2) an opportunity for a kind of initiative and independence and social contacts not often possible at school. Erie's youth programs have followed that guidance.

An Idea, Informed by Practice, Grows into a Movement & the Debate Over Who Belongs

As early as 1892, just 3 years after Hull House started, settlement workers from around the country met to discuss their "new movement." Bravado? Prophecy? Or what Chicago settlement worker of the late 20th century, Ann Seng, used to say: "If you believe it you will see it."[59] Davis reports that by 1891 there were six known settlements; by 1897 there were 74, by 1905, 200+ and by 1910, 400+. They did, indeed, have a movement in the making. Along the way, Jane Addams founded the Chicago Federation of Settlements in 1894, and Robert Woods of Andover House in Boston, co-founded the National Federation of Settlements in 1911.

However, Woods was adamant that settlement houses were non-sectarian endeavors, and therefore, were not to be admitted to membership if they had denominational affiliations. By drawing that line in the sand, many organizations like Erie Neighborhood House, especially with its early sponsorship and ongoing support from the Presbytery of Chicago in its Noble Mission phase, were excluded from the NFS. While there is much discussion, even today, about the distinction between spirituality and religion, the commitment of the Presbyterian Church of Chicago to Erie House, and of many other churches throughout the US, to their settlement houses, is difficult to dismiss as not being true settlements, as Jane envisioned. While they may have begun with a Sunday School program, they soon learned the same lessons the women of Hull House did, that settlement work was the work of the Gospel, with doctrines and creeds of lesser importance. The story of Erie House illuminates this reality and what Robert Woods misconstrued.

Stebner suggests the pointlessness of Woods's position by recalling a comment of Richard Ely, an

American economist and Progressive Era spokesperson. Ely noted that Hull House was criticized for "not floating the sectarian flag;" church-based settlements were criticized for having one. Should we not just unify around common values, Ely suggested?

A Generation of Women Find a New Vocation

The "settlement impulse" as Davis described it, or the engine that energized the Social Gospel Movement, was fueled by a generation of young adults, particularly the first generation of college-educated women, feeling compelled to be useful in ways not previously defined, and understanding the urgent need for reform in industrial cities.[60] A large part of the influence was religious and predominantly Protestant. And, thus, Eleanor Stebner calls her work about the women of Hull House, "A Study in Spirituality, Vocation, and Friendship."

More than half of the settlements were Congregational or Presbyterian. Even Robert Woods, who chose not to open membership in the National Federation to church-affiliated settlements (like Erie House), began his settlement work in the Presbyterian-sponsored Andover House. In contrast to Woods's adamant insistence on separating settlements from any church affiliation, Jane called settlement work a "renaissance of Christianity." But Jane's "Christianity" was that of the "early Christian Movement" of simple fishermen who challenged the rich and powerful by their very existence.[61] If the theology of a "Church" ran along those lines, more spiritual than institutional, Jane viewed them as in sync with the values and objectives of the settlement movement. Or as Stebner argues, "Spirituality and religion are not mutually exclusive. A person (or institution) may be spiritual and religious, spiritual and NOT religious, or religious and NOT spiritual."[62]

In the midst of this renaissance, in 1915, The Noble Street "Mission" became the Erie Chapel Institute. While it would be another 20 years before it would be called Erie Neighborhood House, which sounds more like a social settlement name, the endeavor at 1347 W. Erie drew from and grew into that model, step by step. They did this with the support of what the Presbytery came to call the Mission Extension Board. And "extending the mission" was what they were doing. With few Presbyterians to fill churches in Chicago's inner city, they did not abandon these areas, but instead, extended their mission, the mission of Jesus of the Gospels, to live with and minister to the poor. Stebner points out that Toynbee Hall's Samuel Barnett argued that a mission has for its objective, conversion; a settlement has for its objective, mutual knowledge.[63] And while Addams agreed that settlements and missions were different, she did not disparage one over the other. "I am ready to say a mission is as much a finer thing than the settlement."[64] In other words, she did not see the two as rivals, but rather, workers in the same vineyard.

It would seem that Jane's understanding of how some "missions" in Chicago valued spirituality over dogma, was supported by the fact that, in the case of the Presbyterian Mission Extension Board, after 1890, the work was mostly among Catholic immigrants, as with the Poles and Italians described above, and which continued to be the case with the Latino immigrants that began arriving in the 1950s. While church services continued to be held at Erie House into the 1960s, contrary to Woods's concern about sectarianism, Erie House practiced Jane's idea of Christian humanitarianism seven days a week.

How this partnership evolved through the 100 years from 1915 to 2015 is what follows. It is hoped that scholars, practitioners, church leaders, and activists of today will add the Erie House Story to that of Hull House, and the settlement and social gospel movements, for a deeper understanding of what Jane hath wrought.

Chapter Three: The Angel of the Alleys: Florence Towne Comes to Erie Street, 1914-1951

The Erie Chapel and Chicago: Growth and Struggle, 1886-1915

Since 1886, when what had been called the Holland Presbyterian Church, moved out of a church building and into a structure built at 1347 W. Erie, it had become known, alternately, as the Noble Street Mission or, simply, Erie Chapel. In 1893, in addition to the opening of the World's Columbian Exposition in Chicago, the Erie Chapel Kindergarten was one of 20 new programs founded as part of Chicago's Free Kindergarten Association. By 1895, Erie expanded their building to accommodate that Kindergarten and the other programs described in Chapter Two–an industrial school, a boys' brigade, a junior choir, and a reading room. All of these operated side by side with church services and Sunday School. Poles and Italians had replaced the Dutch, Norwegians, and Germans, and were all working hard in the industries flourishing in Chicago: steel, railroads, metalworking, printing, food processing (i.e., the stockyards, etc.), manufacturing–especially clothing--and selling it in what became iconic department stores.

Edward Dunne (1905-1907), who had served as Mayor, deemed most representative of the Progressive Era in US History, was replaced by Republican, Fred Busse, the first mayor to have a four-year term, 1907-1911.

By 1909, Third Presbyterian Church was struggling for its own survival, so in 1911 it deeded the Erie Chapel property to the Presbytery of Chicago, specifically to the Mission Extension Board. Also, in 1909, The Burnham Plan was published, laying out a vision (at least of the business community) of what the

Photo: Florence Towne (Erie Neighborhood House)

future city might look like. They were either ignorant of Upton Sinclair's publication of 1906, *The Jungle,* or, more likely, were ambitiously putting forth a counter narrative. Clearly, people coming to the Erie Chapel in 1909 were more impacted by what was outlined in the latter publication. That year, a law was passed to limit the working day for women to 10 hours per day. This would, supposedly, give them more time with their children under 14, as eligibility to be legally employed had been capped at 14, in 1899. Still, mom and dad and their older siblings could look forward to finding work in companies such as Wisconsin Steel, International Harvester, or even Riverview Park, that opened in 1902, 03, and 04, respectively. If they worked in the garment industry, as many immigrants did, they were on strike in 1904. In anticipation of, and as facilitator of, The Great Migration of African Americans from south to North, *The Defender,* started publication in 1905.

In a notebook found in the Erie House archives,[65] Mrs. Evangeline Gielow made the following observation. After 1910, she says: "People left the neighborhood (around Erie Chapel) in droves." She documents this exclamation with a conversation she says she had with the area's mailman. He told her that in a 60-day period, 550 families moved out, in particular, to Austin and Logan Square. As those families moved out, the next wave of immigrants moved in. By 1920, Poles coming to Chicago far outdistanced any other country of origin. Mrs. Gielow, and her husband, Walter Gielow, were among the most active board members that Florence Towne would work with, from her first days at Erie Chapel, throughout most of her days as Head Resident. Gielow, a name of German origin, was of that generation of German Americans who prospered and moved away from the central city neighborhoods. For the Gielows it was Lincoln Square, at its eastern most edge with Uptown, and, eventually, Oak Park.

While Walter Gielow served as Erie Board president, Evangeline was serving as president of the Erie House Woman's Auxiliary (EWA) and running the annual Tag Day fundraiser. For a good part of the 20th century, this was where Presbyterian church women focused their energies. In the earliest days, they often ran Sunday Schools, but at the neighborhood houses, that role evolved to fundraising and volunteering in program work. The EWA at Erie lasted longer than most, from the 1920s to the 1990s. For almost 40 of those 70 years, they ran Meals on Wheels and the Thrift Shop at Erie House

For entertainment, the Cubs won the World Series for the second year in a row in 1908. Who knew then how long it would be before that happened again? Films were being produced in Chicago by 1909, long before Hollywood existed. One out of every 10,000 Chicago residents owned a car. These would have been the people who employed Erie Chapel's neighbors, and could probably also afford a drink at the Green Mill (1907-present). Hopefully, they did not purchase tickets at the Iroquois Theater when it burned down in 1903, killing 602 patrons – mostly women and children. As of 1913, the more affluent would have to start supporting their country through an income tax (16th Amendment). And by 1914, some of those taxpayers opened 4th Presbyterian Church, destined to be the spiritual home of some of Chicago's wealthiest and most distinguished citizens. In that same year, Miss Florence Towne arrived at Erie Chapel to serve as Kindergarten teacher and to oversee girls' programs.

Erie Chapel Becomes the Erie Chapel Institute in 1915

In 1915, Erie Chapel incorporated as the Erie Chapel Institute, and Carter Harrison II was finishing his last term as mayor, 1911-1915. Rev. George J. Searles arrived as the new minister and director. The staff consisted of three people: the pastor/director, the boys' worker and the girls' worker/kindergarten teacher (Miss Towne). They had an annual budget of $6,400.

The circumstances surrounding Rev. Searles's "calling" to Erie Chapel were outlined in a letter to him from Rev. Clyde W. Smith, dated August 15, 1914.[66] Rev. Smith was the Director of Immigration & Social Service of the Church Extension Board of the Presbytery of Chicago, at 509 S. Wabash at that time. [The fact that such a position existed in a denominational structure in 1914 is worth noting.] In essence, this is a letter, from one minister to another, providing a straightforward assessment of what to expect if he were to accept the "call" to serve at Erie Chapel. Thomas Templeton and other leaders at Erie Chapel, were clearly petitioning the Presbytery for a minister. Rev. Smith indicates that, as a "Presbyterian church" Erie Chapel would not be getting a minister, as there was only a" handful" of members, too small be a conventional church.

But Smith goes on to point out that he thinks there is important work to be done in the Erie Chapel neighborhood, and that there are good people there to work with--"a credit to any church, excepting none. The devotion they show and their willingness to work is a constant marvel to me." He just wants Searles to be realistic about what he is getting into. He tells him candidly that he is not being called for his preaching, but rather for his leadership and administrative skills. And he is probably Erie's "last chance" to "call" anyone--Erie's last stand to find the right leader. "If Erie justifies itself under your leadership, they will sail ahead and support will be forthcoming for whatever extension is needed." And so, it did, and so it was.

Finally, Smith admonishes Searles to look upon his chance to go to Erie as St. Paul regarded the opportunity to go to Ephesus -- "A great door has been opened unto me," Paul said. And, he closes, just outside the Erie Chapel door is Chicago, proclaiming: "Chicago is the heart of the world!"

Searles went through the Erie door in 1914 and entered into the heart of the world, or at least, West Town.

The following year, on the 26th of September, 1915, a Certificate of Incorporation was filed for the organization of the Erie Chapel Institute (ECI) that was officially recorded on December 1, 1915 by the Secretary of State, Lewis G. Stevenson. The names that appear on the certificate on behalf of ECI are: Thomas Templeton of 112 W. Adams, Walter C. Gielow of 1627 W. Ainslie, and Julius Fulde, of 1448 W. Bryn Mawr. Fulde, of German ancestry like Gielow, had also moved to the north side, to what is now Edgewater. Templeton stayed much closer to Erie, just a little over 2 miles away. There would be an ECI board of 9 or more persons. That first board included Templeton, Fulde, Gielow and his wife, Evangeline, George Peterson, John Menton Freeman, and the Misses Anna Thourson, Emma Rasmussen, Florence Simbert, Florence Price, and Afra Ramey. Rev. Clyde Smith and Rev. Searles were also on the board. In all, there were 7 men and 6 women, very gender-balanced for early 20th century. Then again, the 19th Amendment was just around the corner.

At the time of incorporation, the ECI outlined four goals in the Institute's work with residents:

1. Improve their social condition;
2. Implant high ideals;
3. Protect them from exploitation;
4. Help *them* fight for a better life.

Jane would have approved; she would have especially agreed with the concept of enabling implied in the fourth point. Erie's neighbors are expected to stand up for themselves, with ECI providing the assist. This message itself represented one of those high ideals to be implanted. But neighbors could also be assured of Erie's protection as they prepared to take on the struggle. These themes have been the basis for Erie's *raison d'etre* for its 150 years.

As 1916 dawned, Thomas Templeton died on January 25. This faithful servant of Holland Presbyterian Church, Noble Street Mission, and Erie Chapel, could rest in peace as he had accomplished his goal of securing a new minister and a new name for the ministry he supported through thick and thin. He would have been pleased to know that his sister, Hannah, honored that ministry by leaving a substantial sum in her will in 1933 that would carry Erie forward and allow it to expand again in 1935.

Already in 1916, evidence of the new ECI structure appears in the form of annual reports to the ECI board by Rev. Searles and Miss Towne. Kindergarten enrollment is at 53. The Mothers Club has 30 members with 51 children among them, representing 10 nationalities. So, while Poles and Italians were the largest groups in the area, clearly there were others. There are three Girls' Clubs: Pre-school enrollment was 106; School Age, 65, and Working Girls' enrollment averaged 31. The latter were girls over 14 who could still work, and generally, did. Miss Florence reported that Boys' Work was not going so well due to excessive staff turnover. English classes (ESL) were mostly populated by Poles being taught by volunteers from the Moody Bible Institute, only about 1.5 miles east of Erie. Still is.

It is noted in the annual reports that the work of ECI is greatly supplemented by volunteers—846 during the previous year. It is not clear if this is a duplicated or unduplicated count, but the point is, volunteers were critical to the work of the Institute. Two Presbyterian churches are mentioned at this early date for sending volunteers: Buena Memorial (located on the border of Uptown and Lakeview) and First Presbyterian Church of Oak Park, which is a supporter of Erie to this day. But, even with these volunteers, Rev. Searles concluded his report by saying that

ECI's principal need was money. Expenses in 1916 were $8,258, in spite of a budget set at $6,400.

While Poles may have been attending English classes in 1916, by 1918 there is a note in the financial report regarding the purchase of 20 hymnbooks in Italian. And one of the new church attendees was listed as Mary Josephine Nitti of 1473 W. Grand. [One can only surmise that Ms. Nitti might be some relation to Frank Nitti who became a member of Al Capone's gang in the 1920s.] There were also a number of local stores with the Nitti name on them as late as the 1960s, along Grand Avenue. La Rocco's (or La Roc's as it came to be called), was located at the corner of Grand and Ogden, where you could get great Italian beef sandwiches as well as hot dogs and hamburgers. It was a family-owned precursor to the drive-through chains of today. According to Erie's records, Adelaide Berkeley La Rocco, of 2328 W. Iowa, joined the Erie Chapel in 1918.[67]

The 1918 Annual Report also mentions revenue from Tag Day of $1,697. This may not seem much by today's standards, but at the time, this represented about 20% of the ECI budget. 20% of Erie's budget in 2000 would have been $1.6 million. Throughout the 20th century, Tag Day was a fundraising project organized by the Children's Benefit League to assist their member organizations. Each non-profit organization received boxes to collect money on street corners from the general public. Each donor received a tag to wear as a sign they had given some money to the cause. The amount of money raised was generally dependent on how many volunteers an organization could muster for one-to-two-hour shifts throughout the day, and what type of locations they were assigned to. Erie generally had locations downtown, at six-corner locations in more affluent neighborhoods, and, eventually in suburbs near the Presbyterian churches that supported them and provided volunteers in their town. Tag Day was an annual fundraiser for Erie into the 1990s, when it was decided that the time and organization required versus the amount of money raised was no longer cost-effective. But, for many years, it was a concrete opportunity for Erie's network of church supporters to volunteer on behalf of Erie, near their home or workplace. Over time, maintaining the engagement of that network was the value-added more than the cash proceeds.

As ECI moved into the 1920s, Mrs. Gielow's notebook reveals that the budget had increased to $23,000. She notes that only 2% of that came from the Church Extension Board, and half of that came from the Hannah Templeton estate. The rest the board had to raise. The Chapel congregation in the 1920s was around 420. Meanwhile, program participation continued to grow, making serious demands on the 1886 building that sat at 1347 W. Erie. In spite of adding the third room, and even digging out the basement to add more room, the board decided it was time to start thinking about an entirely new and larger building. In fact, some preliminary blueprints were drawn up as early as 1923. But that dream would take time, not to be realized until the next decade, and under new leadership. Because, after 8 years of service, Rev. Searles resigned in 1922. "Big Bill" Thompson was just finishing his second term as mayor, turning the office back to the Democrats with the election of William Dever.

Miss Florence Gets the Call

Miss Florence Hayden Towne became Superintendent/Head Resident in 1926, having already been on staff since 1914, one year before the Erie Chapel became the Erie Chapel Institute, when she came to teach kindergarten at the age of 28. She was born in Lombard, Illinois in 1886, the year Erie Chapel was built at 1347 W. Erie, and three years before Jane Addams founded Hull House. She was one of two daughters of Henry Beeman Towne of Troy, New York, and Caroline Latham Wilson

Towne (Bama) of Lombard. From the time she became Head Resident, until the new building opened in 1936, she lived on the third floor in a building behind the ECI structure, above the janitor's apartment and a garage. When the current structure opened, she occupied two rooms on the third floor in the area designated for staff quarters.

One year after she became Head Resident, Chicago elected its last Republican mayor, as William Hale Thompson began his third and final term. 90 years have now passed, and no Republican has occupied the fifth floor of Chicago's City Hall. In 1932, descendants of Czech immigrants helped elect their favorite son, Anton Cermak, a Democrat, to serve as mayor. However, he did not serve for long as he was assassinated in 1933, as he stood next to President Franklin Delano Roosevelt. (The unresolved historical question remains: Was Cermak the actual target or was he the unfortunate victim of a bad marksman, aiming for President Roosevelt?) Following the service of an uncelebrated interim mayor, Edward Kelly, another Democrat, served as mayor until 1947.

What happened at ECI, from the time Searles left to when Miss Florence took over is a bit sketchy. Some glimpses emerge from well-kept notes of the Woman's Auxiliary of Erie. We know they started as a group of women from various Presbyterian churches who met regularly at Erie Chapel and Erie House, to support its mission, beginning in 1924. They raised money and had a special focus on mothers and children. From their by-laws:

> *The purpose of this auxiliary shall be to assist the Board of Directors of Erie Neighborhood House to stimulate interest in Christian Service and to secure funds for the Erie community from members of the Chicago Presbytery.*[68]

Membership was open to all women interested in this purpose, but in particular, it was expected that every woman's organization in the churches assigned to Erie House would be requested to send one or more reps to this auxiliary. At that time there were ten Presbyterian churches participating: River Forest, 1st Presbyterian of Oak Park, Fair Oaks (also in Oak Park), Austin First Presbyterian, Edgewater Presbyterian, Buena Memorial, 4th Pres, Wilmette Pres, First and Second Pres of Evanston. With the exception of Austin, Edgewater, and Buena, the other churches were all suburban, reflecting the migration from city to suburb for people of means this early in the 20th century. As the 1920 census indicated, while the population of Chicago had reached 2,701,705, the surrounding eight counties had 5,575,209.

Other notes from the Women's Auxiliary notebook, include reference to the "Pleasant Sunday Evening Club" that met at Erie.[69] The idea of a social gathering on a Sunday evening was carried out at Hull House and many other settlements, when Sunday was the only day off work, and thereby, truly a day of rest. If the local tavern was not your hangout of choice, the settlement house might be. It was certainly more family-oriented. It was noted in 1928, that Erie invited a group of youth from Howell House on South Racine Ave., later to be renamed "Casa Aztlan," as its Pilsen location turned over from Czech to Mexican immigrant residents in the latter half of the 20th century. But, before that, there were Mexicans in Chicago, as early as 1920, in the Hull House Neighborhood. They became known for their colorful Fiesta Ware, pioneered in the kilns of Hull House.[70] They were also renowned for their mural work on the walls of Hull House buildings, all lost to Chicago when most of the Hull House buildings were razed to build the University of Illinois Chicago campus in the 1950s.

In 1928, Auxiliary members remarked on the lack of space to work with the ever-expanding Mothers Club, echoing space complaints that had emerged as early as 1923, when the first blueprint plans for a new building appeared. Ultimately, they worked side-by-side with their husbands to raise money and plan for the new structure to replace the building they visited, at least monthly, for their meetings. In 1930, they called upon architect, Benjamin Franklin Olson, of 19 S. LaSalle Street, to revise the earlier blueprint of 1923. Olson had once worked for the distinguished architectural firm of Pond & Pond, designer of the Hull House buildings and others in the downtown area. His 1930 plans, titled *Chapel and Neighborhood House for the Erie Chapel Institute,* were dated May 12 of that year. Five more years would pass before that design was actualized.

But, on a day to day basis, when told that Erie's food pantry was empty, the women of the Auxiliary reached out to their respective churches for donations of food, and brought back to those churches the stories of the people who needed that food, along with the work of Miss Florence and her colleagues. They included in their meeting minutes, an introduction to the "Erie Tigers," a group of 14 boys, age 16-19, that were organized at Erie, to participate in sports, leadership training, learning art, music, and public speaking.

One of the Tigers, John Vitacco, age 16, wrote an article for their quarterly newsletter, *The Advance.*[71] His article was entitled: "Erie Chapel and its Work." He begins by saying there is a type of "welfare work" that happens in a place called a settlement house, and every "congested neighborhood" has one. He further explains that "Erie Chapel abides with every detail and connection that pertains to the settlement house and also serves as an auxiliary to churches." From this, it sounds like 16-year old John has been tuned into the ongoing argument as to whether church-supported neighborhood houses were actually settlement houses. He goes on to say the Erie Chapel is our "Community Center." He says that immigrants, like his family, "turn in bewilderment to the friendly help offered, tactfully, by men and women of sympathetic judgment." With Erie's "friendly help," he eventually became a doctor.

So, here is the description of settlement house principles — community-centered, friendly, non-judgmental, in service to immigrants coping with a confusing new culture, finding the assistance they need, regardless of their age. Even a 16-year old understood the value of this concept. The connection between church and settlement was not an obstacle to carrying out the humanitarian "mission" of the settlement movement. Rather it was a mutually beneficial arrangement--church members benefitted from their engagement with the poor, as much as the poor benefited from their largesse. On the one hand, they learned that the world was made up of people of different classes, but not so different human qualities. This was the Gospel message and the settlement movement message. And Erie neighbors benefited, not only from the resources that came from supporters to them through the settlement, but also from whatever their benefactors may have absorbed that led them to consider paying a living wage, and modifying their prejudices against people who were different. This was that "education through permeation" that Barnett of Toynbee Hall considered a critical component of the settlement experience.

Perhaps, young John was given an article to read that someone, probably Miss Florence, had saved, that was published in 1925 in a National Board of Missions publication that pertained to settlement houses. The author, Christine Wilson, wrote that Neighborhood Houses have a set of goals that are different from but complementary to churches.

Workers are measuring their success in terms of transformed neighborhoods and individuals, the development of individual social consciousness and action, and by the extent and continuation of

community participation in the Neighborhood
House program. Only a few tested their success in
terms of church membership.[72]

In the same file, there are quotes from the Conference of Neighborhood House Work held in 1925. In one of the papers from this conference, Laura H. Dixon writes: "The Neighborhood House exists to demonstrate the power of practical Christianity."

And finally, Dr. W. Clyde Smith, who wrote the letter urging Rev. Searles to consider the call to the Erie Chapel, said the following in one of his papers:

> *The Neighborhood House goes into the*
> *neighborhood to be part of it, conscious of a*
> *contribution to make, knowing it will receive as well*
> *as give, rejoicing in the opportunity that is given to*
> *know the humanity of which it is a part. It says in*
> *effect to the community – 'Come, let us work and*
> *play and live together, give the best you have and*
> *we will give the best we have, that all of us may do*
> *a bit for the welfare of all.'*[73]

It is evident, then, that Miss Florence had the benefit of knowing and hearing from Jane Addams, herself, as well as leaders and spokespersons in the Presbyterian church, who echoed in their words the concept of the social settlement as the model they expected Neighborhood Houses to embrace. Message received. . . and advanced.

The Open Door: A Place to Come

Early in 1932, in Miss Florence's 6th year as Head Resident, the ECI published a brochure titled "The Open Door."[74] It was 15 pages long, with a different photo and headline on each page. The front cover featured a photo of

Erie's neighbors on the front steps of the ECI building, at "the open door." Inside, a glimpse of the work the ECI was doing in the early 1930's as the Great Depression was unfolding, is laid out. It says ECI was a place where:

- Men and women come with their troubles, and find friendliness, cheer, new hope and courage, and a new faith in Jesus Christ;
- Young people, boys and girls, learn to form right habits, through clubs and classes;
- Little children come to play and learn;
- 15 different nationalities come each week to find an answer to their need.[75]

Next is a photo of Miss Rose with her Kindergarten class of 50. It is noted that 15 years earlier, in 1917, Miss Rose was, herself, a student in the ECI Kindergarten. This example of an "Erie kid" returning as an adult to work at Erie, becomes a common occurrence over the organization's 150-year history. As a contemporary staff person remarked: "Erie never let's go." Subsequent pages of the brochure describe numerous clubs, classes, athletic activities, and summers at Camp Gray -- all aimed to engage neighbors from age 5 to 75, meeting their needs for survival, and giving them hope that they could survive in an America with a 50% unemployment rate, with no streets paved with gold in sight. The brochure documents that, in the three months prior to its publication, 1,054 people came to 1347 W. Erie for assistance, compared with 1,573 for the entire previous year.

Even in the context of this extreme deprivation, every children's club had a "bank account" for the pennies in dues they probably "earned" giving a performance at Erie. Financial management was being taught at every opportunity. The children saved for the purchase of athletic equipment or supplies for art classes. Some even said they wanted to earn money to donate to "construction of the new building." When children were not at school or at work, the door at ECI was open to them. During the day and in the evenings, the boys' library or the game room was open. The invitation was specifically extended, as follows: "Delinquent boys welcome." There were 13 organized clubs and 14 gym classes for boys. While Miss Florence recognized the important work of the women of Hull House in establishing a Juvenile Court system, her goal was always to prevent delinquency in the first place, intervening before the boys' actions required them to appear in Court, Juvenile or otherwise.

Fridays, "The Ministry of the Old Clothes Cupboard" moved into action. Volunteer church women gathered clothes through their auxiliary members. Again, they note that clothing had been distributed to 414 people compared to 165 for a comparable period the year before. While their husbands worked in corporate America by day, they were, no doubt, hearing stories at night from their wives who witnessed "the other America." This assumption is supported by Presbyterian church historian, Rev. Richard Poethig. In his 1995 article, he wrote,

> *Very often the congregation's relationship to the neighborhood house provided the chief experience for its membership's understanding of the problems of the urban working class.*[76]

Poethig also cites the early work of William Shriver, elected to the Presbyterian Board of National Missions in 1907, and who was given charge of creating programs for ministry among immigrants, from 1910 until 1940. Under his leadership, by 1925, the Presbyterian Church in the US was guarantor of 30 neighborhood houses; by 1940, the number had grown to 114. Neither Poethig, or anyone else, is suggesting this ministry was a cure for capitalism, and the unbalanced power structure it creates, that results in the poverty of too many in America, and everywhere else in the world. But neither does it ignore that reality. Even Jesus sadly acknowledged that the poor were not likely to disappear, but he urged his followers to go out among the marginalized and let them know they deserved attention, that they were loved.

While in these early days of ECI, there is not much evidence of the settlement's call to empower their neighbors to take the lead in bringing about the changes in public policy that will be evident in the work of Erie Neighborhood House in later years, the foundation of support for the rights of immigrants as citizens of the human community is well laid. Like Jane Addams, Florence took up her pen and wrote a book in 1940, called, simply, *Neighbors*. While this slim volume does not rank with the writings of the renowned Jane Addams, the following is evidence of how her thinking aligned with Addams and the views of the Presbyterian Church in their ministry among immigrants. In the book she says,

> *I am often asked, 'Do you see any signs of anarchistic tendencies among your neighbors?' . . . I invariably reply, 'No, they are, most of them, too weak and hungry' . . . buffeted about the Relief Station. . . and treated so generally as inferior beings they have about reached the place where they believe they are inferior and have accepted the label put upon them so unfairly.*[77]

As capitalism had collapsed under its own weight with the Crash in 1929, this was Miss Florence's reflection on the work of the ECI in the 1930s, where, in 1931 alone, they served 150,000 people at their wholly inadequate building on Erie Street, with a budget of about $18,000, no endowment, and a paid staff of seven—four, full time and three, part time. Clearly, this could not have been accomplished without the 125, more affluent, church volunteers and the benefit of the New Deal's WPA workers, who were deployed at ECI and Erie Neighborhood House for as long as that program lasted. As Allen Davis noted, settlement workers had their hands all over the New Deal. While they worked at that level, the local settlement/neighborhood house back home became a meeting ground for the two groups the early 20th century American culture defined as enemies. But settlement work created the opportunity for the middle and upper classes and the underclass to learn from each other as neighbors – not in the geographic sense of that word, but in the Gospel sense.

The "Open Door" brochure closed with a list of the members of both the Women's Auxiliary Board and the ECI Board of Directors for 1932. Some of the names on these lists had been active at Erie since the incorporation of the Erie Chapel Institute in 1915; the names of others will appear over and over into the 1950s. The constancy of these Protestant lay leaders made neighborhood houses not only possible, but strong. At the head of this list would be Walter C. Gielow, who was on the board when ECI was incorporated, served as Board president in subsequent years, until his death in 1945. His wife, Evangeline, also served on the ECI Board at the same time that she was secretary of the Erie Woman's Auxiliary (EWA). The president of the EWA was Mrs. A. L. Sawyer from First Presbyterian of Oak Park. Her husband, Dr. A. L. Sawyer, eventually joined her on the ECI Board. The Sawyers would become long term benefactors, and thus, Erie House first floor classrooms are, today, known as the Sawyer Rooms. William G. Dahl and John E. Dahl are listed as board members. These two are of Swedish ancestry. William Dahl, however, was not Presbyterian, but is named in the records of the Evangelical Lutheran Church of America (ELCA). He was probably brought to the Board by his father, John, who may trace his connection to Erie back to the late 19th century, when

Scandinavians lived not far from Erie. Another Scandinavian on the Board was Arthur C. Anderson, not the founder of the well-known accounting firm of Chicago, but perhaps, a Norwegian cousin. Anna Thourson, also dating back to ECI incorporation, served as secretary to the board for many years.

This was the core group that began to dream about a new and larger building to meet the growing demand for services and the need for "a place to come."

A Dream Come True: The Construction of Erie Neighborhood House, 1935-36

The drafts of blueprints for a new building, dated 1923 and 1930, are evidence that the need for more space was on the ECI agenda for a long time before plans could move forward. So, in 1933, when Hannah Templeton bequeathed $100,000 to Erie to honor her late brother, Thomas, the dream was about to become real. Its church connection would ensure Erie would have a home at 1347 W. Erie for the next 80+ years and still counting. Both Hannah and Thomas Templeton were members of Third Presbyterian during the years their church had responsibility for the Noble Street Mission and then built the first structure at 1347 W. Erie for the Erie Chapel Institute.[78]

According to the Erie board's financial report for 1934-35, no new building would have been possible without this infusion of capital. Here is what they reported as "Sources of Income":

10% from the Church Extension Board	2,000
15% pledges from Individuals and churches	3,000
20% from the Community Fund	4,000

Total	9,000
55%, balance to be raised through contributions not yet pledged	11,000
Total Budget	$20,000[79]

By this time, Dr. A.L. Sawyer has joined the Board, along with N. Ray Miller, who served as Chair of the Building Committee, and Dr. Leora Davies who would serve for many more years. In their enthusiasm to begin the planning process for new construction, the board put together a booklet to describe some of the projected elements of the new building.[80] The description begins: "In front of the building is a sunken garden with green grass and shrubbery." Whether this was ever "a sunken garden" is not known. As the building exists today, one does need to walk down a few steps to reach the front door of the building, but there is only a strip of greenery on one side; the rest of the "sunken" area is concrete.

However, several of the projected inside space plans came to fruition. They dubbed a first-floor room the Florence Towne Auditorium, later called Towne Hall, and used as an auditorium space until, more than 50 years later, it was claimed for use by the School Age program. There was a large dining room next to an ample kitchen. That dining room was later dubbed the Sawyer Room. The gym was built on the second floor and named Gielow Gymnasium. Also, on the second floor were rooms to serve 50 Kindergartners. There would be an adjacent, but attached, building, with its own entrance that would be the sanctuary for church services, for its 416 church members. Fittingly, it would be called the Templeton Memorial Chapel, that sat above Towne Auditorium.

As these plans became more and more definite, Erie's family case records underscored the justification for this undertaking. They documented that 16,000 men, women and children participated in 103 activities each month at ECI.[81] There were six full time and three part time employees, assisted by 68 volunteers, working in three adjacent buildings, including 1351 and 1353 W. Erie. This pre-construction booklet closes with testimonials from some of the board members. Dr. J.W.G. Ward notes the faithful, longtime commitment to Erie by First Church of Oak Park. Mrs. William H. Wilson says:

> *I am thankful every day for the privilege of sharing in the work of Erie Neighborhood House, knowing what this house means to its people, of their loyalty and appreciation, how lives are remolded. . .Nothing could be more worthwhile.*[82]

It should be noted that this was the first use of "Erie Neighborhood House" rather than Erie Chapel Institute. This new name would be engraved on the front of the new building.

The Board developed a second brochure called "Questions and Answers About the Building."[83] Here they address the question of why they intend to build at the same location as the 50-year-old ECI building. They point out that 99% of participants and 81% of church members live within five blocks of 1347 W. Erie. They acknowledge that many churches have left the neighborhood.   Erie Chapel has stayed, based on the belief that while the population may "thin out," with some people moving further west, their services will still be needed and people will travel a little further to take advantage of them. So, as early as the 1930s, the concern that neighborhood changes might compel them to move away from 1347 was raised. In a way, this was a kind of foreshadowing of a discussion that would be revisited 50 years later as the neighborhood not only thinned out, but gentrified. First, European ethnics, and later, Puerto Ricans and Mexicans, in fact, moved west and northwest, away from the immediate neighborhood around Erie. Later chapters will discuss the strategies Erie employed to address these changes, and still maintain services at 1347 W. Erie.

During what was projected as a six-month construction period, some programs would operate out of space they were renting in a corner building at 1400 W. Erie. They would utilize space on the first floor, formerly occupied by a drug store, as well as a second-floor apartment. The Assemblea Christiana, an Italian Church across the street from ECI, at 1350 W. Erie, offered space for afternoon clubs and classes. Over the years, Erie rented space from various denominations that occupied that space when even the "new" 1347 building was running out of space. Arrangements were made with a church located at Chicago and Noble, probably the Lutheran Church mentioned earlier, for Erie Chapel services and Sunday School during the interim. Since 1935, that church has been replaced by a different type of real estate.

While the Board explained that the entire Templeton bequest would be needed for the physical structure, they hoped individuals and/or churches would step up to furnish a room, perhaps as a memorial to a friend. Plaques are still visible in the 1347 building as tributes to those who helped Erie move forward in those early days, plaques naming Walter Gielow, N. Ray Miller, Frances Sawyer, and Hannah & Thomas Templeton. This same approach would be used 60 years later to furnish pre-school classrooms for an Erie expansion in 1995.

On April 25, 1935, Erie's architect, Benjamin F. Olson, accepted a demolition proposal from C. J. McGuire Wrecking company of 225 N. Francisco to tear down Erie's existing structures for $350. Building Committee Chair, N. Ray Miller, approved the contract. Correspondence among ECI board members regarding construction matters were written on company letterheads. This fact provides a perspective in two areas. First, the construction of the new building was managed by board members who worked closely with the architect. Second, these board members were "downtown businessmen" who, voluntarily, took time away from their business day to deal with this project for the non-profit community organization they were committed to support. N. Ray Miller worked for Chandler & Montague at 38 S. Dearborn. There was both a Montague and a Chandler on the membership list of the Chicago Board of Trade at the turn of the 19th century. We can only speculate that descendants of these early commodities players merged interest at some point to form the company Miller worked for. Mr. Gielow worked in the insurance industry, apparently in partnership that resulted in Cloidt-Gielow & Dudley, 175 W. Jackson.[84]

While the board members were handling bids and contracts, Miss Florence was not silent. She spoke with the architect to review the general plans, and sent suggestions to the Building Committee. These included her suggestions they heat the building with coal v. oil, and that there be an entrance at street level to access the Chapel and Towne Hall. That suggestion was definitely implemented, which allowed access for various events, like church services on Sunday, that did not require people to trek through program space. She also wrote a letter to Mr. Miller, urging him to consider hiring Herman Reininga for the carpentry work, based on his connection to First Church of Oak Park, a longtime benefactor of ECI. Done. She also hoped the construction project would provide jobs for a few local young men. She named four of them. So, Miss Florence was directly involved in design decisions and paid attention to how this project might benefit the ECI community of neighbors and friends, even before it was finished.

By June of 1935, the contract for the foundation went to Robert Goldie & Co. of 19 S. LaSalle, perhaps, a neighbor of Olson who had his office in the same building. Cost: $43,295.[85] On July 16, 1935, 26th Ward Alderman

Konkowski, proposed an ordinance to exempt ECI from various building permit fees. He gleaned the needed support from his fellow aldermen. Among them were names that were then, or eventually became, prominent in the history of Chicago politics. These included: Bathhouse John Coughlin, who shared responsibility for the City Council's nickname, "The Gray Wolves," during the late 19th and early 20th century. There was William Dawson, founder of the African American version of Chicago's Democratic political machine. Jake Arvey, who eventually rose to leadership in the state Democratic apparatus, is named. Tom Keane was already in place, and would become City Council floor leader under Mayor Richard J. Daley, until Keane went to jail for corruption in the 1970s. Congressman Dan Rostenkowski, Democratic majority whip in the 1970s, could find his father there, as could current State Senator John Cullerton. Erie House would be dealing with Keane, and the Rostenkowski and Cullerton descendants at a later time.

On July 28, 1935, a crowd gathered on Erie Street for the laying of the cornerstone. On it was inscribed: "To the glory of God and the service of his children," a phrase that represented its past, present, and future commitment. The solemn and prayerful celebration of the day was presided over by Rev. William O. Ruby, Assistant Superintendent of the Church Extension Board (CEB) of the Presbytery of Chicago. An invocation was offered by the pastor of Wilmette Presbyterian Church, and a prayer of dedication was led by the pastor of Rogers Park Presbyterian, as Board President, Walter Gielow, set the stone in place. Hymns were sung, featuring a solo by Mrs. Herbert Gielow, Walter's sister-in-law. The sermon connected the work of Erie, described as "enterprise, refuge, inspiration, and earnestness" with the work of Christ. The Postlude was "The Grand March' from Aida by Verdi.[86]

As board members, church leaders, and neighbors were celebrating the beginning of a new era for the Erie Chapel Institute, 1935 proved to be an important year for the New Deal as well. The National Labor Relations Act was passed as well as Social Security. The Congress of Industrial Organizations, the CIO, opened its doors as unions continued their fight for workers' rights in the face of un-heard of unemployment figures. To provide the unemployed with the dignity of some work and a small wage, The Works Progress Administration (WPA) and Federal Writers Project were organized. To take their minds off their troubles, Americans listened to and laughed with *Fibber McGee and Molly* on the radio.

By November, 1935, Gielow notified Miller that the board had authorized completion of the residential quarters on the third floor, at a cost not to exceed $7,000. Instead of living over a garage, Miss Florence could look forward to living over the work she loved. She would just have two rooms – a bedroom and a parlor. The other rooms in the residential quarters consisted of seven bedrooms with a shared bath between, and a kitchen. Other rooms on that floor were likely used for the pastor's quarters. The residential quarters were in use for staff and summer volunteers into the 1970s, but Miss Florence was the only Head Resident who lived there. Pastors no longer lived there after the 1940s.

Once all the construction contractors were selected, the firm of Bradley, Harper, Huss, & Rehm reviewed the contracts for a fee of $50. The total cost of construction was $84,613, and miscellaneous costs were noted as $11,329. When the building was actually completed, a Continental Bank report showed charges against the Templeton Trust at $96,226. These frugal Presbyterians managed to bring construction costs within the range of the Hannah Templeton bequest. Other Erie supporters contributed any additional dollars required to finish the project. This was outlined in a pamphlet entitled "How a Vision of Many Years Becomes a Reality in Our New Building."

The opening paragraph recognizes the generosity of the Templeton family and other friends of Erie who "made possible this demonstration of the blessings that consecrated wealth can bestow on those less privileged." This opening "thank you note" is followed by a tour of the new building, beginning with the "sunken forecourt" envisioned in the early renderings of the project. One then proceeds into the "Friendly Lobby." Here all gather "in the warmth of the beautiful stone fireplace for sociability, counsel, or aid." This room was made possible by Mrs. William H. Wilson, a board member. On one side of the lobby is the auditorium, later named Towne Hall; on the other side is the Mothers' Room, dedicated to Mrs. Frances Curtis Sawyer. On the second floor is the gym, the Kindergarten, the library and the Pastor's conference room. The pamphlet closes with special thanks to the Building Committee, and in particular to the Chair, Mr. N. Ray Miller.[87]

When the new building officially opened on March 15, 1936, Erie Neighborhood House (ENH) had 12 staff, the Depression's end was nowhere in sight, and the WPA, just launched a year earlier, sent 50 workers to Erie House.[88] Franklin Delano Roosevelt had been president for four years and had nine more years to go. Ed Kelly was still mayor and would be for 11 more years. To mark the opening of the new building, "Dedication Week" ran from March 22- 28. On the front cover of the program of dedication week, the years 1886-1936, indicated that 50 years had passed since the first Erie structure was constructed on this site. There was also a detailed drawing of the brand-new Erie Neighborhood House and Templeton Memorial Chapel. Below the drawing is a passage from *John 10:10*: "That they might have life and have it more abundantly." This quotation captures the essence of the purpose of this new edifice – that the people who come to this place may flourish.

Dedication week opened with a service on Sunday afternoon. Dr. Henry Brown of the Presbyterian Church Extension Board presided, and the sermon was delivered by Rev. J.W.G. Ward, First Presbyterian Church of Oak Park. The invocation that day:

We humbly pray that we may be worthy of the memory of the throng of consecrated helpers who have labored here and that we may continue to merit the whole-hearted support of our friends everywhere.[89]

On Monday night, there would be an Open House and Demonstration Night "for our friends outside the neighborhood," pertaining to the numerous churches that supported Erie Neighborhood House. On Tuesday, from 3:00-9:30 would be an Open House for friends in other settlements and neighborhood houses, all other social service agencies and teachers from local schools. Thursday evening was designated "Neighborhood Night – an evening of fun and fellowship for our neighbors." And, finally, Young People's Night on Saturday with a banquet and program.

As beautiful and perfect as everything sounds during dedication week, a month later, April 21, 1936, Miss Florence has penned a letter to Mr. Miller, outlining six building issues that still needed to be addressed. Items of note included the mention of Mr. Savino, who was already working as janitor in 1936. (His wife, Mary, later known to all as "Mom Savino," stayed connected to Erie for the next 50 years.) She is also calling for a fence around the playground, not only to keep the little ones in, but also to keep the older boys out. Miss Florence complains, "Boys from the alley try to peek when the girls are taking showers. . ." This letter is also special as it is one of the few examples found with Miss Towne's actual signature, and it is typed on what must have been new stationery created after the completion of the new building. It says "Erie Neighborhood House, Formerly Erie Chapel Institute" on top, and features the drawing of the new building at the bottom. Also, across the bottom of the page is the line: *Endorsed by the Association of Commerce Subscription Investigating Committee for the Regular Period Ending November 30, 1936.*[90]

According to a 1922 article in *Chicago Commerce*,[91] this "Investigating Committee" was organized in 1912, apparently by a group of businessmen, to evaluate charitable organizations and report on their "worthiness" to receive philanthropic dollars. The evaluation was guided by the following standards for each organization:

1) It was not duplicating work already done by another organization;
2) It was providing effective services to its constituents;
3) It was financially sound and managed its funds effectively.

The author of the article, W.C. Shurtleff, also the Chair of the Investigating Committee, implied that their endorsement was sought after and assured donors their money was being well-spent. They kept detailed files on each organization they endorsed that could be reviewed by anyone contemplating a new organization to ensure they were not duplicating what already existed. Organizations seeking endorsement were required to fill out an application and open their doors to a visit by committee members. This would seem to be a sort of precursor to the Community Fund and United Way of today. No doubt, their three "standards" would be approved by any 21st century foundation.

Thy Neighbor as Thyself – The Depression Wears On

As the work of Miss Towne and her staff settled into their new space, Board President, Walter Gielow, and fellow board members, were contemplating a new brochure to keep the work of Erie Neighborhood House (ENH) in front of their supporters. Gielow solicited the support of N. Ray Miller and board member, Forest MacGibbon, an employee of Marshall Field's department store, in their Stationery Department. (In the days when people wrote letters and used paper, this may have been a prestigious position.) Gielow suggested they contact board member, Harry Moore, who he believed had a large collection of Erie photos. The cover photo of a young girl and small boy holding hands may be from that collection. The line from the New Testament, positioned over the photo, is ". . . and thy neighbor as thy self."

Clearly, ENH was very conscious of the plight of its neighbors. The text notes that "95% of the families attending Erie are either on relief or supported by a WPA job."[92] Relief orders are delayed. The rent goes unpaid. Children are unable to attend school for lack of clothes to wear. It goes on to say that ENH is seeking "to awaken the tiny spark still slumbering and fan it into a flame of new hope and new courage, giving our neighbors a new sense of their value to the community." This pledge of support on the part of ENH is followed by numerous testimonials as to what ENH has meant to their neighbors. One example: "Erie Neighborhood House means to me what the coast guard means to one in peril on the lake."[93]

A photo shows young men gathered in front of Erie, sitting on the front stoop. ..."boys out of school and unemployed with whom we are working in an effort to keep them *out* of Pontiac and Joliet (prisons) by keeping them *in* Erie Neighborhood House." These young men are among the 15,000 men, women and children who were counted in Erie

91

activities the previous year, served by six full time employees, 32 WPA workers and 68 volunteers.

The Church has 421 members, with 350 enrolled in Sunday School. ". . . our aim is not so much church membership as growth in Christian character." This was an important point that church-supported settlements made at every opportunity. Furthermore, some of the names that appear on the Sunday School roster of teachers went on to become community leaders and even founders of important community institutions.[94] Dan Brindisi would found the Near Northwest Civic Committee. Rose Genova was sister to Carmella and Daisy who helped start the Erie Clinic, which evolved into the Erie Family Health Center of today. The Savino's–Joe, Mary, Celia, Michael--contributed to the work of ENH over a 50-year period. Kenneth Rutschman went on to become a missionary in Latin America, and his son Richard served at Latino Youth and at the Chicago Teachers Center in the West Town Community in the 1980s and 90s.

The brochure reports that Erie's annual budget in 1937 was $19,000. A hand-drawn pie chart illustrates that only 40% of their income is known in advance of a budget year. These are funds that come from the Community Fund, pledges by individuals and churches, and the Church Extension Board. The other 60% is represented by a large question mark, pertaining to funds Erie hopes to raise through Tag Day and special appeals.

In 1937, the board filed the necessary paperwork to officially change the name from Erie Chapel Institute to Erie Neighborhood House.[95] And as bureaucracy takes its time, this was officially approved by the Illinois Secretary of State in 1938. 1938 was also the year when scholars at the University of Chicago came up with the Community Areas map, and Erie discovered it was located in West Town, Area # 24. Erie's brochure that year was called "Growing up at

Erie Neighborhood House" and featured a drawing of a boy and a girl that was holding a doll.[96]

Inside, Erie reports on its programs. Under the photo of a child is the heading "Getting a Good Start." It would seem that Erie House had the idea of a head start long before the federal government came up with "Head Start" as the name for their pre-school funding in 1965. The text goes on to say that "it is especially gratifying to mark the progress of those who have truly grown up at Erie." This comment identifies what has become one of the hallmarks of Erie's history. First, it has been the case that children who start in Erie's pre-school, continue in the School Age program, and transition into the Youth Department, literally grow up at Erie. In college, many come back to volunteer and mentor younger children, and after college a good number have become Erie employees, who then place their children in Erie's pre-school. This cycle is recognized at this early stage in the next panel of the brochure titled "Learning Today – Teaching Tomorrow." Miss Florence says to John, "Keep on the way you are going and some day you may be in the position of boys' worker at Erie." She goes on to talk about Dan, who is able to continue his education at George Williams College with a part time job at Erie. This refers to Dan Brindisi, who, as noted above, later founded the Near Northwest Civic Committee, with offices on Grand Avenue, just a few blocks from Erie.

About 7 o'clock in the evening young adults begin to arrive at Erie. There is a photo of a group of young men and someone penciled in names of the ones they recognized: Jimmy La Rocco (recall the La Roc's drive-in connection), John Leverance, Guy La Calamita, Sam Vaccaro, and Sam Benedetto. While Erie counted 17 nationalities among their participants, here is evidence the predominant group was Italian. Each week, these Italians were joined by Poles, Russians, and Greeks in one of the eleven English and

Citizenship classes held at ENH. These classes were sponsored by the Board of Education.

The rationale for what came to be known as the KONC initiative, Keep Our Neighborhoods Clean (KONC), is laid out in this brochure. The vignette that is outlined here also contains several themes that have appeared throughout Erie's history. The clean-up campaign that ENH organized was a response to their frustration from encounters with local politicians, the alderman and the ward supervisor of streets and alleys, who argued that dirty alleys were the fault of the neighbors. But with some direction and encouragement from Erie, those same neighbors got involved in cleaning up those alleys. When someone commented on the improvement the Alderman had made, a member of Erie's Neighborhood Health Club was heard to remark: "The Alderman? Did you think he was doing all this? It's Erie Neighborhood House and its neighbors."[97]

This fact was picked up in an article that appeared in the *Chicago Daily News,* March 4, 1939, with the headline: "Erie Neighborhood House Cleans Up Dirty Alleys."[98] The reporter says: "It took a woman to do what the politicians couldn't do." Florence Towne went door-to-door asking neighbors to get involved. She had Boy Scouts place garbage cans in alleys and organized health clubs and clean-up campaigns. Now this area has the cleanest alleys in the city, was his conclusion, all done by arousing neighborly interest and consideration. While the title does not appear in this article, this work would eventually lead to calling Miss Florence the "Angel of the Alleys."

In addition to the development of health clubs, and cleaning up the alleys, Erie's commitment to the health of their neighbors is further documented with the opening of a free dental clinic at Erie on March 1, 1939.[99] At that time, the only free dental service in all of Chicago was available at the Cook County Dental clinic. So, Erie was the second place, offering a dental clinic through the help of six dentists who each volunteered one half day per week. In addition, on Thursday afternoons, Dr. Sanderson conducted a class to train unemployed neighborhood girls to be dental assistants. In turn, these young women helped out in the Erie dental clinic to gain practical experience. Marion De Vincent, who later became the organizer of the Erie Annual Reunions, was one of these girls. She recalled that when the Erie dental clinic closed, she was able to get a job in a dentist's office downtown.[100]

On November 11, 1939, what Erie called "Demonstration Night," where they had open house and a program to show their supporters what they had invested in, Dr. Paul Johnson, of the Church Extension Board, greeted Erie's guests. Erie participants sang a song that evening that they had composed called "The Dentist's Song." It went like this:

> *For children who can't afford to pay*
> *To have dental care, and so we say. . .*
> *We're glad indeed to contribute to these in such*
> *great need*
> *Children: What would we do, oh dear, without a*
> *dentist here.*
> *Nurses: What would they do, oh dear, without a*
> *dentist here.*
> *Both: Our thanks to you*
> *Mothers: We mothers, too, are so grateful for all*
> *you doctors do.*
> *Our children can have this dental chair, and expert*
> *care, because you share.*
> *Our thanks to you.[101]*

Finally, this brochure reports that Erie's 1938-39 annual participation has grown to 236,971, up 58,734 from the previous year, all coming from within a 6-block radius of Erie House. This is still a duplicated count, where Tony is counted every time he shows up for Boys' Club, but it gives a sense of the sheer volume of activity. And, as noted elsewhere in the brochure, the larger "new" building quickly exceeded its new capacity. The annual budget was $21,517, with sources of revenue as follows:

- The Community Fund Allocatio.   4,845
- Church Extension Board   2,200
- Women's Presbyterial   335
- Estimated Tag Day Receipts   1100
- Other pledges   2600
- Total $10,980
  Balance to be raised from friends $10,537

Walter Gielow was still Board President and William Dahl was Treasurer, with 34 additional board members.

The Church Extension Board (CEB) report for 1938-39 mentions Erie Neighborhood House and notes the opening of the dental clinic with the dental assistant training program. It also mentions other organizations supported by the CEB.[102] These include: Camp Gray (which Erie utilized), the Christian Industrial League at 847 W. Monroe, Christopher House, 2507 N. Greenview, its headquarters until the first quarter of the 21st century, Firman House at 1109 S. Ashland, ministering to Mexicans of the West Side, no doubt the overflow from the Hull House "Pots of Promise" artisans.[103]

In the introduction to its 1939-40 Annual Report, as World War II was already under way in Europe, the Church Extension Board of the Presbytery explains,

> . . .the neighborhood house is the essence of what democracy is and does.It is a world in miniature with its many and varied peoples. If this little world in a neighborhood house can be at peace, there is hope for the whole world . . . Defense claims most

of our attention these days. . . but armies and ships cannot guard our ideals . . . Tolerance, love, good will, unselfishness which call all men brothers, irrespective of race or creed. These are the bulwarks of democracy. . . the philosophy of the neighborhood house leads the way.[104]

1940: *Miss Towne Writes* Neighbors *and Erie Responds to the Challenges of the War Years*[105]

As Erie Neighborhood House began its seventh decade, Chicago had over one million telephones. Miss Towne reported to the Board that 2500 individuals attended 38 different Christmas activities. 204 Christmas baskets and 100 "Mayor Kelly Christmas boxes" were distributed. This is the first mention of an Erie connection with a Chicago mayor. It does not necessarily mean that Mayor Kelly was personally aware of Erie House, but someone got Erie on the list for mayoral largesse. Mr. Gielow is still President of the board and William Dahl is Treasurer. Dr. A.L. Sawyer joined them as Vice President. By 1940, income was up to around $17,500, but with expenses being close to $22,300, deficits were generally a part of the monthly board report. Over time, deficits were either covered by the annual allocation from the Community Fund or by just adding more fundraising appeals and/or events.

One idea for a new source of revenue, that was announced early in 1940, was the publication of a new book being written by Miss Florence. She had written a book published in 1929, called *Sheep of the Outer Fold;*[106] this one was called *Neighbors.*[107] In May of 1940, the board approved publication of the book, and the management of this process was undertaken by Harry Moore, Chair of the Publicity Committee. 3,000 copies were to be printed by R.R. Donnelly (printers of the Chicago telephone directory for many years), with 600 copies pre-sold to cover the cost of printing and binding. By October, 1940, book sales had yielded $566.

Miss Florence dedicated her book to:

> *Our Board of Directors, our Woman's Auxiliary,
> and All Other Friends of Erie Neighborhood House
> whose devoted service and gifts for our
> maintenance have brought, from day to day, new
> hope and courage and a new way of life to these
> whom we call "Neighbors."*[108]

She also acknowledges Rev. J. W. G. Ward of First Presbyterian Church of Oak Park for his gracious review of her manuscript, and "the people of his church who have for many years been devoted friends and generous contributors to work carried on by Erie Neighborhood House." Rev. Ward then wrote in the Forward:

> *If literature means a vivid portrayal of human
> nature, with its passions and struggles, then this
> book, while making no such ambitious claim, is
> truly literature. . . . From personal knowledge of
> the work which Erie Neighborhood House is doing,
> and of the devoted leader, who has given more than
> 25 years of her life to these people, we might
> suggest that a more fitting title for this book would
> be, 'An Angel Amid the Alleys.'. . . We warmly
> commend this volume **to all who are concerned
> about the underprivileged, and who believe that a
> fence at the edge of the abyss is better than an
> ambulance at the foot.**[109]*

It is not possible to summarize her entire book here. It is basically a collection of 16 stories of actual experiences that Miss Florence wanted to share with her readers to illustrate the work of Erie Neighborhood House, and to introduce them to Erie's neighbors. But two of the stories are particularly effective in communicating strategies that have been employed by Erie House, over and over again. The chapter entitled "The H.B. Gang," is a good example of what Rev. Ward meant when he said "a fence at the edge of an abyss is better than an ambulance at the foot." In other words, see what preventive actions you can take before trouble happens, rather than trying to deal with the problem afterwards.[110]

She describes a group of unemployed young men, ages 17-21, that hung around the Erie lobby, generally wreaking havoc and annoying other visitors, day after day, often from 10:30 in the morning until Erie closed at 10:30 at night. Finally, Miss Towne called them together and fed them some ice cream. While the boys generally goofed around while they were eating, Miss Towne observed, "A group cannot sit around a table and break bread without drawing just a little closer to each other." She told them from now on they would be known as the H. B. Gang, and it was up to them to guess what the letters stood for. Then they talked about what the boys could do to help Erie. She ended up asking them to serve as ushers or tour guides for the 400 women who were coming for the Woman's Auxiliary annual Sunshine Luncheon. She prepped them on what to do, and from comments she received, the women were so impressed they thought they were on the Erie staff. By the way, H.B. stood for "Honor Bound," and so they were from that day forward, and some did eventually become staff.

The chapter entitled "The Neighbors March Down Our Alleys,"[111] is the story that gave Rev. Ward the idea for Miss Towne's nickname. It basically relates Miss Towne's concern about the garbage-strewn alleys in the neighborhood and her frustrating and futile conversation with the Ward Superintendent, who blamed the problem on lazy neighbors who did not care. As related above, Miss Towne went to the neighbors and helped them organize the Keep Our Alleys Clean Campaign. In response to the uncooperative Ward Superintendent, Miss Towne said of her neighbors:

> *It is our task to rouse them from their apathy, to challenge them with their responsibilities and opportunities, and then to stand beside them and say, 'I believe in you. Together we will tackle this job and win.'*[112]

Saul Alinsky would have loved Florence Towne. Organizing their neighbors to stand up and speak for themselves has been a recurring agenda for Erie's 150 years – fighting for garbage pick-up, more responsive police, better schools, immigrant rights, alone, or in collaboration with others, Erie House has stood with their neighbors. When they march today, they carry a banner that says, simply, *¡PRESENTE!* It would have been the same in Italian or Polish.

In February, 1941, the board authorized N. Ray Miller to approach the owner of the house just west of ENH about selling it to Erie. The plan was to use money that remained in the Templeton Fund to make the purchase. However, the negotiation proved unsuccessful. This idea remained on the ENH agenda for the next 50 years, but circumstances never aligned themselves to accomplish the acquisition. A developer eventually acquired the property and built an upscale building that was definitely marketable as the neighborhood gentrified in the latter years of the 20th century. Erie always regretted they had missed the opportunity to add this space to the ENH footprint.

In March 1942, the dental clinic marked its third anniversary, having recorded 4,551 visits by 815 different patients.[113] In December of 1942, first mention is made of "the Christmas Store." While format probably varied over the years, the basic concept revolved around donations of gifts by numerous churches, as well as local and downtown businesses. Erie's needy families were then invited to come to Erie, generally to the gym, where toys for their children, handmade winter hats and gloves, and items for the parents were displayed for their perusal and selection. In spite of the word "store," no purchases were required. Volunteers would be set up in another room to wrap the gifts. By the 1980s, the number of gifts donated annually was over 500, enough to share with other social service agencies. The "Christmas Store" was a hallmark of the ENH Christmas celebration for more than 50 years, and was equally a part of the Christmas season at the many churches that gathered gifts, wrapped gifts, decorated the Erie gym, and showed up to volunteer for the event itself.

Some historically significant people were on the Board in the 1940s. Mr.& Mrs. Harry Armstrong of First Presbyterian of Oak Park joined the board earlier, but Harry served as president in the latter half of the 1940s. They would later be succeeded by their son Chuck, and his wife, Phyllis. There would be an Armstrong on the board for the next 70 years. And Chuck would connect Erie with the Union Church of Hinsdale (United Church of Christ), a supporter well into the 21st century.

David Dangler, of Lake Forest, and later, the Gold Coast, and Northern Trust Bank, joined the board in 1945 and stayed on into the 1990s. On the staff, the Savinos were prominent: Dominick was the janitor, Mary cooked for the children and the Board, Celia was hired as part time Kindergarten teacher, and Joe eventually served on the board, with a term as president. Doug Cedarleaf, who would later serve as minister at Erie, is listed in 1942 as a summer worker for vacation bible school. In 1943, he and Mrs. Cedarleaf were listed as Erie Board members. Attendance for that summer was reported as 256: 108 Protestants and 148 Catholics! Twenty years before Vatican II encouraged ecumenism, Erie's Catholic neighbors already knew this was a good idea. Tolerance of religious diversity at Erie went hand in hand with ethnic diversity. Just a few years later, racial tolerance would be tested, and embraced.

By 1943, the 55 WPA workers that Erie depended upon to carry out its programs were withdrawn, as war brought a new type of employment, and wartime production, certainly at great cost, pulled the US out of the Depression. Those neighbors Miss Florence wrote about stepped up to the challenge and volunteers from the community, calling themselves the "Cheerie Erie Workers,"[114] took the place of the WPA. They helped at all levels, especially as the demand for child care increased as West Town's "Rosie the Riveters" took the place of their husbands in the production of wartime goods. In Chicago and other major manufacturing centers, companies that previously manufactured sewing machines, for example, converted to the manufacture of airplane parts. As noted in one of Erie's wartime brochures: "It is true that war has loosened the bonds of want by providing jobs" but this created new problems with many children returning to empty homes at the end of the school day. So, Erie enlarged its services by providing "day care" for pre-schoolers, and after-school care for the older boys and girls, two programs destined to continue long after the war ended, more than 75 years and still counting.

In April, 1943, John Magill resigned as pastor of Erie Chapel. The board voted to extend the call to someone they knew well—Rev. Doug Cedarleaf–at a salary of $170/month.[115] He and his wife, Carolyn, moved in to the third-floor staff quarters at 1347, and resided there until the birth of their first child. At that point, they moved to a house down the street.

That same year, the board voted to purchase two lots south of Erie House that face Ohio Street. Today they are used for a parking lot. In May, Erie purchased a camp on Lake Michigan for $550. It came to be known as Camp Davies, in honor of Dr. Leora Davies, board member and major proponent of healthy outdoor activity for Erie's children and families. Initially it had one two-room building; in subsequent years, two more were added: Cedarleaf Cottage and Bradley Cottage.

In its constant effort to attract more donors, its brochure for 1943, was called "New Patterns for our Neighbors." Various pieces of a dress pattern served as background for Erie programs. These were described as: DENTAL CARE BEFORE THE TOOTHACHE COMES, CLEAN STREETS AND ALLEYS, SAFE PLAY FOR CHILDREN WHEN MOTHER WORKS, GAMES WITHOUT GAMBLING, FUN WITHOUT ALCOHOL, VOTES WITHOUT DOLLARS. (This last item has a definite Chicago ring to it.) The projected budget for 1943 was $24,000, with about $8,800 TO BE RAISED. Appreciation was expressed to the Community Fund, for their allocation of $5,141, and the Chicago Community Trust and the Wieboldt Foundation, with foundation support at $6,318. The mention of two foundations this early was unusual. Large-scale philanthropic support for Erie from foundation sources did not really evolve until the 1980s. Erie also notes its organizational affiliations: The Chicago Council of Social Agencies, the Chicago Federation of Settlements and Neighborhood Houses, and the Social Service Exchange. They are still endorsed by the Chicago Association of Commerce.

As 1944 opened, Walter Gielow was still board president, and Doug Cedarleaf was pastor, with his salary increased from $170/month to $185; Miss Towne made $200/month. (After all, after church services on Sunday, her line was reported to be longer than the one to the pastor.) The budget was up to $31,000.

At the February board meeting, Miss Florence shared with the Board her investigation of a local factory that appeared to be in violation of Child Labor Laws, employing children under 14. She explained that "the situation was cleared up after a few visits and some correspondence."[116] Shades of Jane Addams! Miss Addams was known to pay a visit to Hart, Schaffner & Marx over some "labor violations" as well.

In March, 1944, the Erie board was informed that the Council of Social Agencies was urging Erie to invite "neighborhood people" to the board. Since 1915, when the Erie Chapel Institute was incorporated, and operated with oversight from the Presbyterian Church Extension Board, only individuals affiliated with Presbyterian churches served on the Erie Board. Discussion ensued, but no action was taken at that time. Eventually, this recommendation would be adopted.

Architect Benjamin Olson, who had become a member of the Erie Board, was working on plans to add buildings to Camp Davies. A bequest from the estate of Kate Waterman of $10,000 made these camp improvements possible, and the board authorized construction to begin at the end of April.[117] Miss Florence reported on plans for the new camp, including the problem of finding sufficient lumber, in light of wartime production restrictions, and on a Community Fund allocation that would allow her to hire four more staff to handle increasing demands for Day Care programs. She then read some letters from "Erie boys" serving overseas. The "Erie Girls" published a newsletter in the 1940's called "The Bugler," that was devoted to those serving in the armed forces during World War II. In it they would send news of life at Erie House; they would also post the names of Erie boys who had been killed--names that have already appeared in this text, such as Pfc. Nunzio J. Savino, and Sgt. Thomas P. Vitacco. Al Vitacco and Paul Genova sent letters back, reminiscing about happy times at Erie House. These letters came from all the theaters of the war: Germany, France, Holland, Okinawa, and the Philippines.

Her report also commented that "The 'Negro' situation is becoming more apparent in the neighborhood. It has affected the Chicago Commons neighborhood and it is coming here."[118] It is not entirely clear what "situation" Miss Florence is referring to, but probably pertains to African Americans moving into the Near Northwest side. On the one hand, you could say they had been in Chicago since DuSable founded it, but their presence increased significantly during the Great Migration of 1915-1920. However, these migrants lived mostly on the south side of the city, in the area that came to be known as Bronzeville. The Chicago version of the Harlem Renaissance was under way, marked by the opening of the South Side Community Arts Center in 1941. The 1940's witnessed the publication of Richard Wright's *Native Son*, St. Clair Drake and Horace Cayton published *Black Metropolis: A Study of Negro Life in a Northern City,* and Gwendolyn Brooks' poetry in *A Street in Bronzeville* was being praised.

Their numbers and their voting power had gradually won some concessions from city hall, and in 1940 Chicago appointed the nation's first African American police captain. That same year, what was called the "American Negro Exposition" was held at the Coliseum. By the mid-1940's, the Second Great Migration was under way, responding to the wartime demands for labor in industrial cities like Chicago, and would not be contained on the south side. In 1943, Mayor Kelly appointed the Mayor's Committee on Race Relations, and in 1945 Roosevelt University, nicknamed "the Little Red Schoolhouse," opened its doors and played a major role in educating a generation of African Americans, including the future mayor, Harold Washington. Erie's racial tolerance test would soon be upon them.

In June of 1944, the board began to discuss plans for Erie's upcoming 75th anniversary in 1945. They also agreed to purchase a life insurance policy for Miss Florence. Finances were improving. The Waterman bequest was followed by two others, and the Tribune Charities and Beidler Trust joined Wieboldt and the Chicago Community

Trust as foundation support continued to grow. And finally, after numerous reports to contributors that "Erie has no endowment," one was established. 1944 was also the year Erie House got a zipcode; it was 22. The Erie phone number was Monroe 2413.

1945: The Social Gospel Shines at Erie and a Bright Light is Extinguished

It turned out that 1945 would be a momentous year for Erie Neighborhood House, and not just because they were celebrating their 75th anniversary, or because World War II came to an end. Just a year earlier, Miss Florence had reported to the Board that "The Negro situation is becoming more apparent in the neighborhood." That "situation" took on an ugly visage early in 1945. An African American family had moved into the Erie neighborhood. They were John Strong, his wife, son, and a niece, who took up residence at 721 N. Throop. They were part of the post-World War II second wave of the Great Migration of African Americans leaving the rural south to re-settle in northern cities.

They did not receive a warm welcome on Throop Street, just two blocks from Erie House. Shortly after their arrival, rocks were thrown through their windows, and later a fire bomb threatened their lives. In the context of this horrific treatment, one neighbor, John Vilna, stepped up and invited them to services at Erie Chapel on Sunday, February 18, 1945. Rev. Cedarleaf had already heard about the violent attacks and he was prepared to challenge this violence and move against it. A graduate of North Park Seminary just a few years earlier, he and his wife had been inspired to come to Erie House when they heard a talk about the work of Erie Neighborhood House, given by "a white-haired lady," who spoke at North Park during the Christmas season, calling for social justice and mercy. This was Miss Florence, of course.

It has become evident since then that "a number of pastors, educated at North Park in the early 1940s, committed themselves to urban ministry and the cause of social justice."[119]

Acting on that commitment, Cedarleaf's sermon that morning was titled "Vandalism on Throop Street."[120] He passionately confronted the racially motivated violence directed at the Strong family. He called upon members of his congregation to "love their neighbors as themselves" and resist the temptation to fear those who are different. Then he called upon his mostly white congregation to demonstrate that they were prepared to *show* their commitment to follow Jesus' "second most important commandment." He invited them to get up and escort the Strong family home. The majority of the congregation, 135 in all, followed him and Miss Towne as they led them from Erie House to Throop Street. They sang "Lift Every Voice and Sing" and carried signs that proclaimed "Christianity Means Love Your Neighbor" and "Democracy Means Liberty and Justice for All." When they reached the Strong's front door they sang "Blessed Be the Tie that Binds" and presented the family with a Bible, and a clear message that they would always be welcome at Erie House.

This all transpired 10 years before Rosa Parks refused to move to the back of the bus on December 1, 1955, an action that has been said to launch the civil rights movement. But history has taught us that movements are born over time, and that there are many steps behind the scenes before it becomes public. What happened at Erie House in 1945 was another example of that truth. In that all-white ethnic neighborhood, a minister and settlement worker provided the leadership, but there are no leaders without followers. Certainly, racism did not disappear from that corner of West Town on that day. In fact, Cedarleaf and Towne received numerous letters full of vitriolic accusations and hate-filled threats; they also received letters of encouragement and unsolicited donations "from around the world."[121] However, an important message was delivered. There is ONLY a *social* Gospel. It was read, it was heard, and it was lived at Erie Neighborhood House.

The next day, this event was reported on the front page of the *Chicago Sun-Times,* by journalist, Fletcher Wilson, with an article titled "Love Thy Neighbor as Thyself." Not long after, *Time* magazine picked up the story and ran a piece on page 54 in the religion section, March 5, 1945, titled "With Dismal Regularity."[122] It opened with the first verse of Psalm 126 (Douay Version), "Unless the Lord build the house, they labor in vain who build it." Rev. Cedarleaf was making that very point about the House called Erie. A photo of Cedarleaf and Miss Florence leading their neighbors down the street, with the American flag unfurled behind them, accompanied the article.

That article was even seen by Walter Gielow's son, Bob, still serving in the Navy, as the war would not be over until August. He knew of his parents' strong connection to Erie House and wondered about the impact of this event in a letter home. Not exactly "the shot heard round the world," but, as Kurt Peterson put it,

> *Cedarleaf stood as a prophet on the threshold of one of America's great social movements, publicly denouncing racism and economic injustice years before the civil rights movement caught fire.*[123]

This prophet lived at Erie House until 1948. From there he went on to pastor several Covenant churches, including North Park on Chicago's northwest side, serving the Albany Park community. He was honored by the Chicago branch of the NAACP, and in 1998, he and Carolyn received the Irving C. Lambert award in recognition of their commitment to urban ministry.

When V-E Day arrived on May 8, 1945, Erie Chapel was open all day, as neighbors gathered to give thanks to God and share a meal together. Miss Florence was already making plans to hire returning servicemen to staff the Boys' programs. While some of them took advantage of the GI Bill and went to college, others would be glad for work at Erie until they found other jobs. When V-J Day came on August 14, 1945, Erie was well into planning for its 75th anniversary to be celebrated on November 9, 1945.

To mark the occasion, Erie published a brochure called "Notes of Encouragement: 1870-1945."[124] Each historical benchmark was represented by a musical note. The years on the notes included:

1870 – the Holland Presbyterian Church,
1886 – construction of Erie Chapel at 1347 W. Erie,
1915 – Incorporation of Erie Chapel Institute,
1933 – Hannah Templeton's 100K bequest,
1936 – opening of the current Erie Neighborhood House building,
1940 – the Cheerie Erie Workers step up to replace WPA workers,
1942 – The Community Fund began to subsidize day care at Erie throughout the summer
1943 – Erie purchases Camp Davies
1945 – "All God's Children Got Wings," recalling the action for social justice Erie had taken to welcome the first Negro family to the neighborhood in the midst of a hostile reaction by others.

The last note was imprinted with the year 1946 and pertained to the final paragraph of the brochure: "The Next Step Ahead." Miss Florence envisioned two steps: first, engage our returning servicemen with jobs and volunteer opportunities; second, engage our teenagers in programs of service "big enough to appeal to their spirit of adventure and daring."

Of course, there were photos throughout. There was a picture of neighbors standing in front of the old ECI building, 1886-1935, a photo of the interim location at Erie and Noble, 1935-36, and finally a photo of the 9-year-old building that had opened in 1936. There were darling children everywhere, and there was the photo that had appeared in *Time* magazine, when Erie marched.

The budget for 1945, shown on the last page, was $34,523. The largest source of revenue was $9,775 from the Community Fund, the second largest was $6,200 from pledges of individuals and organizations, and the third largest stream of revenue was $4,500, "contributed by the neighbors." Erie had an investment portfolio that was 60% government bonds and 40% stocks.

The next day, on November 10, 1945, *Chicago Tribune* reporter, Rita Fitzpatrick, wrote an article titled "Erie House – the Story of a Great Venture." She started with a quote, saying,

> *For 75 years, Erie Neighborhood House has been 'a house by the road where the race of men go by . . . and in.' It has been a home, a cultural center, a school, a playground, and a chapel for men, women, and children of many nationalities. . . a corner of America. Last night it celebrated its diamond anniversary . . . 75 years of hardship and happiness. . . the story of a great venture.*[125]

Sadly, a man who had been faithful to the great venture for 48 of those 75 years, was not on hand for the big celebration. Just two days later, Erie House would lose one of its greatest friends and benefactors. Walter Gielow passed away, at age 65, on November 12, 1945. Mr. Gielow's name was on the incorporation papers for Erie Chapel Institute in

1915, and he continued to serve on the board for the next 30 years, serving as board president since 1930. From a notebook kept by Mrs. Evangeline Gielow, it was clear that the couple was around Erie as early as 1910.[126] According to the bio included in the program for the memorial service Erie held for Mr. Gielow, he lived in the neighborhood before he and Evangeline married. He was born July 14, 1880, and was confirmed at the German Lutheran Church at Noble and Chicago, when the surrounding community was German and Scandinavian.[127] He was eventually drawn to Erie Chapel and, at the age of 17, (in 1897) he was leading the choir; by 20 (in 1900) he held an officer position in the church. Given this long connection, it is not surprising that the task of building the new Erie Neighborhood House in 1935 benefited so much from his leadership. For more than half of his 65 years, he devoted time and energy to this place and this work. The Memorial Service program closes with these words:

> *During his many years as Chairman of our Board of Directors and member of our church session, he has endeared himself to all who knew him. . . May we follow in his footsteps since: 'the path of the just is as a shining light. . .'[128]*

At the Erie board meeting the following month, Robert Gielow, son of Walter and Evangeline, joined his mother on the board, and continued the Gielow connection into the next decade. As a tribute to his many years of service, the board decided on a plaque, with Walter's name on it, that hangs in the Erie lobby to this day. Dr. Sawyer moved from Vice-president to president; Herbert Johnson became VP and Harry Armstrong, Treasurer.

The End of an Era: The Passing of Miss Florence

In the ebb and flow of settlement work, following the remarkable events of 1945, Erie House finished the decade at a more everyday pace. As Erie marked its 75th year, and Miss Florence her 31st year, she described the mission or purpose of Erie Neighborhood House in the annual report non-profits filed with the Illinois Secretary of State. (In 1946, that was Edward J. Barrett.) She stated:

> *We are a neighborhood house ministering to the physical, social and mental needs of our neighbors on every level, from the Nursery School to Old Age Pensioners, with no discrimination as to race, color or creed. The program of activities is* the usual settlement house program *with special emphasis on working with the neighbors to make a better neighborhood.*[129]

Early in 1947, the board picked up on an earlier discussion about adding one or two community residents to the board. At the recommendation of Rev. Cedarleaf, Erie neighbors, Mr. & Mrs. Stanley Stollars, joined the board. From that point forward, there was a continued commitment to have neighborhood residents join the reps from Presbyterian churches on the Erie Board, but the Presbyterians still dominated, well into the 1980s.

In May of 1947, Erie church member and House volunteer, Margie Schramer, received an award from the State Street Council for the most hours of volunteer service in neighborhood house work in the Chicago area—definitely a Cheerie Erie worker. That same year, Erie did a salary survey of pay rates at other neighborhood houses. Robert Gielow reported that Erie was lagging behind the going rate. The board agreed to move Erie's rate from 85 cents/hour to $1.00/hour.[130]

Erie sent congratulations to Third Presbyterian Church on the occasion of their 100th anniversary. By 1947, it was struggling to hold on to its location at Ogden and Madison, as the neighborhood was changing. It is no longer there.

1948 brought plans for repairing and improving Camp Davies. Board members and the Woman's Auxiliary pledged $1,500 to help with this project, as they so often did whenever Erie asked. There was a charge for attending camp: $7.00 for one week for *school-age children not yet working;* working children were asked to pay $11.00. Erie's 1948 budget was up to $42,835, but it was reported to the board that Erie's deficit was the largest ever at $4,300.

It was also the year that Dominic Savino, who had been caretaker at Erie for 15 years, passed away. His position was offered to his son, Joe, and Mrs. Savino's hours as cook for the children's programs were increased. Miss Towne and Miss Marie Norem (staff) and board members Harry Armstrong and Herbert Johnson were appointed delegates to the Chicago Council of Social Agencies. In the Fall of 1948, Doug Cedarleaf responded to a call to pastor a Covenant church in Spokane, Washington. Upon his departure he said:

> *My lot has been a happy one, surrounded as I have been with loyal and understanding friends as well as situations that challenged my best thought and effort . . .these past six years.*[131]

While the Pulpit Committee searched for a new minister, two other events happened at the end of 1948 that have longer term significance. First, a Youth Council held its first meeting on October 1, 1948. A Youth Council has operated at Erie House ever since, for more than 70 years, underscoring Erie's commitment to honor input from neighbors themselves, and to engage youth in leadership

113

roles that would keep them coming to Erie, where they had a voice that was heard.

Second, an important relationship began when Laurence Carton joined the Erie board in December of 1948. He was a principal in the law firm of Gardner, Carton & Douglas, founded in 1910. This firm has offered Erie pro bono counsel ever since, again, for more than 70 years. The relationship continued, even when it merged with Drinker, Biddle & Reath of Philadelphia in 2006. The East coast name was adopted, and the merger resulted in making Drinker Biddle one of the 70 largest law firms in the country.[132]

As the decade came to a close, the Board had the Erie property appraised for insurance purposes. The value was estimated at $320,000. Erie's investment portfolio was valued at around $36,000. The Wieboldt Foundation increased its grant from the previous year, as did the Community Fund, and the deficit was down to $1,165 from $4,200. The chronic search for someone to staff Boys' Work was once again on Miss Towne's agenda.[133]

A new kind of recognition came to Erie House in 1949. It began in April, when Miss Florence addressed a letter to Mrs. Burm of the Volunteer Bureau at 123 W. Madison. Her letter outlined the dedication of Mrs. Vincenzo Savino (Mary/"Mom") to Erie House and the work of her and her family in the neighborhood. The letter, with the information that follows, was forwarded to the American Mother Golden Rule Foundation. The story of the Savino family could be the story of many immigrant families. But what made her family story unique is how she credits Erie House with her family's success in America.[134]

Mrs. Savino arrived in the US from Italy in 1919. By 1928, she and her family were connected to what would have been the Erie Chapel Institute. They joined the church, and eventually she became a Deacon and her husband, an Elder. Mr. Savino landed the job of caretaker of the ECI, and then the ENH building; Mary was in charge of the kitchen. She was one of the key organizers of the Cheerie Erie Workers after the WPA ended. At the time, she said: "We cannot help like the staff, but there are things we can do. We will do it with all of our hearts because we love Erie." Miss Towne notes that Mrs. Savino was especially sure to include Negroes in the volunteer group. She was there when Rev. Cedarleaf led the march on behalf of the Strong family in 1945, and took the minister's message to heart. The Savinos raised two girls and two boys in the neighborhood, all of whom finished high school, not the most common occurrence in those days. Celia went on to graduate from college and had been heading up Erie's Kindergarten since 1945. Miss Towne closed her letter by saying:

> *She has a brave spirit and seldom lets anything discourage her. I have often referred to her as 'the Saint' of our Neighborhood House and Church because of her devotion, love, understanding, and sympathy, and her zeal in serving her fellow man.*[135]

There is no evidence in the record that the foundation ever did anything with this information. However, it is not a stretch to imagine that this letter somehow made its way to the State Street Council who, joining with the Welfare Council of Metro Chicago, named Mary Savino "Mother of the Year for 1949." It probably did not hurt that the president of the State Street Council that year was Joel Goldblatt. Regardless of their State Street store, Goldblatt's flagship store at 1615 W. Chicago was still headquarters. No doubt, Mr. Goldblatt had heard of Erie House, and through the promotion by Miss Florence, Mrs. Savino. At age 51, she was chosen from among 600 nominees that gave a million hours of service to the 249 agencies affiliated with the Welfare Council. The award was presented to her at a luncheon held at the Palmer House, attended by 1500, including Mayor Kennelly, who had replaced Mayor Kelly two years earlier.

But lunch at the Palmer House was not the end of it. In October, 1949, an article appeared in *Readers Digest,* titled "Why Chicago Feted Mrs. Savino," by Karl Detzer. The article related the following information, summarized here: "The Mother of Erie Street" was born in a small town near Naples in 1898 and came to America when she was 20. She married Dominic Savino and moved to a flat next door to Erie Street Settlement. Eventually, they switched from the local Italian Catholic Church and joined Erie Chapel. Both she and her husband found work there, but she volunteered many more hours, beyond her work day. She is described as helping neighbors of all creeds and ethnic origins. When asked why she does this she replies: "You gotta live til you die. So, you live good." Her philosophy on race: "Jesus don't hate colored people."[136] One might surmise from her comments that the question that guided her life was: "What would Jesus do?"

The Savino children gradually moved out of the neighborhood. Joe, for example, moved to Oak Park. But Mom lived on Erie Street until she died. In 1978, Erie House hosted an Open House in her honor to mark her 50 years of service. When she passed away, at the memorial service, former executive director, Rev. Ross Lyman, said: "And so we thank Mom for her deep and consistent love. . . for to be with her was to be more motivated, more refreshed and renewed."[137]

While it is surmised that Miss Florence was behind the scenes, orchestrating the initial tribute to Mom Savino, she herself was drawing some attention. Shortly after the *Readers Digest* article appeared, Miss Towne was invited to go on the air for the Community Fund's Sunday morning radio program, "Meet the Churchman," or in this case churchwoman. On March 8, 1950, James Supple, religion editor for the *Chicago Sun-Times,* wrote an article, "Erie

House–It's Neighborliness in Action." He refers to Erie's neighborhood as a slum, to Erie House as a settlement and a Chapel. He wrote,

> *This unique blend of religion and social work is largely the result of the interest of Miss Florence, Head Resident for 26 years. . . Erie House is helping people who lacked all the usual opportunities for economic and cultural advancement, and find here a glimpse of democracy, friendship and Christian Faith.*[138]

Another tribute to Miss Florence appeared in the November 10, 1950 issue of *The Erie Spirit,* a kind of in-house newsletter. Under the headline: "Our Best Friend," accompanied by a photo of that friend, the article sings her praises as follows:

> *Miss Florence. . . has never failed to be the guardian angel of all those who have come to know her at Erie. To us, Erie means Miss Florence.*[139]

As 1951 dawned, The Erie board had 31 members, many of them couples. Harry Armstrong, of Elmwood Park, had moved up to president. Besides Mr. Armstrong and his wife, other long-termers on the board included David Dangler, Dr. Leora Davies, Mrs. Walter C. Gielow, Mr. & Mrs. Haarstad, Mr. & Mrs. Herbert Johnson, Mr. & Mrs. N. Ray Miller, Benjamin F. Olson, Dr. & Mrs. Sawyer, Miss Anna Thourson, Mr. & Mrs. A.D. Williams, & Mrs. Wm. H. Wilson. The long-termers made up more than half of the board. The 1950 list also says where they are from: River Forest (3), Oak Park (4), Lake Forest (3), Evanston (5), Wilmette (1), Glen Ellyn (1), Elmwood Park (1), Chicago (8). So, with 70 % living in the suburbs, the Erie Board reflected the tsunami that was the post-war move out of

Chicago to the suburbs. But it is also important to note that, by and large, the suburbs represented were among the more affluent ones, where time and money were available to support mission work in the city. That is not said to demean this level of support. These folks could just as well have stayed home and spent their money elsewhere. They did not. Besides their attendance at Board meetings at 1347 W. Erie, they also made the trip in to provide hours and hours of volunteer service. Examples include Meals on Wheels, the Erie Thrift Shop, the Christmas Store, Tag Day, Mayfair and numerous other fundraisers; and, in addition, for the women, attending monthly Auxiliary meetings and the Annual Sunshine Luncheon.

Mr. & Mrs. Glen Graham of First Presbyterian of Oak Park joined the board in January of 1951. Mrs. Graham was the daughter of the Sawyers, another example of succeeding generations of the same family serving on the board and supporting Erie. Bob Gielow, another second-generation board member, was chairing the Boys' Work Committee that year and introduced Bob Oliver as the new director. At that time, Boys' Work included 21 clubs run by four full time and seven part time staff. Activities included: alcohol education, wrestling, print shop, newspaper, gym, and outdoor sports. Evidence of these productive programs, however, should not lead to a conclusion that all was rosy all the time at Erie House. The top item on the agenda of the House Council that year was: How to deal with boys involved in an incident that resulted in broken chairs and records. Even Miss Florence's boys would still be boys.

On February 12, 1951, Miss Towne's 65th birthday, she received a birthday telegram from Fr. Bob at St. Boniface Catholic Church, at Noble & Chestnut, and was hailed for marking her 25th anniversary as Head Resident of Erie with an article in the *Chicago Daily News*, "Erie House Head on the Job for 25 Years," by Frank L. Hayes.[140] The article praises her and Erie House for their racial tolerance, and cites Miss Florence's invitation to Father Daniel Cantwell, chaplain of the Catholic Labor Alliance, to speak at a large community meeting at Erie on this topic. Cantwell would later head up the Catholic Interracial Council of Chicago.

Just a few days later, the President of the Chicago Federation of Settlements, Elizabeth Pfeiffer, was a guest at the Erie Board meeting. She congratulated Erie Neighborhood House, on behalf of 34 other settlement and neighborhood houses, for Erie's excellent work in the neighborhood and cooperation with other Federation members. So, 62 years after the founding of Hull House, there were 34 more organizations, based on that model, operating in Chicago. As members of the Chicago Federation, they represented another characteristic of settlement work – the willingness to collaborate.

In April, long-time board member, Arthur Haarstad (1874-1951) passed away. Haarstad was an example of someone who came to Erie as a child, a Norwegian immigrant, and then grew up to come back and serve on the board as a supporter of the place that had meant so much to him in his childhood.

Volume 1, Number 1 of "The Erie Crusader" came out in April, 1951, described as "the official organ of the ENH House Council."[141] The editors are Anthony Volpe and Mrs. Savino; Business Manager: Harry Armstrong–a joint effort of staff and board. One of the writers was Tony DeVincent, who grew up at Erie, and then returned to serve as staff in the boys' programs. This is a professionally printed, 8.5 X 11, publication. The top headline reads: "Groups of Varied Backgrounds Work Together at Erie." The article that follows explains that while most of the neighbors are Italian, many are Polish, and some are Negroes, people migrating from Appalachia, and even some Japanese families. In all, Erie served three races and 22 nationalities, all regarded as simply, neighbors. Lorraine

Gawrych was one of those neighbors who lived in the 1400 block of West Erie Street, and was a volunteer at the annual Mayfair fundraiser. She also rented apartments in her building to Erie staff. She wrote how grateful she was to Kindergarten teacher, Celia Savino, "for the guidance and treasured hours you gave my child."

The Presence of some Japanese participants at Erie House in the late 1940's or early 1950's, was confirmed by a visit from a Japanese woman, who came to the House in 2006 and asked if anyone was available who could give her a tour.[142] She explained that her mother had come to Chicago from the internment camps in the west, as there was nothing to go back to in California after the war. She walked into Erie House, desperately looking for work. She met Miss Towne, who immediately gave her a job helping out in the office. She said her mother told her that story as a child, of how grateful she was for the kindness of this woman, and this place.

In the Fall of 1951, the board meeting was attended by the new pastor of Erie Chapel, Donald Decker. With a deficit of $3,879, the Board was projecting a 1952 budget of $63,000. David Dangler admonished the board that they were too dependent on Miss Towne to do all the fundraising. They needed to shoulder more responsibility for pledging funds, and more importantly, reaching out to other individuals and churches to help with fundraising. This was a timely argument, as Florence Towne, the Angel of the Alleys, passed away on September 30, 1951, at the age of 65. After 37 years, 25 as Head Resident, Erie House was going to have to get along without Miss Florence.

The outpouring of condolences and memorials was a fitting tribute to a life full of service. In the ENH archives,[143] are numerous obituaries and tributes, from newspapers and newsletters. What was saved amounted to 15 handwritten notes of condolence, 2 telegrams, 19 typewritten letters, many from other settlements and from companies that did business with Erie House. Many are listed here, not only to show their respect for Miss Towne, but also, because they provide historical data on churches supporting Erie, and on settlements and where they were located in 1951.

From just a sample of condolence messages:

- *Isabel Pifer*, Benton House, 3052 S. Gratten, Bridgeport;
- *Carmine Marconi*, an Erie kid;
- *Winifred Lineberg*, First Presbyterian of Lake Forest;
- *Myrtle Good*, a friend from high school;
- *The Girls of the Junior Westminster Guild*, 1st Presbyterian of Oak Park;
- *Rev. David Bronstein*, Peniel Community Center, 3839 W. Lawrence;
- *Relinda Wittelle*, Chair, Women's Committee on Adequate Housing, 69 W. Washington;
- *Dick Covlison*, seminarian who spent a summer of impactful work with Miss Florence;
- *William H. Brueckner*, Executive Director of Chicago Commons, 955 W. Grand, refers to Commons' site, at Emerson House, working with Erie House;
- *William Hammond*, Executive Director, Ada S. McKinley Community House, 3201 S. Wabash; Hammond: "Miss Towne's passing is a great loss to the Settlements in Chicago. The contributions she has made, however, will live long in the memory of those who know Erie Neighborhood House."
- *Rev. Willian Scholes*, Head Resident, Christopher House, 2507 N. Greenview;
- *Rev. John L. Regier*, Head Resident, Howell House, 1831 S. Racine (later, Casa Aztlan);

- *Esther Brinkman*, Firman House, 235 W. 53rd Street;
- *Rhoda (Mrs. Jack) Pritzker* (Aunt of Illinois Governor, J. B. Pritzker, 2019), President, The Association for Family Living, 28 E. Jackson. Miss Towne served on their board;
- *Robert K. Hill*, Clerk of the Session, Fourth Presbyterian;
- *D.H. Darweld*, President of the Board, Laird Community House;
- *Rev. Thomas Lineweaver*, Jones Memorial Community Center, Chicago Heights, IL;
- *The Division of Americanization and Adult Education of the Chicago Public Schools* saluted Miss Florence in their newsletter, praising her work in helping her neighbors become citizens.

Curtis Reese, President, Chicago Federation of Settlements and Neighborhood Centers, shared the following tribute in memory of Miss Towne:

> *Florence Towne was an active member of the Chicago Federation since its early beginnings. She willingly carried responsibility in the Federation, because she realized the importance of planning and working together. She saw citywide and national problems in terms of her "neighbors." Her concern for and devotion to them was always uppermost in her thinking and planning. How often have we heard her say, "And what will this mean to our neighbors?"[144]*

There was a memorial service held at Erie House on October 2, 1951, and one held at First Presbyterian Church of Oak Park on November 4. At that service, a eulogy was delivered by Rev. Egbert M. Hayes. An excerpt follows:

*The perfect tribute to Miss Florence can be
achieved only as each of us of different race, class,
condition and nation who has been blessed by
association with her, tries loyally to carry on in her
spirit. . .We thank God for the countless number in
the Erie neighborhood who have responded to her
faith and begun to live the abundant life.*[145]

Attendees also included Florence's nephew, Perry Towne
Smith, who explained that he had come with his brother Alan
Searles and sister, Carolyn Searles Witt. Alan and Carolyn
had been adopted by Rev. George Searles and his wife, when
their birth mother, Mary, Florence Towne's sister, died. So,
Miss Florence's pastor at Erie Chapel Institute through 1923,
adopted her niece and nephew. Years later, in 1992, Rev.
Alan Searles and his wife Bonnie, sent a letter to Erie House,
recalling how his dad's connection to Erie had plunged him
into life there as well, and left an indelible mark on his life.
He remarked that the lines on the plaque that was placed in
the lobby after her death said it so well: ". . . anyone can tell
where she has been by all the little lights she leaves
behind."[146]

There is an undated and uncredited newspaper
clipping in the archive file that shows a photo of Miss
Florence, 1886-1951, and offers what is probably one of her
greatest tributes. It begins: "Sunday, September 30, 1951,
Chicago's second Jane Addams, Head Resident of Erie
Neighborhood House, passed away at the Wesley Memorial
Hospital at the age of 65."

From the service at Forest Hill Cemetery: "A burden-
bearer lies asleep, for all her work is done . . . She did her
work and did it well." And now the Erie House board would
need to take up David Dangler's challenge, taking on full
responsibility for Erie Neighborhood House until a new
Head Resident could be found.

Chapter Four: Rev. Ross Lyman: An Era of Professionalization, Innovation and Community Organizing, 1952-1977

Preparing for a New Head Resident

As Miss Florence would have wanted, Erie held its annual Demonstration Night, on November 9, 1951, with the usual purpose of participants demonstrating to supporters what a fine return on investment they were receiving. The program for the evening featured a framed picture of Miss Florence, with the caption: "Because of Her." Inside, was a poem called "Our Creed." Just an excerpt, certainly reflects the beliefs Miss Florence lived by:

> *We believe all men are our brothers*
> *And within our neighborhood*
> *That which separates us from each other*
> *Also cuts us off from God.*
> *Here at Erie all are equal*
> *Striving for a common good.*
>
> *We believe unselfish service*
> *Should be every Christian's goal.*
> *As we gladly share with others*
> *So, we find ourselves made whole.*[147]

At the first meeting in the new year, the board agreed to set up a Florence Towne Memorial Fund. Some of the donations would pay for a plaque to be hung in the lobby, next to the fireplace. Surplus funds would go to supporting Presbyterian seminarians. Staff member, Marie Norem, was appointed interim Head Resident, in consultation with Rev. Dean Collins of the Church =

Reverend Ross Lyman (Erie Neighborhood House)

Extension Board. Harry Armstrong continued as board president and Anna Thourson as Secretary; Bob Gielow, Walter and Evangeline's son, became Treasurer.

At the first meeting of 1952, the board was presented with the Community Area 24 (West Town) Report, submitted by The Executive Secretary of the Division of Education and Recreation.[148] Whether this was a division of city government or some other entity is unclear. But the report is about Erie House and was undoubtedly based on data provided by Miss Towne some time before her death on September 30, 1951. It is useful in providing a profile of the Erie House the new Head Resident would find, when selected.

The report notes that the ENH board has 43 members, mostly Presbyterian, and a Women's Board. Its stated purpose: *"To maintain and conduct an organization to minister to the spiritual, moral, mental, and physical needs of our neighbors with no discrimination as to race,*

color, class or creed."[149] The "community served" is
bounded by the Northwestern railroad tracks to the south
(400 north), Chicago Avenue on the north (800 north),
Paulina on the west (1700 west), and May Street on the east
(1100 west). It was noted that these boundaries reflected a
desire not to overlap with nearby settlements: Emerson
House to the west, Northwestern University Settlement to
the north, and Chicago Commons to the East. This
consideration suggests how dense the West Town population
was, if four agencies could all be less than a mile from each
other and still have plenty of people to serve. If you reached
out another half mile to the west, there was Onward House,
and 10 blocks north of that was Association House. This
was probably the densest cluster of settlements in
Chicago.[150]

Miss Towne's profile of the ethnic and racial mix of
the Erie service area in 1952 was as follows: Still
predominantly Italian on the south, and Polish to the north;
interspersed are a few African Americans, Japanese,
Scandinavians, Germans, Mexicans, and migrants from
Appalachia. She counted 25 nationalities in all. She noted
that substandard housing was the neighborhood's number
one problem and disgrace, followed by drinking and
gambling. She does not mention unemployment or
underemployment as a possible factor related to the first
three.

Five departments are identified:

- Little children/primary/kindergarten;
- School-age boys and girls;
- Teenagers;
- Young adults;
- Adults.

Some units merged and others created smaller subdivisions,
but these were, for the most part, departments or programs

that represented programming at Erie since 1915, and would persist for the next 70 years. The physical plant that housed these programs was described as church, auditorium, club rooms, gym, kindergarten, library, wood shop, and living quarters for nine residents, plus two playlots. Erie also ran its own camp, Camp Davies.

These programs were staffed by nine full time and five part time employees with additional workers added for summer programs like camp. "Some" had BA degrees; only one was a "trained social worker." They served 1,136 "registered" participants, 60% under the age of 18; 30 were enrolled in Kindergarten. Of 506 adults, 320 were women. The game room served numerous unregistered participants. Erie worked closely with two schools, Otis and Carpenter, and was a member of the Northwest Side Community Council.

The final component of this report was called an "evaluation." With the passing of Miss Towne, Erie was at a turning point. She had strong convictions in two areas: the importance of religion and morality in Erie programs, and her equally important conviction that neighborhood improvement was also the work of the settlement, especially by working for improved housing and higher relief standards. While the former was not always shared by others in the settlement field, the latter certainly was. Overall, the report concluded, methods for achieving the goals of helping the people and improving the neighborhood were changing as new techniques were developed. This was the reality that would face the new Head Resident.

Rev. Ross Lyman Gets the Call

At the March, 1952 board meeting, the Search Committee recommended the hiring of Rev. Ross Lyman of Pittsfield, Massachusetts, as Pastor and Head Resident, at a salary of $4800 + a house for his family to live in, pension, and moving expenses, effective May 15, 1952. In what would be his dual role as executive director and minister, he bridged the gap between sacred and secular in neighborhood house work. Lyman was born in Kansas, but raised in upstate New York, the son of a clergyman. He was a graduate of Drew Seminary and former director of Madison House in Madison, New Jersey. While at Drew, he met Rev. Ben Richardson who later recommended him for the position at Erie House. The board approved and a new era at Erie Neighborhood House would soon be under way. As an indication of Lyman's interest in professional preparation for his new assignment, he requested permission to attend a few conferences shortly after his start date. He would attend the conferences of the National Council of Presbyterian Neighborhood Houses, the National Federation of Settlements, and National Council of Social Workers.

Upon his arrival, he assessed the need for some cleaning and improvements at the House, and he visited the camp. He then set out to develop his staff, adding several new positions.[151] These included Rev. Francisco Casas, Associate Pastor, in recognition of the arrival in the neighborhood of the first wave of Puerto Ricans, along with a few Mexicans Miss Towne had identified as present in her 1951 report. Rev. Richard Presser was named Program Director, and Rev. Ben Richardson, an African American, and friend of Lyman from seminary days, was named Director of the Remedial Adjustment Center, a kind of group work/gang intervention center. This was, no doubt, more reverends than Erie had seen since its inception. He also hired six McCormick seminarians to work part time. All of this led to a budget proposal for 1953 of $71,000, up almost $4,000 from the previous year. Over a 20-year period, revenue had increased eleven-fold.

Apparently, the Community Area Report's suggestion that times were changing, was not the only place where this was being discussed. In November, 1952, a meeting was called of Neighborhood House Board Presidents, Head Residents, and staff of the Church Extension Board (CEB). The CEB was being asked to draft a 3-5-year plan to assist neighborhood houses in developing a vision for their future. This meeting would gather input on questions to be addressed by this plan. For example:

- What is the underlying purpose of a neighborhood house?
- Are we able to serve the needs of our local community?
- Do we meet the standards of program and operation satisfactory to the Presbytery, the Community Fund, and the Welfare Council?

In the tradition of storytelling that Miss Towne established in *Neighbors,* Rev. Lyman shared one at the November board meeting. Six months into his position this experience gave him the flavor of life at Erie. He told the story of David Hinchcliff, age 82, who recently stopped by Erie House, and showed Ross a certificate indicating that in 1888 he had been enrolled in the Third Presbyterian Church School and was taught by Miss Mary Templeton, no doubt a relative of Erie benefactors Thomas and Hannah Templeton. Ross said they had tea together.[152]

A New Direction for Neighborhood Houses

In 1953, there were 48 people on the ENH board, 33 of them from the suburbs; there were 19 couples. Harry Armstrong was still president, Herbert Johnson VP, Bob Gielow, Treasurer. Long-time secretary, Anna Thourson, stepped down from that office at the end of 1952, and was replaced by Mrs. George Reel. At their January, 1953 meeting, the board heard highlights from *The Neighborhood House Policy Statement of the Inner-City Church Extension*

Board, Presbytery of Chicago, January 2, 1953.[153] This statement was the result of the meeting convened the previous November, and marked a turning point in the underlying goals the Chicago Presbytery envisioned for its neighborhood house work. The three areas that were highlighted were: Purpose, Emphasis, and CEB Responsibilities.

> **Purpose:** *Through its neighborhood houses the Presbyterian Church expresses its concern, and, as part of the community, works with the people, their problems and opportunities, to achieve for them a healthier, happier, and more abundant way of life.*

Nothing particularly new here.

> **Emphasis:** 1) *Spiritual growth (emphasis on "spiritual" not "religious," as in dogma); 2) Strengthening of the individual, family life, and community organization.*

A better neighborhood had always been a goal of neighborhood house work, but this wording suggested a new approach. The Statement spelled it out this way.

> *The importance of vital community organization to the strengthening of democratic principles and values cannot be overemphasized. Houses should take an active role in community organization movements which have the approval of the Community Councils Division of the Welfare Council. In the process of working toward respectable, safe, and well-integrated communities, local lay leadership should be developed to assume the major responsibilities for this work.*[154]

Perhaps the Presbytery was taking its cue from the Welfare Council, since that organization seemed to have enough interest in community organization to evaluate the credibility of "community councils." Whether this was the case or whether their own deliberations led them to promote "community organization movements," and simply use the Welfare Council as back-up, is hard to say. But strategic shifts in thinking are often percolating in several different places at the same time. It is possible that someone was reading Saul Alinsky's *Reveille for Radicals,* or was familiar with his work in the Back of the Yards neighborhood. Something or someone was stirring the waters, and Erie, along with the other neighborhood houses, was being encouraged to wade in.

Responsibilities of the Inner-City Unit: As it had since the turn of the century, the Church Extension Board was to be there to help the neighborhood houses do their work, to:

- *foster program development,*
- *encourage churches to provide financial support,*
- *become educated regarding inner city mission work, and*
- *help locate head residents, staff, and new board members.*[155]

The Erie House response to this new mandate was not immediately visible. In fact, it would be another 10 years before community organizing was an active component of its work. But the seeds were planted here. It was also a slow process of engaging more "local lay leadership" on the ENH board. The neighbors had always been heavily involved in programs and fundraisers as volunteers, like the Cheerie Erie Workers. But leadership in the form of decision-making took a little longer.

What was happening in Chicago and the neighborhood around Erie House during the Ross Lyman years in the 1950s, like the statement of the Presbytery, would become more a part of the Erie House story in the 1960s and 70s. However, to understand that later period it is essential to look at the history immediately preceding.

The 1950s in the US and Chicago

To say that American policy toward immigrants has been on a roller coaster ride for 200 years would be an understatement. In spite of the lovely verse at the foot of the lady with the lamp, the US has consistently wrestled with who gets to come, to stay, and to become an American. A melting pot or a multi-cultural society, America struggles with a continuing identity crisis. It is this crisis that the neighborhood houses that the Presbytery of Chicago supported were established to address. Eighty years into it, in Erie's case, the continents of origin began to change, but the needs to be met had not, nor had the animosity some of their neighbors experienced.

As the second half of the 20th century opened, the United States would become involved in the Korean War, marking the first of 70 years of US involvement in war somewhere on the Asian continent, far east or middle east, spilling over into the 21st century. Few would seem to be as impactful at home as World War II, but each would involve loss of life, would result in immigrants from new places, and new ethnic and religious prejudices. The US has been schizophrenic when it comes to Asian immigrants. It passed exclusion acts to bar Chinese immigrants in the early 20th century, put Japanese *Americans* in internment camps during World War II, and by the end of the 20th century, businesses were using HB1 visas to recruit those clever Asians to meet their demand for computer skills they claimed American-born workers lacked.

At the same time, neighboring countries to the south, in the Caribbean and Latin America, were experiencing their own upheaval, some of which resulted from US interference in governments there. In some cases, the US acted to topple governments they perceived as inimical to US interests. Or, as in the case of Cuba, the US supported a government that was inimical to the interests of many of its own people. Thus, the Cuban Revolution in 1959 was led by Fidel Castro to overthrow the Batista regime. In either case, the resulting situation compelled many of their residents to look to the US for political freedom or refuge, often coupled with the search for economic opportunity. The push/pull dynamic of immigration had changed little since European ethnics fled to the US a century or half century before, for similar reasons. More recently, the journey might be geographically shorter in the case of Latin America, but no less harrowing. Whether crossing an ocean or a desert, people fleeing for their lives and their children's lives, risk an uncertain end to avoid a certain one. If their lives are not in immediate danger, they believe their children's lives will hardly be worth living if they don't strike out in search of economic opportunity.

A member of the National Economic Advisory Council was once heard to say, "The day immigrants no longer want to come here, is the day we should start worrying about our economy." Certainly, the 1950s were not the economic boom period of the late 19th century. In fact, manufacturing employment in Chicago peaked in 1947. But it was a time for overall prosperity for many who were perceived to make the move from lower class to middle class, even if it would take a while for that reality to become known and felt. No one was predicting the dramatic decline of steel on Chicago's south side and in neighboring Indiana. Earlier in the century, a first generation of Mexican immigrants had settled in on the southeast side, establishing Our Lady of Guadalupe parish, and taken those back-breaking, but high-paying, jobs at Southworks and Wisconsin Steel. Their sons and daughters went to college and also became community leaders because of those jobs their fathers left their home country to take. Ask Mary Gonzalez, a Pilsen leader in the 1980s and 90s, who then stood for the generation after her that came for the same opportunity just in time to see it slip away.

Agri-businesses that replaced many family farms needed to fill harvesting jobs second and third generation Americans were no longer willing to do. Slavery was not coming back, but there were migrant workers that lived in conditions that could be described as just one step above slave quarters, by 20th century standards. The migrant workers could take those farm wages back home and live a little better. The Braceros program facilitated that. Eventually, many decided they could stay in the US, get different jobs, or start their own businesses, and do even better. Others came north working along the railroads, and ended up in Chicago, like the Velasquez family of Azteca Foods. Whatever their final place of employment, they came to work. Thus, they came to contribute. Many are among the estimated 11,000,000 undocumented who have been living among citizens for years, as their neighbors.

So, does America not need to acknowledge that they import immigrants when they need them? But in general, whether they come on their own or are recruited, if their skin is a different color, some of their neighbors want them to go home, or stay home in the first place. Immigration policy in the US suffers from what Jim Wallis has called America's original sin– racism.[156]

When Ross Lyman arrived at Erie House in 1952, he initially found the same immigrant groups Miss Florence had worked with – Poles and Italians -- and some migrants, African Americans, for the most part, along with some transients from Appalachia. But that was about to change. West Town, this worn out port-of-entry neighborhood, was about to experience one more wave. Puerto Ricans and Mexicans would gradually become the new neighbors, and fellow church-goers. These Latinos were predominantly Catholic, as were the Italians and Poles. That, however, was not a new experience for Erie House. The time of serving fellow Protestants had pretty much moved on, as the Dutch and Norwegians moved on, even before the 20th century began. As was revealed in the numerous letters of condolence Erie received, Miss Florence was known and respected by at least one local Catholic pastor, at St. Boniface, and she had not hesitated to invite a Catholic priest to speak at Erie, if he had something worthwhile to say about social justice. What would change was the relationship with Catholics on an institutional level, that became more intentionally collaborative. For example, Erie partnered with the pastor of Holy Innocents Church, the principal of Santa Maria Addolorata School, and sat next to delegates from St. Boniface Church at the Northwest Community Organization's Congress each year. These new relationships converged under that Presbyterian mandate to get involved with local community organization movements. This began to take shape in the 1960s, so that follows in future pages.

Chicago, in the early 1950's, was busy switching from streetcars to buses in its public transit system, and then making it easier to avoid public transportation all together by building the first of its expressways; the Edens Expressway opened in 1951. Television had become the new babysitter, as children were mesmerized by Kukla, Fran and Ollie, a Chicago original, and Garfield Goose who imagined himself to be King of the United States. For the older kids, there was Mr. Wizard, of the world of science, not Hogwarts. Children would soon have other options as Chicago's public television station opened in 1955 as the Window to the World (WTTW, Channel 11). Meanwhile, Erie planned for its 85th anniversary.

135

Also, in 1955, Richard J. Daley became mayor for the first time, a job he would hold until he died in 1976, 21 years later. In other words, he was pretty much the only mayor Erie would know during Rev. Lyman's time as Head Resident. During his time in office, Daley would turn the Democratic Machine into the Daley Machine that won local elections on all levels, and even helped on the national level to put John F. Kennedy into the White House.

His was also an administration that tolerated, if not promoted, racism. In the 1940s, one of Chicago's own, Carl Hansberry, father of playwright Lorraine Hansberry, initiated a series of lawsuits that ultimately led to the Supreme Court striking down restrictive covenants as unconstitutional in Shelley v. Kraemer (1948). The covenants were a tool of the real estate industry to limit where African Americans could live or own property in Chicago.[157] To the extent that the restrictions it imposed created a tight-knit community, it could be called Bronzeville; in its role of limiting opportunity, it bore the more pejorative name of the Black Belt. As restrictive covenants were eliminated, more middle class African American families began to move to other parts of the city.

One of the programs Daley initiated in the 1950s was a new form of restrictive housing opportunity. This was the corridor of high-rise public housing built along State Street on the south side, such as Stateway Gardens and the Ida B. Wells apartments, the Jane Addams cluster on the west side, and the Cabrini-Green buildings on the near north side. Naming them after such distinguished Chicagoans as Ida B. Wells, Jane Addams, and Mother Cabrini, did not alter the racist purpose of containing African Americans in these "projects."[158]

While such racist policies impacted life in Chicago, the civil rights movement was being born in the south. Ironically, a Chicagoan was prominent in catalyzing that movement when Emmett Till was beaten and murdered by southern white racists in 1955, and his mother, with the help of Johnson Publishing's *Jet* magazine, made sure everyone knew it. That incident, coupled with the Supreme Court decision to strike down "separate but equal" in Brown v. the Board of Education (1954), set the scene. Ten years after Rev. Cedarleaf and Miss Towne marched to Throop Street to stand for civil rights, the Montgomery bus boycott took place.

At the time, many of these events seemed to be happening far from Erie's doorstep. But this was the backdrop, in fact the foundation, of the community organizing movement that was headed for West Town and many neighborhoods in other large cities in the US. Building on the lessons learned from the civil rights movement, and linking that to the ethnic/church organizing of Saul Alinsky in Chicago's Back of the Yards neighborhood, combined to provide a powerful strategy to give Erie's neighbors the tools to fight city hall. They did so, regularly.

Puerto Ricans and Chicago: Va Y Ven

The island of Puerto Rico had come under US control as a result of the Spanish American War in 1898. Puerto Rican migration to Chicago began in earnest in the late 1940s. Their move to the mainland United States was facilitated by the fact that the Jones Act of 1917 conferred citizenship on Puerto Ricans, just in time to draft 18,000 of them to serve in World War I.[159] The push/pull migration dynamic in this instance had a unique twist to it. In 1947, the US Bureau of Employment and Migration was established to encourage Puerto Ricans to leave the island to relieve "overcrowding." This is not to be confused with the type of overcrowding we associate with densely populated urban neighborhoods, or schools with too many children in a classroom. The analysis that was done of the situation in Puerto Rico concluded that the agricultural economy, primarily dependent on sugar cane, could not provide sufficient jobs. Therefore, two things should happen: some people should leave, and the economy of Puerto Rico should be "industrialized" to provide better jobs. It turned out this also provided an opportunity for US companies to open factories there, providing "better" jobs, but not as well-paying as those on the mainland. At the same time, there were recruitment agencies in Chicago that encouraged Puerto Ricans to come to Chicago to take jobs in the steel industry and other manufacturing firms in need of workers. Both men and women responded, but women were also recruited to work as domestics. So, both the push off the island, and the pull to Chicago were orchestrated by the US government and those they appointed to govern on the island.

The earliest enclave of Puerto Ricans in Chicago lived in Lincoln Park, more or less along Halsted and Clark, between North Avenue (1600 north) and Armitage (2000 north). To put a personal face on it, this is the area where Congressman Luis Gutierrez was born and lived until he was 15.[160] At that point, in 1968, his parents decided to move back to Puerto Rico, to their birth home of San Sebastian, in the northwest corner of the island. During his college years, Luis returned to the US, and eventually Chicago, to live in Humboldt Park. His story is an example of what Gina Perez calls the "Va y Ven" (go and come) that characterized the Puerto Rican "transnational" experience.[161] This was also facilitated by a relatively reasonably priced ticket on Pan American Airlines, for flights between San Juan and Chicago, making Puerto Ricans one of the first waves of immigrants/migrants to fly to their "better life" in America.

By the time Luis Gutierrez settled down with his wife in Chicago in the 1970s, Puerto Ricans had been displaced from Lincoln Park by rising real estate prices. This is why Perez's *Near Northwest Side Story* focuses on the Puerto Ricans of West Town, Humboldt Park and Logan Square.

These were the neighborhoods that absorbed Puerto Rican migration as it peaked in the 1950s, and where the second generation, born in the US, like Gutierrez, grew up or spent their young adult years. For most, they were years of struggle. No doubt the jobs they secured in manufacturing paid more per hour than they could earn in Puerto Rico, but at the same time, the cost of living was much higher. And then there was the immigrant experience of discrimination, denial of a voice in the city's political infrastructure, or jobs in places like the police and fire departments, and incidents of lack of respect and abuse by the Chicago police department.

As frustration over lack of economic opportunity built up, it came to a head when a young Puerto Rican man was shot and killed by the police in June of 1966. For two days, June 12-14, Puerto Ricans "rioted" on Division Street. While what was then Manufacturers Bank, at the corner of Ashland and Division, bricked up their windows in response, the Chicago Human Relations Commission held hearings, heard complaints, small changes slowly took place. Back in the neighborhood, Puerto Ricans began to organize their own community infrastructure as organizations like Caballeros de San Juan, the Spanish Action Committee of Chicago (SACC), Aspira, and the Ruis Belvis Cultural Center came into existence. Two years later, at the time of the Democratic Party Convention in Chicago, what came to be known as a "police riot" broke out in downtown Chicago as the police moved against Vietnam war protesters. Some 50 years later, Laquan McDonald was gunned down by a Chicago policeman, firing 16 shots at this young black man. Some patterns resist change for generations.

The Legacy of the Lyman Years at Erie House: The First Decade

As Lyman got to know his staff during his first two years at Erie, together they evaluated what most needed his attention and what the staff thought was important to meet the needs of the Erie community in the 1950s. In June of 1954, they wrote up what they called "Statement of Purpose of Erie Neighborhood House, as Developed by the Staff." They stated:

> *Erie Neighborhood House's purpose is to foster religious, social, physical, and educational growth among those whom we serve.*[162]

They described their service as directed to neighbors, volunteers, and Church members, regardless of nationality or creed. This statement did not vary much from what had always been stated as Erie's purpose, except insofar as underscoring the idea that Jane Addams often argued for, that the service and education go both ways. Those who identify as the providers of service, benefit as much as those being served. If they are open to it, they will learn about people different from themselves, and yet the same. They will experience the lessons of the New Testament by spending time with their neighbors who may be financially less fortunate than they, but spiritually and culturally, were still their neighbors, with a wisdom of their own to share.

The usual programs are described, as serving children from pre-school through high school as well as adults with English Classes and other types of adult education. In addition to these typical programs that had been part of Erie for 75 years, the Statement suggests some additional services: counseling, leadership training, providing training opportunities for college students, in education and social work, and working on community problems, such as housing (which had been addressed by Florence Towne as well), and lastly, doing the research required to determine the best methods for helping people.

1954 was also the year that Erie House and Erie Chapel would begin functioning under separate budgets. Whether this came about due to pressure from funders who wanted assurance their funds were not supporting a church, or whether Lyman just viewed it as a good organizational decision, is not clear. Nevertheless, since then it has not been even a potential issue. One of Lyman's other proposals was that Erie establish a partnership with Jewish Vocational Services (JVS) who could help Erie residents with getting jobs. He also addressed the job situation at Erie, arguing for the expanded outlay for salaries to bring on better trained staff and increase capacity for supervision of volunteers. This included adding an assistant minister who would help out at both Erie Chapel and Erie House. He felt it was in Erie's interest to deploy, if not employ, graduate students in certain part time positions, who came with more education but low or no cost.

In January, 1955, the Erie board received "Community Area 24 (West Town) Report," submitted by Robert L. Neal of the Welfare Council, of which Erie House was a member.[163] It appears that the purpose of this report was to provide profiles of social service organizations by community area. The report notes the West Town area is in transition, with new arrivals from the Ukraine, Puerto Rico, and Mexico. It notes the new vocational guidance program at Erie, in partnership with JVS. It proclaims in dramatic terms that, "for the first time in the history of the neighborhood," Catholic and Protestant churches, and representatives from the various nationality groups, came together at Erie House to work on the problem of housing. This is early evidence of a characteristic of Ross Lyman's leadership in broadening Erie's reach. It was an example of his desire to partner with others, especially with other religious denominations, and to put Erie on the map as a place where collaboration was welcome and public policy discussed. While this ecumenical collaboration was a hopeful sign, there were prejudices that continued to disappoint. Lyman shared with the board in May, 1955, that following a fire that left several families homeless, Erie, Association House, and Chicago Commons worked together as Protestants, united in providing services to all in need. He was dismayed at "the aloofness" of the Catholic church to people who were not parishioners. "Evidence of racial prejudice against victims of the fire was disturbing."[164]

The report also noted that Erie had followed through on its commitment to carry out research to guide their work, mentioning two research projects: 1) "The Contribution of Neighborhood Study to Programming in a Neighborhood House," to be published in a social work periodical (which was not named); 2) a study on resources in housing. Along with this research, Erie had developed a connection to a neighborhood association. It is presumed this refers to the Conservation of Property Association (COPA), incorporated in 1953. Leaders of COPA were introduced at the February, 1955, Erie Board meeting. The board heard of the rationale for this organization from Dan Brindisi, a former Erie employee, and founder of the Near Northwest Civic Committee, with offices in the Erie neighborhood. It turned out that Erie kid, Brindisi, represented another contribution of Erie House to the rich neighborhood organization story that was intertwined with the story of West Town and Chicago in the latter half of the 20th century. Joe Orlando, owner at that time of Orlando Glass on Ashland and Erie, and a neighborhood resident for many years, explained that COPA represents "those of us who do not want to run to the suburbs. We are staying."[165]

For the program year, 1953-54, Erie had 1,958 enrolled participants. This is an unduplicated number, compared to the duplicated numbers of attendance v.

enrollment used during Miss Towne's time at Erie. Fifty-nine per cent were children under the age of 18; 26% were age 18-60; 15% were over 60. The budget for 1955 was $65,794, with $18,250 (28%) from the Community Fund, $41,944 (64%) from individual or church contributions, and $5,600 (9%) in earned income.

The report closed with an evaluation that praised Erie for "significant progress in neighborhood relations and for providing leadership in "founding" ("finding" would be more accurate) a neighborhood organization. It viewed as positive, an increase in training for staff, and gave particular credit to the Executive Director (first time this title used in place of Head Resident) for his contribution to "improving the position of Erie House," as well as the Program Director, Robert Armstrong. All in all, the report gave the Erie Board cause to be pleased with their choice of Head Resident/Executive Director.

A 1955 brochure, titled "The Erie Story," re-caps the historical stages of that story: It begins with Holland Presbyterian Church in 1870, the Noble Street Mission of Third Presbyterian in 1882, incorporation as Erie Chapel Institute in 1915, and its renaming as Erie Neighborhood House, when it opened its new building in 1936. Its mission in 1955:

> *The doors of Erie Neighborhood House are open to both the troubled and the triumphant. It is at once a sanctuary and a source of mission. One comes into it out of a busy world seeking refuge, strength, and peace, and goes back into the world to share these spiritual gains.*[166]

Before leaving 1955, it is worth noting that Erie House finally joined the National Federation of Settlements, that at the time of its founding in 1911, banned church-affiliated settlements from its membership. Apparently, after 40+ years, that ban had been lifted. On the other hand, Erie had always been a member of the Chicago Federation of Settlements, and was represented on the Executive Council of that organization in 1955. And, 1955 was the year that Jim & Lynn McClure joined the Erie board. They came with connections to Erie's connections. They lived in Oak Park and belonged to First Church of Oak Park, a supporter of Erie House since 1915. Besides that, Jim worked for Gardner, Carton & Douglas, Erie's pro bono law firm since 1947. The year ended with the sale of Camp Davies to the camp's neighbors for $500. This was a financial decision, based on the reality that Erie saved $5,000 that year by using other camps instead of running its own. New officers for 1956 would include Bob Gielow as president, Benjamin Olson as VP, Lynn McClure as secretary, and David Dangler as Treasurer. All except McClure were time-honored names at Erie; but time would make the McClures honored as well, as they were active with Erie House for the next 40 years.

New construction was under way in the neighborhood in 1956. The new Carpenter School was being built at Racine and Erie (now Ogden School), and a new Santa Maria Addolorata School (now Rauner Charter High School) was being built at Ohio and Ada, directly behind Erie House. Church and school had been forced to relocate when they were displaced by the construction of the Kennedy Expressway. The Welfare Council was offering a "School for Board Members," and Board president, Gielow, was encouraging Erie board members to attend. Mrs. Armstrong reported that the opening of a Thrift Shop was under consideration, both as an ongoing fundraiser for Erie, and to provide clothing at a low cost to residents. That idea did become a reality and was part of Erie programming for years, an early version of what later came to be called "a social enterprise."

The Pilot Club was committed to funding rehab, of what are now the Sawyer rooms, to become a teen center. The Woman's Auxiliary raised $500 at their annual Sunshine Luncheon, and was proud to have sold 1200 pounds of pecans to raise $400. Pecan sales became another Erie tradition. All of that was helpful, but Lyman estimated that some significant deferred maintenance issues needed to be addressed. He proposed a capital campaign to raise the needed $65,000. A new boiler was installed, repairs were made to the boys' locker room, and $4,000 was spent on tuckpointing and painting. David Dangler secured a $5,000 contribution to the capital campaign from the Chicago Community Trust.

The story was told earlier of how Miss Florence helped a Japanese woman, a refugee from a US internment camp, with a job at Erie. In 1956, there was a Hideko (Decco) Tamura on staff, Dr. & Mrs. Nakamura joined the Erie Board from Austin Presbyterian Church; Elizabeth and Margaret Okayama entertained the December board meeting with Christmas carols, during Erie House's little known "Japanese period."

The Erie "Reunion" is Launched

As the West Town Community Area Report of 1955 had noted, the area was once again in transition, with European ethnics beginning their exodus to the suburbs, and immigrants from Latin America beginning to move in. This did not happen overnight, but it sparked an interest among some of the Italians, in particular, to grab hold of nostalgic memories of "growing up" at Erie House. A committee was formed and the "Old Timers File" was compiled of names going back as far as 1900, described as having mostly Polish and Italian names, with the latter being the larger number. They ended up with 138 names: 77 were Italian, 16 Polish; 42 still had "local" (not suburban) addresses. The planning committee had several names that show up in Erie's history on a regular basis, such as, Dan Brindisi, Tony and Marion DeVincent, John Vitacco, LaRocco, and Savino. LaCalamita and Spacucello were attached to Santa Maria; Duda, was a neighborhood Polish family name; and Mrs. F. Bibro, formerly of the building at Erie & Noble, that Erie House rented from time to time, was eventually associated with St. Boniface, where her daughter, Sharon, was active until that church closed in 1990. Letters went out in April of 1957 calling for an "Erie reunion" in the form of a dinner-dance to be held at Erie. Over the years, this effort at a reunion continued, eventually taking place at the DeVincent farm in Michigan. Last known contact with the leadership of this group was in 2003, indicating a strong enough attachment to Erie House to last approximately 47 years.

The Oak Park/River Forest Connection

Also, in April that year, an article appeared in an Oak Park newspaper titled, "Talents of Villagers Provide Joy, Happiness for Erie House Tots." It went on to say how many residents of Oak Park and River Forest were involved at Erie House. Oak Park shares its eastern border with Chicago's western one, between North Avenue and Roosevelt Road. River Forest is just west of Oak Park. Mr. & Mrs. Allin K. Ingalls and Dr. & Mrs. John Vitacco were from River Forest; Mr. & Mrs. Edward Dudley, Jr., Mrs. Andrew Kanelos, Mrs. William H. Wilson, Mrs. Elmer J. Featherstone, Mr. & Mrs. A.G. Bitzer, Mr. & Mrs. Harry Armstrong, Mr. & Mrs. Harold Swenson were listed as residents of Oak Park. Dr. & Mrs. Sawyer, and Mr. & Mrs. Glen Graham, were still members of First Presbyterian in Oak Park even though they had moved to Elmhurst, and Mrs. Oscar Pearson had moved to Glen Ellyn. Rev. Lyman and his family lived in Oak Park as well, as did board members Jim & Lynn McClure, and legal counsel, Laurence Carton. Board members in later years also came from Oak Park through Fair Oaks Presbyterian church. These were, and continued to be, longstanding connections for Erie House.

In May of 1957, Erie entered into a unique partnership with the United Cerebral Palsy Association of Chicago to provide counseling services to adult cerebral palsy victims. Lyman recommended taking on this project as a 3-year commitment, arguing that "a Neighborhood House is set up to serve disadvantaged groups and offers multiple types of services already." While this was certainly true, the project did not meet another important criterion of settlement house work -- to serve their local community. It was not continued at the end of the 3-year contract.

The Community Area 24 Report of 1957,[167] commented on several changes at Erie since the report of the previous year. First, this phrase was added to the Statement of Purpose: "In achieving our purpose, much emphasis is placed on helping our board, staff, and neighbors to *learn and use the skill of democratic decision-making* so that such an approach becomes part of our living fiber." Second, in spite of an overall decline in the number of teens in the neighborhood, reported in the 1950 census, Erie had doubled their teen participation, so that teens represented 25% of Erie participants, enrolling 133 boys and 87 girls. The report suggested this was due to hiring a better qualified staff, coupled with an overall increase in staff salaries that had been recommended by the Community Fund. Third, the report commended Erie for their summer program, visiting the homes of Puerto Rican families to explain Erie services and make them feel welcome as the newcomer neighbors. Fourth, Erie's work with COPA, and interest in developing local leaders to address housing issues, was praised. Erie's budget for 1957 was noted as $70,962, with the endowment fund at $52,036. As to the future, the report alerted Erie to the potential impact of the JFK Expressway that was cutting a path through the old ethnic neighborhood, cutting across church boundaries, and generally, accelerating further departure to the suburbs.

In 1958, Erie was finally able to deliver on their promise to provide a house for Lyman and his family. Since he and his wife and son, Paul, had arrived in 1952, they lived in an apartment in Oak Park, above the McClures. Then Greg and Beth came along and they needed more space. "The Manse," as it came to be called, located at 1033 Superior in Oak Park, was purchased for $24,750 in March. Securities were sold to help with the purchase and a mortgage was secured for $13,500 from Oak Park Trust & Savings, at 5%. Lyman was the only Head Resident/Executive Director to live there. When the Lymans moved on it was sold.

The Clinic Takes Off One Year after It Starts

In the minutes of the January Board meeting of 1957, a brief note is made of a new service Erie was offering to the community. This bullet point in Rev. Lyman's report actually marked an historic moment in Erie's history. As in the case of many such moments, no one at the time imagines that it is a historic moment. It is reported that a Dr. Snyder, from Glenview, is beginning to provide *pro bono* medical services, on an occasional basis, using space at Erie. Carmella Genova Jacob, an Erie participant, was a cancer patient of Dr. Snyder, and apparently shared with him her love of Erie House and the good work it was doing in her neighborhood. From their conversations, the idea of a clinic at Erie House was born. In consultation with Erie staff, an agreement was reached that the goal was to develop a service that was

> . . . *closer to the residents of the neighborhood, can win their confidence, can encourage them to obtain medical referrals to other clinics and at the same time, rendering them initial medical care.*[168]

During the following year, Carmella passed away, but 4 other volunteers began to work with Dr. Snyder. One of them was Carmella's sister, Antoinette (Daisy) Genova (Braucher), a psychiatric nurse at the Veterans' Hospital; another was a trained med tech. What they were learning about the health needs of Erie's new Puerto Rican neighbors and some of the elders staying on in the neighborhood, the medical aspects of social problems low income people face, led Dr. Snyder to come back to the Erie Board on March 8, 1958, with a proposal for "a cooperative medical project between Erie Neighborhood House and Northwestern Medical School," as follows:

- the Northwestern University Medical School would have 3 interns work at the Erie Clinic, two afternoons a week;
- Staff would grow to 4 doctors, 2 nurses, a lab tech, and a medical social worker;
- Lab services would be established;
- Hours would be expanded from one afternoon a week to two;
- Space improvements needed at estimated cost of $1,100;
- Would need to secure license from Board of Health;
- Intended to implement new health care nurse-practitioner strategy;
- Will make the effort not to interfere with other programs using the same space.[169]

As context for this expansion, Dr. Snyder shared the short, but active, one-year history of the clinic. He described its role to date as educational and preventive and as a dispenser of medications. He noted they had given out 400-500 polio vaccinations in the summer of 1957, even when the vaccine was not available at many doctors' offices. The clinic had tried different hours, but as of March 1958, was open mainly on Wednesday afternoons. Dr. Snyder, working with three volunteer health care professionals, on average, was serving 30-40 people each day it was open.

Dr. Edward Peterson, Director of Northwestern Medical School Clinics, explained that if the agreement was approved, starting in May, 1958, the med school would send 3 senior students to work under Dr. Snyder. Two of the students would work in the examining room; one would make house visits. He outlined the advantages of this proposed cooperation for both NU and Erie.

For NU, this would be:

- an opportunity to further expand the growing recognition by the medical profession of the effect of sociological problems in physical illness,
- give the school an ideal field area easily accessible to the school, located just two miles to the east of Erie House.

For Erie, this would provide:

- a much-needed service close by,
- access to the Comprehensive Care Clinic at NU to which neighborhood people could be referred when extensive treatment was indicated,
- an opportunity to add to Erie's work with local residents, a broadening and deepening of service
- an opportunity for Erie to be a pioneer in this type of health care work[170]

The ad hoc committee of board members that heard this presentation asked their questions and received satisfactory answers. An important understanding was reached regarding the screening of patients. Those who presented themselves for service would be assisted based on three possible scenarios: 1) They were in need of immediate care; 2) they could not afford health care elsewhere; 3) They were from the Erie House service area only (at least initially).[171] Bottom line, as Erie staff were most aware of and sensitive to the local population, they would do the patient screening. Based on this understanding, the committee voted unanimously to approve this proposal and to vote on it at the next Board meeting. It was approved, and proudly noted that this was the only clinic in a settlement house attached to a medical school.

This was the humble beginning of what is now the Erie Family Health Center (EFHC), with 13 sites throughout the Chicagoland area. Their headquarters today is at 1701 W. Superior, where they share a building with their co-founder, Erie Neighborhood House. EFHC occupies the third and fourth floors, while ENH uses the first floor for administrative offices, and the second floor for 10 pre-school classrooms. It turns out that 1957 was "the beginning of a beautiful (and successful) friendship." (as Humphrey Bogart said to Claude Rains at the end of *Casablanca).*

Closing Out the 1950s

Another beautiful and successful friendship was emerging in terms of Erie's work with COPA around the housing issue. Rev. Lyman reported to the board in June, 1958, that he had taken the initiative to invite two Puerto Rican ministers from a small church on Milwaukee Avenue, where Erie ran a Puerto Rican outpost to provide casework services, to attend a COPA meeting. In his words, "the effect was transformational." As the mostly white COPA members came to realize the shared interest of these ministers to cooperate with the COPA and Erie agenda to improve the neighborhood, the usual blaming on "those people" was completely undermined. Plans were under way for a meeting with 50 Puerto Rican landlords and tenants to meet with reps from COPA for further discussion of local housing improvements. Ross commented that "this is just one of the contributions Erie has attempted, not only to improve housing but to deepen neighborliness."[172]

Erie Launches Thrift Shop, RAC, and Meals on Wheels

Before the closing of the decade, three more Erie initiatives took off. On December 5, 1958, Erie opened the Thrift Shop that had been under discussion for some time. Churches were encouraged to donate items and volunteer to sort. That same month, Erie announced plans to open what they called a "remedial adjustment center" (RAC) that would be under the supervision of Rev. Ben Richardson, an African American colleague of Rev. Lyman. This "clinic" was targeting services for "troubled youth" who were prone to joining gangs and getting involved with the Juvenile Justice System. It had at the heart of its mission the principle of prevention that Miss Florence had always championed. In the case made for this program, Erie argued that it cost $1200/year to keep a boy at St. Charles, a juvenile detention center; it cost $30/ year to engage a boy at Erie House to keep him out of the system. It was a powerful ROI (return on investment) argument. Last but not least, discussion was under way for another new program idea, called "Meals on Wheels" (MOW), to provide hot meals to neighborhood shut-ins.

When MOW actually did roll out in 1959, it was thought to be the first program of its kind in Chicago. Volunteers, initially, all from churches, prepared meals in their church kitchens and then warmed them in the Erie kitchen when they arrived. They started with serving one hot meal two days a week to 16 individuals. Later it would expand to five days a week, and 30 individuals. MOW was the result of the finding of the Erie Clinic that elders, in particular, were showing signs of malnutrition. While remedying that problem was the initial impetus, the other benefits included providing some fellowship for those suffering from social isolation, as well as fellowship for the volunteers who worked together to provide this service. Finally, it provided that opportunity for suburbanites to keep coming into the city, staying in touch with the realities of urban poverty, and at the same time, seeing Erie House at work every week.

Erie Woman's Auxiliary (EWA) in the 1950s

Notes from Erie's Woman's Auxiliary (EWA) suggest they also had a busy year in 1958. Mrs. E.J. Featherston was president. Thirteen years after his death, Walter Gielow's widow, Evangeline, was still active at Erie. She gave the Treasurer's report in January to the 62 members present. Pecan sales were under way; Tag Day netted $2,840. Donations were approved at $150 to ENH and $50 to the Chapel. They heard reports on the new clinic development, the plans for the McGuiness Memorial Woodworking Shop, the Cerebral Palsy program, and from Mrs. Mae Lyman, regarding the new Thrift Shop, which would draw a good number of EWA members to volunteer. Lynn McClure was elected president for 1959. They closed their meetings and the year with the *Mizpah Benediction*: based on a passage from Genesis: "May the Lord watch between you and me when we are out of each other's sight." (New American Standard Bible)

A New Decade Begins: The 1960s

In February, 1960, Erie hosted a tour that gave Lyman the opportunity to introduce the new staff he had brought to Erie House. Ross underscored the professional preparation of Erie's senior staff. Bob Armstrong, Program Director,

153

had a Master's in Group Work from the University of Pittsburgh, on staff since 1953; Rev. Ben Richardson, Director of RAC, was a Harvard grad, specializing in work with youth; Cecilia Campbell, Director of Community Services, was a graduate of UCLA. The work of these professionals was complemented by employees hired from the neighborhood to make, what was hoped to be, a good professional and cultural blend.

That March, an article appeared in the magazine called *Presbyterian Life*. The title was "The Church that Commutes to its Mission Field," subtitle, "United Presbyterian Suburbanites from Oak Park Act as Part-time Staff of Chicago's Neighborhood Houses."[173] The article highlights the work of First Presbyterian Church of Oak Park on the occasion of its 75th Anniversary (founded in 1884). According to the author,

> *First Church of Oak Park has spent much of its energy building a genuine missionary interest for the inner city into the heart of congregational life.[174]*

First Church pastor, at that time, David B. Watermulder, added the following reflection:

> *If the suburban church were a cozy, comfortable club, it would be a terrible thing. Instead, the church is a continuous discipleship which is never wrapped up in a little package.[175]*

The article goes on to explain that Pastor Watermulder chairs the neighborhood house unit of the Church Extension Board (CEB) of the Presbytery of Chicago, and joins 58 other Oak Park members serving on boards of eight United Presbyterian centers in the city. Harry Armstrong is identified in the article as one of the members of First Church who had joined 40 years earlier, and shortly thereafter, joined the Erie House board, serving six years as its president. There is also a photo of Keturah Phelps, providing speech therapy to a participant in Erie's cerebral palsy project. Mrs. Phelps is the mother of Lynn McClure, Erie board member and president of Erie's Woman's Auxiliary in 1959. Once again, multiple generations of the same family, as well as the same church, connect with Erie House--"a continuous discipleship."

While *Presbyterian Life* highlighted one form of discipleship, from the point of view of the Presbyterian church, Robert Armstrong, an Erie staff member for seven years, wrote a paper in June of 1959 for his Ethics & Society class.[176] Armstrong was one of the first staff hired by Ross Lyman when he took the job of Head Resident in May of 1952, and Erie's first professionally trained social worker, who also lived at the house for his first nine months on the job. In his paper, he offers some observations regarding changes that were made by Lyman – changes that pertained to both staff and board that he believed benefited them as well as local residents. He noted two developments under Lyman's leadership: 1) An overall upgrading of staff, hiring people with academic and professional credentials, and raising salaries; 2) An invitation to staff to attend board meetings, making them feel more respected, and giving board and staff an opportunity to know each other.[177] Armstrong believed that the crossing of class lines at the board/staff level facilitated crossing the same kind of line at the neighborhood level. This, he argued, was an important contribution of settlement house work. This practice has continued to the present day.

Armstrong also observed that at Erie Chapel, the church worship service per se was not the total meaning of ministry. In fact, he found that the most active church members were those involved in the "total ministry," as they were also active in work at the House. He concluded:

*If we can bring people to the point of a comfortable
class identification, and at the same time develop in
them a capacity to cross class lines, and be
concerned that mobility between class groups be
maintained, we are doing as much as can be done
to actualize Christian values in the urban
civilization in which we live.*[178]

In July of 1959, it was announced that the
commitment of the Lyman family to Erie House was about
to expand, as Evelyn Lyman, Ross' sister, would be joining
the staff in September. Miss Lyman was a nurse and was
leaving her position of eight years as director of the Christian
Center in Pittsfield, Massachusetts. Her job description:
supervise the Thrift Shop, Meals on Wheels, and two adult
programs; she will also serve as a social worker and make
home visits. But, observers at the time saw that job evolve
until she became the day-to-day overseer of all that
transpired at Erie House. She lived in an apartment on Erie
Street, just a block away, in a building owned by Erie
supporters. It turned out that this was the beginning of the
rest of her life.

As Miss Lyman came in, two key staff among Rev.
Lyman's first hires in his plan to upgrade the professional
qualifications of Erie staff, moved on. Cecelia Campbell was
marrying Erie's young assistant minister, Duane Holm, and
moving to Scotland. Robert Armstrong also left at the end
of 1959.

On November 11, 1959, Ross Lyman submitted a
report titled *Ten Year Prospectus*, in response to a request
from the Welfare Council. The report was to address two
areas: 1) a statement of policy indicating the agency's long-
range prospectus; 2) Erie's three new programs in that
context: Remedial Adjustment Center (RAC), Meals on
Wheels (MOW), and the Puerto Rican Outpost. Since the

Outpost program was deemed no longer necessary, it had been discontinued and, therefore, would not be addressed.[179]

In what might be described as a Statement of Purpose as well as Policy, Lyman provided the following:

> *Erie Neighborhood House and Chapel is a ministry of the Presbyterian Church in the inner city, whose purpose is to meet the spiritual, health, civic, moral, and cultural needs of the people of our defined geographic community. We do this through pastoral ministry, group work, recreational programs, case work, health clinics, and remedial adjustment services. . . without regard for race, color, or creed. In our total ministry we are committed to that creative pioneering that will more meaningfully interpret our faith, more effectively relieve human woe, and enrich the lives of the people we serve.[180]*

There is nothing particularly new about this statement except the addition of RAC as a new approach to work Erie had been doing to keep boys out of trouble, at least since Miss Towne had arrived on the scene. What is more striking is the inclusion of the Chapel as part of the statement of purpose. Certainly, the chapel and its minister had always worked closely with the Head Resident of the House, but with the Head Resident actually being a minister, the overall work is now defined as a "ministry" v. a "settlement house." Some would say this description and use of a word with such religious connotation made Erie less of a settlement house and more of a mission, exactly as Robert Woods had argued when he banned church-affiliated neighborhood houses from the National Federation of Settlements. On the other hand, Jane Addams would probably not have been adverse to a referral to settlement work as a "ministry." In *Twenty Years at Hull House* she spoke often of how respectful work

157

with the poor reflected the message of the New Testament, and was an active expression of Christianity, as she understood it.

In regard to projecting where Erie House would be in 10 years, Lyman was reluctant to estimate that, in light of the Erie context of a changing neighborhood. He begged the question by saying it was likely many programs would continue, and some new ones may need to be added–kind of vague, to say the least. However, in its 89th year at that point, Erie had already proven its sustainability, and the 1950s was not the first era of change Erie had adjusted to. Ironically, he was actually on target. Regardless of the racial and ethnic changes, most of Erie's programming, designed to serve the needs of immigrants living in dilapidated housing, in need of better jobs, would be just as relevant with Latino immigrants as it had been with Europeans. The language would change, techniques for delivering programs would evolve, but Erie had another 40 years before the neighborhood would change so much that their geographic "neighbors," just outside their door, would no longer need their services. At that point, it would become clearer that "neighbor" was a concept that was never meant to be limited by geography.

As the new decade began, the Erie endowment fund was valued at $96,000, an encouraging rate of growth in 15 years, guided by savvy board members. And because they were savvy, they turned over management of the endowment fund to Continental Bank in 1960. There would be many years in the future when just the interest from the endowment would help the House move forward in difficult financial times. The fact that Erie had an endowment was often the envy of other non-profits who had no such back-up.

Lyman's Second Decade

Marvin Brown, an African American group worker at Erie, put together a report on West Town that offered a demographic context, as of 1960.[181] He noted that 25% of Puerto Ricans in Chicago lived in West Town or the neighboring Humboldt Park. Southern whites, who Erie observed in the neighborhood in the 1950s, showed up again in the 1960 census. Brown noted that "Negroes" had been in West Town since the 1930s; in the Erie Service area since 1945. That number would begin to grow in the 1960s.

As ethnic groups changed, the housing stock had not. There was no evidence of any new construction after 1930; the type of housing that remained, was predominantly, 2- and 3-flats, with an abundance of mixed-use properties that had retail at the street level with apartments above. This included many "Mom & Pop" corner stores on residential blocks. In 1960, only 21% were owner-occupied, and only 60% had complete plumbing facilities. 22.8% of apartments still shared a bathroom located in the hallway between the units. Aside from all that, 74% of the structures were considered sound, a fact that supported an argument for rehab versus demolition, as the community formulated its housing improvement agenda. Of the 16,000 persons in the Erie 4 X 6-block service area (Grand to Chicago, May to Paulina), 41% (6,560) were children under the age of 18. It was no wonder that local public schools were bursting at the seams, and the new Carpenter School was desperately needed.

This community snapshot did not significantly alter programs at Erie House or its support of COPA in advocating for improved housing. However, ESL students were now Spanish-speakers, the need for staff who could speak Spanish would continue to increase over the next 10 years, and gradually become bicultural as well as bilingual. One other area of service that changed somewhat was the focus of case work on providing assistance to families in coping with the government's welfare system, filling out the paperwork and troubleshooting issues that were preventing benefits from kicking in. This was partially due to the fact that incoming Puerto Ricans were citizens, and thus, automatically eligible for such government services. What was not new was the demand for assistance in finding jobs. In the early 60s, Erie was serving about 120-150 families a month under the heading of Welfare Services.

Erie Chapel, on the other hand, made significant changes to accommodate its first Spanish-speaking members, by welcoming former members of La Iglesia de San Marcos that had not ever had a really permanent home in West Town. Unexpectedly, this congregation was mostly Mexican, but the hope was that, with a service in Spanish, Puerto Ricans would come to Erie Chapel as well. To extend a further welcome, the "Erie Chapel Chimes," or Sunday bulletin, began to include a *Noticias de la Iglesia* section. In spite of all these efforts, Erie Chapel was faced with the same challenge they had for the last 70 years – their new neighbors were predominantly Catholic.

Erie House Finances

Before going on to Erie programs and neighborhood developments in the 1960s, this might be a good place to address the Erie budget, with its varied sources of revenue. Income for 1960 was reported as $98,993. Here is the budget growth picture in round numbers:

1915	-	$ 6,400
1920	-	23,000
1935	-	20,000
1945	-	34,000
1955	-	65,000
1960	-	99,000

One might conclude from this that Ross Lyman was a crackerjack fundraiser. By 1955, three years after his arrival, the Erie budget had almost doubled from 10 years earlier. In the next five years, it went up 50% more. What did the increase reflect? One problem in interpreting this data is that government contract revenue was often not reflected in the budget reports at Board meetings. Private revenue sources included the Community Fund, the single largest contributor, Foundations and Trusts (a steady but small source, lacking much growth since they began in the 1930s), churches, individuals, and fundraisers. Church financial support is complicated to measure. That category usually pertained to checks written on a church account. However, many members of churches donated as "individuals," bought tickets to fundraisers, or contributed through church-related organizations such as the Woman's Auxiliary. Finally, it has always been a challenge to put a dollar amount to thousands upon thousands of volunteer hours church members and neighbors contributed to Erie programs and fundraisers.

So, what is known in 1960, in terms of private revenue, is that the Community Fund allocation was $24,940; Foundations and Trusts contributed $3,500. Fundraiser results were as follows: Thrift Shop: $4550, Tag Day: $2750, and Mayfair: $900, for a total of $8,200. These activities and events were primarily the responsibility of the EWA, in addition to their annual pecan sales. Churches: $8,200; Individuals and firms: $32,000. That totals $76,840 in round numbers, leaving a balance of $22,160 unaccounted for. These are not numbers from accounting reports, and again, there is no report on government sources that paid for most of Child Care programming. But the point here, is to indicate rate of growth, the value of regular fundraisers, and the role of the Community Fund in contributing about 25% of Erie's budget. In addition, it seems relevant to point out that the revenue accounted for in the category, "churches," was likely an underrepresentation of their financial contribution. It also illustrates a reality that fundraising events need to be evaluated for the ROI value of manpower vis-à-vis dollars raised. In 1961, its 91st year, the Erie budget first achieved the 100K threshold at $108,679.

The 1960s as Context

For Erie Neighborhood House and the West Town community of Chicago, the 1960s would mark the unfolding of the community-based organizing movement and locally developed affordable housing. The national back-drop for this was the heightened civil rights movement led by Dr. Martin Luther King, Jr., still mostly focused in the South, but strong enough to convince President Lyndon Johnson, a Southerner himself, to sign into law the Civil Rights Act in 1963. That was the same year of the now renowned March on Washington and King's "I have a dream" speech. Even before that speech drew national attention, an Erie House connection, Anna Grace Sawyer, was connecting with Dr. King.

On March 3, 2000, Kerry Taylor, a researcher at the MLK Papers Project at Stanford University (founded by Coretta King in 1985), emailed Rose Blaney at the Presbytery of Chicago. Taylor had come across correspondence between Anna Grace Sawyer (AGS) and Dr. Martin Luther King (MLK) from 1960. Regardless of the purpose of Ms. Taylor's inquiry, her finding certainly makes an interesting Erie House story. What made their way to the Erie House files,[182] were copies of nine hand-written pages of correspondence from AGS to MLK, followed by three type-written pages in reply. What made it of particular interest to Erie House was that this was a "Sawyer." Anna Grace was the sister of Dr. Alva Sawyer, an Erie House supporter and board member in the 1930s. She was the aunt of the Sawyers' daughter, Betty, who married Glen Graham. The Grahams followed the Sawyer tradition by becoming major benefactors of Erie, a tradition carried on in the next generation by Anna Grace's grandniece, Marj Schuham.

The first letter from AGS to MLK was sent from her address at 424 Elgin Avenue, Forest Park, IL, (just west of Oak Park) to Dr. King at Ebenezer Church, Auburn Ave., Atlanta, GA, and postmarked September 1, 1960. Her greeting: "Honored Man-of-God, Dr. King." She tells Dr. King that she has heard from a friend, a Lillian Smith, regarding *"the heroic Negro students' non-violent sit-ins. I have been deeply stirred by this Christian ethical plan against long years of unjust discrimination."* She goes on to share her opinion of this activity. *"What admirable training these students are acquiring under the Congress of Racial Equality (CORE)."*[183] Aware that CORE leader, James Robinson, was in prison she hoped he would be released soon to carry on his "Christ-like and Gandhi-like" non-violent work. She says she is enclosing a check, and that perhaps, it can be used for Mr. Robinson's defense. She wrote again on September 6, this time saying that her friend recommended dividing her donation of $2,000, with $1,000 going to CORE, and $1,000 directly to Dr. King *"in support of your work on Negro voting rights."* She went on to say that she hoped his work could arouse *"static white church people"* to overcome racial prejudice.[184] There was nothing static about Anna Grace.

She received a first reply on September 9, from James R. Wood, Administrative Assistant to Dr. King. Wood noted he opened her "warm & sincere letter" in Dr. King's absence, confident he will react as I did to your deep concern for conditions here and abroad. *"Your letter will bring him inspiration and encouragement. It is his life's desire to attain, in the words of Mohandas Gandhi, the 'beloved community.'"* The second reply, from Dr. King himself, arrived on September 26, thanking her for the $1,000 donation to his work. He went on to say that he received many letters, but occasionally, one came to hand *"which conveys more than the written word reveals. The warmth of your letter is penetrating and I feel inspired."* [185]

Sixty years later, readers might be inspired by the depth of understanding of this suburban woman, whose story suggests that some of Erie House's supporters were not simply supporting an institution connected to their church denomination, but were, indeed, followers of the Social Gospel preached by Jane Addams and lived by Florence Towne. Anna Grace Sawyer named what she believed, that King was, indeed, a Man-of-God to be honored.

Meanwhile, Richard J. Daley, "static white church (Catholic) person" that he was, was building Cabrini Green and the Robert Taylor Homes to do his best to segregate low-income African Americans in public housing. And, in the light of Brown v. the Board of Education, a very successful boycott of Chicago's public schools was organized in support of the demand for desegregation of those schools. Circumstances such as these, had Dr. King heading north.

In 1967, the Chicago Freedom Movement emerged under the leadership of educators and activists like Al Raby and Timuel Black. Dr. King came to Chicago, as his own understanding of the racism that thrived in urban areas, while seemingly more subtle than Jim Crow in the south, was an undercurrent ready to break into the open. In 1966, both the Marquette Park violence against Dr. King and the civil rights marchers there, and the Humboldt Park "rioting" on Division Street, that followed the killing of a young Puerto Rican by a police officer, were evidence of this. And this was not the end of civic unrest in Chicago in the 1960s.

In 1968, Chicago was the scene for two more headline-making protests. In one, non-violent protesters against the war in Viet Nam were attacked by police during the Democratic National Convention in Chicago, under directives from the mayor. The other outburst, mostly on the west side of Chicago, occurred following the assassination of Dr. King in April. A rampage of arson and destruction erupted, expressing grief, frustration and rage at the loss of this remarkable man who had brought so much hope to

African Americans all over the country. He was gone, taken from them in violence, and they were angry. And then anger was stirred up once again in 1969, when Chicago police killed leaders of Chicago's Black Panther Party, under a directive of the State's Attorney, Robert Hanrahan.

To some extent, Erie had a pivotal moment, facing the issue of racism in its neighborhood back in 1945, when Rev. Cedarleaf and Miss Towne marched to Throop Street. From that moment forward, African Americans were welcome at Erie House, as staff members, volunteers, and participants. This does not mean everyone in the neighborhood took that same position, but they had the model for an alternative response in their institutional neighbor down the block. And around the city, positive programs emerged to seek other, non-violent responses— Operation Breadbasket in 1965, Leadership Council for Metropolitan Open Communities and the Puerto Rican Parade Committee, in 1966.

And before the 60s were over, two more groups of Americans, who were often pushed to the margins, found their voice. Women rose up and formed the National Organization of Women (NOW) in 1966, and women of Chicago followed with their own chapter of NOW in 1967. By 1971, the first women were elected to Chicago's City Council. It only took 101 years before Erie House witnessed that. And in 1973, the Supreme Court handed down Roe v. Wade. As far as women's rights were concerned, settlement houses recognized and depended upon the leadership of women, from Jane Addams and Florence Towne to the present day. To round out the decade, in 1969, the Stonewall riot in New York is often credited with starting the movement for LGBTQ rights.

All in all, it was a momentous decade. These events may not all be evident in the details of Erie's history, but the sons and daughters of this decade of movements came to work at Erie House and other settlement houses, products of an earlier movement, and protagonists for the next.

1950's Start-ups Flourish in the 1960s

An Update on the Clinic from Dr. Snyder

In January of 1961, Dr. Robert Snyder reported to the board on the progress of the clinic since Erie partnered with the NU Medical School in 1958.[186] To share the good news, he used the metaphor of the unlikely growth of a plant in an unfriendly environment, and the pleasure it gives when it flourishes regardless. This was the story of an outpatient clinic "planted" in a settlement house located in the "asphalt jungle" of a depressed area of Chicago. He reported that medical students wanted to serve at Erie, making it the first of NU's outpatient clinics fully subscribed. He attributes that success, initially, to the convenience of proximity, just two miles from school, but also to the location in a well-established agency, at 88 years in the same neighborhood. This context gives patients confidence they will be treated with respect in a dignified atmosphere, where they often already came for other services. That, in turn, added to patient rapport with their physician. Furthermore, this clinic is close to home. This addresses their reluctance, as new arrivals in the city, to venture downtown to deal with large institutions, even if they had the carfare to do so, which, Dr. Snyder understands, they don't.

Med students are learning about different cultures and how to work with patients who are unfamiliar with health care systems and medical care in general. They are exposed to the maturing experience that the responsible role a family physician in a neighborhood clinic has proven to be. They have also realized the advantage of working at a location where other services that supplement medical attention are available under the same roof – a dental clinic, clinical psychologists that do testing and counseling, tutoring available to adults and children, and a Meals on Wheels program to address nutritional needs of elders and shut-ins. Finally, their work is facilitated by neighborhood resident volunteers who greet their patients and put them at ease.

Some of the demographics Snyder shared were that 50% of their patients were Puerto Rican, about 25% Southern white, and 25% Poles and Italians. They were able to see about 50 patients per afternoon session, or 100 per week. Staff at this point consisted of 1 supervising physician, 3 senior med students, 4 nurses, 5 lay persons who were all volunteers. He acknowledged that while they primarily worked in the youth department and arts and crafts room, they were spilling over into more rooms as well. These rooms became the lab, the pharmacy, and the immunization rooms, but in 45 minutes were transformed back to program spaces immediately after the clinic sessions ended, twice a week.

Since the medical clinic had opened, another connection was made at Northwestern to re-open a dental clinic at Erie. The first one had opened in 1939. In 1960, Dr. Arthur Elfenbaum, Emeritus Dean of Oral Surgery at NU's Dental School, volunteered his time to organize the clinic and a dentist from Deerfield donated a full set of dental equipment. Snyder concluded by reporting that this model of locating clinics at settlement houses was spreading throughout the country.

By 1968, 10 years after Dr. Snyder made his pitch to the Erie board to partner with the NU Medical School, one of his key arguments had clearly been well founded. The medical School was just as impacted by their work in a neighborhood clinic as the neighborhood itself. The medical students urged the university to add an evening option on Thursdays, recommended fluency in Spanish be a consideration for admission to medical school and, that the school offer a medically-oriented Spanish course as an elective in Sophomore year.

Meals on Wheels in the Headlines

Not only was the clinic doing well, but two other programs received positive media coverage in 1962. "Meals on Wheels Brings Cheer to the Needy" was the headline for a story by Jean Dietrich that appeared in the *Chicago Sun-Times,* March 11, 1962. A nice spread of photos accompanied the article featuring volunteers preparing meals in the Erie kitchen, and then walking down a snowy street to deliver them. Dietrich wrote, "You are ill and old and poor and alone. . . but 4 times a week friends will be dropping by with a warm meal and some conversation." She noted that the program had started in 1958 and had been run by church volunteers, who, in 1962, came from the following churches: Glenview Community Church (United Church of Christ), Wilmette Presbyterian, Highland Park Presbyterian, and Morton Grove Community Presbyterian Church. After four years of operation, they were delivering an average of 17 meals a day, four days a week. One couple on welfare said they received an allowance of 75 cents a day for food; they paid Erie volunteers 20 cents, only to help cover the cost of milk and coffee that had to be purchased; the rest of the meal was donated by the churches.[187]

Remedial Adjustment Services

The lead article of the May 15, 1962 issue of *Presbyterian Life*, was titled "Antidote for Delinquency."[188] The magazine's cover featured a photo of Rev. Ross Lyman, Executive Director, and Rev. Ben Richardson, Director of Remedial Services of Erie House, in conversation with teen boys, at night, in front of a local hot dog stand. Remedial Services was the latest name for a program that began in

1958 as "the remedial adjustment center" and was devised to work with youth who were not participants at Erie, but were often getting into trouble and ending up in the Juvenile Justice System--who in popular parlance were called juvenile delinquents. The Erie program was designed to go out and meet the boys, learn the issues that were impacting their lives, and bring them to Erie for the type of service most likely to be an "antidote" to their problem. This could be psychological, educational, or medical, or all of the above. The Remedial Services "staff", many of whom were professionals volunteering their time, would refer them to the appropriate service at Erie, or elsewhere if needed. Lyman and Richardson had made the rounds of the Presbyterian churches to find their volunteers; 46 professionals responded.

The goal of RAS was to get youth off the street before they became delinquent. Their motto was "it is important to correct juvenile delinquency, but more important to forestall it." In what they called the "Christian view" their objective was to look for solutions that were "restorative." One could see some foreshadowing here of an approach to dealing with problematic youth behavior in 21st century "restorative justice" programs, initiated at a number of public schools, and deployed again by Erie House in their work in Little Village.

Erie Woman's Auxiliary (EWA) in the 1960s

In the light of these accomplishments, Lynn McClure offered a tribute to Mae and Ross Lyman at a meeting of the Woman's Auxiliary, on May 14, 1962, the occasion of their 10th anniversary at Erie. She noted that they were known and loved in the neighborhood and by staff. It was due to Ross's leadership and Christian commitment that Erie was successfully coping with the many changes in the neighborhood. One of the key elements of his success was that he made volunteers feel valued for their contribution to the overall ministry of Erie. Certainly, the EWA felt valued. By 1962, the members represented 28 churches; typical attendance ranged from 50 to 75 at their monthly meetings.

Throughout the 1960s, Church support was stronger than ever. The Erie Woman's Auxiliary broke their own attendance record in 1964 with 250 attending the annual Sunshine Luncheon. The core group of the EWA consisted of 84 delegates from 30 Presbyterian churches, only nine of which were still in the city. First Church of Oak Park alone had 11 representatives, while most churches had only two. The families with the longest history on the Erie House Board, were also found to be active with the EWA. With this organization's involvement with the Erie Thrift Shop and Tag Day, they raised thousands of dollars for Erie House each year. Nineteen churches were represented on the ENH Board in 1965, and 13 more were listed as supporting, for a total of 32 Protestant Churches[189] involved one way or another, through volunteer work, or donations, or both. 1965 was also the year that Erie House was one of 16 agency members of the Chicago Federation of Settlements to receive funding from Lyndon Johnson's War on Poverty.

The ABCs of the 1960s: Activism, Bickerdike, and Catholic Nuns at Erie House

A is for Activism, Alinsky-style

While programming at Erie continued to adjust to its new neighbors, a new organization came on the scene that would take Erie into a new area of "service" and an updated version of the Social Gospel – community organizing. In 1962, The Northwest Community Organization (NCO) came into being in West Town. It was initially organized through the Catholic churches, more specifically, through the efforts of Monsignor Jack Egan, and with the full approval of

Cardinal Meyer, who headed up the Chicago Archdiocese at the time. Egan made the rounds of local pastors to secure the level of financial commitment that would be needed to pay staff and get the organization off the ground. He was successful in raising $54,000. But to better understand how Jack Egan came to do this work, and ultimately how Erie Neighborhood House connected with NCO, one has to go back at least eight years, to 1954, when Fr. Jack Egan met Saul Alinsky. Sanford Horwitt's *Let them Call me Rebel,* is an excellent source for understanding these connections.[190]

How Did the Catholic Churches and Protestant Neighborhood Houses Get to 1962?

Saul Alinsky had become infamous for his work in the Back of the Yards neighborhood in Chicago in the late 1930s. He began there connecting union leaders, who were fighting the meatpacking companies for better wages and working conditions, with Catholic and Protestant pastors. When those pastors showed up on the picket line, it proved to be an unbeatable combination that brought the Swifts and Armours to the negotiating table, and won many of the provisions the unions had been fighting for. From the lessons of that victory, workers and parishes went on to transform their neighborhood into a much more pleasant place to live with the ongoing support from their own neighborhood organization, the Back of the Yards Neighborhood Council (BYNC). It was initially headed up by Joe Meegan, who was introduced to the strategic tool of community organizing by Saul himself.

In subsequent years, Alinsky was not happy about how some things had evolved in the Back of the Yards community. To say that the neighborhood was not welcoming to African Americans would have been an understatement. But with the founding of his Industrial Areas Foundation (IAF) in 1940, he had moved on to focusing on fundraising to support other community organizing ventures, in particular the work of Fred Ross in California who had found a protégé with a lot of potential in San Jose, by the name of César Chávez. He had financial support for his earlier work in Chicago from Bishop Sheil, and as it turned out, the hierarchy of the Catholic Archdiocese of Chicago would once again become a resource in support of community organizing in the city.

Alinsky and Egan first connected in 1954.[191] While born in New York, Egan grew up in Chicago's North Side Irish community. After ordination, as Horwitt describes him, "he gravitated to the Catholic left in Chicago." In other words, he spent time with a movement in the church that expressed itself through organizations like Young Christian Workers (YCW), Young Christian Students (YCS), and a program for young married couples called the Christian Family Movement (CFM). Perhaps, only in Chicago would a Jewish community organizer receive a letter from a French Catholic theologian, who then connected him with an Irish Catholic priest, who was welcoming the founder of the Little Brothers and Sisters of the Poor to his city from France. But Jacques Maritain wrote to his friend, Saul, in the hope he could work with Fr. Egan, when Fr. Voillaume came to town. Chicago has been a mission home to the Little Brothers and Sisters ever since, but more was wrought through a partnership that took off that day than either Egan or Alinsky might have expected.

In the context of this story, it is not possible to review all the steps in between. Suffice it to say that Egan knew which monsignors to talk to that eventually led him to a conversation with Cardinal Stritch, and at the right moment brought Alinsky into that conversation. The right moment was a call from Msgr. John McMahon, pastor of St. Sabina's on Chicago's south side, to Jack Egan. In the mid-1950s "if you were a Catholic pastor on the South or Southwest Side of Chicago, you were concerned about saving your parish from the possibility – even the probability – of a mass exodus of your white parishioners."[192]   While Back of the Yards' answer to this problems was to adopt an anti-Black agenda, McMahon was interested in a different approach. He talked to Egan about a large-scale community organizing strategy, that hoped to ensure integration versus flight, and had already been in touch with Catholic Charities about contributing funds, also pledging money from his own parish treasury.

Meanwhile, Cardinal Stritch passed away and was succeeded by Cardinal Meyer. Meyer appointed Egan to a full-time position as executive director of the Cardinal's Conservation Committee, and Egan set up a meeting between Cardinal Meyer and Alinsky to talk about McMahon's proposed project. "He allowed us to do it," is how Egan described Meyer's message, delivered to the pastors of the Southwest Side. This was the impetus for the development of the Organization of Southwest Chicago or OSC, and Alinsky put Nicholas Von Hoffman to work as the lead organizer. But less one assume this was all done by Catholics, another young organizer was drawn to Chicago. His name was Ed Chambers. He came from working in Harlem, living in a settlement there called Friendship House, to work with the man who had written *Reveille for Radicals*. In 1959, he became one of Alinsky's organizers for OSC. One of his assignments: find out where the Protestant churches are.

One of Chambers' early contacts was the Reverend Bob Christ at Seventh Presbyterian. He had come to Seventh in 1954, after completing the urban studies program, at McCormick Seminary. After numerous conversations with Chambers, Von Hoffman, and Alinsky, he came to this conclusion.

Nick, Ed, and Saul in their own way offered people like me and some others who were hungry to make

*our mark in the world a way to do it . . . And we
were, I think, authentically concerned about some
of the wrongs, but the way we were going at them
was so trivial that we knew it was only a finger in
the dike. . . What Saul had to offer was a device, a
methodology and a vision that something could be
done.[193]*

So, in spite of the fact that many Protestant clergy in
the 1950s were suspicious of Catholics in general, (and vice
versa) and the role of the Archdiocese in particular, Bob
Christ, himself, started meeting with Catholic clergy
involved in the OSC project. He also began to work with the
leadership and members of his own congregation to develop
buy-in to this newly minted ecumenical movement.
Eventually, Rev. Christ was joined by more than a dozen of
his Protestant church colleagues. Within the space of little
more than a year, Alinsky and company had ushered in a new
era in Catholic-Protestant relations in Chicago. Years before
Vatican II, there was evidence that Chicago could become a
shining example of ecumenism.[194] The point of telling this
story and the next, is to explore the broader Chicago
backdrop of community organizing that Erie House would
be drawn into. Saul Alinsky, Jack Egan, and BOTH Catholic
and Protestant clergy set the scene for the scenario that
resulted in a collaboration with Catholic priests like Fr. Tony
Janiak, pastor of Holy Innocents, Rev. Ross Lyman, and
others, to embrace and invest in the Northwest Community
Organization in West Town in 1962.

By the late 1950s, Jack Egan was practically a full-
time intern at the IAF. Their next project would be to create
The Woodlawn Organization (TWO), probably one of
Alinsky's most celebrated accomplishments after Back-of-
the-Yards, and with a much more civil rights-friendly
outcome. Once again, it began with a Catholic pastor. This
time it was Martin Farrell, pastor of Holy Cross in

Woodlawn. At the start of the 1950s, Woodlawn was about 60% white; 10 years later, it would be more than 95% black.[195] Farrell wrote to Alinsky, pleading for help to organize this neighborhood. Like McMahon before him, Farrell approached Catholic Charities and secured $50,000 through his friend, Msgr. Vincent Cooke. Next, the IAF, Holy Cross Parish, and First Presbyterian of Woodlawn, whose co-pastors (Ulysses Blakely and Charles Leber) were a black and a white, became Farrell's allies. They approached the Field Foundation for funding. While that funding did not come through, the Churches did. Cardinal Meyer committed $50,000/year for three years. The Presbyterians committed $22,000. The latter contribution was not without controversy. There were a good number of Protestant church leaders who found Alinsky's approach to organizing difficult to accept – especially his focus on self-interest as the basic motivator for humans to act, and his insistence on attaining power and exercising it, as the only effective strategy for achieving social or economic justice. He was updating the Social Gospel, but many did not see it that way and/or found it difficult to accept. Nevertheless, it was based on Jesus' words: "I come to cast fire on the earth, and would that it were already kindled." (Luke, 12:49).[196]

Acceptance of that interpretation was championed by two more Protestant ministers. One, Doug Still, arrived in Chicago from California in the late 1950s to assume a key position with the Protestant Church Federation. Some of his time in California had been spent with the Migrant Ministry, where he was educated about the plight of the poor farmworkers by César Chávez, Fred Ross, and Alinsky, who enlightened him with the message that it was unlikely that Christian love alone would dissolve the differences between migrants and growers. With this experience fresh in his mind, he arrived in Chicago, just as Alinsky needed another ally among Chicago Protestants.

Still found his own ally in Rev. David Ramage, head of the urban church department of the Presbytery in Chicago. Still made sure that he and Alinsky met, and in Ramage's own words, he was "wowed" by Alinsky's persona and message.[197] By 1960, not without much more argumentation to combat Protestant opposition, he believed he had to make the decision as to whether to support the Woodlawn project or not. But also, by this time, the civil rights movement, led by Dr. Martin Luther King, Jr., was in the news and in front of clergy everywhere. Thus, Alinsky's "grand strategy" in which a black community organization would help lead the way toward the integration of Chicago," was difficult to ignore. The old notion that institutional churches could help the oppressed through services alone needed to shift to a place where churches supported community-based organizations in their fight for economic justice. Steering the Presbyterian Church, in particular, toward a commitment to urban social action, became his agenda. Ramage put it this way:

> *I became a major factor in strategizing and developing the framework and policy for the United Presbyterian Church, starting in Chicago, and ultimately beyond, to embrace Alinsky's style of community organization as a basic, legitimate, and non-paternalistic mission of theology for the urban church.*[198]

The commitment of the $22,000 was the first step in the new strategy.

NCO: *Beneficiary of Ecumenical Collaboration and a New Understanding of Urban Church*

The historical connections just laid out, provides the context for how NCO emerged in West Town. It illustrates how both Catholic churches and Protestant Neighborhood Houses worked together to embrace a new strategy for the urban church – community organizing. Fr. Egan called on the Catholic churches and got 22 pastors to commit funds and to call on Saul Alinsky to come to West Town. At the same time, Protestant leaders like Doug Still and David Ramage, were taking the message to their Protestant representatives in the inner city, the neighborhood houses. With Ramage in a key position at the Chicago Presbytery, neighborhood house executives, like Presbyterian minister, Ross Lyman, at Erie House, clearly heard the message, and more importantly, embraced it. In fact, with Erie's connection to COPA since the early 1950's, they were at an advanced stage of readiness.

A description of the Northwest Community Organization (NCO) appears in the finders' guide to archived NCO materials at the Chicago History Museum:

> *The Northwest Community Organization (NCO) was a coalition of neighborhood organizations based on the northwest side of Chicago for the purpose of assisting in the resolution of community problems and to encourage diverse peoples to live and grow harmoniously together.* [199]

A further explanation of purpose indicates NCO intended to "manage rather than suppress conflict." How conflict was viewed by Saul Alinsky was both the secret to his success and a source of criticism. He once called "politeness," the "venereal disease" of the middle class. Use of these terms did not always endear him to church leaders. But he consistently argued that anger was the best catalyst to get people to act rather than just complain, arguing that action, more than words, was needed to bring about change. Therefore, go forth and rub raw the skin that is covering up potential conflict, he was known to suggest.

An early encounter between Tom Gaudette, the man Alinsky installed to get NCO going, and the local ward committeeman, Matt Biesczat, illustrates his point. Biesczat was invited to a community meeting organized by NCO, in February of 1962, to hear the community express their concerns about matters that needed the attention of the political establishment. His response to Gaudette, and indirectly to community leaders was, "Look, sonny, I own this area. I decide what is going to happen." Then he stalked out. This was one of the early incidents that made people angry, resentful of the suggestion that somebody "owned" them, ready to be *im*polite, only a *quid pro quo*, after all. The group decided to go over his head, marched to City Hall, and secured the zoning changes citizens wanted for *their* neighborhood.

NCO opened its storefront office at 1109 N. Ashland, and worked from that address from 1962 until it closed in 1994. The NCO boundaries were as follows: Fullerton on the north (2400), the Kennedy Expressway on the east, Kinzie (400 north) on the south, and Kedzie/Kimball (3200/3400) on the west. Within those boundaries, in 1962, lived an ethnically diverse community of 160,000 -- Poles, Puerto Ricans, Italians, Ukrainians, Germans, African Americans, Mexicans, Russians, Latvians, Cubans, and Norwegians. According to the 1960 census, 25% of the city's Puerto Rican population, close to 8,000 people, lived in West Town. It was home to 22 Catholic and 60 Protestant churches, six settlement houses, four hospitals, 18 Catholic, and 22 public, grammar schools and a YMCA. Residents worked in the Kinzie industrial corridor, Goose Island, and along Elston Avenue. It was an area of old housing that suffered from neglect, but was so well built in the first place, that much of it was salvageable. It was worth re-investing in, as would be evident some 25 years later, but banks were redlining West Town then, withholding those reinvestment dollars. It was a neighborhood on the edge of its last great wave of immigration, turning from white to brown. It was an area with so many vacant lots it was the constant target of urban removal plans over a 25-year period, until it renewed itself. Through NCO, the churches and the settlements, and a determined blue-collar community of residents, who turned off their TVs to go to community meetings, the area stabilized itself. And then the gentry took it back, without a word of thanks.

During their 32 years of operation, NCO organized ordinary residents, identified both grassroots and institutional leaders, and trained them in the Alinsky model to work effectively to achieve the goals that they, themselves, defined. These included:

- Working to improve housing;
- Challenging block-busting real estate practices to grab property at bargain prices by scaring people into fleeing from people of color moving in;
- Working to improve public schools and offer more bilingual education to serve the Hispanic populations that were settling in West Town and Humboldt Park
- Fighting off arsonists seeking to cash in on insurance at tenants' expense;
- Urging CPS (Chicago Public Schools) to build a new high school to replace the outdated Tuley (that is the Roberto Clemente HS of today);
- Devising a strategy to control future housing development on vacant lots by helping to start a non-profit, community-based housing development organization called Bickerdike Redevelopment Corp. (1967);
- Publishing *The Northwest Community Observer*, a bilingual monthly newspaper to keep its members and neighborhood residents well informed about the

issues of the day and how NCO was working to address them;

- Addressing the need for good local jobs by helping to create the Industrial Council of Northwest Chicago (ICNC) to focus on retaining local industry.[200]

At its peak, NCO was comprised of more than 200 local organizations that sent reps to its annual congress that voted on resolutions to set the organizing agenda for the coming year, and elected the NCO Board. But the core of the organization, where the work got done, was with the nine civic organizations that were actually staffed by NCO organizers. Depending on the size and level of activity of the "civic," an organizer might be assigned more than one. Organizers also staffed NCO issue committees. The Education Committee would be an example of a standing issue committee, along with Housing and Crime/Police Relations. Other committees were ad hoc, coming into being to address a "hot" issue, such as the Campaign for a New Tuley High School.[201]

While the money raised from local Catholic churches paid the salary of Executive Director, Tom Gaudette, that first year, Egan could not get all the parishes to renew their financial commitment. The settlement houses stepped up. Erie House, Association House, and Onward House, all paid for an NCO organizer who would be based at their House, with some duties to perform there. But, in reality, they were mostly full-time NCO staff. They attended weekly staff meetings at 1109 N. Ashland, and worked under the supervision of Tom Gaudette and his successors. These positions were also supplemented by seminarians recruited, for the most part, from McCormick, the Presbyterian seminary in Chicago. In later years, they were joined by the Jewish Council on Urban Affairs (JCUA) volunteers and Jesuit volunteers.

Erie's connection with NCO was an early one. As Gaudette made the rounds recruiting members, he would have encountered Rev. Lyman at Erie, possibly at a COPA meeting, and gotten a positive response. So, by the time of the first NCO Congress, on February 17, 1963, Ross Lyman served as "Speaker of the House," or master of ceremonies for the day, a very visible role, and prestigious for Erie House to have such recognition among its peers. It also helped the image of NCO to show it had the confidence of the leader of one of the oldest (93 years) and distinguished organizations in the neighborhood. Coverage of the Congress by *The Northwest Herald,* on February 23, reported on the NCO elections and featured a photo of Ross Lyman handing over the gavel to the first NCO president, Fr. Tony Janiak, Pastor of Holy Innocents Church, just two blocks from Erie House. He, and one of the other officers, were also active COPA members, the civic that was supported by Erie House. COPA, Erie House, and NCO were deeply intertwined from day one.

The *Chicago Tribune* called Fr. Janiak "an activist priest" in his obituary, December 12, 2000, following his death on November 21, at age 83. "He was always organizing people to fight injustice," said Auxiliary Bishop Timothy Lyne.[202] Certainly, this description fit with Fr. Janiak's time at Holy Innocents and his involvement with NCO. A native of Cicero, IL, Janiak was ordained in 1942. He arrived at Holy Innocents as assistant pastor in 1949, and was subsequently named pastor. He was succeeded by Fr. Edward Pajak who was also active with NCO.

There was good reason that Gaudette found fruitful territory for the leadership and growth of his organization in the Erie neighborhood. This was the era of Mayor Richard J. Daley and urban renewal, or as West Town residents called it, "urban removal." Urban planning theory at that time identified "old" as "bad." That applied to housing and even entire neighborhoods. *IF* "old" was the problem, then

181

the solution was demolition–of individual buildings and entire blocks. This approach was popular with developers and realtors who made money re-building and selling the replacement housing or commercial property. The new development was seldom accessible to former residents, even if they could "hang around," so to speak, to move back in, as prices would put that possibility out of reach. Thus, urban renewal displaced people, with little regard for where they were to go when their house was taken and their neighborhood swept away, often along with their churches, social clubs, and community connections. In Chicago, West Town and NCO would resist, just as Jane Jacobs did when she fought for the preservation of Greenwich Village in New York, documented in her book, *The Death and Life of Great American Cities*. There she made her case for all the valuable characteristics of "successful neighborhoods," that were often old and in need of investment and improvement, not demolition. According to Jacobs,

> *American downtowns are not declining*
> *mysteriously, because they are anachronisms. .*
> *.They are being witlessly murdered, in good part, by*
> *deliberate policies . . .under the misapprehension*
> *that this is orderly city planning.*[203]

Mayors of the older industrial cities were often champions of urban renewal for several reasons. First, there was higher property tax revenue to look forward to from newer properties. Second, urban renewal brought federal dollars to their budgets with the opportunity to take some off the top, "for administrative purposes." Third, if you knew how to wield power, and Richard J. Daley did, you could ignore some of those pesky rules about who is supposed to benefit from these federal dollars. And finally, urban renewal became a handy tool for pushing out the poor and the people of color, usually one and the same, that racism suggests "don't belong," or make unreasonable demands regarding their rights. Daley embraced urban renewal for all of these reasons. Urban renewal went hand-in-hand with his plans to use public housing as a strategy to keep African Americans in narrowly defined areas.[204]

His "government policies" went hand-in-hand with private real estate practices called "block-busting."[205] This was a scare tactic used by unscrupulous realtors that would knock on the doors of white homeowners, warning them that they better sell now and get out before African Americans, or Puerto Ricans, moved in. If owners heeded this scare tactic, they tended to sell their homes at below-market prices. The realtors would then turn around and sell them at an inflated price to an African American buyer.[206] Even more heinous were practices of landlords that burned down their buildings to collect insurance. In fact, West Town of the 1970's became the target of an FBI investigation that uncovered an "arson-for-profit ring" that was active on streets like Cortez, just east of Ashland (1600 west).

But NCO's first big fight was with the Richard J. Daley administration over plans for a development at the intersection of Division/Ashland/Milwaukee, the heart of Polish Downtown, and extending east to Noble Street (1400 west). In this case, white ethnics were being challenged rather than people of color, but all the other elements of urban renewal were the same. NCO organized community meetings focusing on carrying out "a people's planning process." The theme: "Homes or High-rises: Which Plan do you Want?" The Department of Urban Renewal (DUR) was proposing to build three high-rises. The people, through NCO, proposed low-rise homes, more in keeping with the character of the neighborhood. They held meetings attended by Mayor Daley and put on the pressure for their plan. In these early days, Daley actually came out and met with people in the neighborhood. He even attended the first NCO Congress. But, as NCO grew stronger and more confrontational, he would only meet in his office; eventually, he refused to meet at all. The final outcome was a compromise. Noble Square was built with one high-rise, instead of three, and the rest of the site was filled with low-rise townhomes. The NCO plan also included a co-op ownership structure.

It finally opened in 1969. Few of the Poles who had been displaced came back to live in Noble Square. Instead, upwardly mobile African Americans, wanting out of the Cabrini-Green public housing project to the east, made up the majority of Noble Square residents. They also turned Noble Square into one of the most progressive precincts in the ward, consistently voting for independent candidates for mayor and other offices. This, undoubtedly, was an outcome that neither the mayor, DUR, or the local community anticipated.[207]

The lesson NCO and local residents learned from the Noble Square experience is the necessity of being at the planning table much earlier, in order to prevent the clearance in the first place, and/or, be at the front end of what was being planned for the vacated space. Bottom line, prevent DUR from even thinking about urban renewal for the NCO neighborhoods.

No sooner had the community succeeded in revamping the Noble Square plan, when the need for a pre-emptive defense arose again in the form of what came to be known as the Erie-Eckhart project that emerged in the mid-1960s. The targeted area was bounded, more or less by Chicago, Noble, Huron, and the Kennedy, just south of Noble Square, and just north of Erie House.[208] Eckhart came from the name of the park located at Chicago and Noble, across the street from the target area. All of this was within the Erie House service area. These were Erie participants who would be impacted directly. The area included Throop Street, home to a number of African American families, since the Strongs moved there in 1945, an important moment in Erie history commemorated in the previous chapter. There were Puerto Ricans and Mexicans along Huron. These were members of St. Boniface and Santa Maria Addolorata parishes, but also participants at Erie House. While Polish parishioners of Holy Innocents tended to live west of Noble, they were not so naïve as to think urban renewal was going to stay east of Noble forever.

This was also the area served by COPA. Their worst nightmare, the fear that the city planned to demolish their neighborhood, had returned (or never left) to haunt them once again, and they were determined as ever, to live up to their name, as "conservation of property" became the goal of a neighborhood planning process, what *The Northwest Herald* called a "do-it-yourself" plan. The Erie-Eckhart initiative was intended as a first step in community control of the development process, and Erie House was all in. Together with NCO they shared the cost of hiring Peter Williams as community organizer to work with COPA, local residents, and the churches involved in the "Erie-Eckhart Neighborhood Improvement Project." The goal was to develop plans focused on renovation and reinvestment, including plans to build homes on vacant lots. Another lesson learned: too many vacant lots make a neighborhood vulnerable. NCO estimated that there were 800 vacant lots in West Town. Fr. Janiak voiced this realization when he said, "Our success in the demolition of deteriorated buildings frightens me. We need to think of a solution, some positive programs."[209]

Janiak continued to speak out on the threats to the neighborhoods NCO was fighting to defend. On January 13, 1965, he was quoted in the *Humboldt Journal*:

> *Believe me when I tell you, you can fight city hall and win. NCO knows because NCO has done it.[210]*

He emphasized the role of a strong organization committed to maintaining and upgrading the neighborhood, with the grassroots support of the people and the help of professional organizers. He challenged the clergy, insisting that they all get involved, and be ready to march in picket lines. Aware of the tensions this type of call to action might arouse, he put out the rhetorical question: *qualms of conscience about pressuring people?* And followed with the admonition to: *remember the pressure that the powers that be are putting on you and your congregations.*[211]

As reported in *The Northwest Community Observer,* February 21, 1965,[212] Lyman did not step back from NCO after handing the gavel to Fr. Janiak at that first Congress. He is identified in this article as First Vice-President and Finance Committee Chair of NCO. By the end of 1964, NCO had raised $53,000 for their 1965 budget of $65,000. After the first two years of funding from local Catholic churches, funds were now coming from Protestant denominations, local businesses, and individuals and fundraising events. The Charles Merrill Trust of the Presbyterian church gave $11,000; the PRCU (Polish Roman Catholic Union) and the Polish Women's Alliance gave $3,500; Businesses donated $14,000. As he shared with the Erie House Board, Lyman was clearly pleased with these outcomes. He said, "I think our success is directly attributable to our good program of activity in the neighborhood."[213]

Also quoted in this article was Clarence Lipschutz, NCO Planning Committee Chair. He stated a core belief that underscored the community's Erie-Eckhart proposal, and all the work of NCO:

> *This project has been organized and developed from the bottom, by the residents of the neighborhood, while others have been organized from the top, and ignored the citizens. You can't ignore the residents; it's their community. This is*

*responsibility at the local level, where it belongs,
with government providing only the means to allow
us to do this, and not do it for us. It shows that
democracy really works when the people exercise
their rights.[214]*

Erie House was also doing well. As the NCO
Congress in February, 1963, successfully launched the
organizational work in progress, community organizing
became one of Erie's strategies for serving the community,
for the next 20 years, working hand in hand with COPA.
Lyman kept the Erie board in the loop concerning the
connection with NCO. At the board meeting following that
first NCO Congress in February, 1963, he let them know that
Erie's Rev. Prosser was chairing the NCO Housing
Committee. He assured them that both the Catholic and the
Presbyterian church were supporting NCO, and a
community organizing strategy. As Erie board president at
that time, Bob Gielow later reflected,

*Ross was an unusual individual. He at first seemed
to be a rather intellectual type of person. But I
think that, as time at Erie House passed, he became
more and more influenced by the neighbors, and
was very good at organizing and working with the
community.[215]*

Most of the usual programs for children and adults
continued in the House, while NCO and COPA grew
stronger and more effective in addressing neighborhood
problems outside the House. Rev. Ciro Rocco was assisting
Rev. Lyman with the Chapel services for the Latino
community. A teen job training and placement program for
part time jobs was being developed with the support of
Montgomery Ward, and the intention of motivating youth to
finish high school. Therapeutic services were added to group

work in conjunction with an intensive training program for staff and volunteers that took place during the summer of 1964. One of the participants in that program, Bob Johnson, stayed on at Erie, and did some work with COPA. In 1965, when Peter Williams was hired, Bob succeeded Tom Gaudette as Executive Director of NCO -- another Erie House contribution to the organization. Also, in 1965, Lyle Franzen became the new Assistant Pastor of Erie Chapel, and supervisor of group work. He was a graduate of McCormick Seminary and the Jane Addams School of Social Work at the University of Illinois Chicago. With Noble Square redesigned, and the city's "Erie-Eckart" plan deferred, Peter Williams continued to work as Erie's NCO organizer.

1967 would be an especially important year for Erie House and their neighborhood. But before the story of the neighborhood self-help solution for blight and defense against urban renewal unfolds, Erie had a very special visitor in 1966. Pulitzer Prize-winning poetess, Gwendolyn Brooks, Writer-in-Residence at Illinois Teachers College North (now Northeastern Illinois University), came to Erie to read to the children from her poems. This came about in connection with a work-study program that brought students from the college to tutor Erie children. In 1966, Work-Study was a brand new, federally funded program, and Ms. Brooks brought her distinguished presence to the kick-off event for the reading program this new funding facilitated. As Erie's good work became more prominent in the 1960s, often through its engagement in public policy issues, honors, like this, came to Erie House more and more often. Excellence in programs went hand-in-hand with public awareness through engagement in public policy. Prominence fades if excellence is not maintained and advanced.

B is for Bickerdike Redevelopment Corporation: Born out of the Necessity for Local Control

NCO and Erie House had learned that the mentality of planners and developers was that if there are six vacant lots on this block, why not just tear down the 6 buildings that remain and gain a larger space to re-develop. The concept of "in-fill" housing was yet to be developed or promoted. That would be a feature of the community's plan for the "positive action" Janiak called for, along with renovation of existing property. But, as the community focused on implementation of *their* Erie-Eckhart Plan, in the Fall of 1965, they encountered four major problems:

- The unwillingness of lenders to make loans for renovation;
- Local owners did not have the resources to renovate their buildings without loans;
- No general contractors were willing to build on vacant lots without mortgages available;
- Absentee slum landlords resisted improving unless pressured, and did only the minimum repairs.[216]

It became obvious that the do-it-yourself plan was going to require a "do-it-yourself" developer. So, research began on how this might be accomplished. At that time, there were no templates, no models for locally initiated community development. The 1970s would see an "explosion" of not-for-profit community development corporations (CDCs), but these were early days. Erie House, leaders from local churches and civics, consulted with lawyers, FHA officials, and the Community Renewal Society. CRS was one of the few church-based/community-focused organizations that started in Chicago even before Erie House, and had some experience in community development.

In March 1966, NCO, and now, Monsignor Jack Egan of the Office of Urban Affairs of the Catholic Bishop of Chicago, hosted a meeting at the rectory of Santa Maria Addolorata parish, just south of Erie House, to present the concept of this not-for-profit entity, that would be community-controlled, and develop housing for local residents. They won the pastors' support and assurance that the resolution to be presented at the NCO Congress in May, 1966, would pass. While both the local planning and the ultimate solution for challenging urban renewal was formulated by and for the Erie-Eckhart area, NCO worked to carry this model throughout the entire NCO area. Consequently, Erie House became more widely known, and at the 1967 NCO Congress, delegates elected Rev. Lyle Franzen, Erie minister/social worker, as the new NCO president. In the midst of this newer type of recognition at Erie House, Mrs. Evangeline Gielow was receiving a silver tray from the Erie Woman's Auxiliary for her 50 years of service to Erie. Moving forward with innovative strategies, but not afraid to look backward to recognize other kinds of excellence, was a hallmark of Erie's success in being a neighbor among neighbors.

In its own publications, Erie also promoted NCO and their connection with it. In June, 1967, their newsletter at that time, *Erie Encounter,* reminded their readers that ENH had been a member of NCO for 5 years. It had grown to encompass 168 member organizations, serving 145,000 people in West Town. The newsletter article explains how Erie's own COPA tackles issues first. Then, if they need more help, they bring the matter to NCO for broader support and muscle. Therefore,

> *Erie has committed the energy of its staff to further the work of NCO in the conviction that this effort is helping people to establish their own goals, develop*

political skills, and achieve pride in their community.[217]

Finally, in November, 1967, Bickerdike Redevelopment Corporation (BRC) was officially incorporated. According to the Laurence Carton Papers,[218] Erie's *pro bono* attorneys helped with the legal paperwork. The locals chose the name after a small park called Bickerdike Square, that was located on Ohio Street, between Bishop and Armour, next to Otis School. That park was named after George Bickerdike, the original owner and developer of the area known as the George Bickerdike Subdivision. It was not a name that rolled easily off the tongue, but it was a name that earned respect as one of the most successful non-profit CDCs in the country. The initial board included residents from the Erie-Eckhart/COPA area. Jack Irving and Juan Sierra were members of COPA from Santa Maria; Rev. Lyman from Erie House; and the successor to Tony Janiak at Holy Innocents, Fr. Edward Pajak. Peter Williams served as part time staff that first year, still funded by Erie House and NCO.

Community organizing kept the pressure on, with support of the fledgling Bickerdike as a number one priority. The organizing process and the local development process were interconnected; one would not prosper without the other. In 1968, in the midst of the redlining fight, BRC secured its first mortgage loan for a property at 1515 W. Huron, around the corner from Holy Innocents. But what was really needed was to find a way to keep the cost of financing home purchases low enough that more local residents could afford to buy. Fortunately, Section 235 of the 1968 National Housing Act, included an interest subsidy for home ownership. Prior to this, the federal government, through its Federal Housing Administration (FHA), only subsidized home mortgages for houses built outside the city, for a predominantly white population.[219]

In 1968, BRC built its first two new homes, both two-flats, and both privately financed. The first one, at 1476 W. Ohio, in the Erie Service area, is still there. It was sold to a Santa Maria parishioner. The return on the investment of the Catholic parishes had begun. While this was the "positive program" that Fr. Janiak hoped for, it still needed the support provided by COPA and NCO to pressure absentee landlords to fix up their buildings, so that the neighborhood where Bickerdike would be building continued to improve around it.

Consequently, COPA and NCO members took building owners to housing court. They picketed their homes, when necessary, as well as the homes of local bank officers that continued to "redline" the neighborhood, refusing to make home mortgage and rehab loans available to their depositors. They were happy to take local money in, but not to loan it back. Too risky, they argued. Of course, some would say that it was rude to show up on a banker's front lawn, on a Saturday morning, in his suburban neighborhood, with flyers and picket signs. That was Saul Alinsky's point. The time for politeness was over. The future of urban neighborhoods across the US was at stake, as redlining became a national issue. It was eventually addressed with the passage of the Federal Home Mortgage Disclosure Act in 1975. That fight was led by Chicagoan, Gale Cincotta, as the president of the National Peoples Action, headquartered in Chicago. NCO and its members, along with the Organization for a Better Austin (OBA), helped to form NPA. While Cincotta was from OBA, NCO's president, at that time, Ed Stefaniak, of Wicker Park, stood next to her every step of the way.

C is for Catholic Sisters: From Around the Corner at Santa Maria Came the "Nun in the World" of West Town and Erie House

In October, 1967, Ross Lyman nominated Sister Antonelda (later known as Sister Marian Dahlke, when many sisters returned to their baptismal names) to serve on the Erie board. Sister was a member of the School Sisters of St. Francis and principal of Santa Mara Addolorata (SMA) school at 1337 W. Ohio. When church and school rebuilt at Ohio and Ada, in 1960, after being displaced by the Kennedy Expressway, the School Sisters were called upon to staff the new school. By this point in Erie's history, the settlement had worked with many Catholics. The Poles and Italians, who made up most of the participants in Erie programs since the beginning of the 20th century, were generally Catholic. A few Italians had become members of the Presbyterian Erie Chapel congregation over the years, but most remained cultural Catholics, if not regular church-goers. Rev. Lyman had worked closely with the two pastors of Holy Innocents, Fr. Janiak and Fr. Pajak, as members of NCO and COPA, and in the founding of Bickerdike. So, by the late 1960s it was not new to work with Catholics, but the close working relationship that developed between the sisters at SMA and Erie House was unique.

While the priests at Holy Innocents, the Polish parish, were engaged with community organizing and well-acquainted with Erie House, at Santa Maria, the Italian parish, it was the sisters that made the stronger connection – to NCO and to Erie House – more actively than the priests. For example, Sister Antonelda probably earned the attention of Rev. Lyman, leading to her nomination to the Erie Board in 1967, as a result of getting to know each other at COPA meetings. The sisters were there. In fact, at the time of an important COPA/NCO meeting with DUR, in March, 1966, there were six sisters from SMA on the attendance sheet.

But more importantly, the COPA president sent a letter to Sister Antonelda, March 22, 1966, thanking the sisters for their great job in helping with the turnout of 80 people for that DUR meeting.[220]

This was the post-Vatican II era when many orders of sisters stepped outside their convents to become, as a popular book of the time suggested, "the nun in the world."[221] For the previous 100 years or so in the US, most religious women either taught in parochial schools, ran Catholic colleges, or were nurses and hospital administrators. This began to change in the 1960s, as did so many other things in America in that pivotal decade. As the sisters at Santa Maria stepped up to volunteer at Erie, and encouraged their students to go to Erie after school, Rev. Lyman extended a warm welcome.

In 1969, he hired Sister Annette Ferriano (Now Mrs. Annette Ferriano Wood) as Director of Erie's Head Start program. She had been teaching first grade at Santa Maria since 1967, but had read about Head Start, begun as part of Lyndon Johnson's War on Poverty, and was interested in working in this new program for pre-schoolers.[222] When Mae Lyman mentioned the opening at Erie, she expressed interest, and got a call from Ross to come in for an interview. He offered her the job on the spot, a job she held until 1972. Sister Maureen Hellwig (that was me) and Sister Millicent Stukel served as chaperones for the summer day camp at Winnetka Presbyterian Church in 1969, accompanying the Erie children on the bus ride to Winnetka each day. Sister Mary Lou Carney worked directly with NCO, as staff.

Sister Terese Brown (now Ms. Sanchez) had arrived at Santa Maria in 1963, a year before Sister Antonelda, to teach the middle grades. She recalls that she and some of the other sisters heard from Msgr. Egan about the Urban Apostolate, an organization that encouraged sisters to become involved in their neighborhood.[223] She was at the right place to follow that calling. She eventually left teaching, replaced Sister Ann Seng at Community House in Cabrini Green, and then returned to West Town to work in the neighborhood with Dave Moore, a staff person from the Division Street YMCA, to provide a program to address the growing drug addiction problem among teens in the neighborhood.[224] In solidarity with Erie House, the sisters shopped at Mayfair, tagged on Tag Day, and volunteered in the Christmas Store.

Sisters were also moving out of convents to live in the neighborhood. Sister Millicent and I lived at 1419 W. Grand Avenue, and Sister Annette and Sister Susan Rosenbach lived at 1472 W. Erie. Their building was owned by a woman who had an arrangement with the Urban Institute to rent her units to their participants. These were people who came to Chicago for what was sometimes called the "urban plunge," to learn about issues facing low-income people of color, for the most part. Ferriano said, "It made for interesting neighbors."[225] When Sister Susan moved on, Sister Terese moved in. Evelyn Lyman lived in the building next door, owned by Erie supporters, Mr. and Mrs. Gawrych. When Sister Marian celebrated her Jubilee, her 25th anniversary as a sister, Rev. Lyman attended the service at Santa Maria church.[226]

One of the area's local aldermen at the time was Tom Keane, Mayor Richard J. Daley's powerful floor leader in the City Council. He often complained that sisters should be home praying rather than out protesting. He was definitely not happy with "the nun in the world." But Erie House and NCO were delighted. And, Sister-as-community organizer, was evolving as a new ministry in the 1960s. The School Sisters of St. Francis, current and former members of the congregation, came in and out of life at Erie House for the next 50 years.

The Closing of Erie Chapel

One more historic moment, amidst a decade that was full of them, took place in 1968. The Erie Chapel, a congregation of the Presbyterian Church that went by that name since 1886, closed its doors on Erie Street, and merged with another small Presbyterian congregation in West Town to form the Erie-Waldensian Church. 118 years of urban ministry, however, did not end. It was embedded in Erie Neighborhood House. Furthermore, the Erie House connection with the Presbytery was well represented when James J. McClure, Jr., a member of the Erie House board since 1955, was elected Moderator of the Chicago Presbytery for 1969. The Presbytery described itself at that time as "the governing and judicial body for 143 Presbyterian churches in Cook, DuPage, and Lake Counties, with approximately 89,000 communicant members."[227] McClure represented many Erie House connections. He was a member of First Church of Oak Park, he worked for Gardner Carton & Douglas, was the first president of United Christian Community Services (UCCS) when it formed in 1967, and was serving on the board of the Chicago Federation of Settlements.

Bickerdike Succeeds in Becoming "The Positive Program"

By 1970, George Knight had become Director of Bickerdike, and he and community leaders met with the Regional Administrator of the FHA (Federal Housing Administration) to work out a plan to use Section 235 extensively, to build in-fill housing on the abundant vacant lots. What Fr. Janiak had perceived as a serious liability, would be turned into an opportunity, through neighborhood ingenuity, faith-based commitment, community organization, a little help from the federal government, and

$10,000 in seed money from Erie Neighborhood House to shame banks into stepping up with mortgages. Initially, FHA authorized six Section 235 homes. On July 25, 1970, groundbreaking for the first home took place at 1431 W. Erie. All six homes sold in 1970. Each home with 3-4 bedrooms, sold for $24,000 with a down payment of only $200. With the subsidized interest rate, monthly payments were as low as $148. Local market demand was very strong and Bickerdike went on to build 100+ Section 235 homes throughout the NCO area. As incidences of FHA foreclosures on 235 buyers began to escalate in other cities, and even other parts of Chicago, BRC's program did not have that problem. Knowing that they were dealing with first-time home buyers with limited means, and understanding their accountability to the community to make this program work, BRC offered buyer preparation workshops and pre- and post-purchase counseling. Consequently, foreclosures were the exception.

In September, 1970, Bruce Gottschall, came to Erie House. Like Peter Williams, he was on the Erie payroll, staffed COPA, went to NCO staff meetings, and worked with the community volunteers that staffed the clinic, ensuring ongoing accountability to the community. However, he was also considered Director of Bickerdike. Gottschall came to Erie House from the SSA program at the University of Chicago, where he had met George Knight. When George moved on to work for the Federal Home Loan Bank, basically to launch the Neighborhood Housing Services (NHS), he told Bruce about the opening. Having spent two years in the Peace Corps in Lima, Peru, Gottschall brought his fluency in Spanish to his job at Erie. He also supervised students, an ever-present group, recruited to work and learn at Erie since the early days of Lyman's administration. One of his proteges was Tom Behrens. He also worked for NCO, but is better known for founding the Night Ministry in Chicago, a program that serves homeless youth. Not an "Erie kid" like Dan Brindisi, but an intern that moved into the group of Erie Alums who have made a difference in the lives of ordinary people in need.

An article appeared in the *Chicago Tribune,* December 12, 1971, stating that in addition to developing $1.3 million in new construction of homes, the success of BRC had begun to turn around people's view of their neighborhood. Gottschall noted that 37 homes had been completed by the end of 1970, with 50 more pending. Housing was filling those vacant lots Fr. Janiak had worried about. Urban Renewal was pushed back, until another threat would present itself a few years down the road.

Subsequently, Bickerdike would move on from building single family homes to addressing the insufficient number of decent, affordable rental units, using another federal program called Section 8. Once again, one of the first clusters of these rental units, all to be no more than two stories, and built on vacant lots, was developed on the corner of Huron and Noble. Fr. Pajak contacted the former parishioners of Holy Innocents that owned the land, moved out of state, and had given up hope of ever selling their lots. They sold them to Bickerdike, and another long run of successful new construction, Section 8 rentals, took place throughout West Town.

In 1975, Gottschall went on to become Executive Director of Neighborhood Housing Services of Chicago, a position he held for 35 years, until he retired in 2009. Their office was in West Town, in walking distance from Erie House. While NHS helped homeowners keep their homes, Bickerdike continued on, building affordable homes and rental units, rehabbing and managing hundreds of existing units, establishing its own management company, and its own Humboldt Construction Company. When it celebrated its 50th anniversary in 2017, it had become one of the most successful, not-for-profit, affordable housing developers in the country, and was still headquartered in West Town. It prospered under two long-term executive directors. Bob Brehm took the job in 1979, having learned about Bickerdike during a Northwestern University internship with NCO's Community 21 neighborhood planning office. He was succeeded in 1995 by Joy Aruguete, who was still there to celebrate in 2017.

Erie's role in the early days of Bickerdike was critical. They provided staffing, an office and seed money for the first homes. Ross Lyman was on the board at the time of incorporation, Erie Board member, Bob Wiley was president of the BRC board in 1969, and ENH Board member, Jack Irving, served after Wiley, 1970-71. Jack was one of those other Catholics from Santa Maria Addolorata, but who found his way to Erie House primarily through COPA. Their support of BRC was a major contribution to the stabilization of the Erie neighborhood, and from there throughout East Humboldt Park. In addition, even with the gentrification that finally took over, with the benefit of subsidized Section 8 rents, many low-income families have had the opportunity to stay and enjoy all the new amenities, including improved schools and increased attention to public safety. Furthermore, they represent a small victory for diversity.

The 1970's: A Change in Erie Leadership Begins

Meanwhile, every day at the settlement saw the sun go up with the arrival of pre-schoolers, and set with young men shooting hoops in the gym. Literally, hundreds of school age children were tutored in between – by college students, and by the ever-faithful suburban church members who came into the city to tutor on Saturdays during the school year, and hosted the children at their suburban locations in the summer, with an education/recreation "day camp" experience. Some churches even organized families who volunteered to have Erie kids stay at their homes. A community in Warsaw, Indiana hosted 192 children during the summer of 1970.

Clearly, education had become a major focus of the settlement, more than casework. As Evelyn Lyman reported repeatedly at board meetings in the 1970s, people came to Erie every day seeking help in finding employment. She understood that as jobs became more technical, and less labor-intensive, educational credentials were more and more critical for gaining adequate employment. In the 1970's and 80's, this meant finishing high school; in later years, the focus would move to college admission and vocational training.

The focus on education also went the other way. Erie knew it needed to start early. Over the years, early childhood education had many names, different funders, and multiple purposes. From the earliest days of Erie Chapel Sunday School, young children were important. When Kindergarten was promoted by Hull House, the Erie Chapel opened its own, and that brought Miss Florence to Erie in 1914. When the House opened its new building in 1936 there were pre-school classrooms, and when Rosie the Riveter went to work during World War II, Erie took care of her children. While the TV shows of the 1950s portrayed moms staying at home, most of those homes were in the suburbs. In Erie's neighborhood, many moms had no choice but to work. The reality was that all-day child care was not only an educational investment in pre-schoolers, "the head start" to get them ready to be successful in school, but it also allowed parents to work toward incomes that would eventually help those pre-schoolers go to college. Day Care was an economic engine as well as an educational strategy. It was also a magnet.

As Day Care parents got to know Erie House, they learned about and took advantage of many other services. Erie provided English classes, GED for adults, health care services at the medical and dental clinics, and citizenship classes for those eligible to seek that status. They learned about COPA and NCO, and how to be citizens engaged in democratic decision-making to determine their own future. They might even get a Bickerdike apartment. Thus, the whole family could be educated at Erie House. From Erie's perspective, this was the pathway out of poverty. Over the next 20 years, the pressure would grow to expand pre-school to serve more than 35 children. Sister Annette spoke of the need to expand when she reported to the board, as early as 1970. Changing neighborhood demographics also appeared first through the youngest families, and already in 1970, Sister Annette was assisted by Alicia Flores Puente, a Mexican woman, and Georgia Dennis, an African American. She understood it was important for children to see teachers who looked like them.

In 1971, after serving as president of the Bickerdike board, Robert Wiley, from Wilmette, returned to become president of the Erie Board. Sister Marian moved up to VP. As late as this, names on the board still included: Sawyer, Graham, Olson, Armstrong, McClure, Bristol –names that had a 20 to 30-year run on the board. Lynn Mc Clure reported on Tag Day revenue at $6,370, and reminded everyone that Erie Had been participating and benefiting since the Children's Benefit League started tagging in 1908. How many fundraisers go on for 60+ years? With Mr. & Mrs. Curtis Ward (of Montgomery Ward) on the Erie board, their donations of merchandise for Mayfair had that fundraiser matching Tag Day, bringing in $6,300. By 1974, that was up to $8,400, with Tag Day bringing in $7,400. But Ross warned that, overall, institutional church donations were down. Even the Erie Woman's Auxiliary listed membership from only 12 churches in 1974, down from peak membership from 30+ churches. Undoubtedly this was also being affected by the next generation of church women at their place of employment on weekdays, as well as the shrinkage of overall church membership. By the end of the

1970s, Erie would need to step up their dependence on Foundation support to offset the gradual end of the Golden Age of Church support. More in the next chapter.

Bruce Gottschall reported that the Methodist Church had donated $5,000 in additional seed money to keep the new construction program moving along, and three of the new BRC homes had been purchased by Latino families. As a result of NCO's successful campaign for a new high school, Clemente high school was opening at Division and Western in the Fall of 1971. He informed the Erie Board that NCO had a new Executive Director whose name was Shel Trapp, formerly of the Organization for a Better Austin, and husband of Anne Trapp, who worked as Administrative Assistant at Erie for more than 10 years. He succeeded Don Elmer who had succeeded Bob Johnson.

1974 brought changes to Erie's community organizing department. Bruce Gottschall left to work for the Federal Home Loan Bank to start the process of setting up Neighborhood Housing Services of Chicago. In his place, Ross hired Merri Steinberg. Ms. Steinberg was fresh out of college with a degree in Latin American Studies and the ability to speak Spanish. She was also Jewish, a first for Erie House, and from New York. In an interview in 2019, she explained that after six months, she confided with Ross that she did not find the job of community organizer a good fit for her. However, she loved working at Erie House and proposed that her responsibilities shift to working for Bickerdike, working more in the home-buyer counseling area of BRC. So, seven years after its founding, working for Bickerdike still meant being on the Erie House payroll and having your office there. Lyman agreed to pay the first $10,000 of her salary, but after that she would have to raise the funds, which she did by writing proposals to foundations.[228]

In the Day Care program, Sister Annette Ferriano had moved on and Steve Stein stepped in briefly. But,

Angela ("Angel") Carroll, who had been hired by Ferriano as a teacher, two years earlier, became Day Care Director during 1974, and maintained that role for the next 20 years. As she assumed her new role, enrollment in Day Care was about 90% Latino, with Mexicans joining Puerto Ricans to increase the Hispanic population in the area. She recalled,

> *We were initially funded through Head Start. When that program began, it served low income parents with no work requirement, and was generally a half day program. When they added a work requirement, they still kept income eligibility so low, that it was very difficult to find eligible families. When Title XX came along, it was full day, and with much more realistic income guidelines for working parents. It also funded after-school care. Overall, Title XX contracts were generous, allowed us to add supportive services, and eventually made child care the largest line item in the Erie budget. The only drawback–generous funding called for onerous paperwork.[229]*

Reports to the Erie Board and EWA show more and more Latino names on staff as well. By 1975, that Day Care contract was at $90,000, about 25% of Erie's $360,000 budget for that year. Money well spent, according to neighborhood resident, Lorraine Gawrych, who felt compelled to write to the *Northwest Herald,* to, as she put it,

> *. . .write a little article of gratitude to the staff of Erie Neighborhood House, who devote their lives to making happy, wholesome personalities of our children, and I am sure my feelings reflect those of all the parents living in the neighborhood.[230]*

It was reported that $130,000 came from churches, what Ross described as a declining number, but still 36% of the budget. "The rest" came from United Way (formerly, the Community Fund), which would put their contribution at $141,000 or 39%. So, in its 105th year, Erie was still at 75% private support. By 1995, those percentages would be reversed. It is not clear where fundraising events were included, but the old standbys continued to increase their take during this period. With the backing of Montgomery Ward, Mayfair proceeds over a three- year period looked like this: 1974: $8,930; 1975: $9,650; 1976: $12,750.[231] A sample list of the type and volume of merchandise Ward's and their suppliers provided is an indication of why lines formed around the corner on the day of Mayfair, especially with an unemployment rate of 7%. In 1976, Erie received:

- 300 winter coats;
- 5 dozen infant sleepwear sets;
- 62 dozen articles of boys' and men's clothing;
- 43 dozen outfits for infants;
- 1200 toys;
- 132 pairs of Cool-Ray sunglasses;
- "a lot" of houseware.[232]

This was described as 140 truckloads of merchandise – all offered to Erie neighborhood residents at dramatically reduced prices. Tag Day, was still hanging on, generally bringing in some amount between $6,000-$7,000 each year; the Thrift Shop was up to around $12,000/year.

In 1975, one of Erie's champion fundraisers and supporters, Mrs. Walter Gielow (Evangeline), announced her retirement from volunteering there. This is the woman pictured in her long skirt, a pre-World War I fashion statement, doing her part for Erie on Tag Day, the woman who 8 years earlier received a silver tray from the EWA for her 50 years of service. At just year 58 of that service, she rested. The plaque in the Erie House lobby at 1347 has Walter Gielow's name on it. This was understandable since, at the time of his death in 1945, he had been a major supporter who helped coordinate the construction of the "new" building. It might be long past the time to honor the additional 30 years of service of Evangeline Gielow with another plaque. Finally, an unpredictable, but always welcome resource was the bequest. In 1977, the estate of Esther Dean Griffis left Erie $15,000.

Urban Removal Plans -- One More Time!

On the neighborhood development front, as Bickerdike was just picking up steam in its new construction program in 1973, yet one more threat of urban removal surfaced. This pertained to that part of West Town/NCO that was east of Ashland (1600 west), roughly between North Avenue (1600 north) and Kinzie (400 north), just west of the Kennedy Expressway. The southern end of this area was COPA and Erie territory. It once again came from downtown, with no local consulting involved. "The Chicago 21 Plan," was put together by what was called the Chicago Central Area Committee (CCAC), a group of business people. They employed Skidmore, Owings, and Merrill, a major architectural firm, to work out the details. It sprung from their perception that the neighborhoods on the immediate edges of the downtown, or "central area," posed a threat to the continued success of the center. They based this potential threat partly on the fact that these neighborhoods and their housing stock were old – that argument was made out loud–and partly because they were non-white–an argument that stayed behind closed doors. And, once again, the local community pushed back. COPA was on it, but this time it had its big brother, an even stronger NCO than in the days of the Erie-Eckhart project, to fight back. The Chicago

21 Plan became an organizing issue for all of NCO, with the mantra: Today it's them; tomorrow it's us.

Initially, NCO, representing the East-of-Ashland/ West Town portion of the Chicago 21 Plan, joined with other neighborhoods that were also affected, namely, Cabrini-Green (African-American), and Pilsen (Mexican), with the east end of NCO being a little more diverse. The south Loop was also a target, but no organized group came forward to join the protest. This was, for the most part, old railroad yards and the adjacent properties that had not been healthy since railroads began their decline, as federal highways facilitated more flexible transport of goods by truck. While a woman by the name of Marian Stamps, from Cabrini, emerged as a strong leader on this issue, over the long haul, the two more organized neighborhoods, West Town and Pilsen, persevered to win a position that put the local communities into the planning process. Their message had been: "We plan for ourselves, thank you. Been doing it since the 1950s, and will do it again."

By some time in 1974, tired of having their meetings interrupted by protesters and having to cross picket lines, the CCAC came up with a strategy they believed would get the protesters off their back in the short term, giving them the time and space to prevail in the longer term. It started with a challenge. The CCAC argued that even local planning needed the services of a professional planner, at an estimated cost of $25,000. They agreed to put $12,500 on the table, for each neighborhood, if the local communities could raise the other half. They had one year to do it. That, they thought, was the end of that. NCO and Pilsen Neighbors took up the challenge.

On December 12, 1975, a photo appeared in the *West Town Herald,* showing NCO leaders receiving a check from CCAC executive director, Jack Cornelius. They had done the unexpected and raised their $12,500. Featured in the photo was NCO President, Bob McCann, two residents of the East-of-Ashland area that had been active in the fight and the fundraising-- Josephine Koziol of Fry Street, and Loretta Landowski of Thomas Street--along with the pastor of St. Boniface Church, Fr. John Hillenbrand. This was the church at the corner of Chestnut (900 north) and Noble. It had always been friendly to Erie House as early as the days of Miss Florence, but had emerged as a lead institution in the NCO/Chicago 21 fight. Also, in the photo, was Bud Kanitz, Director of the Industrial Council of Northwest Chicago, that represented mostly manufacturing firms that lined the Kinzie corridor at the south end of the Chicago 21 Plan target area. Companies were not interested in being removed either, and, as ICNC had been started by NCO, joined the pushback campaign. No doubt, part of the $12,500 came from their members. But as legend would have it, as the 11th hour was approaching for the fundraising deadline, and the campaign was a little short, Father Hillenbrand stepped up with a check from the church to close the gap. Monsignor Egan would have approved.

The final figure in the picture was Monsignor Geno Baroni of the National Center for Urban Ethnic Affairs (NCUEA). This was an entity of the Catholic Church, recently formed, in acknowledgement of the reality that for many years, the Catholic Church in the US was comprised of numerous ethnic groups–immigrants–that should be recognized and supported in their urban neighborhoods. In many cities, the 1970s was the decade of the "Last Hurrah" for urban European ethnics. But late to the game or not, NCUEA came forward to help NCO with the Chicago 21 challenge. This Center helped NCO find the right professional to oversee the local planning effort they told the CCAC they would undertake. Baroni sent Marcy Kaptur, a graduate of the urban planning program at the University of Wisconsin-Madison, and a veteran of community engagement in her hometown of Toledo, Ohio. She moved to Chicago and became the facilitator of a neighborhood planning process, aimed at producing what came to be called the *Community* 21 Plan. Upon returning to Ohio, she became a Congresswoman.[233]

While Erie House was less directly involved in this effort than St. Boniface, it was clear that all of their effort in getting Bickerdike started on in-fill housing could have been overwhelmed by the downtown planners who were thinking hotels and high-rise apartment buildings. Furthermore, Community 21 was yet another example of the community's insistence that they have some control over local development, and create entities that were accountable to the community, professionally staffed or not. Kaptur was in sync with that agenda and worked side-by-side with community residents, and under NCO's watchful eye.

The Community 21 planning process got under way in 1976. NCO opened the Community 21 Planning Office at 1400 W. Chestnut, across the street from St. Boniface Church, so that Kaptur had a place to work in the heart of the Community 21 area. The building they moved into was owned by George Franklin, BRC's executive director, at that time. Intertwining connections continued. That same year, Richard J. Daley died, after serving as Chicago's mayor for 21 years.

In 1977, Ross Lyman marked his 25th anniversary as Executive Director of Erie House. He informed the board that he wanted to take on a different role, as Director of Development, to work full time to raise funds from churches, individuals, and foundations. He recommended that Merri Ex, who had been working at Erie House for about 2.5 years, be given the role of "administrator" with the title of Associate Director. In a short time, this became Executive Director.

Chapter 5: Merri Steinberg Ex: From Community Organizer to Executive Director, 1977-1984

Starting Out at Erie House

Merri Steinberg was born in Staten Island, New York, a descendant of Polish and Russian Jews. She attended Newcomb College and Tulane University for her undergraduate work. She became interested in learning Spanish and spent a summer in Mexico, then pursued a Master's Degree in Latin American Studies at the University of Wisconsin in Madison. From 1971 to 1972 she spent time at the University of Madrid. Friends, including her future husband, Mitchell Ex, drew her to Chicago. She had heard about Saul Alinsky during her student days in Madison, thought community organizing sounded like interesting work, and applied for that job at Erie House. Ross Lyman was interested in her credentials, in particular her ability to speak Spanish, as more and more Latinos were coming to Erie for services. The 1970 census revealed that Hispanics made up 39% of West Town's population, mostly Puerto Ricans at that point. By 1980, West Town would be 57% Hispanic, of whom 23,500 were Mexican. She started her community organizer job at Erie on October 4, 1974, at the age of 22, and in her words, "shared a closet of an office" with staff from Bickerdike that was located under the stairs, just off the lobby.[234]

Her assignment, like that of Bruce Gottschall, whom she replaced, was to work with COPA and NCO. At that time, Don Elmer was NCO Executive Director. By then, Bickerdike (BRC) was led by George Franklin. There was also an architect by the name of Bruce Reid, and Bob Houston who coordinated construction. Fortunately, they were not generally all in the office at the same time. Partly due to her proximity to BRC staff, and

Merri Steinberg Ex (Erie Neighborhood House)

partly due to her dissatisfaction with the organizing position, she went to Ross about changing jobs after her first 6 months. She recalled, "I loved the settlement house milieu, but was uncomfortable with the male-dominated environment at NCO, and their practice of having staff meetings at 10:00 at night that often ran until 1:00 or 2:00 in the morning."[235] On the other hand, she thought she might be helpful in providing supportive services to the families BRC was working with, whether they were buying one of the 235 homes, or were tenants in the FHA foreclosure buildings that BRC was rehabbing at that point.

Lyman agreed to the change and said he would front the first 6 months of her work with Bickerdike, but that she would have to raise the balance. She approached foundations, and got a positive response from the Wieboldt Foundation, assisted by a "few Presbyterian connections" there. ENH board member, David Dangler, also helped with her salary with funds from a trust that he managed. In her work with Bickerdike, she met Fr. Edward Pajak, pastor of Holy Innocents and BRC board member. "This was my first experience getting to know a priest; we became good friends," she said.[236] Besides being introduced to working with Catholics, she also had to learn about "Protestantism and their mission." It was a cultural learning experience on many levels.

In June, 1977, when Rev. Lyman sensed she might be considering moving on, he asked her to consider becoming his successor instead. So, after one year as Associate Director, she became executive director in 1978 when she was 26. Ms. Ex recalls that Lyman had to go to the Presbytery for "permission" to hire a non-Presbyterian. It was not a problem, but he needed to ask. It is not known whether that continued to be an issue, but, in reality, she was just the first of all the subsequent executive directors that were not Presbyterian either – two were Catholic, and two were of different Protestant denominations.

Chicago and West Town, 1977-1984

In 1977, things were changing in Chicago as well. When Richard J. Daley died in office, actually his doctor's office, in 1976, he had not prepared for or named a favorite to succeed him, eventually. With no plan in place, the party turned to another 11th ward politician, Alderman Michael Bilandic. He first served as acting mayor and then won the special election in 1977. During his two years in office, he was no one that Erie House would have to deal with. Pundits played on his name to describe his time in office–he was Mayor Bland. At least that was the case until he went from bland to outrageous, when he directed the CTA elevated trains, during a snowstorm, to by-pass the stops in south side African American neighborhoods to rush white folks to their jobs downtown. This *faux pas* handed the mayor's office to the first woman to hold that position, Jane Byrne. Besides being able to criticize Bilandic for his racist insensitivity, she promised the moon and the stars, in terms of positions in her administration, to African Americans and Latinos, courting the Puerto Rican community of West Town and Humboldt Park along the way. What actually happened, given her lack of experience in governing, is she fell back on the good-ol'-boy network of the party to serve as her advisors. So, while many Chicago women were thrilled with having a woman as mayor, their enthusiasm waned fairly quickly. Byrne was a disappointment, and voters expressed their frustration by limiting her to one term.

Electing Byrne was a relatively small step away from typical machine control of mayoral elections, as she was a "party regular." The next step was much bigger. In 1983, Chicago elected their first African American mayor, Harold Washington. He won, first, by insisting on a major voter registration campaign, (especially in the African American community) before he would even agree to run. Second, with his charismatic style, he turned the Black vote completely away from the machine, a journey they had already begun during Daley's last two terms.[237] Third, he convinced rising young Latino political leaders, like Luis Gutierrez and Jesus "Chuy" Garcia, that their communities would be better off with him in office than a representative of the Democratic machine. The Latino vote gave him just the edge he needed, as people of color out-voted the white minority for the first time in a mayoral race.

With this political upheaval in the background, two organizations that would be of importance to Erie House came into existence in 1978. The Center for Neighborhood Technology (CNT), one of the first local non-profits to take environmental issues seriously, started with an agenda to reduce energy consumption and clean up industrial waste. Erie benefited from one of their energy audits and retrofits to reduce utility bills while Merri Ex was executive director. The MacArthur Foundation also came on the scene and became a source of philanthropic support for Erie House for many years. In 1979, Erie House rejoiced with their Polish neighbors when John Paul II, the first Polish pope visited Chicago.

As Merri was well aware that Evelyn Lyman ran Erie House, in terms of day-to-day programming, she focused on her task of raising funds other than from churches, which was Ross Lyman's job. She had to admit, having the former director, semi-retired but still around, looking over her shoulder, made for a somewhat awkward situation, but she got through it. She also came to realize that she needed to understand how to construct a budget as a real planning tool. She knew there was a 200K government contract to cover Day Care, they waited to see the size of the annual Community Fund (United Way) allocation, and then pumped the churches for their contributions. Fundraisers like the Spring and Christmas appeal, Tag Day, and Mayfair filled in the rest, along with a steady flow of funds from the

Thrift Shop. The total was still under a million dollars when she started.

"So, I went to my dad, who was a CPA, and asked him to teach me how to construct a budget," Merri said. "And, fortunately, I had Anne Trapp in the office to help me with all that." [238]

The other key responsibility of an executive director is to work closely with the board. In those days it was required to be 51% Presbyterian. On the other hand, the United Way, for one, was encouraging recruitment from the neighborhood for the board. And, in fact, directives from the Presbytery urged the same–at least for the other 49%. In Erie's case, this certainly meant including Latinos. Initially, Lyman had invited the Latinos he knew best to join the board, generally meaning Erie staff. Sister Marian and Jack and Mary Ann Irving were among the first to populate the non-Presbyterian, but white, category; Marj Bosley, from 1170 W. Erie, and Mary Burns, clinic volunteer, represented African Americans on the board. Gradually, other Latinos and non-Presbyterians would be recruited, but it was a slow process.

The struggle in the Latino category was based on two problems: 1) the predominantly suburban, white board, and their director, just did not know who to ask; 2) the local Latinos, a working-class community, were not always comfortable sitting in a decision-making position, with strangers of a different class and ethnicity. Erie was not the only non-profit organization to face this challenge. Only when the executive director position was filled by Latinos, did the recruitment of Latinos for the board make some significant progress. Middle class Latinos who became executive directors, knew other middle-class Latinos, thus addressing the ethnic issue, and reducing the discomfort that class differences can create. The one place where *Latino, local*, and *working-class* were addressed simultaneously was through the requirement of federally funded child care that a program parent have a seat on the agency board. Over the years, some of the women who filled this position stayed on the board, even when their required spot was filled by a different parent. Whether Head Start thought of it or not, it became a leadership development opportunity.

During Merri's first year, Bickerdike held its first annual membership meeting at Erie House. Founded in 1967, it apparently took 10 years to reach a critical mass sufficient to have a "membership" meeting. It had a board from the beginning, and its president in 1977 was Jack Irving, also a member of the Erie Board, a member of COPA, and a member of Santa Maria Addolorata Church. He lived on May Street at the eastern end of the Erie neighborhood, had a wife and 3 children and owned a small trucking business. He exemplifies the wisdom that suggests, if you want to get something done, ask the busiest person you know. Mr. Irving began the meeting by sharing some BRC history, and honoring all who had a part in getting it going. This included NCO, Rev. Lyman (also a BRC board member), and Erie House, as an institution that provided the seed money that made the first few BRC housing deals possible, and provided free office space in those early years. Father Pajak stepped forward and presented a plaque to Mr. Irving, thanking him for his 10 years of dedication to Bickerdike. Board elections followed; Irving, Lyman, and Pajak were re-elected; new members included: Bud Kanitz, Industrial Council of Northwest Chicago, Father Hillenbrand of St. Boniface, and Josephine Koziol, resident of Fry Street. The new members were all veterans of the Chicago 21 Plan fight, and having pushed back on outside interference in the neighborhood, were prepared to support what was the positive program of local plans and local control, like Bickerdike--"the solution."

In May of the following year, 1978, Erie House transferred its accounts from Continental Bank to Northern Trust. No reason is given for the change, but one might surmise that long-time Erie Board member, David Dangler, a vice-president at Northern, might have had something to do with it. Regardless of the original business reason, Northern Trust became a partner in one of Erie's most successful programs, TEAM, a youth mentoring program that was launched during Merri's administration in the 1980's. More to come on that later in this chapter. But, since 1978, in addition to their support of TEAM, Northern Trust has invested time as well as money, through the service of several of their executives on the Erie Board, such as Victor "Sy" Nelson and John Van Pelt, following David Dangler.

1978 was also the year that one of Erie's longest-term employees came to work at Erie. Ema Peña began her 40-year employment at Erie, initially, as a clerk-typist. This was before there were computers and when carbon paper was used to make copies. She also helped Pops Lopez with the Erie Drill Team, active during the Merri Ex years. The Drill Team lasted about seven years, until Ema and Pops married, had a daughter, and focused their time on being a family.

Urban Planning and Community Organizing – Oil and Water?

Three blocks away from Erie, at the Community 21 office, Marcy Kaptur had finished the neighborhood plan. It was printed and bound in an attractive format as *The Plan for Improvement: 1977-1980,* and was full of information on the state of the neighborhoods east of Ashland, outlining both obstacles and opportunities for future improvement. Residents who had been engaged in the process with Ms. Kaptur, made it very clear to NCO that they would not have this document sitting on a shelf and gathering dust. They wanted NCO to back them up on implementation of as many recommendations in the plan as possible. To see to that, they believed that someone needed to be hired to be their "neighborhood planner." This was not an all-together popular idea among the NCO staff. With the exception of Kaptur, who was "just a consultant," planners were still, in organizing parlance, "the enemy." The organizing staff mostly associated planners with those who worked for the city at DUR. But Fr. Hillenbrand, whom the organizing staff did have great respect for, was taking the lead on this. So, the job was posted and interviews were scheduled. One of the applicants, Lynne Friel, was an employee of Bickerdike, and known to the NCO staff; the other was Maureen Hellwig (i.e. the author of this book). As a former NCO board member, a resident of the Community 21 area for 10 years, and someone just completing a Master's Degree in Urban Planning at the University of Illinois Chicago, it was a credible candidacy. Fr. Hillenbrand cast the deciding vote, and I was hired.[239]

Community Organizing at Erie, 1977-1984: Still Going Strong

Community organizing continued to be an Erie program during Merri Ex's time as executive director. Organizers that worked for her were Peter Earle, Hiram Lozada, and Josh Hoyt. All were bilingual. The main issues they worked on—sometimes through COPA, and sometimes more directly through NCO— were housing and schools, with police and welfare close seconds. Since NCO had come into being 16 years earlier, important strides had been made in housing with the creation of Bickerdike, in their fifth year at this point. However, that did not mean that slum-type housing throughout the neighborhood vanished overnight. On the other hand, some of it vanished as a result of arson. In the Community 21 area, especially in the 1400 and 1500 blocks of Cortez Street (1050 north), there were far too many suspicious fires. Eventually, the FBI got involved and an arson-for-profit ring was uncovered and put out of business.

But before that, intensive block club organizing, multiple trips to housing court, and finally, a meeting of 100 people in Mayor Richard J. Daley's office, got the job done. Between the heinous actions of arsonists, general slumlord neglect, and the earlier construction of the Kennedy Expressway, that had taken out 1600 units of housing, West Town lost about 22% of its housing stock between 1960 and 1980. Of what remained, the median value of a single unit home was $23,518, less than half of the city median.[240]

Erie always had a working relationship with its two local schools, Otis and Carpenter. Parents knew Erie House as the place their children were kept safe and engaged after school. They and their school principals often attended COPA and NCO meetings. But by the late 1970s, the local leadership that led the fight to either keep programs from being taken away, or to add programs that were needed, was African American and Latina. Carpenter had a fairly large African American population. It came from the Northwest Tower Apartments, a high-rise at 1170 W. Erie, built in 1970, right across the street from the school, and from the longer-term African American residents that lived along Throop Street since 1945. Ms. Nancy Patterson, of Throop Street, was a neighborhood activist who earned her position as President of the District 8 Advisory Council; Carpenter was the school her children attended. Another public-school parent activist, and Erie House volunteer, Virginia Moreno, focused on securing and retaining bilingual programs at the local schools. As a mother of many children, this was certainly an issue related to her self-interest. Moreno was among the earliest Mexicans to live in the Erie neighborhood and become involved at Erie. Erie's organizer worked with both of these women leaders as they developed their slogan: STAND AND FIGHT, UNLEASH YOUR MIGHT, QUALITY SERVICES IS OUR RIGHT![241]

At one point, however, Josh Hoyt's organizing strategy at Otis School upset Fr. Pajak, long-time community leader, friend of Erie House, and friend of Merri Ex, since her days of working with the Bickerdike board. As Merri recalls, "I had to pull Josh back and insist he re-think his approach."[242] Eventually, Hoyt moved on and served for many years as the executive director of the Illinois Coalition on Immigrant and Refugee Rights (ICIRR), of which Erie House was an active member.

COPA was also still an Erie organizer responsibility, and in 1980, their 27th year, they held their annual meeting at Erie House. The slogan on the program read: "In Unity is Strength/*La Union Hace Fuerza.*" COPA had learned how to speak Spanish, and they fought for their relatively new African American neighbors in the 1170 high-rise, assisting them in getting a rent-increase withdrawn and the management agent fired. This old-time organization's evolving openness to people of color was a direct result of their affiliation with Erie House, where their organizers came from, and where people of color were clearly welcome. ENH had been doing its best to carry forward the commitment made under the leadership of Rev. Doug Cedarleaf, in 1945, to never discriminate against African Americans who came to live within Erie's boundaries.

Erie interacted with African American residents in several ways: their children were welcome in Erie Day Care and after school programs, their teens came to the youth program, Carpenter School parents were supported by ENH, residents of 1170 got jobs at Erie (Marjorie Bosley for one). And, 1170 residents saw people who looked like them at Erie. One of the pre-school teachers, Georgia Dennis, was Black, Marj Bosley was an admin for the Day Care program, Mary Burns was a longtime volunteer with the clinic, Nancy Patterson of Throop Street was a COPA leader, Valery Shepard was an After-School staff person who eventually became program director. There were others.

COPA activities were highlighted in the Community 21 Newspaper, the bi-monthly publication of the neighborhood planning office, that was distributed widely in their East-of-Ashland service area. In the April/May, 1980 issue,[243] it was reported that COPA won two new bilingual teachers for Otis and Carpenter. District 6 School Superintendent McMasters, stood before a crowd of 150, as COPA leaders told her what needed attention at their schools. They met with the new District 13 police commander, Joe McCarthy. Residents already had complaints about McCarthy, that he arrested every kid he found on the street, based on the assumption that all kids were gang members. This was his first community meeting, where, according to the article, he came off arrogant and insensitive as he said: "Well, this is a poor neighborhood; you don't pay as many taxes, so you don't get as much protection[244]." COPA leaders, Regina Quintana and Joe Orlando, grilled him into a ruffled state, and Joe sent him off with these words: "Yes, we know this is a tough district. And if you don't like it, go back to Belmont (A more affluent north side district) where you came from."[245] He only lasted two years in the 13th when he was promoted to Deputy Superintendent of the Bureau of Gang Crime Suppression. Not what Joe Orlando had in mind.

COPA's ad book had 30 participants, including such local businesses as: Avila's Bakery, Farmacia Real, El Buen Gusto Bakery, Williams' Live Chickens, Meyers Dept. Store, Morgan Paint & Wallpaper, La Superior Carniceria. The Chicago-Ashland Business Association (CABA), which had been rejuvenated as an active chamber of commerce by the Community 21 planner, also bought an ad. Holy Innocents, St. Boniface, and Santa Maria all participated. Erie House bought a full page and NCO saluted COPA as "its oldest civic."[246]

While the fight for the neighborhood continued, the Erie Pre-school program continued to prepare 3 and 4-year-olds to do well when they arrived at Otis or Carpenter. Then they would come to Erie after school for recreational and educational programming until their parents came from work to pick them up. If they had teen siblings, they could come to Erie in the evening, from 5:00-8:00, hang out in the gym, sign up for boxing or woodshop classes, or go to monthly dances. Adults also got time in the gym, signed up for the men's club or the single moms' discussion group, and/or attended ESL classes to improve their English.

In 1980, 23 years after it was founded, "the clinic," now known as Erie Family Health Center, Inc., still operated out of Erie House. The settlement support was in the form of donated overhead, space, and an annual operating grant. More major funding was provided by public and private grants. The clinic leadership was working toward a more autonomous status, and a larger space outside of Erie House. That was the plan. Meanwhile, they had the reputation of providing the highest quality care at the lowest possible fee. A team of nurse-practitioners, a newly developing career niche in the health care field, was functioning as the primary caregivers, with some physicians available part-time and for consultation. They also had an educational mission that focused on nutrition, pre-natal care, family planning, adolescent sexuality, child health and women's health. At this point they were open Monday through Friday from 9:00-5:00 and two evenings a week. They had moved far beyond the fold-up clinic that disappeared and reappeared in shared Erie program space. There was a staff of 9: 5 locals, including such Erie stalwarts as Magdalen Ellsworth, Eva Hernandez, and Mary Burns; 4 nurse-practitioners, one of whom, Sally Lundeen, served as the clinic's Director.

Meals on Wheels was still rolling, and welfare rights was both a service and an organizing issue. A Puerto Rican woman, Carmen Santiago, sat at the front desk to greet people, and made the transition from a plug switchboard to a 20th century office phone system. Anne Trapp and Ema Peña ran the office, typing and crunching numbers.

1980 A Big Year for Erie House in the Press

In 1980, Erie House drew the attention of a reporter for the *Reader*. Bob Daily wrote an article titled "The House on Erie Street," dated February 22, 1980. It was a 3-page, in-depth article, written, the author claimed, from the perspective of a skeptic who thought what he had heard about the work of Erie House was "too good to be true."[247] He chronicles his meeting with Marge Schramer, who started volunteering at Erie in 1943, 37 years earlier. She then became a paid staff member, who worked with the church volunteers that came to Erie 5 days a week to deliver meals to neighborhood shut-ins. The Meals on Wheels program, begun in 1959, was in its 21st year. He ends up being drafted to help pack up food, and then accompanies two of the volunteers on their delivery route. As he sees the dingy, barren living conditions, and the loneliness of the shut-ins, it becomes clear, if not for the daily meals and visits, many of these folks would be in nursing homes or dead.

He next visits Mom Savino in her third-floor rooms at Erie. She tells him she started at Erie 52 years ago, in 1928. As newly arrived immigrants from Italy, they lived across the street from the first building that housed the Erie Chapel Institute. Crossing that street, and meeting Miss Florence, shaped the rest of their lives. Her husband worked as janitor until he became ill and died in 1952. As Miss Florence had just passed away a few months earlier, Rev. Lyman invited Mrs. Savino to take over her two rooms on third floor, and then she became the cook for the Day Care program. Her son, Joe Savino, served several years on the Erie House board.

His final interview was with Executive Director, Merri Ex. She cited the neighborhood problems as: unemployment, poor housing, large numbers on public aid, and too high a dropout rate, at 70% for Latinos, at Wells

High School. She explained that Erie deals with most of these problems with programs and services. We have helped children raise their reading levels, helped youth go to college, found people jobs, provided day care so parents can work. But Erie also affiliates with other organizations like Bickerdike, for housing, and NCO– organizing people to speak up and challenge the powers that be for failing to serve the local neighborhood. "We are proud of our community organizing program at Erie," she emphasized. "Erie is an exciting place to be – nothing miraculous, just steady hard work and enthusiasm."[248]

Just up the street, at Noble and Chestnut, was the Community 21 office. This was another place and project Erie was affiliated with. The neighborhood planning office was opened by NCO to implement the "Plan for Improvement" that Marcy Kaptur had authored, and was working on a solution to a neighborhood eyesore and danger to life and limb. They were called "vaulted sidewalks." They were/are only found in the oldest neighborhoods, close to downtown, and were a by-product of the city's engineering feat of installing sewer lines above street level to address the flooding problem of building on what was once a swamp. As a result, houses that once had been at street level found their first floors below that level. Sidewalks were raised, or vaulted, to be even with the street, leaving hollow areas below. After more than 100 years, they were collapsing, leaving gaping holes and crevices everywhere. It gave the neighborhood that bombed-out look that tends to depress real estate values. As city hall often ignored this neighborhood altogether, except when they had urban renewal clearance plans, they ignored this problem as well. When approached about repairs, they offered the city's "50/50" program where the owner shares half the cost with the city to put in a new sidewalk. The problems with applying this idea to vaulted sidewalks were manifold; here are a few:

- These sidewalks were in the oldest/poorest neighborhoods of the city where many owners could not afford to share the cost or, in the case of absentee owners, did not care;
- The cost of replacing a vaulted sidewalk was at least 10x more than an ordinary sidewalk;
- The reconstruction challenges of repairing vaulted sidewalks called for a public works approach that would take on an entire block at a time, replace all the sidewalks at once, not one parcel at a time.

Getting the city to take responsibility for the vaulted sidewalk problem in the Community 21 area had become an issue that all NCO members were committed to resolve. Thus, the community organizers that worked at ENH/NCO were involved in fighting for this objective. As early as 1976, the idea of the city using federal Community Development Block Grant Funds (CDBG), to pay for the public works project that was needed, was viewed as a potential solution. The city finally agreed to address the issue, and the vaulted sidewalk replacement began on Cortez Street in 1979. In 1980, Alex Polikoff, Director of BPI, the public interest law firm that had just won the landmark Gautreaux case that successfully challenged the discriminatory practice of concentrating public housing in African American communities, decided to cover this story in the BPI Magazine. Polikoff knew about the vaulted sidewalk fight because Community 21 residents had consulted with him to explore possible legal action against the city. "The Incredible Vaulted Sidewalk Saga" [249] featured photos of children standing in the middle of a vaulted sidewalk cave-in, and also featured photos of the many ordinary residents who fought long and hard to rid their neighborhood of this blight. They included the pastor of St. Boniface, Fr. Gene Gratkowski (who had succeeded Fr. Hillenbrand), his parishioners, like Josephine Koziol and

Mr. & Mrs. Casimer Patryn, Cesar and Gigi Perez, Mary Gibbons, Paula Perez of Cortez Street, and Loretta Landowski of Thomas Street. They all shared those Erie House values Merri Ex spoke of – steady, hard work and enthusiasm -- and deserved to be on a magazine cover for winning a major city concession to deploy CDBG funds in their neighborhood. Such a project, in such a place was, of course, exactly what CDBG funds were intended for.

Another article appeared in the *Reader,* December 19, 1980. Hank De Zutter wrote "A Cold Christmas in West Town: God help us *every one.*" He outlined the inadequacy of welfare checks to cover basic expenses, an ENH organizing issue. A photo of an Erie family, Mrs. Cuellar and her two daughters, accompanied the article. De Zutter talked about the journalistic habit of writing stories at Christmas about the "poor Cratchits," but too often omitting the mean Scrooge –politicians, bureaucrats–who have "kept Illinois public aid grants the lowest among the northern industrial states."[250] Earlier in the year (May 10, 1980), this same public aid issue led to photos of Erie kids appearing in *The Defender,* Chicago's historic African American newspaper. And finally, on December 29, 1980, a *Chicago Tribune* headline read: "Latinos unite to obtain clout in school policies." COPA education leader, Margarita Cabrales, was quoted.

This extensive press coverage is noted because it is an important vehicle for non-profits to support their work. If they don't know your name, they can't write it on a check. If they don't know your name, pols might not take your call. Emolument and empowerment – one is needed to facilitate the other.

Reaganomics: How to Survive when Government Funding Gets Cut

With the election of Ronald Reagan as president in 1980, the so-called "war on poverty" came to an end and the "war on the working poor" began. Erie House, along with other social service organizations, began to experience what came to be called "Reaganomics." Both Day Care and After-School programs were affected, programs that enabled parents to work. Social work positions were eliminated, parent involvement funds were drastically cut, and a reduction in the food contract meant no breakfast for After-School participants on full days. Family eligibility would no longer be determined by ENH staff, but by bureaucrats. Program providers would be reimbursed on a per diem attendance report, rather than for actual cost of providing the service every day. If just one or two participants were out sick, funding was reduced for that day, even though the cost for the teachers working with the remainder of the classroom remained the same. Teen employment would suffer due to cuts in CETA. So, Merri asked board members to write to their congresspersons, to inform them of the negative impact these cuts were having on Erie's participants, and Erie parents boarded the bus to Springfield to plead their case with state legislators. They got them to override Gov. James Thompson's veto of the state's match of Title XX funds. Erie was forced to lay off staff, but also decided to subsidize Day Care with $43,000 in private funds. Many agencies would wait too long to make the hard decisions about layoffs, and many more would not have the option of sufficient private funds to deploy as a subsidy.

Erie made this decision, even though, on the private revenue side, there was more bad news. Because Montgomery Ward's had a bad year, there would not be a major donation of goods to be sold at Mayfair, meaning the fundraiser was likely to suffer from reduced sales. In fact, as predicted, revenue from Mayfair was around $12,000, down from $19,000 the year before. The good news to offset some of the cuts was a $30,000 bequest from a Grace Lewis, and $5,000 from the estate of Clair Lenert; stock was donated at a value of $19,000. First Church of Oak Park contributed $5,000 to support Erie's employment services, and Tag Day brought in $8,200, one of its highest results. With 50 new names solicited from board members, the Christmas appeal netted over $50,000. This represents a good picture of how Erie House managed, time and time again, when public dollars were cut. Erie and their church partners, (living and deceased), scrambled to hold on, through their time and money, until the political winds shifted again. Erie would also take advantage of advice from a business consultant, provided by United Way, to focus on foundations and new and better fundraising events, to supplement the work Ross Lyman was doing raising money from the churches. It also became a budget goal to keep a healthy balance between public and private revenue. While this did not eliminate vulnerability to shifts in government funding, it proved to be more of a safety net than many non-profits enjoyed, who often worked with ratios like a 90/10, or even 95/5, of government-to-private funding. And, last but not least, it was time for a new volunteer recruitment plan–the churches, the neighbors, the seminary, the university interns– always represented a stalwart strategy, but also one that needed regular maintenance. The steadiest source of volunteers according to Ms. Ex, was Erie's Woman's Auxiliary, and Erie was one of the last settlements to have an Auxiliary, still active in the 1980s.

Finally, Erie House joined other member agencies in deciding to separate from United Christian Community Services (UCCS), the umbrella structure United Way had imposed upon eight social service organizations in 1967, so that they could pass along one lump sum to UCCS and let them divide it into smaller grants to the member agencies. It was not working from the member agency point of view. Association House left first; Erie and other agencies followed. Immediate benefits were clear. Under UCCS, Erie's annual share in 1980 was to be $105,000; on their own, their United Way grant would be $150,000. They did the math. By 1982, as United Way understood the need to compensate, as best they could, for the federal cuts, Erie's grant went to $200,000. This was all private money from companies and their employees that passed their philanthropic giving through United Way.

The upshot of all these efforts was that Erie would close FY82 with a balanced budget, overcoming the projected deficit of $35,000. But prospects for FY83 were not good. Projected deficit for that year was at $74,000, almost 10% of the $750,000 annual budget. The board approved this budget, but with the caveat of a six-month evaluation to determine if more lay-offs were required.

Arrivals and Departures

On the arrival side, late in 1981, Jack O'Kieffe, of Wilmette Presbyterian Church, joined the Erie board. He eventually served for more than 25 years. He and his wife, Connie, became generous individual donors as well as helping to organize fundraising events to help Erie. Early in 1982, Lois Quinn and her husband, longtime MOW volunteers, joined the Erie Board. Blanca Almonte was bringing the Family Focus program to West Town, occupying a storefront in the Erie Neighborhood. Tom Brindisi was assuming the mantle of leadership from his dad, Dan Brindisi, as the director of the Near Northwest Civic Committee. His dad had become director right out of college in 1942, and ran the agency for 40 years. The NNCC still partnered with Erie House in a number of areas, especially bringing together local school principals, pastors, and

Bickerdike staff to discuss community challenges and solutions.

On the departure side, Evelyn Lyman announced her retirement, after 20+ years at Erie House at the end of 1981. Erie Family Health Center Director, Sally Lundeen, announced that the clinic, housed at Erie since its founding in 1957, was preparing to become a financially independent entity, effective June 30, 1982, and anticipated moving to its own space. They eventually moved to the vacant building previously occupied by the failed City Savings at Chicago and Paulina, almost two years later. However, it still needed Erie's help in this transition. This would include continuation of payroll administration for the first two months of the transition and a $10,000 loan at the time of the actual transition, with a negotiated schedule and terms for payback. So, here was a risk that Erie took on, even in light of its own financial challenges, to commit resources to an entity it created, to let it go forth and, hopefully, prosper. It turned out to be a worthwhile risk, evident, when EFHC invited Erie House to its 60th anniversary in 2017.

As Mobil Oil bought out Montgomery Ward's, the Mayfair fundraiser, after a 20-year run, was cancelled in 1982, never to return. Partially, to cover the loss of Mayfair, and partially to honor Jim and Lynn McClure for their 30 years of service (1952-82) to Erie House in so many capacities, a dinner/fundraiser was planned in their honor at the Oak Park Club for spring of 1983.

Point/Counterpoint: Affordable Housing and Early Signs of Gentrification

In the area of housing, two significant developments occurred that appeared on Erie's agenda. They were both representative of patterns that would continue over the next 20 years. Bickerdike, under the leadership of its executive director, Bob Brehm, was breaking ground on 20 affordable rental units in July, 1982, subsidized under the FHA Section 8 new construction program. The way this program worked, tenants paid that portion of market rate rent that was assessed as affordable to them, based on their income and family size. The Section 8 subsidy made up the difference so that the owner was actually receiving the market rent. In Bickerdike's case, they used the difference to pay off their construction costs and then invest in the next project to build more affordable housing. BRC built a total of 454 of these units, between 1982 and 1990. They were built on vacant lots, throughout West Town and East Humboldt Park, with generally no more than six to eight units in a cluster, and no more than two stories high. Bickerdike has continued to own and manage these units, with the help of tenant councils, since they were built. Some of the sites are in neighborhoods like Wicker Park that, by 2000 were completely gentrified. Most lower income families were displaced from privately-owned buildings as rents escalated with sales prices and property taxes. The Bickerdike units, and a handful built by the Chicago Housing Authority, are the only affordable units that remain, allowing lower income families to stay in place and enjoy the amenities of a reinvested neighborhood.

The other development that Merri reported to the Erie board, was the purchase of six large, corner buildings in the Erie neighborhood, including the one where Erie rented space, at 1400 W. Ohio, by a man named Jim Hines of Creative Realty. This was a challenge to that local control of reinvestment so highly prized by COPA, NCO, BRC and Erie. It was a red flag of more to come as this new owner, by raising rents significantly, was forcing families to move out – out of the building, and perhaps, also out of the neighborhood. This prompted a discussion of Erie's future in the neighborhood as well. It was early days, but this topic would be re-visited more than once in subsequent years.

Erie House has had many newsletters over the years, by many different names. Some copies of these communications made it into the Erie archives; others were lost. The newsletter of 1982, "El Sol," Volume 2, No. 10, August, 1982, had survived.[251] Page one of six, "Topics from the Top," featured an interview with Erie's person at the top, Merri Ex. The interview was conducted and written up by Charles Sallay, a 17-year old senior at Wells High School, with his reporter position funded courtesy of the CETA Summer Youth Employment program. He asked Ms. Ex for her perspective on how Erie House was doing. Her answer was that Erie had a great deal of support from their local community. Erie had numerous volunteers from the community, and they stepped up to help with their own fundraisers in whatever way they could manage. As to Erie's future, she said, "I don't think one of Erie's goals is to grow."[252] That was how it looked to her in 1982; by 1992 that would change. As to problems facing the West Town community, she named lack of sufficient decent and affordable housing. But on the "good news" side of that dilemma, Bickerdike was building new, subsidized apartments right at the corner of Noble and Huron. She also regarded the opening of a Family Focus West Town center as more good news for the neighborhood.

With MOW entering its 25th year of service in 1983, Erie hosted a tea for the volunteers. On the occasion, Anne Trapp composed the following poem:

> *Erie wants to sing the praises*
> *Of the gracious volunteers*
> *Who've provided good nutrition*
> *To our aged through the years.*
> *Who've delivered food in snow storms*
> *When the weather's minus ten.*
> *Who've put up with strange behavior*
> *From the clients now and then.*
> *We know there are two aspects*
> *Of nourishment you are sharing:*

A hot, delicious meal
And a generous dose of caring.[253]

No doubt, it was some of that "generous dose of caring" on the part of Erie House, towards its volunteers, that kept them coming for 25 years. The staff leadership team in 1982, also spent time discussing how Erie was perceived by the community, and how to continue to enhance that image. Members of the team included: Angel Carroll, Steve Koll, Alice Cook, all from Day Care, Paulette Fried, from Counseling, Gregorio Gomez, Youth Dept., Roman Rodriguez, Anne Trapp and Merri, from Administration.

As board members took their seats in September, 1982 for their first meeting of FY83, they were reminded Merri Ex was beginning her 5th year as executive director, and that the goal was to raise $60,000 in private revenue. Some of that would come from the clinic that would start reimbursing Erie for funds they borrowed for their transition. This was made possible due to a grant the clinic received from the Chicago Community Trust for $240,000. The Trust also awarded Erie House $40,000 for their teen program. In comparing private income for FY83 with FY82, it was up slightly from $418,000 the previous year, to $476,700 in FY83. Almost half of that was from United Way, at $208, 000. Revenue (interest) from the Endowment came next at $75,000. With Congregations at $50,000, that source of funding still outweighed foundations, at $30,000. However, Foundations were up 10K from the previous year.

Family Focus would be opening their West Town center at 1450 W. Chicago on October 1, 1982. Family Focus began in 1975, in conjunction with the Erikson Institute and Loyola University. This is a place where mothers can drop off their children under three to be cared for while they attend classes, run errands, or whatever they have to do. Both Erie House and Erie Family Health were to work closely with Family Focus, taking referrals from them for other services their participants might need. Merri also reminded board members that a decision needed to be made as to how to use the two vacant lots they had acquired at 1339 and 1341 W. Erie. Should Erie build an annex, create a playground, or deed the lots to Bickerdike for affordable housing? Due to a second type of collaboration, with the Center for Neighborhood Technology, Erie would be receiving funds from the Amoco Foundation to carry out an energy retrofit at 1347, with an eye to long term savings on Erie's gas bill. There was a story about this project in the *Reader*.

Board member, Harry Olson, asked for an update of the discussion on gentrification that Merri initiated at the last meeting. She reported that efforts to work with realtor, Jim Hines, had reached an impasse. He continued to advertise his apartments outside the community, at rents that were double what tenants paid for comparable units in the area that he had been calling "Little Italian Village." NCO held a public meeting about this, and it was evident that this issue was illustrating divisions emerging among residents. Some owners saw Hines' actions as boosting property values they would benefit from; others worried that the price of vacant lots would escalate to the point that Bickerdike would no longer be able to afford the land they needed to build their subsidized units. How this would impact Erie was also of concern.

Meanwhile, research at the Community 21 office had revealed that many of the vacant lots in West Town were owned by the city, becoming the receiver of properties that had been abandoned by owners, failing to keep up their property taxes, and never paying off liens the city attached to the property when the city had assumed responsibility for demolishing the abandoned building. In July 1984, Merri sent a letter to Alderman Nardulli, requesting that city-owned lots be made available to BRC for affordable housing. It was hoped that availability of these city-owned lots, for free, or at least at reasonable prices, could be a strategy to off-set the loss of privately-owned lots to a gentrifying market. After all, the argument was made, many of these lots used to have buildings with affordable rents that should be replaced.

Minutes of the January, 1983 board meeting indicate Erie was making progress on its private revenue goal as Lyman reported on donations of over $10,000 from Lake Forest and Winnetka churches, due to the efforts of Jerry Fox. Fourth Pres gave $4,000, and $2,000 was coming in from Glen Ellyn. The Christmas appeal revenue was up to $70,000 with 90 new contributors. The Thrift Shop brought in $5,000 and stock dividends yielded $5,000. Board members were urged to "learn another language while you cook," and buy the Erie House bilingual cookbook, *El Buen Gusto,* on sale for $6.00. In May, income from the dinner/fundraiser in honor of the McClures was reported as $15,000. Over 300 attended to honor this couple, who shared their thoughts on their attachment to Erie. Lynn stated:

> *I would have trouble sleeping at night if I hadn't done something for my fellow man. I sometimes don't get the house cleaned or the ironing done, but those things don't matter when somebody is in need.*[254]

Jim added:

> *I see my family, my practice of law, my work with the Village, and Erie as of one great pattern that connects. It has meaning because I feel that I'm doing what I should be doing.*[255]

Board Members were invited to visit the BRC construction site at Noble and Huron to see the first Section 8 rentals in progress. The Erie Woman's Auxiliary planned to celebrate the 25th anniversary of Meals on Wheels in November, 1983. That same year, The Children's Benefit League, sponsor of Tag Day, was celebrating its 75th anniversary. Two Erie women were listed in the program as past presidents: Evangeline Gielow (1941-42) and Lynn McClure (1968-1970).

On May 27, 1983, a request for funding was sent to First Church of Oak Park, jointly submitted by Merri Ex, Bob Brehm, executive director of BRC, and Tom Brindisi of Near Northwest Civic Committee, asking for $5,000 to pay for a feasibility study of a potential joint project in housing and economic development. The grant from First Church came through. In the area of housing, Bickerdike was contemplating the takeover of a 51-unit apartment building at 2049 W. Pierce, in what is known as the Wicker Park area of West Town. The building was a HUD foreclosure, and was likely destined for demolition, the fate of two apartment buildings across the street. Many low- income families were displaced and the land became the site for high-end single-family homes. Bickerdike wanted to save this building, and keep the units in this building affordable, at least to moderate income families, with the possibility of converting the building into a housing cooperative. In an atmosphere of hostility toward low-income residents of color, that was generated by the gentry-dominated Wicker Park Neighborhood Council of the early 1980s, it was hoped the idea of a form of ownership, rather than just another low-rent apartment building, might appease the "neighbors." This plan was eventually implemented, with a good number of current residents buying into what became known as the Woolman-Washington Co-op, and functions as that to this day. The Section 8 program was used to subsidize this project as well.

The economic development idea was based on Bickerdike's experience with their Humboldt Construction Company, formed in 1981, to hire local people – some who already had construction trades skills, and others who would apprentice to learn. Humboldt was a subcontractor on many BRC projects, and also was awarded a grant from the city to run a senior home repair program. Perhaps it was time to start another community-based business to provide more local jobs. This vision was eventually realized in El Mercado, a supermarket located at 2701 W. North Avenue. It operated as El Mercado for several years, as a subsidiary of BRC. There is still a grocery store at that location, but it is privately owned and rents the building from BRC.

The $5,000 received from First Church, was matched with $5,000 from Woods Charitable Trust, to support the proposed community organizing work. As promised, Merri was writing proposals to foundations to increase private revenue. Proposals to churches for projects represented a variation on the more traditional general operating support Lyman had been raising.

Erie Launches Another Model Program: TEAM

In the Fall of 1983, a new concept in youth programming at Erie was being developed, by staff members Gregorio Gomez and Carolyn Newberry, to address the high dropout rate of 64% among Latino students at Wells High School, located 4 blocks from Erie House, at Ashland and Augusta. This kind of statistic was known to Erie from local sources. But they were confirmed in a study published in 1984, called *Los Preciosos,* written by Dr. Charles Kyle. Kyle found that the reasons for leaving school included:

- Gang pressure and fear of violence (The Gang Crimes Study Commission Report of 1983 identified 24 gangs operating in West Town);
- Students were told by an administrator or counselor to leave school;

- 28% of female students left due to pregnancy and inability to find adequate childcare;
- 25% cited low achievement, loss of interest, and truancy as reasons.[256]

Gomez and Newberry were consulting with Manuel Izquierdo, an assistant principal at Evanston Township High School. They would name this program TEAM (Tutoring to Educate for Aims and Motivation). It was designed to not only provide tutoring, but also mentoring, to help students aim for success, and have the motivation to get there. Initially, TEAM targeted sophomores, the most vulnerable year for dropping out, but eventually, students from all four years participated. Both student participants and their parents signed an agreement to participate in a minimum number of tutoring sessions and volunteer hours, and to share grade reports. Volunteer mentors, themselves successful adults, would be recruited, initially from churches, to come in one night a week, during the school year, to spend a couple of hours with their mentee. This was a match-up for the entire school year. As it turned out, some mentors stayed with the same student all four years, seeing them through to graduation. That was the goal. In the first year, 1984, they had 20 participants.

The program drew important support from two sources. First, it caught the attention of Marjorie Lundy, a vice-president at Northern Trust Bank, Erie's bank, and a source of Erie board members. The bank not only provided funding for TEAM, but also became a source of those volunteer mentors, an opportunity they promoted to their employees. Northern has been a consistent funder ever since, 35 years and counting. Second, Glen Graham, longtime Erie board member, created a scholarship fund to help TEAM graduates who were college-bound with their expenses. These proved to be resources well-spent. When TEAM participants were graduating from high school at the

95% rate, the program shifted its focus to college admission, eventually bringing that rate to the 90th percentile as well. Over the years, the pool of mentors was expanded beyond Northern Trust. An important addition was added in the 21st century, when Erie reached out to the engineering community for math tutors. Not only did students do better in math, but they were introduced to a new career. Word spread to more engineering firms and the mentors from that field grew. As a result, Erie/TEAM has seen several of its students pursue and complete degrees in engineering ever since. When they return after graduation to speak to their successors in the TEAM program, the students see someone who looks like them, who grew up in the hood, and now works for NASA. Maybe they could do the same. It is NOT impossible, is the important realization.

Besides starting to plan for TEAM, Erie House was the only organization in Chicago to receive a "Young Volunteers in Action" grant, one of the few CETA programs left under Reagan. YVA involved recruiting and training 100 low-income youth, and placing them in volunteer positions at Erie and other agencies. The program only lasted one year, so it is difficult to evaluate how participation in YVA impacted Erie's programming in the long run. But certainly, the notion of youth volunteering and service learning was evident at Erie House and became a core element of TEAM.

Issues in the After-School Program

While the story of Erie House is full of successes, there are always bumps in the road along the way. Such a bump presented itself in December, 1983, and was not resolved until the following March, 1984. The issue that surfaced, was an allegation of "child abuse," actually described as "inappropriate touching." A parent contacted the program funder, the city's Department of Human

Services (DHS), who opened an investigation. Merri Ex contacted Erie's legal counsel at Gardner, Carton, & Douglas. The strategy that emerged was presented at the December 16 board meeting. The proposal had the following steps:

- Suspend the After-School Program as presently staffed, effective Dec. 16;
- Lay off the After-School staff indefinitely, using up vacation and sick leave;
- Accommodate children in other Erie programs during the usual hours parents need the care;
- Form a study group to restructure an acceptable program with consultation of parents and ENH Board;
- Study group will consist of 2 Erie staff, appointed by ED; 3 parents chosen by parents, and 3 board members appointed by the president;
- Lenora Cartright, Commissioner of DHS will sit with the group.[257]

In the course of the study group's deliberations, they received a "list of demands" from "Erie House Concerned Parents and Community" regarding After-School. The document was in English and Spanish and included the following points:

- Appoint a Hispanic Director (Executive Director or After-School Director was unclear):
  o Need someone sensitive to our culture;
  o This is mostly a Hispanic community and mostly Hispanic children in the program;
  o If Hispanic children are used to get money in your proposals, a Hispanic should write and sign these proposals.

- Develop a new committee to hear staff &
  community suggestions; we have lost confidence in
  the existing structure;
- More Hispanic community representation on the
  Board; the existing structure is paternalistic;
- Reinstate staff:
  o We recognize their sensitivity to our children's
    needs;
  o Our children feel secure with these people;
  o They were unjustly treated.[258]

There are no details regarding any response to these demands, but the After-School program remained suspended until March. When programming resumed, some staff were allowed to re-apply. The child abuse allegations were investigated and addressed to the satisfaction of DHS. While there is no record of a response to changes in the board and the administration, Merri Ex submitted her resignation later that year, and the next executive director of Erie was Latino. The board had already committed to adding more locals and, therefore, more Latinos, but, as noted earlier, it was a slow process.

In the Fall of 1984, Merri wrote to Nancy Johnstone at Youth Guidance to confirm Erie's agreement to join them in submitting a proposal to establish a model demonstration for youth in the southeast end of West Town. In what was to be a collaboration with several agencies, including Association House, Erie would provide family counseling services. A letter was also sent to Sally Lundeen, director of Erie Family Health Center, notifying her that the Erie board had accepted her proposal to start paying down the balance of what they had borrowed from Erie House, at the rate of $3,000/month. The balance owed as of June 30, 1984 was $27,227.

In October, 1984, Ms. Ex submitted her resignation to the board. In response, a Search Committee was formed, to be co-chaired by Chuck Armstrong and Bob Swikart. It also included Mary Burns, Jerry Fox, Manuel Izquierdo, Marie Leslie, Jim McClure, and Yvette Nazario.

As she prepared to depart, she submitted a report on Erie's community organizing activities to Martin Adams at the Woods Charitable Trust. While she reported on a continuing need for this work, especially in regard to school issues, she acknowledged that the future of community organizing as an Erie program was in question. The position had been vacant since April, 1984. A job description was developed and posted, but there was no hire on record before Merri left. What was not in question when Merri left at the end of 1984, was that Erie's budget was $900,000, and the board was considering the possibility of hiring a full-time fundraiser before the end of FY85. She had accomplished her goal of opening the door to new resources from the private sector for Erie Neighborhood House.

Upon reflection in 2018, Merri Ex shared these thoughts:

> *I believe that my bilingual skills made it possible for Erie House to make significant progress in connecting with its Latino neighbors, and becoming recognized as a Latino-serving agency. I also became convinced, from my years at Erie House, that the strength of settlement houses as a whole, rests with their capacity for collaboration, their commitment to be a catalyst of new strategies for service and empowerment, and their willingness to then spin them off to make their own way.[259]*

Chapter Six: Rafael Ravelo: An Era of Expansion, Collaboration, and Facing the Threat of Gentrification (1985-1997)

Before beginning the story of Rafael Ravelo's time at Erie House, it is important to update the historical context for his work, i.e., what was happening in Chicago and in West Town by the mid-1980s. For one thing, when Ross Lyman arrived at Erie in 1952, just as 1950 census data was coming to light, the population of the city was 3,620,962; by 1980, the census data that would be available to Ravelo, when he started at Erie, revealed that the city had lost over 600,000 people, while the surrounding counties of the Chicago metro area, had gained about 2,000,000, a stark illustration of the extent of the flight to the suburbs, as well as the trend of suburban life as a first choice, skipping over any time in the city at all. The real challenge facing major cities, like Chicago, was not shrinkage in size alone, but that people of means were leaving the city behind, to those without. In addition, those with means who continued to embrace urban life, would bear a heavier and heavier burden, as taxes rose to provide support for their poorer neighbors. This turned out to foster more and more animosity, over wider and wider class divisions between top and bottom on the income scale, with a smaller and smaller middle class squeezed between. What that smaller middle class was reluctant to acknowledge was that their self-interest was much more closely aligned with the "lower" class than the much wealthier upper class, which eventually came to be characterized as the "one percent."

Life in Erie's part of West Town in the 1980's pretty much reflected the life of those left behind. But, by the mid-1980s, other parts of the area would experience the phenomenon of "the return," a return to an interest in urban living and the attraction of grand old

Rafael Ravelo (Erie Neighborhood House)

buildings that could be acquired for a reasonable price. On the other hand, the earliest arrivals also included those who had never left the city, like "refugees" from Lincoln Park and Lakeview (Boys Town), where prices were escalating at a more rapid rate than in West Town. They were not heading for the neighborhood right around Erie House, at first, but to Wicker Park, just a mile to the northwest. There they found the housing, built by the more prosperous Norwegian and German immigrants, described in earlier chapters, who had moved up Milwaukee Avenue almost a century before. There, they had spent their wealth on spectacular mansions. Some had, more recently, been turned into rooming houses, but those first "urban pioneers" were up to the task of restoring them to their original splendor.

Based on the observation of this writer, who lived there at the time, these early residents included a fair share of gay men and a number of artists. The latter came for the rents that continued to be reasonable, but were often blamed for the gentrification. Both of these early groups did not drive displacement like the ones who followed 10 years later. They tended to enjoy the diversity of the neighborhood as well as the architecture. They joined the local civic organizations for the same reasons as their Polish and Puerto Rican neighbors. And they were just as upset with District Commander McCarthy, when he suggested that people who lived in West Town did not deserve the same level of police protection as more affluent areas of the city. In fact, when Mr. Ravelo took the job at Erie House in March of 1985, he lived in Wicker Park.

He had the opportunity to enjoy two more years of a progressive mayoral administration under Harold Washington, and would witness the election of Chicago's longest-serving mayor, Richard M. Daley, elected in 1989. There would be no other mayor until 2011. In 1992, Democrats would take back the White House with the election of Bill Clinton, who served until 2000. The Governor of Illinois when Ravelo arrived at Erie in 1985, was James Thompson, a Republican. In 1991, he was replaced by another Republican, James Edgar, who served for the next eight years. By Republican standards in place 30 years later, Edgar would be defined as a "moderate." He proposed policies that supported immigrants and the working poor, and had the capacity to negotiate with those of the other party. In other words, he governed.

The year Ravelo joined Erie House, a guy named Michael Jordan joined the Bulls, and, for a little while, a basketball star replaced a gangster as a Chicago icon, known round the world. Oprah Winfrey was just getting started on her path to becoming one of the richest women in the world, and did not choose New York or Hollywood, but Chicago, to build her Harpo Studio. In 1987, the Mexican Museum of Fine Art opened in Pilsen, the heart of the Mexican immigrant community for many years, a community that was already starting to overflow up Ashland Avenue to the Erie House neighborhood, becoming the next wave of Latinos that Ravelo's Erie House would be serving.

Chicago's Mexican Heritage, Riding the See-saw of US Immigration Policy

Of course, the Mexicans in West Town, or even in Pilsen and Little Village, were not the first Mexicans to arrive in Chicago. That is said with the same assurance that most Chicagoans are not very clear on that reality, but instead, lump all Mexicans in Chicago with most recently arrived immigrants. In fact, the first wave of Mexican immigration came to Chicago in the mid to late 1910s, almost parallel with the Great Migration of African Americans from the south to the north.

The push factor for some of them was the Mexican Revolution, the ongoing fighting and changing of regimes, from 1910 to 1920. The pull factor, as for most immigrants, was economic –para comer, por pan–for bread. There were jobs to be had in agriculture, especially picking sugar beets in the Midwest, jobs with the railroads, that literally carried them north, and eventually in the steel and meat-packing industries on Chicago's south side. Thus, three Mexican enclaves, or colonias, developed in Chicago: South Chicago, Back of the Yards, and the Near West Side; and two developed in northwest Indiana: East Chicago and Gary. In each of the three Chicago enclaves, Mexican Catholics established a core parish. The first Mexican Catholic Church in Chicago was Our Lady of Guadalupe, established in South Chicago in 1924. On the Near West Side, the "Hull House Colonia," took over St. Francis of Assisi on Roosevelt Road, that had been built by German immigrants, used by Italians, and came to the Mexican community around 1930. Lastly, Immaculate Heart of Mary opened in Back of the Yards in 1945. The Cordi-Marian Sisters, who came from Mexico, and the Claretian Fathers, ministered to the Mexican Catholics of Chicago in those early days. It took almost 60 years, but in 1983, Placido Rodriguez, born in Guanajuato, raised in St. Francis of Assisi parish, and ordained as a Claretian, became the first Mexican-American auxiliary bishop for the Archdiocese of Chicago.

Besides their religion, Mexicans brought their art to Chicago. At Hull House, in the early days of the Near West Side *colonia,* Adrian Lozano, clearly influenced by the Mexican muralist movement (Diego Rivera, etc.), painted a beautiful mural that was lost when Hull House was torn down to make way for the University of Illinois Chicago campus in the 1970s. Only a photo of it remains in the University of Illinois Chicago collection.[260] There were also pottery-makers at work at the Hull House kilns, making what came to be known commercially as Fiesta Ware. That story is documented and illustrated in *Pots of Promise.*[261] The Muralists moved on to Pilsen, where conversations were under way in 2019 to establish historic districts to preserve these murals and the 19th century architecture some of them are painted on.

Some workers realized they could work in the fields of the Midwest in the warm months, and then get a factory job in the city during the winter months, rather than traveling back and forth to Mexico in between. Most who came to Chicago migrated from three Mexican states: Jalisco, Guanajuato, and Michoacan, and from that former Mexican state – Texas.[262] As this pattern developed, their "home states" became Illinois and Indiana.

The story of Mexican migration to the US has that pull/push dynamic in US immigration history of pulling them in when the US needed them, and then harassing and sending them back when they did not. Mexicans called those who pulled them in, *enganchistas,* "the ones who hooked you."[263] These were contractors who recruited workers, for a fee, often on behalf of the beet growers, in particular; they took a percentage of the workers' wages as well. More than satisfied with their Mexican workers, employers lobbied the government to exempt them from the 1924 Immigration Act. This Act was predominantly aimed at excluding Asians, but also set quotas for immigrants from other countries the US did not plan to "welcome" any more. For Mexicans, the door mat still said *"Bienvenido."* However, when the economy of the US crashed in 1929, that welcome mat was withdrawn, and there was a widespread movement to "assist" Mexican immigrants to "repatriate." In other words, deportation became the policy. Thousands of Mexicans returned to their country of origin, whether it still was thought of as "home" or not. When workers were once again in demand during the high production years of World War II, 1943-1945, the *Braceros* program welcomed them back. 15,000 came to Chicago during this period, and also to towns like Aurora, Joliet, and Blue Island, Illinois. And then, after the war, there was the "Operation Wetback" initiative to find *braceros* who had overstayed their "welcome," and send them back to Mexico once again!

Regardless of this schizophrenic public policy, Mexicans both stayed and kept coming to Chicago. Here is the story by the round numbers, the Mexican population of Chicago and its metro area over time:[264]

1910:	1,000	Chicago	
1930:	25,000	Chicago	
1960:	55,600	Chicago	
1980:	369,000	Metro Area	
1990:	547,850	Metro Area	
2000:	786,000	Metro Area	530,000 just in Chicago
2010:	961,000	Metro Area	578,100 just in Chicago

The huge jump in numbers between 1960 and 1980 shaped the story that was unfolding as Mr. Ravelo arrived in West Town to become the Executive Director of Erie Neighborhood House in 1985. In Mexico, the value of the peso was down, unemployment was up, and people headed to Mexico City, in search of opportunity. This search led to a population explosion in the capital, as the population of 5 million in 1960, rose to 17 million by 1984.[265] Plan B was to head for the US. This trend would continue during Ravelo's administration. From the 1990 Census to 2000, the percentage of Mexican Americans in all of Cook County increased by 69% and the percentage in Chicago increased by 50% in that same period. The number of Mexicans in Chicago surpassed the numbers in Houston and San Antonio, Texas. The *colonias* that swelled in numbers on this immigrant wave were Pilsen and Little Village (South Lawndale) that, by 1990, had a combined Mexican population of 100,000. One area that received the initial "overflow" was West Town and Erie House–just a 12-block journey up Ashland Avenue from 18th Street to Erie Street. By 1990, West Town had a "Latino," combined Puerto Rican and Mexican, population of 53,241. This placed it third in Chicago's community areas with large Hispanic populations. Little Village was first with almost 69,000, and Logan Square was only slightly ahead at 53,693. Chicagoan, Carlos DeJesus,[266] used to comment that Los Angeles had its Chicanos, New York had its Puerto Ricans, but Chicago had "Latinos." In other words – all of the above.

There was one more piece of legislation that affected Mexican immigrants, those that Erie House served, and those who came to work there. It was the Immigration Reform and Control Act of 1986, signed into law by President Ronald Reagan. First, it declared it was illegal for employers to knowingly hire undocumented workers. Their businesses could be subject to raids by the INS and they could be fined. Secondly, the act legalized all undocumented immigrants who had arrived in the US prior to January 1, 1982. Message: Dear Employers: You can keep the undocumented workers you already have, just don't keep hiring anymore. But Reagan and the Congress did not exactly get the result they were shooting for. The good news for the 5 million undocumented thought to be living in the US in 1986, was that they now had the opportunity to become citizens if they wished. The surprising news, perhaps only to Reagan, was that by 2013, the estimated number of undocumented immigrants in the US had risen to 11.1 million. *Pan* is a powerful motivator; then add escape from violence, as immigrants from other parts of Latin America sought safety in flight. And so it goes–the story of America for over 200 years.

Erie House Gets its First Latino Director

Erie's first Latino executive director was himself an immigrant, but from Cuba. After the Castro-led revolution in 1959, in the context of so much uncertainty, some families sent their children off the island, as what they thought of as an interim strategy, to keep them safe. Young Rafael, age 13, left in the care of the Christian Brothers, who were his teachers in Cuba. Thus, he became part of a group later referred to as the "Pedro Pan" children. By the time this Peter Pan operation was ended by President Kennedy, in 1961, it is estimated that about 14,000 Cuban children had been airlifted off the island. For many, the trauma of being separated from their families was not "interim." It lasted for years, and some never saw their families again. Ravelo recalled that his mother was in her early 30s when he was taken from his family. He did not see her again for 20 years, he said, and it was painful going back to a family that grew up without him.[267]

By the mid-1960s, he was studying theology and psychology in Medellin, Colombia, became a Christian

Brother, and then completed his Bachelor's degree at St. Mary's University in Winona, Minnesota in 1970. Having left the Christian Brothers, graduate school brought him to Chicago to pursue a degree in social work at the School of Social Service Administration (SSA) at the University of Chicago, from 1975-77. An internship brought him to West Town for the first time when he got some of his clinical experience offering individual and family therapy at Clemente High School, at Division and Western, about 1.5 miles from Erie House. After completing his Master's, he went to work for Youth Guidance at Chicago's Bowen High School in South Chicago, one of the Mexican *colonias,* in the early days of Mexican migration.

By the time he applied for the job at Erie House, he was serving as Assistant Director of Youth Guidance. His boss, Nancy Johnstone, encouraged him to apply and wrote a strong letter of recommendation. During an interview with him in February, 2018, he recalled that his competition was Blanca Almonte, already well known to Erie in her role with Family Focus. Nevertheless, his experience and personal warmth won over the search committee, and he felt welcomed by veteran board members like Chuck Armstrong, Jim McClure, and David Dangler. His work began on April 1, 1985. In May, he was introduced to the Erie Woman's Auxiliary, by then president, Marjorie Schuham, who represented the third generation of the Sawyer/Graham family tree of faithful supporters of Erie House.

New Beginnings

In Ravelo's first few months, he hired Barbara Castellan as Associate Director, and then put her in charge of carrying out an agency Needs Assessment. He wanted each of five department directors interviewed to identify both short and long-term needs of their programs. In the report that followed this assessment, before getting into the assessment of each department, a preface laid out some general ideas that pertained to Erie House as a whole. Under the heading, TRADITION, the report claimed:

> *Erie's adaptation of programs to the cultural framework of changing immigrant populations and its responsiveness to emerging needs of residents through comprehensive programs are worthy of replication.* [268]

In addressing PHILOSOPHY, the report suggests that this has evolved over the years, from a "taking care of" mindset, to a broader focus that adds empowerment to caring. Erie had made the effort to educate and encourage its participants to take control of their own circumstances and work for systemic change that would remove barriers to their economic success, and a better life overall. This work is enhanced by the involvement of community residents as volunteers on every program level. Their knowledge of the community helps Erie to understand what needs to be done, and their work at Erie educates them on how to do it better. The integration of these local volunteers with more affluent volunteers, that came from many suburban churches, is a unique form of education and empowerment, challenging both racism and classism. With 52 staff, 66 board members, and 150 volunteers, Erie had the human resources to continue its history of success. Erie has also shown a remarkable ability to initiate, nurture, house, and then spin off, new community-based organizations like NCO, Erie Family Health Center, and Bickerdike.

Some of the key RECOMMENDATIONS that emerged from the Assessment were as follows:

- Computerize!
- Pursue more foundation and corporate funding;

- Expand pre-school services, understanding that adding more slots means finding new/additional space;
- Hire some full-time staff with different credentials to move adult programming beyond ESL and GED;
- Hire more staff, and raise more funds, for the successful TEAM mentorship program;
- Increase efforts to work closely with Erie Family Health Center;
- Increase staff training in order to keep fostering empowerment;
- Support counseling staff to work in key areas that need attention: battered women, alcoholism, single parenting, and acculturation; and
- Pursue question raised about establishing a youth employment program in-house.[269]

So, Ravelo had this agenda to start with, and would add more items along the way. As this story unfolds in this chapter, it will become evident that the first six bullet points were clearly and successfully addressed. Of the last three, staff training was ongoing, counseling ran into funding problems and had to be re-structured, and a youth employment program, except for "Summer Jobs for Youth," was never attempted on a year-round basis.

In 1986, Erie's new Director experienced one of many anniversaries to come, with a celebration commemorating Erie's 50th year in its current building. A Golden Anniversary Committee was formed to plan an event that would take place June 7, 1986. The members of this committee were all staff members with a long attachment to Erie: Virginia Moreno, Carmen Santiago, Angel Carroll, Anne Trapp, Susana Ortiz, and Ema Peña Lopez. The last two on this list still worked at Erie House in 2019. An award was presented to Marge Schramer for her many years of service, since the 1950s. A historical exhibit was prepared, and, of course, there was food – tacos, Puerto Rican rice, lasagna, fried chicken, hot dogs, salad, and dessert. Twenty-nine churches and pastors were on the guest list, and 43 names from the Woman's Auxiliary, as well as a long list of local addresses of Latino families that Erie now served. Sister Mary Beth Minkel, who had replaced Sister Marian as principal of Santa Maria School, was also on the list.

Just before the anniversary celebration, a letter arrived addressed to Anne Trapp. It was from Marjorie Whitney Brass, who, at that time, lived in Riverside, IL. She wanted to share her memories of Erie House that began in the early 1930s, when Dr. Leora Davies, an early ENH Board member, later associated with the Erie clinic, brought a group from her church high school group (Holy Redeemer Lutheran) to volunteer at Erie, when Erie was still in the old ECI building. In the 1940s, her mother, Mrs. Fred Whitney, was a member of the Woman's Auxiliary, and she would sometimes accompany her mother to a Sunshine Luncheon or other event. She remembered Florence Towne and Mom Savino. She and her mom attended Demonstration Nights, when Erie program participants "put on a show" for all of their church supporters. They went to Mayfair, worked at the Thrift Shop, and prepared food for Mothers Club picnics and children's field trips. She remembered Camp Davies, named after her mentor, and pecan sales! She observed the arrival of Ross Lyman and his young family. "For more than 20 years, he led us gently but firmly." In general, she notes, *there was always a warm welcome at Erie*, and clearly this applied to church volunteers as well as program participants. Then she explains why:

> *It seems to me that Erie has been blessed with*
> *exceptional leadership and dedication of directors,*
> *staff, board, auxiliary, neighbors, and friends. . . a*
> *long record of service and inspiration. . . Many of*
> *us have been recipients of letters or words of thanks*

253

*from Erie, but we have been richly blessed by our
associations there. . . we have been inspired and
consoled.*[270]

This was Rafael Ravelo's, and every executive director's
challenge, to maintain and develop an institution that
inspires and consoles its participants–neighbors, staff, and
volunteers.

For 29 years, Erie Family Health Center (EFHC), the
new name for "the clinic," did *their* work of inspiration and
consolation, in the spirit of their founder, at 1347 W. Erie.
But in 1986, the clinic said good-bye to its birthplace, and
moved to a building at 1656 W. Chicago, only five blocks
away. The planning for this move began when Merri Ex was
director, but took much longer to be implemented than
anyone expected. Erie House was patient, and even
financially supportive, every step of the way. Parting was,
indeed, a "sweet sorrow," but the clinic director at that time,
Joanne Gersten, and Ravelo, agreed to continue to work
together, a promise that was well kept.

In June, 1986, Ravelo made his first annual report to
the Erie Board. He informed them that three major areas of
emphasis had emerged:

1) The **Needs Assessment** was carried out by the new
   management team he put together;
2) **Staff training/professional development** was
   under way with the help of some outside
   consultants;
3) An **overall restructuring of the agency** was
   accomplished that would enable Erie to have clearer
   relationships among programs and staff, improving
   levels of accountability as well as lines of authority;
   monthly all-staff meetings were introduced.

New staff included:

1) An **Associate Director** to oversee programs, Erie's first, except for the one year Merri Ex held that title when she was transitioning to Executive Director;
2) A **Training Coordinator** to provide staff development;
3) A **"Fundraiser,"** that became Director of Development (when Ross Lyman retired), and whose job it was to develop a fundraising plan, research prospective donors, and help with proposal-writing.[271]

To indicate his commitment to a new strategy for fundraising, he gave the board a list of the 18 foundations and corporations Erie planned to approach for FY86-87. Finally, he reported on building improvements accomplished, such as the lobby improvements, roof repair, re-purposing the clinic area, and remodeling of the after-school area; improvements yet to come for the pre-school area that would be funded by Title XX. He closed his report with the observation of settlement house directors for almost a century, that while they were greatly under-resourced (with a budget of $1 million), for the scope of work, the job got done because of the talent and commitment of the staff and volunteers.

Restructuring Gets Under Way

Under a department heading of **"Community Services,"** the Thrift Shop, Pantry, and Meals on Wheels were grouped together. **"Counseling Services"** also became a separate department with a focus on further development of "family systems theory" as a working philosophical base, and a plan for aggressive outreach – taking them into area schools and increasing their visibility in West Town and Humboldt Park. In fact, "increasing Erie's visibility" was a major theme of Ravelo's leadership.

As part of the restructuring, youth programs like TEAM became a youth *department* with a more cohesive approach to serving high-risk adolescents, a particular interest of Ravelo's. A proposal submitted to United Way to serve youth, ages 13-21, also in June 1986, included some sobering statistics. Erie reported that at least 24 gangs were known to be active in West Town, representing 34% of all the gangs in Chicago. This fact was accompanied by the observation that these gangs were becoming more violent *as guns became more accessible.*[272] Events happening well into the 21st century would illustrate the escalation of a situation identified a generation earlier. No doubt, that for at least 100 of Erie's 150 years, it has been pulling hundreds of youth off the streets and away from that accessibility. But thousands never made it there; some succeeded on their own; many did not.

The other complicating factor in the lives of Chicago youth, was the failure of the Chicago public school system (CPS) to keep them in high school. The study, called *"Los Preciosos,"* by Dr. Charles Kyle, cited above, had pointed to a 70% dropout rate at West Town's two high schools, Wells and Clemente. Under Ravelo, Erie proposed the following strategies:

- Offer a Teen Drop-in Center;
- Provide an open gym in the evenings (Read: *Hoops as port of entry*);
- Develop more goal-centered programs like their TEAM mentorship program;
- Engage in advocacy on behalf of and with the youth themselves, to fight for policy changes they needed, to have a future.[273]

Estimated cost: $100,000. This was undoubtedly an underestimate, but funders, too often, did not want to face the real cost of a comprehensive, effective strategy. And, non-profits wrote proposals to "fit the guidelines."

As the 1985-86 Needs Assessment indicated, and Ravelo reported, adult education services needed attention and would be reorganized under the *Instituto Educativo*. Basically, Erie heard from staff and students that the ESL and GED classes offered through the City Colleges of Chicago (CCC) were less than satisfactory. The CCC had taken over this responsibility from CPS, as the entity that was supposed to be serving adult learners. As in the case of teens at local high schools, the dropout rate for adults enrolled in City Colleges programs was disturbingly high. In fact, until new leadership came into place, from outside the system in the early part of the 21st century, the completion rate for associate degrees, certificate programs, or remedial services, had been stuck at 7%. As was often noted, no community-based service provider would have survived, if that was their level of accomplishment.

So, in the 1980s, Erie set out to offer its own adult education program. By April, 1987, *Instituto Educativo* had 876 adults enrolled, with an average daily attendance of 200. In the context of a better organized, more culturally sensitive program, students were progressing much faster. A further benefit for the students was the location of their classes in a multi-service agency that could help them address many other challenges in their lives that often prevented them from completing programs and earning certificates. Erie understood that, in immigrant communities, a teacher and a classroom were not enough, as reflected in a student testimonial from that time:

> *My opinion about Erie House is that it is a house*
> *with many opportunities. Especially for the mothers,*
> *there is free baby-sitting for our children. This way*
> *we can study better. Besides this, the teachers are*
> *very patient with us and help a lot so we can*

257

prepare ourselves for better futures and better jobs.[274]

While **"Child Care"** was not in need of restructuring, the director and staff of that department were engaged with other settlement houses, and neighborhood child care providers like North Avenue Day Nursery, that were organizing to challenge Governor James Thompson's veto of the legislature's $3 million day care appropriation, for sites that provided pre-school and after-school care with Title XX funds. A community meeting, co-sponsored by Erie House, Onward House, Taylor House, and The Nursery was held at Erie House on September 30, 1987, to press for one of two actions: to get the governor to rescind his veto or get the legislature to override it. The governor did not attend, but agreed to send a representative. Elected officials that did attend included State Senator, Miguel Del Valle, State Reps, Joe Berrios and Myron Kulas, and Aldermen Terry Gabinski and Luis Gutierrez. Eventually, the governor's veto was overridden. Collaboration and advocacy went hand in hand. It was not always a winning strategy, but, since 1962, from the early days of working with NCO, Erie House generally lived by this strategic approach.

La Casa de la Cultura

From even earlier days, in the settlement tradition established by Hull House, and especially, Ellen Gates Starr, the Erie House papers are full of descriptions of performances presented by participants. The children danced and sang on demonstration nights, the youth imagined themselves the Rogers & Hammerstein of Erie Street, house bands formed, children's art was on display in the classrooms, and the occasional mural appeared on Erie's walls. The arts were also a means of sharing and honoring one's heritage and culture. In 1987, Erie envisioned combining some professional performances with a little fundraising, and proposed a series of three concerts to be held at Erie. They called the series *"La Casa de la Cultura,"* through which "Hispanic artists will musically interpret their countries in a rich tapestry of vocal and instrumental mediums and folkloric themes."[275] The premier concert was set for January 31, 1987 – An Evening with Esther Mejias, featuring The Puerto Rican Folklore Ballet, *"Yucayeque."* (*yucayeques* were small villages in early Taino culture). Mejias was discovered and first brought to Chicago by the Old Town School of Folk Music, when it was still located at 909 W. Armitage Avenue, in Chicago's Lincoln Park area.[276] On August 14, 1985, the folkloric dance troupe was written up in the *New York Times,* having performed as part of the Lincoln Center Out-of-Doors Festival. Not too shabby for a settlement house in Chicago to draw such talent.

There is evidence that great effort went into contacting every individual and organization Erie knew to invite them to this event. Press releases were issued in English and Spanish, and requests for financial support were submitted to numerous companies and foundations. Tickets were sold at $10 and food could be purchased at the event. Bottom line: they took in $1,318. With expenses of $895, they managed a profit of $423. Lesson learned: in the non-profit world, a quality event that is often a source of great pride, is not necessarily a source of significant revenue. Erie would host numerous events featuring Hispanic talent, and artists representing other cultures, but it would be 2005 before it found a program that was its most successful fundraiser.

Engaged and Dedicated Board Members

Both Merri Ex and Rafael Ravelo mentioned in their interviews some challenges in working with the Presbyterian-dominated board, with a religious culture of

Protestantism that was not their own. However, both would also acknowledge that Erie benefited from some amazing individual Presbyterian leaders on the Erie Board. What is particularly striking, is the length of time individuals stayed on the board, and the commitment of multiple generations from the same family.

In 1987, Erie took a moment to honor the three generations of the Sawyer-Graham-Schuham family. Their story appeared in the Fall edition of the *Erie Neighborhood House News*. With the name changes, this generational commitment, that was passed down through the daughters, might be missed. Dr. Alvah Sawyer and his wife, Frances, got involved with Erie House in the early part of the 20th century, when Miss Florence was Head Resident. Their involvement was related to their membership in the First Presbyterian Church of Oak Park, another long-standing connection with Erie. Dr. Sawyer became a member of the Erie House board and served at least one term as president. Mrs. Sawyer was active in the Erie Woman's Auxiliary and served as president there. Her daughter, Mrs. Betty Graham, pointed out that in her mother's time, Auxiliary meetings were important and popular social events, where the ladies dressed up in their best to attend. In those days they met in the Erie Chapel. Her mom shared that Florence would jest, "We pray and spill coffee in the same room."[277]

Due to the generosity of the Grahams, who came to serve on the Erie board through the Elmhurst Presbyterian Church, the first-floor west wing of the building was being renovated. This new space would be known as the Sawyer Room, as the plaque just outside of it pays homage to Mrs. Graham's mother. It would become a place for After-School programming during the day, and the meeting room for the Erie Board and Woman's Auxiliary when they gathered at Erie in the evenings. In 1987, Mr. Graham was vice president of the Erie Board. Mrs. Graham, like her mother, was active with the Woman's Auxiliary, and had spent 15 years volunteering at Erie's Thrift Shop. Following in her grandmother's and mother's footsteps, Marjorie Graham Schuham, served as president of the Auxiliary, and, with her husband, Richard, served on the Erie board. Marjorie also volunteered with Meals on Wheels.

Mrs. Graham explained that their loyalty to Erie was based on their commitment to education, of both children and adults. So, in addition to providing funds for the room renovation, the Grahams started a scholarship fund that supported youth who wanted to attend college. That fund has been a core element of the TEAM program at Erie House.

Others who represent this multi-generational commitment: Walter and Evangeline Gielow and their son, Bob; Harry Armstrong and son and daughter-in-law, Chuck and Phyllis Armstrong; Benjamin Franklin Olson and Harry Olson, Gerald Fox and his son, Steve Fox.

Chuck Armstrong said that when he first came to Erie with his parents, Miss Towne was still living on the third floor of Erie House. He remembers her coming to speak at First Church of Oak Park when he was a child, and talking about the Polish and Italian immigrants. That was back in the 1930s. He and his wife, Phyllis, joined the board in 1960 and got their church at that time, the Union Church of Hinsdale (United Church of Christ), to become active supporters of Erie. He served as president twice, and after 30 years on the board, commented:

> *I really like Erie House because it has always been on the cutting edge of programs. Erie is an innovative leader and it has always helped people to learn to help themselves.*[278]

However, this dedication was not limited to "church couples." Ravelo observed that one of his most active and supportive board members in his early years at Erie was Jeff

Holcomb. When he started at Erie he was a single guy who worked as a trader. He used to come to the Erie gym and just shoot hoops with the young males who inhabited the Erie gym most evenings. Eventually, he joined the board. When Erie announced a new school-age program, called Project Smart Kid (PSK) he committed to organizing a cocktail party to raise funds. The party raised $12,000 – at that time, an Erie record for a single event, organized single-handedly by one person. It was no wonder Ravelo nominated Holcomb for the United Way Heart of Gold Award, which he won, in 1988. Besides winning that award, Jeff Holcomb served as Vice-president of the Erie board in 1988. Ed Schimmelpfennig was president, and James McClure was Assistant Secretary. He had now been on the board more than 30 years.

But on May 23, 1990, Erie lost one of its longest-serving board members and volunteers, Evangeline Gielow. She was 101, and described by her son, Bob, as "imperturbable." Mrs. Gielow first became acquainted with the Erie Chapel Institute through her husband, Walter, who grew up in the Erie neighborhood. Her enrollment in the Chicago Musical Academy (then run by Flo Ziegfeld!), brought her to the city from her hometown in Tennessee. She and Walter served together on the ECI and ENH boards until he died in 1945. Then she served with her son, Bob into the 1960s. She took a turn as president of the Children's Benefit League in the 1940s and, when the Children's Benefit League marked their 80th year in 1988, Evangeline could claim to have witnessed about 70 of those 80 years. She was active with the Woman's Auxiliary for 50+ years.

Also, in 1988, Ross Lyman celebrated his 35th year at Erie House, still serving as Development Director, since he took on that role when Merri Ex replaced him as executive director in 1977. However, he retired shortly thereafter, as Jeanne Gettleman was named Director of Development in April, 1989.

Project Smart Kid (PSK)

Project Smart Kid (PSK) was announced in Erie's newsletter in the Fall of 1987.[279] Funding proposals submitted in 1989, laid out Ravelo's description of this program as follows:

> *PSK was a comprehensive educational support and dropout prevention program designed to improve the academic performance of under-achieving elementary school students and enhance their social and emotional development.*[280]

In this proposal seeking funding for PSK, Erie cited a number of impressive sources to support the need for a program like PSK. This proposal came from a Development Department now under the leadership of Maureen O'Connor Hestoft, a graduate of Northwestern University. Making the effort to find credible sources is one of the arts of proposal-writing that was cultivated by Erie as it pursued a private fund-raising strategy focused on foundations, in addition to churches. Citations used to support this proposal came from:

- Gary Orfield, *Latinos in Metropolitan Chicago: Study of Housing & Employment,* Monograph #6, Latino Institute, 1983.
- G. Alfred Hess, Jr., *Bending the Twig: The Elementary Years & Dropout Rates in the Chicago Public Schools,* Chicago Panel on Public School Policy & Finance, 1987.
- Lori S. Orum, *Making Education Work for Hispanic Americans: Some Promising Community-based Practices,* National Council of La Raza, 1988.

In addition to the usual statistics about levels of poverty in West Town and the high dropout rates at local high schools, the sources Erie consulted pointed out that 45% of the students at Otis Elementary, and 68% at Carpenter, were reading below the norm. The sources also confirmed what Erie already knew, that parents with limited formal education and ability to speak English, were hampered in communicating with their children's teachers, and sometimes even with their own children, as the divide between first and second generation widened in the context of US culture v. parents' home country. PSK proposed providing tutors to improve reading and offering weekly family therapy sessions. Tutors were recruited from Wells High School, who received stipends, translating into the after-school jobs these teens needed. There were also some volunteer tutors recruited from Francis Parker School in Lincoln Park, where Associate Director, Barbara Castellan's children attended school. In 1991, Dolores Raya, one of the PSK tutors from Wells High School, was named a Golden Apple Academy Scholar. The scholarship she won would help her to achieve her goal, she said, to become an elementary school teacher. Once again, Erie proved that volunteers benefit as much as the ones they come to serve.

The success and innovativeness of PSK was recognized when PSK received the Local School Improvement Award from the Citizens Schools Committee on May 23, 1990. This award was noted in an Erie proposal for PSK submitted to Joseph Hickey of Hickey Capital Management, 208 S. LaSalle. Hickey was a friend of Ed Schimmelpfennig, Erie board member and past president, and was persuaded to donate $25,000 through the E. J. Logan Foundation, to support PSK.[281] Given that Hickey was baptized at 4th Pres, this was as much a church donation as a foundation grant. The intertwining of these two sources was an example of the opportunities available to church-based settlements. Besides this gift, and the $12,000 from Jeff Holcomb's cocktail party noted above, United Way provided a Priority Grant of $91,497, $30,737 was allocated from Erie's United Way base grant, and $10,000 came from Chicago Tribune Charities, for a grand total of $156,586. Six figure programs were becoming the norm during the Ravelo years.

Impact of 1986 Federal Amnesty at Erie

By 1989, Erie was experiencing increased demand in the Adult Services area, as the undocumented residents of Chicago, who were given legal status by President Reagan in 1986, when he signed the Immigration Reform and Control Act, were needing help to prepare for citizenship. There were government funds available, under a program called SLIAG (State Legalization Impact Assistance Grants), which Erie used to hire additional staff and to rent space in the basement of the church across the street. Initially, Erie received $300,000 to prepare 1500 adults, over two years, to take the citizenship test. While Erie had been serving immigrants since its inception, this marked the start of a much more formal citizenship program that addressed the need for both educational and legal services. West Town had one of the highest concentrations of amnesty applicants in Chicago. Consequently, when Erie opened the program with its first 300 slots, 1,000 people applied.[282] Classes met four nights a week, in the House and across the street, as applicants needed to learn/improve their ability to read and write English, prepare for an interview in English, and study American History. Regional workshops were held to introduce applicants to the overall process, with attorneys present to evaluate and protect participants from any issues that might get them in trouble during the process. Erie House collaborated with other organizations through the Illinois Coalition of Immigrant and Refugee Rights (ICIRR), to carry out the massive task.

In January, 1990, *The Chicago Reporter* published an article headlined: "Classes pose hurdle for new immigrants."[283]   The writer was addressing an observation of a significant drop in enrollment in SLIAG classes. The findings in this article foreshadowed the long fight to shift more SLIAG and other public funding to CBOs to teach adults, and away from the City Colleges of Chicago and CPS. The rationale for the shift was based on the finding that CBOs demonstrated better performance and higher cultural sensitivity. The reporter stated,

> *Although the community groups have had less funding, they have handled twice the number of students as the City Colleges which got $2.2 million, and the public schools, which got $4.9 million, the largest contract in the state. . . Community groups taught 24,000 students by last September (1989) compared to 7,000 at the City Colleges, and 5,000 at city schools.*[284]

With these kinds of statistics, community-based organizations that offered adult education, as well as various types of job training, formed a coalition called CATE (Community Action for Training and Education). Led by Erie Neighborhood House and the Polish American Alliance, through their consistent advocacy in Springfield, adult ed funders like the Illinois Community College Board (ICCB), eventually began to make larger grants directly to CBOs, not just community colleges. It was an important victory for adult learners and their CBO advocates. As part of CATE's advocacy, they invited an obscure but supportive state senator to address one of their meetings. Before the session, voices were murmuring: "Barack who?" After hearing him speak, they made a note of the name "Obama."

Groundwork Laid for Expansion of Child Care and Strategies to Address Gentrification

On May 12, 1989, the United Way announced its special focus on the issue of affordable child care. The fact sheet that accompanied this announcement, undoubtedly played a part in the unfolding of state government mandates to expand child care services. Fortunately, funding was also made available to support implementation of the mandate. This is not always the case. Three years later, the data and the mandates and the funding would shape Erie House's decision to start down the road to its greatest growth spurt since the construction of the new building in 1935-36. This would be the acquisition and development of the property at 1701 W. Superior, in order to quadruple the size of its pre-school child care program and add another classroom for school-age.

Here is the data United Way put out pertaining to the "Chicago Area" in 1989:

- 40% (178,000) of working women have children under the age of six;
- 66% (330,000) of working women have school age children;
- Of these, 25% are single parents;
- By 1995, expect 2/3 of mothers with pre-schoolers will be in the workforce;
- Market rate day care can absorb 20-30% of a family's income;
- 17% of all Chicago children live in poverty;
- Existing affordable day care options meet only 25% of the need;
- 33% (112,000) of children ages 6-12 are left home alone after school.[285]

With Erie House only able to accommodate 40 pre-schoolers at 1347 W. Erie, this was a call to step up and do more. Call acknowledged in 1995.

But, before specific plans began for that expansion, Ravelo worked with board and staff to address some hard questions. In addition to the Needs Assessment Ravelo initiated, almost as soon as he arrived at Erie, a Strategic Planning Committee, with members from the board and the staff, was also formed. This group concerned itself with the potential impact of gentrification on Erie Neighborhood House, and examined the question of how Erie should respond to the displacement of their participants, as Erie entered its 120th year of service. It was noted that, over that 120 years, strengths and weaknesses had emerged. Their key conclusions can be summarized as follows:

- Erie's small service area, a port of entry, was effective for many years, but also limited Erie's ability to expand outstanding programs, affect public policy, and pursue some funding opportunities;
- Erie has addressed community needs with effective programs, but the dominance of direct service programming, has focused Erie's fundraising and staffing on sustaining those programs, and not enough on increasing resources to do the advocacy work that is sorely needed as well;
- Both board and staff need to better reflect the community Erie serves.[286]

The committee also made some observations about how the community of Latin American immigrants being served in the 1990s was the same, and yet different from, the immigrants of yesterday. On the one hand, just like European immigrants before them, they were escaping political oppression, poverty, and lack of economic opportunity. But unlike their predecessors, simply "working hard" no longer yielded adequate wages to support a family. Thus, the oxymoron of "the working poor", with median incomes of roughly $12,987 per year.[287] With their language barriers, and the loss of many manufacturing jobs, they were relegated to low-wage, unstable, service jobs with no benefits. These were jobs that had not benefited from the labor union victories of the late 19th and early 20th centuries. With the dramatic high school dropout rate local youth were reducing their chances of "next-generation-success" that earlier immigrant groups experienced, including their own Mexican-American ancestors, in the first half of the 20th century.

So, given the challenges faced by Erie's current immigrant participants, and the addition of a new class of gentry outside Erie's front door, the question was raised: will the Erie mission change? Options on the table:

1. **STAY:** Remain at the present location, serving the changing neighborhood as it becomes more affluent
2. **MOVE:** Follow our current disadvantaged clients as they move out of the neighborhood.
3. **A HYBRID OF STAY & MOVE:** Remain at the current location, but also establish outposts in the neighborhoods where prior local residents relocate.
4. **EXPAND SERVICE BOUNDARIES:** So, we can stay, but serve the people where they are.

Options 3 and 4 eventually won out. However, to help address these options at the time, Erie had formed a unique partnership. The work of that partnership unfolded as the "Chicago Neighborhood Experiment."[288]

"Chicago Neighborhood Experiment" (CNE)

As the board was informed, this venture was based on a partnership; the lead partner was The Chicago Council on Urban Affairs (CCUA) and their executive director, Ann Seng (a former member of the School Sisters of St. Francis, the order of nuns that served at Santa Maria). Laurina Uribe was hired as a consultant to coordinate CNE activities, and she wrote the final report. Initial funding of $37,000 was secured from the Chicago Community Trust and Northern Trust Bank. By the end of the project, the total raised was $152,000, with more funding coming from the Joyce, Stewart Mott, and MacArthur Foundations, plus $15,000 from the Illinois Department of Commerce and Community Affairs (DCCA) and $15,000 in CDBG funds from the Chicago Department of Planning. It only took about 40 years for government to spend dollars to assist neighborhoods to plan for themselves, rather than demolish them. It was a moment. But, in the long run, the neighborhood was saved, only to succumb to market forces, that would eventually take over in lieu of the Department of Urban Renewal.

The general concept behind the CNE was to come up with an economic development strategy that, in the face of emerging gentrification, would improve the income of local residents, so as to avoid being displaced, as rents escalated. An interesting group of people were recruited as "partners" to assist in the development of this strategy. They included:

- Mary Ritchie, Director of CABA (Chicago Ashland Business Association);
- Ralph Bogan, CEO, National Security Bank; Robert McKay, VP;
- James Cosme, Principal, Otis School;
- David Peterson, Principal, Wells High School;
- David Luna, Latino Institute;
- Larry Rosser, Chicago Capital Fund;

- George Kaledonis, Chicagoland Enterprise Center
- Larry Pressl, Fulton-Carroll Consulting Group (from the Kinzie Industrial Corridor);
- Virginia Ojeda, VP McDonald's/EVO Enterprises
- Blanca Almonte, Family Focus;
- Carlos Hernandez, Bickerdike's Mercado project;
- Dan Joranko, NCO;
- Maureen Hellwig, community resident for 22 years, urban planner with connections to NCO and Community 21 project;
- Maria D'Amezcua, Wells PTA president & president of Mexican American Business & Professional Women.[289]

From Ravelo's perspective, the CNE project was an effort to position Erie House to be proactive, to protect their low-income neighbors from rampant displacement, or at least, soften the blow. He said:

> *Erie House will always serve its neighbors by meeting their immediate needs. But the Chicago Neighborhood Experiment has an additional goal: to plan for the future, before it is upon us. We cannot stop gentrification, but we can influence its effects on the residents of West Town.*[290]

The first step in the project was to sharpen their understanding of what the neighborhood was up against. The project turned to the Voorhees Center and the Center for Urban Economic Development (CUED) at the University of Illinois Chicago (UIC). John Betancur was a UIC scholar/activist who provided the following definition:

> *Gentrification, the taking over of a low-income neighborhood by high-income 'intruders,' is the product of an urban re-structuring in which low-*

income people, already sorely pressed by the loss of jobs in the manufacturing sector, now lose their home communities to highly paid professional and service workers whose incomes enable them to buy and rehabilitate aging buildings.[291]

Further research and discussion around gentrification led to the conclusion that initial strategies to address gentrification, that had focused on development of affordable housing, so low-income people could stay, were insufficient. There needed to be a strategy that addressed income as well. Even Bickerdike, who had effectively pursued the affordable housing strategy, was currently pursuing a companion economic development project, called El Mercado, to support small food retailers and provide local jobs. But retail jobs could not provide the kind of income that manufacturing did, offering relatively low-skill jobs with relatively high wages. Those jobs were either being replaced with technology or being transported/exported elsewhere.

Based on this understanding, the project moved forward with the following organizing assumptions:

1) Providing stable, high-paying jobs in the neighborhood would permit residents to stay that would maintain economic and ethnic diversity through "market forces";
2) Significant numbers of residents would be interested in organizing and undertaking an effort to stay;
3) Significant numbers of employers would be interested in undertaking efforts to stay if neighborhood desirability improved;
4) Some downtown companies would hire from West Town, if they were introduced to this opportunity, and workers had the skills they needed;
5) Both short and long-term strategies were needed to make this happen.[292]

In other words, strategies were needed in the short term, to hold a finger in the dike; longer term, the flood waters needed to be re-directed. The one was a more local effort; the other, on the scale of a public works project. Finally, social service and economic development programs would need to work in tandem with advocacy for different public policies.

Based on these assumptions, Ravelo announced that Erie House was adding a new Economic Development Department, as of January, 1989.[293] Short term strategies needed to be undertaken right away. In the first phase of taking inventory on current demographics, the project used and updated the *Community 21 Plan for Improvement* (1977) and data gathered by UIC for Bickerdike. They contacted June La Velle, Director of the Industrial Council of Northwest Chicago (ICNC) to get a handle on what was going on with industrial real estate, as so-called "loft" developments were snatching up old manufacturing properties.

The longer-term policy changes turned out to be complicated by inadequate, even hostile, local political representation that would unfold in 1995. Even that complication would be challenged by the groundwork laid in 1990, as community residents and businesses were engaged in the process through focus groups.

In the final report, published in March, 1990, the following major strategy directions were laid out:

1. The Partnership will assist in the formation of a Leadership Development Institute (LDI) oriented to the educational, employment, and social-support needs of 50 target-area, low-income residents per year.
2. The Partnership will assist in building ongoing relationships with 5 neighborhood-based industrial firms, to support their retention in the

neighborhood, and 5 major Loop corporations, with the goal of securing their commitment to hire LDI grads.

3. The Partnership will assist in the research & design of means to acquire control over as much real estate (land & buildings) as possible. [Partly BRCs job already][294]

Much of what Erie learned from this project, as well as the Needs Assessment Ravelo had called for earlier, shaped the first five years of the 1990s.

Conclusions Reached

After what was probably about 18 months of study and reflection, the options Erie's leadership decided to pursue, beginning in the last 5 years of the 20th century, were a combination of the ones laid out above, particularly Options 3 and 4. Option 3, to remain at the present location, but establish outposts where Erie's priority of assisting low-income immigrants could be continued, was one of the choices. That eventually became Little Village, but other areas were considered as well. Option 4, to expand service boundaries beyond Erie's long-term description of an area just a half mile square, was also adopted. In Erie's experience, people would travel a little farther for excellence. Option 4 was basically making that official.

But in addition to the stay/move options first laid out, the CNE pointed to programmatic considerations as well. The ultimate decision to dramatically expand the child care program at the pre-school level addressed the "travel for excellence" assumption, and supported the working poor who needed affordable child care. It allowed mom and dad to work, increasing family median incomes and providing more to put toward rising rents. A new programming commitment was made to economic development that would lead to:

1. A workforce preparation program to help participants access better jobs;
2. A renewed partnership with Bickerdike to develop a new type of affordable housing, with the concept of an Erie Community Land Trust as a secondary strategy; and
3. A Leadership Development Institute (LDI) that would empower residents to take the reins of their survival in a gentrifying environment.[295]

The latter was not exactly the Alinsky-style approach of the early days of NCO, but it did underscore the same notion Alinsky had -- that ordinary people had the capacity and desire to shape their own destiny – with a little help from their friends.

As Time Goes By – Erie House Celebrates 120 years

There were two events to celebrate this important milestone. One took place in May, called "120 years of Caring," and one in September, 1990.[296] In May, the party was at Goose Island Brewery, in the "Goose Wing" at 1800 N. Clybourn. Erie had a new Director of Development, Maureen O'Connor, who helped to plan this event, and a new logo, the one with dancing figures in turquoise. While the revenue from this event was modest, the real gain was in attracting the support of Goose Island owner, John Hall. He eventually became an Erie board member and generous supporter for the next 30 years.

The second event was designed to celebrate the ethnic diversity of West Town and Erie's long history. The schedule of entertainment included: The Clemente High School Steel Band, *Estudiantina* (a Mexican singing group), a German children's choir, Polish dancers, *El Taller de Bomba Y Plena de Puerto Rico,* and Shanta the Storyteller. There would be bocci ball, a Double "Dutch" jump rope demonstration, Italian ice, Polish sausage, tacos and Puerto Rican rice. Over 500 people attended and shared memories that went all the way back to Florence Towne. Those who could not come to Chicago for the celebration, sent along letters where they shared what they remembered about Erie. They are too numerous to include all, but here are a few excerpts from their remarks.

Vincent Genova -- remembered 1940-41 and wonderful times at Camp Gray in Michigan

John Hughes -- was a student pastor at Erie Chapel in 1940-41, became pastor of Lakeview Presbyterian Church, where he later encountered Rose Genova Stortzman and Daisy Genova Braucher, sisters to Carmella, co-founder, with Dr. Snyder, of the Erie Clinic, in 1957.

Doug & Carolyn Cedarleaf -- left Erie 42 years ago for Spokane, WA, and just celebrated their 50th wedding anniversary. Remembered Miss Florence, Mom Savino, and those ham actors, Tony DeVincent and Vincent Genova.

Ted Roos -- been traveling with the Community Renewal Society chorus to Leningrad and Scandinavia. Feeling very Swedish, and reminded that few could make music like the Erie bunch. He admonished: "Keep on singing."

Rose Genova Stortzman -- to her, "Erie House represents the joy of human love." She recalled: the stand we took against racial prejudice, led by Doug Cedarleaf; Miss Florence's story time, with sound effects, plus songs for every occasion, and "The Christmas Doll." She was 8 when the new building opened in 1936. Miss Florence was her godmother, whose secretary, in the late 1940s, was Japanese. She remembered Miss Florence's companion, Miss Fanny Remer, who Rose described as a sort of "bodyguard." Basically, she reflected, "Besides home, this is where we lived."[297]

The 120th drew coverage by the *Sun-Times* and *Chicago Tribune.* On Sept. 5, 1990, "For 120 years, Erie House has soothed the unsettled," was the headline for an article by John McCarron in the *Tribune.* He noted that Erie's roots go back further than Hull House, and says, "Settlement houses gave new Americans a toehold. . . There they could learn English at night and leave their children by day." He goes on, "For all its good works, Erie may finally be up against a wave of newcomers it cannot help: yuppies."[298]

Ravelo's response to this observation, reflects the serious study and discussion under way in regard to Erie's future. "We are seeing displacement as buildings are sold and rents go up. We are looking at the possibility of opening satellites in the neighborhoods where our participants have been forced to move, or we could move Erie House all together. No one wants to talk about that option." Mc Carron closes with, "Even a settlement house gets unsettled after 120 years."[299]

On their own anniversary literature, Erie takes the opportunity to remind everyone of their history and lays out their current mission statement for the 1990s, which, again, reflects the strategic direction the CNE suggested:

> *Erie House maintains a consistent standard of*
> *excellence in serving low-income individuals and*
> *families in this largely Latino community, by*
> *promoting their self-sufficiency and fostering*
> *community economic development and stability.*[300]

Later in the year, in the Fall of 1990, I joined the board along with Esther Nieves. Both of us would eventually transition from board member to staff member. Another name that shows up that year on the staff roster of 49 people is Ric

Estrada, working with a youth peer-counseling program. Esther and Ric would serve back-to-back terms as executive director from 1997 to 2010.

While Erie always honors its past and celebrates its anniversaries, it is also continually opening new doors, experimenting with innovative programs. So, in its 120th year, Erie launched a new child care program. It was called the Day Care Family Homes (DCFH) Network, and in the context of Erie's community economic development strategy, its purpose was twofold. It was designed to: 1) serve working parents of even younger children, 6 months to two years, and 2) help women to start their own business as licensed, professional day care providers. These goals would be accomplished with support through a network of peers, and under the guidance of an organization that had been doing pre-school since they opened their Kindergarten in 1893. The Day Care home was not the new idea, the Network was. Erie had learned that too many of these woman-owned, small businesses had failed on their own. In the context of the Network, with Erie House, like Big Mama, in their corner, showing them the ropes, the success rate of these businesses increased dramatically. Moreover, Erie House helped them to get a contract with the city, so they could serve lower income families, and then managed that contract on their behalf. Erie had a line item in the contract to help cover the cost of a Network Coordinator, and the bookkeeping involved in managing the contract. It was a win/win.

In July, 1991, Ravelo announced that he had just been awarded a Community Service Fellowship by the Chicago Community Trust, that would support the opportunity for him to study youth entrepreneurship experiments, at home and abroad. Shortly thereafter, he offered me a job as Director of Community Economic Development. He had gotten to know me through our work together on the Chicago Neighborhood Experiment.[301]

Could a Housing Co-op Strategy Be One of the Answers to Gentrification?

During 1991 and 1992, Erie was gathering information on housing co-ops to educate staff and community leaders.[302] Research revealed an article from *Cooperative Housing Journal:* "Mutual Housing Associations: Expanding Housing Cooperative Potentials," December 14, 1990, by Carr Kunze. Around this same time, a new organization emerged called the Chicago Mutual Housing Network (CMHN), a non-profit supporting the development of housing cooperatives. It began in space provided by the Center for Neighborhood Technology (CNT), at their Wicker Park location, about two miles from Erie House. Erie House had been associated with CNT in the 1980s when they brokered an energy audit and low-interest loan to Erie House, from the Amoco Foundation, to do an energy retrofit of Erie's building.[303] In December, 1991, CNT staff members, Michael Freedberg and Gail Schecter, published a report: "The Tenant Ownership Project: Preserving Affordable Housing through Alternative Ownership Strategies for Low-income Families." This work was prompted by such data as appeared in a *Sun-Times* article on August 4, 1991, titled "Area Home Values Climb." The article reported on significant increases in home values, 1980-1990, by community area. *West Town showed a 211% increase*; Logan Square, 138%; Humboldt Park, 95%.

Clearly, this data correlated with the CNE report's red flag concerning gentrification. CNT was announcing that the Tenant Ownership Project would provide one-stop technical and training services to tenants in Chicago interested in "collective home ownership." They outlined a nine-step co-op conversion process and provided a comparison of rental housing to limited equity co-op housing.[304] No doubt, the availability of this kind of technical assistance, the support of CMHN, and

Bickerdike's own experience with co-ops, from their work developing the Woolman-Washington Co-op, all shaped Erie's path to consideration of this option as a strategy to address the continued loss of affordable housing options in West Town. The co-op idea would continue to evolve through 1995.

But on Friday afternoon, January 17, 1992, longer term strategies were displaced by an extraordinary phenomenon. Multiple gas explosions occurred at 21 locations less than one mile from Erie House, in the area NCO used to call Marshall's Corners; yuppies were calling it River West by then. The explosions occurred on both sides of Milwaukee Avenue, between Grand Avenue (550 north) and Chestnut Street (900 north), running parallel to and just east of the Kennedy Expressway.[305] Two people died, and two were hospitalized with serious injuries. Forty people had to be evacuated from their homes in the bitter cold. Erie Neighborhood House and Northwestern University Settlement House (NUSH) partnered with the city's Department of Human Services (DHS) to provide disaster relief services. Erie offered children's clothing and household items from its Thrift Shop and food from its Emergency Food Pantry; NUSH offered crisis counseling and also food. Barbara Castellan, acting director while Ravelo was away on his fellowship, made calls to the McCormick Tribune and Continental Bank Foundations requesting some emergency funding. But, in the Erie House tradition, the churches stepped up with cash and food donations. First Church of Oak Park, Elmhurst Presbyterian, churches in Lake Forest, Glen Ellyn, and Wilmette packed up station wagons and drove supplies into the city to aid the victims of the explosions. The Sunday School at River Forest collected 50 bags of groceries.

While 1992 opened with neighborhood drama, Erie programs acted out their parts on a smaller stage. But there was excitement a few weeks after the explosions when the

Youth Options College Fair welcomed three times the number of students and parents than they had the year before; a total of 300 attended. Dennis Puhr was hired as director of the After-School Program and creatively blended PSK into his new strategy that he named El Barrio Nuevo/The New Neighborhood. Mr. Rogers was alive and well at Erie House, where being a neighbor was an ongoing invitation and commitment.

A Housing Action Group, later called the Community Alliance for Strategic Action (CASA), was organized to engage more neighbors to work with Erie on that affordable housing strategy. But they were not just a think tank. They collected 200 signatures in support of a city ordinance that had been proposed years earlier, but was finally making it to the City Council floor for a vote. The ordinance would facilitate local acquisition of city-owned vacant lots adjacent to their property, for as little as $1.00 and some processing fees. The idea was originally proposed by the Community 21 Planning Committee in the early 1980's.[306] Ironically, it was Alderman Terry Gabinski, not a close ally of Erie House or Community 21, who sponsored the ordinance which passed. Lesson learned: Some good ideas get implemented when you least expect them to, and later than you ever imagined possible. Ten years after it was initially proposed, Erie residents were still pushing for local control, and ANA (Adjacent Neighbor Acquisition) was another tool to maintain that control, another "solution" that Fr. Janiak had been calling for to deal with the great number of vacant lots that he already concluded could be obstacles or opportunities in the late 1960s. The Bickerdike solution, infill housing, was the best solution, but ANA rewarded residents who stayed in the neighborhood with a side yard– next best.

In addition to organizing the Housing Action Group, the new Economic Development Department was also moving forward on the employment issue and the

Leadership Development Institute (LDI), that the CNE report and Erie's strategic plan called for. United Way Priority Grants for 1992 would be focused on workforce development programs. So, Erie wrote a proposal for a new program called Pathways to Success (PTS), and was rewarded with a 3-year grant totaling $1.25 million. This allowed Erie to hire two staff: William Acevedo, as PTS Coordinator, and Pam Johnson, as Administrative Assistant.[307] Alfonso Cortes was hired to work on the LDI. One Puerto Rican, one African American, one Mexican, in that order–the diversification of staff Ravelo had called for.

The initial program that Erie had proposed had two sectoral components. One was a bank teller training program that was quite successful. This was at a time when there were still numerous local banks, not just branches of bigger banks. Bob McKay, a VP at National Security Bank, and an Erie Board member, worked with staff to engage other local banks in supporting this employment initiative, that focused on these local, neighborhood banks. Two factors influenced this decision: First, local banks were easier to get to, and second, the work environment was less intimidating than a larger bank downtown. Banks provided staff to conduct trainings at Erie House and to prepare students for their interviews. They also pledged to give PTS graduates priority in selection for job interviews. No guarantees they would be hired, but at least they got a foot in the door. The PTS curriculum ran for 10 months, with classes meeting two evenings a week. There was a kick-off dinner on September 9, 1993, sponsored by Northern Trust and Manufacturers Bank, with State Senator Miguel Del Valle as keynote speaker. After that, representatives from about 16 local banks in West Town, and surrounding community areas, gathered for lunch at Erie, quarterly, to get an update on the program, and enjoyed the opportunity to network with each other. Another successful Erie collaboration was under way.

Looking at the list of participating banks 25 years later, 10 of the 16 no longer existed.

The second component of PTS was designed as a "bridge" program. Erie House was certainly among the first, if not *the* first, to use the term. This type of program was designed to bridge the gap between the skill levels generally achieved through ESL or ABE classes, and the next level of reading and math skills needed to access sectoral skills training and/or some entry level jobs. Unlike basic level remedial classes, bridge programs have a "contextualized curriculum." In other words, while the student continues to work on reading and math, their assignments pertain to the career path they are working towards. For example, in a health care bridge, students study medical terminology and read about health care occupational situations. They are also given practice tests for the skills training program they plan to enter, which greatly enhances successful admissions. And finally, workplace skills like decision-making, problem-solving, and teamwork are also addressed.

In 1993, Erie was experimenting with bridge classes to prepare people for training in a few manufacturing sub-sectors, training that was offered by other CBOs like the Jane Addams Resource Corporation, Greater West Town Project, and Chicago Commons. This approach was not as successful as the bank training program in this first round, but was revisited in 2006, and, along with a health care bridge, took off in PTS Phase II, with a focus on CNC jobs (Computerized Numerical Control) in the manufacturing sector.

Overall, Erie was successful in its workforce development efforts, especially with immigrants, due to its cultural sensitivity and the array of support services available to the participants. At Erie, people were seldom using only one service at a time. Child care, health care, counseling, tutoring, etc. were there to facilitate successful workforce outcomes, and vice versa, as child care parents found out about PTS and used it to find a career path and improve their incomes.

That summer, as PTS was getting organized, Erie received news that Evelyn Lyman had passed away on July 23, 1992, at a nursing home in Missouri, at age 82. She had played a critical role at Erie from her arrival in 1959 until she left more than 20 years later, in 1981. A memorial service was held for her at Erie House on September 15. People who had known Evelyn and worked with her came to pay their respects: Merri Ex, Chuck Armstrong, Jim McClure, Angel Carroll, and Mary Burns all said a few words of tribute. As a salute to Miss Lyman, a quote from a George Bernard Shaw composition, called "Legacy," appeared in the program. This is an abbreviated excerpt:

> *This is the joy in life, being used for a purpose. . .*
> *Being a force of nature. . .I am of the opinion that*
> *my life belongs to the whole community, and as I*
> *live, it is my privilege to do for it whatever I can*
> *and be thoroughly used up when I die. For the*
> *harder I work, the more I love. . . Life is no brief*
> *candle to me. It is a sort of splendid torch, which*
> *I've got a hold of for the moment, and I want to*
> *make it burn as brightly as possible before handing*
> *it on to future generations.*[308]

That same year, Evelyn would have been sad to know, Erie closed its Thrift Shop, due to an increase in rent for the space Erie could not justify paying. It was hoped a more affordable space would be found where it could be re-opened. That did not happen. The Thrift Shop was displaced, a victim of the same gentrification its patrons were experiencing.

The Capital Campaign for Child Care Expansion Gets Under Way

But as one program closed, Erie was well into its newest venture, on the road to child care program expansion. In May of 1992, Ravelo convinced the Erie Board to approve the launch of a capital campaign to develop the property at 1701 W. Superior. While the board had some reservations about their ability to raise $500,000, they stepped up to the task. Jack O'Kieffe would take office as board president in September, and provided the leadership the board needed to get the job done. O'Kieffe was a Session member at First Presbyterian Church of Wilmette, and had been on the board for about 10 years at that time. He was VP for Sales in the Chicago office of Stifel Nicolaus Company, a regional brokerage firm headquartered in St. Louis.

By October, 1992, Erie was gathering support letters to help secure the approval of this expansion by state and local governments, to get the public support they needed to accompany their capital campaign. Letters came in from the Erie Family Health Center, Family Focus, Gardner, Carton & Douglas, the Private Bank, Emerson House, North Avenue Day Nursery, LEED Council, Casa Central, and Association House. In December, the Executive Director of the Illinois Facilities Fund (IFF), Trinita Logue, announced that four child care centers in the Chicago area had been selected for a statewide initiative to help low-income workers. They were Erie Neighborhood House in West Town, Chicago Commons in Humboldt Park, Christopher House in Uptown, and Community Mennonite Day Care in Markham, IL. It should be noted *that three out of four of the centers chosen were settlement houses.* The IFF exists to help make expansion programs more affordable by keeping the cost of financing construction cheaper than what the private banking industry offers. Following this

285

announcement, Alderman Ted Mazola introduced an ordinance to rezone 1701 W. Superior.

An article appeared in the *Chicago Tribune*, February 10, 1993, with the headline: "Lots of eyes on day-care expansion try," by Wilma Randle.[309] Randle gave a good overview of the importance of child care and the state of Illinois' failure to address it. She made the argument that Erie House heard every day, "If I don't have a safe place for my children to stay while I work, I can't work." Child care that is subsidized, and therefore affordable, is unquestionably one of the key services that allows low-income parents to join the full-time workforce. And Center-based child care is generally more reliable than a sitter, willingness of family members to do the job notwithstanding. And yet, Randle reported, in 1992, DCFS estimated the state was serving only 22,000 of the 200,000 eligible for subsidized child care! The Department of Health later broke this down by community area. West Town had 265 slots for 2,259 eligible children; Humboldt Park had only 85 slots for 2,140 eligible children. These dismal statistics were backed up by a report published by The Center for the Study of Social Policy in Washington, DC that ranked Illinois 35th among the states in providing adequate child care services. No wonder Voices for Illinois Children gave Illinois a D-minus in child care. Voices Director, Jerry Stermer, went on to point out that child care addresses two very critical needs. First, it provides important early childhood education, giving youngsters that "head start" on learning. Second, the income from and the dignity of working, will allow parents to provide that child with the support they will need all along the way to successful adulthood.[310] Indicating that Erie shared this perspective, Ravelo added:

> *Throughout our history, Erie Neighborhood House*
> *has maintained that child care that is within the*

economic means of our neighbors allows them to work and provide the income and security their families need to lead well-functioning lives.[311]

No doubt, the fact that the IFF and DCFS put resources on the table, made the Erie House expansion possible. But there were other elements of this project that also contributed to its success. These were finding a building and partnering with the Erie Family Health Center to develop it. In a built environment like the West Town of 1992, there were few parcels of vacant land large enough to build a new facility of the size that would be required. So, rehab of an existing building would be preferable. Finding such a building, in a desirable residential area, with convenient public transportation nearby, was a dream come true. The building at the corner of Superior and Paulina, just four blocks from Erie House, was such a building. It had been a place where cardboard boxes had been manufactured, at a time when industrial uses got mixed in with residential uses, without serious objections. In fact, before cars were so available, having the factory walking distance from your house made total sense, especially if it was not a smelly, smokestack operation. But as manufacturing changed and moved up and out, this building was abandoned and sat vacant for many years. But prospects for the owner to sell were looking brighter in 1992. When ENH and EFHC came shopping, there were other potential buyers that were looking for old industrial buildings to convert to loft apartments. As luck would have it, or the will of the God of immigrants and Presbyterians, the owner preferred to sell to the Erie partnership. He told them that his family had done well because of the workers they hired from this neighborhood. If another generation of workers could use his building to get the child care and health care they needed, then he wanted his building to house that kind of service. He wanted to pay it forward.

The second element, the partnership with Erie Family Health Center, was also key. As Rafael recalled, 1701 was a large, four-story building and would have been a lot for Erie House to take on by itself. As fate would have it, the clinic was looking to move from their space at Chicago and Paulina, and this move of just one block would certainly keep them in the area, which was one of their requirements. Furthermore, both agencies could see the advantage of having one building where low-income families could get affordable child care and health care side by side. So, the agreement was struck. Erie House would occupy the bottom two floors and the clinic the top two. That agreement was the basis for eventually setting up two "condominiums" as the way to structure ownership and management of the property.

It also helped that this was not "the clinic" that Erie had started 36 years ago. By 1992, EFHC was the second largest community health care center in the state and had the third largest WIC program. It was a nationally recognized model for the integration of health care and substance abuse treatment. In 1992, it served 14,335 individuals, 90% of whom were below the poverty level, and 48% were on Medicaid. Only 6% had private insurance. 83% were Hispanic.[312] Their campaign goal was $2.2 million!

Boyer/Hoppe Associates were hired as architects for the project that would take about one year to complete. The first major donations to the Capital Campaign, besides the O'Kieffe kick-off donation of 50K, started to come in. Wilmette Presbyterian, the O'Kieffe's church, gave $10,000. Mr. & Mrs. Jack Mabley (*SunTimes* reporter) gave $5,000, and $8,000 came in from the Palatine Presbyterian Women's Mission Committee. These and other donations totaled $100,000–20% down, 80% to go.[313]

Another Erie House Initiative for 1993: Youth Options Unlimited

Thus far in the1990s, Erie completed the Chicago Neighborhood Experiment and issued the CNE report, began to explore affordable housing co-ops, launched Pathways to Success to address employment, securing $1.25 million to do so, and became one of four applicants approved by the IFF to expand its child care program, requiring the acquisition of a new building and the launch of a capital campaign. While all that was going on, Rafael won a Community Trust Fellowship and was away for a year. When he returned, in the Spring of 1993, he announced one more initiative, the formation of Youth Options Unlimited (YOU).

As Ravelo described it, this was a collaboration of 10 social service agencies in West Town, offering a new model of service for youth. When it started, YOU included Casa Central, Association House, Emerson House, Onward House, North Avenue Day Nursery, Northwestern University Settlement House (NUSH), Erie Family Health Teen Center, Family Focus, and the Infant Welfare Society. It was funded by a grant of $1.7 million over two years. Two clusters of agencies were formed, and Erie led the southeast cluster. Bonnie Capaul, a former ENH board member and local resident, was hired to coordinate the southeast cluster. But the cluster concept was abandoned the following year and Erie and Capaul led the full collaborative. The concept involved making a bus available for each cluster, allowing youth to travel to the agency with the programs of interest to them, and/or to secure services they needed, not available at their home agency. A schedule of options would be revised and published on a quarterly basis.

In addition to YOU, Erie was involved in another collaboration for youth programming, working with Emerson House, just 4 blocks west of Erie House. This collaboration involved an innovative project at Wells High School, known as "School-within-a-School." A third collaborator was the Street-Level Video Project. Street-Level's primary interest was to produce work about issues of youth culture, education, jobs, family, and gangs, and to change the perception people have about youth, inside and outside the community. Artists and youth worked together to create videos to stimulate a dialogue about social and cultural issues in the community, *el vecindario.* Key collaborators were: Denise Zaccardi of Community Television Network, Lucy Gomez from Emerson, Olga Lopez from Erie House, and Nilda Ruiz Pauley. Pauley was a Wells teacher, engaged with School-within-a School, and a long-time resident, as well as director of her own dance company, "Lasting Impressions."

To sum up, in his Executive Director Report, that appeared in the ENH News, Spring, 1993 edition, Ravelo said:

> *Growth, expansion, excitement, collaboration and integration – all of these words have a new, special meaning to us at Erie House today. Two major programs (child care expansion & YOU) soon to start will affect the way we have conducted business for over a century.*[314]

Red Ink and Red Flag at United Way

While Erie House's United Way (UW) base allocation for FY93 was still substantial, at $250,271, they received a letter from UW on June 10, 1993, alerting member agencies to future reductions due to reduced intake from member companies. Looking back, the historic importance of Community Fund/United Way funding for Erie House, comes through by examining this fund's contribution as a percentage of the overall Erie budget.

- 1930s: 20%
- 1945: 25%
- 1955: 28%
- 1960: 25%
- 1975: 36%[315]

In terms of dollars, by 1982, Erie's base allocation hit the 200K mark. In 1983, it represented 50% of all *private* revenue. As Priority Grants came into existence in the early 1990s, Erie benefitted with awards exceeding a million dollars. Consequently, this 1993 announcement was not to be taken lightly.

How this warning, in 1993, played out over the next 10 years, is illustrated in the following data, that shows an eventual 50% reduction.

- FY93: $250, 271
- FY94: $208,631
- FY95: $194,881
- FY96: $185,061
- FY97: $181,118
- FY98: $162,456
- FY99: $149,624
- FY00: $156,282
- FY01: $156,282
- FY02: $156,282
- FY03: $126,588[316]

Fortunately for Erie, during this same period, public funding was increasing significantly, primarily due to the child care expansion, and, to a significant but lesser extent, with public dollars flowing to YOU, PTS, and adult education in general, and immigration services in particular. Erie also continued to expand support from foundations and corporations, reaching over a half million dollars in FY93, or 26 % of the budget. That offset a gradual decline in financial support from churches and United Way base grants. So, this was the financial situation Ravelo worked with as Erie House was expanding and experimenting during his time as executive director. In the context of this historic shift in revenue sources, the Capital Campaign met its goal, and Erie's budget climbed into the millions by the end of the century.

Both new and older board members helped to make this happen. John Hall, owner of Goose Island Brewery, joined the board in 1990, and became a generous donor. As noted, Jack and Connie O'Kieffe kicked off the Capital Campaign with a donation of $50,000. Bob McKay, of National Security Bank, was replaced on the Board by the new president, James M. Quinn, and Dr. Anne Doege, a pediatrician at EFHC for 20 years, joined the board. Local resident, Norma Gonzalez, came on representing CASA.

In spite of all of this United Way doom and gloom, Erie got one more major gift in 1993. The Community Economic Development Department was awarded a second 3-year Priority Grant, this time, for its affordable housing proposal – the development of 40 units of a scattered-site housing cooperative, in partnership with Bickerdike Redevelopment Corp., now a 26-year-old organization with an extremely successful track record. No one had any idea in 1993 how this proposal would turn into one of the most stressful moments in Erie history. It would be a Charles Dickens moment: . . . *the best of times and the worst of times.*

Transitions and celebrations: By the end of 1993, Barbara Castellan left Erie to take the position of Executive Director at Gads Hill, another settlement house. She was replaced by Esther Nieves, who moved from board to Associate Director. In accepting her new position, Nieves said:

*The array of programs offered at Erie House seek
to create a setting in which the individual becomes
a contributing member of society and a person
imbued with a sense of self-esteem and pride. . .
Erie House is a significant institution, not only in
West Town, but throughout the city.[317]*

Tim Bell was hired as Literacy Coordinator for Adult
Ed. Kent Unruh, who came to Erie House as a Mennonite
Volunteer, was hired as Computer Specialist. Nancy
Gonzalez came on board as Clinical Coordinator for El
Barrio Nuevo, and Carmen Santiago, Erie's receptionist,
celebrated 25 years at Erie.

1994: Honors All Around

1994 was a year of more honors for Rafael Ravelo.
This was a tribute to him, but also a recognition of what
Nieves had observed about Erie House. Its reputation had
moved beyond its old neighborhood boundaries, even
beyond West Town. As further evidence of this broadening
awareness of Erie House, Erie youth appeared in a special
on WTTW, Chicago's public television channel, and the
director of counseling was interviewed on WBEZ, the city's
public radio station.

Because of his role in establishing the Youth Options
Unlimited (YOU) collaborative, Ravelo was one of 15 social
service agency directors invited to make a trip to Northern
Ireland to visit youth centers there. In June, 1994, it was
announced that he was named *United Way of Chicago's
1994 Executive Director of the Year*. This was the 8th year
this award was made "to honor outstanding leadership at a
Chicago-based non-profit human service agency." United
Way cited Ravelo's role in organizing the West Town
Directors Group that then launched YOU, as well as the
plans he initiated to expand child care, and partner with Erie

Family Health Center to develop the Erie Community Center at 1701 W. Superior. They noted he had been awarded a Chicago Community trust fellowship in 1991, and praised him for promoting agency stability and teamwork among the Erie staff. In presenting the award, Dean Taylor, Chairman of United Way of Chicago stated:

> *It's clear that when people want action, they turn to Rafael Ravelo. He leads with intelligence. He leads by example. Erie House is a model of the good that can be achieved through team work, cooperation, and determination.*[318]

It was fitting that Ravelo received this award in 1994, as two of the major projects initiated during his administration were taking giant steps forward. On May 26, just before his award was announced, Erie celebrated a "groundbreaking"/ribbon-cutting ceremony at 1701 Superior. This launched the year it would take to rehab the building for Erie's child care expansion and the new home of the EFHC. Mayor Richard M. Daley attended and praised the model of combining child care and health care in the same building. The new executive director of EFHC, Angela McLemore, was also on hand, noting the new location would double the space for their headquarters and clinic. McLemore was EFHC's first African American director, a graduate of Northwestern and Yale. According to the clinic's fact sheet for the occasion, in 1994, they had 150 employees that were 90% bilingual, and a budget of $7.5 million. Born at Erie House in 1957, there was no doubt the clinic had become a well-functioning adult at 37, doing what every parent hopes for, surpassing them (at least in size, in this case).

On June 30, Erie's Annual Report for FY94, announced that Erie would be partnering with Bickerdike to develop a 40-unit, limited equity, housing co-op.[319] This initiative was under the direction of Erie's Economic Development Department, with community residents providing leadership through CASA (Community Alliance for Strategic Action), and planning was being funded by that United Way Priority Grant.

If this was not enough to keep an executive director busy, plans were under way for celebrating Erie's 125th anniversary in 1995. There would be two main events to mark this anniversary: 1) In May, there would be a Grand Opening Celebration at the new Erie Community Center; 2) In the Fall, there would be a gala at the Drake Hotel, which was also hoped to be a significant fundraiser, the first of its kind for Erie House. Ravelo also noted in the Erie News, summer edition, that during its 125 years, Erie had depended on a dedicated board of directors. Chuck Armstrong, who was marking his 30th year on the board, and David Dangler, his 50th, were both presented with the Erie "Spirit Award." Also, six former board members were made Honorary Life Trustees: Glen and Betty Graham, Laurence Carton, Jim and Lynn McClure, and Gerald Fox.

More award-making was on Erie's agenda in 1994 through their annual "Community Awards Business Breakfast." This event was in its 6th year and was described by Erie's Director of Development, Bill Pfeiffer, as an opportunity to inform local businesses, both retail and manufacturing, of Erie's educational and economic development activities and to solicit their support. It was also an opportunity to honor the success of local business persons in the presence of their business and community neighbors. From its inception, the cost of the breakfast was underwritten by National Security Bank. This bank had a representative on the Erie board for several years and helped to launch the PTS bank training program, eventually endorsed by 19 other banks. It had come a long way since the 1970s, when NCO had challenged its redlining practices.

In 1994, the awardees were local Latinx entrepreneurs: Virginia Ojeda and Zully Alvarado. In 1980, Ojeda and her husband were the first Chicago Latinos to own a McDonald's. By 1994, they had 4 in the West Town and Humboldt Park areas. Virginia earned her degree from Northern Illinois University and worked as a regional manager for the A&P grocery chain. She also worked for the Illinois Department of Children & Family Services and the state's Department of Commerce. In 1991, she had been named National Businesswoman of the Year by the US Hispanic Chamber of Commerce. In her spare time, she served on the boards of LULAC and SER, both Latino-serving organizations in Chicago.

The second awardee, Zully Alvarado, was born in Guayaquil, Ecuador. She came to the US from Ecuador when she was nine years old. She had been a victim of polio and was not able to walk, until, through the kindness of a Catholic missionary, she was brought to Chicago for treatment. She regained her ability to walk, stayed on with a foster family, and eventually earned her college degree in speech pathology and early childhood development. But by the late 1980s she was drawn to fashion design and merchandising and began designing shoes for people with hard-to-fit feet, that look fashionable, not orthopedic. She began showcasing her work at Chicago Originals, a retail incubator that was started in 1988. Eventually, she and a partner bought the incubator and, by 1994, were representing nine small businesses that produced clothing, jewelry, art, textiles, and, of course, shoes. She served on the board of the Chicago Foundation for Women from 1985-1993, and on other boards of organizations that serve women and Latinx. She was included in *Crain's* "40 under 40" feature in September, 1994. Years later, she moved to Gary, IN, and in 2011, founded "Causes for Change International" that provides things like wheelchairs to disabled people in remote areas of the world that lack access to such necessities.

Attendees at the breakfast also heard a keynote address from Ronald Temple, new Chancellor of the City Colleges of Chicago, and a presentation by Erie youth entrepreneurs regarding their new start-up tee shirt production company, "Always New." Israel Perez, nephew of Maria Perez, Erie's Director of HR for many years, was in this youth group. He went on to become principal of Yates School in West Town, in 2016.

One more activity was squeezed onto the calendar in the Spring of 1994. It was a fundraiser called "Opera Night at Monastero's," and was the brainchild of Board president, Jack O'Kieffe. This family-owned, Italian restaurant was located on the northwest side in the Sauganash area of Chicago. One of the things they were known for was hosting an opera night that featured young opera students from the Bel Canto Foundation. Jack approached the owner, about using their banquet room, with the Bel Canto singers, for an Erie fundraiser. With the O'Kieffe's underwriting part of the costs, the first event netted about $16,000. The event was repeated several times and was a popular social event with board members. But Erie continued its struggle to balance the benefit of broad engagement of board members and volunteers with the much-needed benefit of a larger revenue stream. That goal would not be realized for another 10 years.

Having survived the Spring of 1994, Erie was pleased to welcome some good news and a special guest in the Fall. Governor Jim Edgar (R) announced that $1.1 million in grants will fund the first-ever, state-sponsored program in the nation to help immigrants and refugees become citizens. This was a kind of forerunner to the "New Americans Initiative" of 2005. Erie benefited from these funds to support their work with immigrants seeking citizenship, work they had been doing since 1870, but with renewed focus since the Reagan amnesty in the late 1980s.

On October 18, Illinois's US Senator, Paul Simon (D), visited Erie House. Joining Ravelo and Nieves in greeting Senator Simon, was Tim Bell, Director of Adult Education. Bell was front and center because the issue Erie wanted Senator Simon to address was the federal allocation of funds that came to the state for adult education. This was part of the ongoing fight, since 1990, over the allocation of millions of dollars in SLIAG funds to entities like the City Colleges, when the performance numbers indicated that non-profits like Erie did a much better job. In 1994, the Illinois State Board of Education (ISBE) was in charge of allocating federal funds for adult education. They awarded the City Colleges of Chicago about $30 million. The CCC then passed through only $500,000 for numerous CBOs to share. Simon was asked to support a change in policy that would give CBOs direct access to federal dollars. Based on their performance, which they knew to be far superior to the CCC, they could receive much more funding than was currently available to them. Erie House alone, had served 500 adult ed students in FY94, and expected that number to grow to 700 in FY95.

Appreciation for Erie's work in this area was expressed by the students themselves in a 1994 publication called *Portraits*, described as "a text of authentic writings by Latino students in ESL classes at Erie." A few samples follow that comprise the strongest testimony for the change in funding policy Erie was advocating for:

> **José Araya**: "I know how to read and write. . .It is the most beautiful thing in the world... To not know how to read and write is like walking in the darkness."

> **Sylvia Bermudez:** "I am a student at Erie House. . . I like to invite anyone who feels stuck in their life

and wishes to progress forward, to come to our
school to ask for help."

Patricia Campos: "So, it is necessary to study. . .
this is the way we can liberate ourselves from bad
jobs, poverty, and discrimination. . . we need
education." [320]

Whether Simon had a direct hand in the policy
change or not, the policy did change, and ISBE shifted more
federal dollars to CBOs. In December, 1994, Tim Bell and
Erie took the lead in convening 30 organizations,
representing different immigrant groups, to plan an
immigrant education conference. At the conference they
laid out a strategy that began with immigrant education
about their rights, moved on to education of the public about
immigrants, and finally, education of legislators.   They
planned to speak at church forums, hold town hall meetings,
and then rallies and marches. By June of 1995, Erie House
was one of 18 organizations that raised money for a
Washington Post "Justice for Immigrants" ad. Erie Adult Ed
students raised $1,000. Initially, they joined with 59 other
organizations to purchase the ad.   By October, the
"Washington Post Campaign" had gone viral, with 500
organizations contributing $100,000 to buy a full-page ad.

Whether it was Paul Simon or some other elected
official, Erie House was seldom shy about encouraging visits
and photo ops with powerful, and mostly sympathetic
political actors. It was just one strategy among many. Nor
was it shy about going after those who presented themselves
as adversaries, as the next story illustrates.

The Fight for the Erie Co-op: "The Best of Times and the Worst of Times "

Once the 1993 United Way Priority Grant for affordable housing projects was secured, the limited equity co-op that Erie and Bickerdike had proposed began to take definite shape.

Erik Nordgren, a bilingual, former Peace Corps Volunteer, was hired to fill the position of community organizer for the Economic Development Department. While Pathways to Success was rolling along successfully, the importance of community engagement and support for the investment in 40 units of housing, would be a different type of project. Little did Erie House know how different, or how much "community engagement," positive and negative, was on the horizon.

CASA leadership formed the Erie Co-op Steering Committee in April 1994, and suggested that Nordgren head out into the community to interview people and start getting reactions to what Erie and BRC had in mind. He was also assessing the potential interest and eligibility of families that might become co-op members. He reported that of 54 people interviewed, 44 would be eligible based on work status, family size, income, current rent paid, etc. That did not mean they were all interested in moving in, but it was important for Erie leadership to know they were matching the elements of the project to the characteristics of potential co-op members. Erie was also engaging key players in other local community organizations, to invite them to a community meeting in August, 1994, to provide information on the co-op concept and ask for their support. Nordgren provided the following list of those committed to have representation at the meeting:

- Tom Vitton, Near Northwest Civic Committee
- Fr. Alex and Marj Bosley, Santa Maria Addolorata

- Eva Guttierrez, Holy Innocents
- José Alatorre, Northwestern Settlement
- Debbie Both, Onward House
- Carlos DeJesus, Latinos United
- Noble Street Condo Association: Jay Capaul
- Mickie Maher, Eckhart Park Supervisor
- Sister Mary Ellen, The Julia Center
- Francisco Ramos, Centro San Bonifacio
- Bickerdike Tenants at Huron & Noble
- Members of CASA and the Co-op Steering Committee[321]

The plan was to also invite the candidates for 1st Ward Alderman that had announced for the upcoming election on February 28, 1995.

While Erik was out meeting people, he encountered Bryan Boyer, who identified himself as a member of the 1400-1500 Huron Street Block Club, which later extended itself to become the Eckhart Park Neighborhood Council. He informed Erik that his group was opposing a project sponsored by Habitat for Humanity, a non-profit that had been hired by the CHA (Chicago Housing Authority) to develop scattered-site public housing in West Town. He said that his group would challenge Erie's project as well. He refused to distinguish what would be a privately-owned co-op, developed by two respected local organizations, targeting a different income group, where occupants would be co-owners, not tenants.

His group spoke up at the August community meeting, expressing their opposition, while many others expressed their support. Of the two aldermanic candidates, Victoria Almeida, stated her support; Jesse Granato, was ambivalent. Over the next few months, Boyer and Granato worked out a plan they hoped would de-rail the co-op. Unbeknownst to Erie or BRC, they developed and circulated a petition that would place a referendum question on the February 28 ballot, when people came out to vote for alderman. The wording of the referendum was as follows:

Should the Bickerdike Redevelopment Corp. build cooperative housing within those areas of the first ward which are within the area bounded by Racine on the east, Damen on the west, Grand on the south and Division on the north?[322]

The referendum was on the ballot in 11 precincts of the 1st Ward, which roughly represented 4000 voters. Of those voting on February 28, 50% +1 YES votes were required in support of the co-op for the referendum to pass. With only two months until the election, Erie and Bickerdike had to mobilize support quickly. A meeting of what came to be known as the "Affordable Housing Referendum Campaign" was called for January 10, 1995. Meanwhile, Rafael put in a call to Granato, in an effort to get him on record as to what was behind the referendum, make him defend himself. Ravelo also pointed out that the wording of the referendum question was inaccurate. This was an Erie House project, with Bickerdike as the developer partner. Of course, Erie was quite sure that their name was left off intentionally, due to the established credibility of this 125-year-old institution, and the hope that people would think of Bickerdike, like Habitat, as another developer of "public" housing for the poorest of the poor.

On January 20, Granato wrote a letter to Erie, in response to Ravelo's call, and he also addressed a letter to 1st Ward voters. In the letter to Erie, he promised to use the name of Erie House in relation to the co-op from then on. In the letter to voters, he claimed he wanted to make sure the community knew about the project, saying "an informed community is a better community." Of course, he himself, was at the August, 1994 community meeting, and at an Erie-sponsored aldermanic Forum in November. Erie had believed in "an informed community" long before Granato. He said he was using the referendum for education. He did not comment on the question raised regarding the fact that no other private housing developers, active in West Town, were required to "inform the community" about their plans or submit to a referendum. In this letter to 1st ward voters, he stated, **"I also want to assure you that if the community supports this cooperative housing plan, after they have been fully informed about it, then it will have my support also."** [323] It was assumed that a YES vote would indicate such support, and so that is what Erie and Bickerdike set out to ensure.

The agenda for the January 10,1995 meeting was: 1) determine the components of a winning strategy; 2) ascertain people's commitment to implementation of that strategy; 3) assign tasks. In order to win, the following tasks were outlined in Nordgren's notes:

a) The Erie/Bickerdike partnership had 3 weeks to register voters who were Erie allies;

b) The partnership needed to develop its message and get it out there: "Housing for working people; co-op = ownership; vote YES for working families!"

c) To get the word out and demonstrate support for the co-op, Erie would circulate its own petition as a counter-measure to Granato's. Wording for the petition: *"Because home ownership is important for neighborhood stability and quality family life, I support the efforts of Erie House and Bickerdike to build co-op housing for working families in the first ward."*

d) To make sure residents knew that this was an Erie project, and that they understood what this specific co-op housing plan looked like, a Co-op Fact Sheet needed to be developed. A sample text was presented, and variations on this would appear in various pieces developed for the campaign:

ENH, now in its 125th year serving West Town, is working with community residents to plan new housing, to be built in the first ward, that will meet the needs of working families who want to remain in the neighborhood. About 40 units are planned which will be located in 2 and 3 story buildings between Division, Damen, Grand and Racine. Families who wish to live in this housing will purchase shares in a cooperative corporation and become co-owners of this housing along with other shareholders.

e) Door-knocking teams, buttons, youth to help distribute flyers were needed;

f) A press conference should be planned with allies present, along with a media strategy, for both English and Spanish-language media;

g) There must be phone calls the night before the election, and palm cards for the day of.[324]

For anyone familiar with how elections work, and then how they work in Chicago, they will recognize the expertise behind this plan.[325]   Erie's Associate Director, Esther Nieves, a veteran of Harold Washington campaigns, stepped up to personally lead the campaign, along with CASA leaders from the community. Erie crafted and carried out a campaign that Boyer and Granato never imagined possible.

For the next four weeks, door-knocking teams were out every weekend. The referendum press conference was set for January 22, to be attended by Fr. Klajbor from Holy Innocents and Fr. Pelosi from Santa Maria, Efrain Vargas from BRC, CASA leaders, Carlos Colon, Adolfo Perez, and

Martha Franco, the Co-op Steering Committee, and reps from ICNC and the Julia Center. Executive Director, Ravelo, the Director of Community Economic Development, and Nordgren from the Erie staff were ¡Presente! Articles appeared in the local paper, CBO newsletters, and the *Chicago Tribune*.

On January 23, 1995, under the headline: "Erie vote: Blueprint for a fight," Melita Maria Garza described the referendum as a "political football" even if he (Granato) argues he just wanted to generate more discussion. In this same article, State Senator, Miguel Del Valle criticized Granato for misleading voters by leaving out Erie's name, "a pillar of the community that is spearheading this project." "The referendum is totally irresponsible panic-peddling," Del Valle said. "It is a very clever strategy to get people to come out to vote against the measure, and for Granato." The article concludes with a testimonial from Anita Zajac, a Polish American single mom, and member of the Erie Co-op Steering Committee, who argued for "the need for a broader range of housing options for lower income workers in a neighborhood that is gentrifying and raising rents."[326]

On that same date, Steve Neal, in his *Commentary* column for the *Tribune,* wrote:

> *Seeking to play one group off against another isn't leadership. Bringing people together ought to be the role of the 1st Ward's new alderman.*"[327]

In a publication called *New City,* a pundit wrote under the heading "This Week's Biggest Losers": "Jesse Granato, proposing a stealth referendum on Erie House's West Town development, landed the first ward candidate in *agua caliente.*" The story was also picked up in Spanish language newspapers, *La Raza* and *Exito!,* as well as *Extra,* a local bilingual paper.

The press coverage was encouraging, but elections are won with votes, not headlines. To get those votes, Erie and BRC needed to make sure voters really understood what they were voting on. The Co-op Fact Sheet, written in English and Spanish, that was carried door-to-door, highlighted these points:

- Who was Erie Neighborhood House, a good neighbor for 125 years;
- What a co-op building would look like appeared as an illustration of a 3-flat;
- Emphasis on working families and ownership;
- Info on monthly costs to co-op members, ranging from $355 for a 1 bedroom to $546 for 4 bedrooms, below market, but only affordable to working families;
- Eligible annual income range: $12,000-30,000;
- Facts about rising rents in West Town, up 212%;
- Wording of the referendum with precinct numbers where it would appear on the ballot;
- Testimonials from local residents and pastors;
- Info on who was funding the project from the private sector: United Way, Campaign for Human Development (an arm of the Catholic Church), & an Episcopal Church Economic Justice grant;
- **Punch 152 to vote YES![328]**

About 46 volunteers made up canvassing teams that hit all 11 precincts in 2.5-hour shifts of door-knocking on weekends. Posters were placed in stores in the Chicago/Ashland shopping area and every local settlement house displayed them. Passers, runners, and closers with poll watching credentials were recruited for election day. A final rally was held in the Erie gym on February 22. The gym was packed with over 300 people, standing room only.

Senator Del Valle was the keynote speaker, commending Ravelo and the Erie House staff and community members for their commitment to advocating for this important housing initiative, and standing up to the falsehoods that were spread by opponents. There were other events planned to celebrate Erie's 125th anniversary that year. However, this was by far, the most impactful way to mark Erie's dedication, not just to providing services, but to fighting for their neighbors' rights.

ON ELECTION DAY, FEBRUARY 28, 1995, THE ERIE CO-OP CAMPAIGN WON 9 OF 11 PRECINCTS!

In a follow-up article on March 17, 1995, *Tribune* reporter, Garza, described how "the massive public relations campaign," by Erie Neighborhood House, resulted in voters approving the idea of the co-op in the February 28 election.[329] She noted that "Alderman Granato" said he would now support it. From that day on, Bickerdike and the city's Department of Housing moved forward with plans for the co-op, and Erie, exhausted but re-energized, went back to planning for the Grand Opening of 1701 W. Superior and 125th anniversary events.

Attention returned to the co-op in March, 1996, when Erie organized a public meeting for people interested in becoming members of the co-op, and plans were under way for a groundbreaking in August. Construction for what was now planned as 30 units, was slated to begin in September. As was custom in Chicago's City Council, any project that needed their vote was subject to "aldermanic privilege." This means that if the local alderman does not approve of the project, the rest of the aldermen would vote NO as well. So, in May, 1996, a year after the referendum, that Granato said he would honor, he exercised that "privilege" and voted NO.[330] Everyone, including the Department of Housing staff, who had spent thousands of hours working out this deal, and set aside $2.8 million to fund it, were stunned. Granato's excuse for now voting NO was that the deal included tax increment financing, brought in to the deal to make sure the cost of a share was affordable enough. As a result, the co-op members would not have full equity up front. Therefore, he said, this was not the same deal that the referendum pertained to, but rather a "bait and switch" situation, and he was off the hook. It did not matter that the referendum was a vote for the concept, not the financing deal, nor that his logic did not recognize that people buying houses with a mortgage did not have full equity up front either. Erie did their best to challenge Granato's decision, rounding up letters to the mayor from Roger Fox, head of United Way, and Mary Heidkamp from the archdiocese's Campaign for Human Development, but to no avail.

In a July, 1996 *Tribune* article, Linda Contreraz, a key leader on the Erie Co-op Steering Committee, and campaign activist, told the story of her displacement from West Town, where she had grown up.[331] Before gentrification she was paying $350/month; after, rent for her apartment rose to $800. She noted with deep regret that the Erie Co-op would have housed 30 families, in 7 buildings, on 12 vacant lots, at a price they could afford, and that made them co-owners, not renters. It would have allowed them to stay in the neighborhood where they attended church, had access to affordable child care at places like Erie House, and could enjoy the amenities of a safe and pleasant neighborhood.

In response to Linda's story, the theme of Erie's Fall, 1996 newsletter was "What's at Stake in the Fight for Affordable Housing in West Town?" In one of the articles, Ravelo gave this response: "By losing the people who have made the community what it is, this ethnically and economically diverse community is losing its soul and character."[332] As Ravelo reflected on the co-op years later, "It was a dream that never came true. Granato's action cost us dearly."[333]

Based on an article that appeared in *Extra,* April 10, 1997, it is clear that community leaders tried to keep the co-op alive for almost a year after Granato's NO vote in city council. They had staged protests in front of his office and collected 300 letters in support of the co-op, but Granato would not be moved. He continued to reference Bryan Boyer and his Eckhart Park Community Council as "the community" he was accountable to, and not the Erie community. Lower income residents had won the referendum battle, but the gentry won the final siege, at their expense.

Celebrating Other Dreams

About two months after the referendum victory, Erie marked its 125th year, with another major accomplishment for 1995. On May 19, Erie hosted a Grand Opening Reception, "Building Our Future," at the 1701 W. Superior building. The Capital Campaign received a nice boost that same month, when the Manse in Oak Park, that had been home to the Lymans, when Ross was Director, sold for $249,000. For the first time, donation by credit card was available.[334] This event gave Erie the opportunity to show off building progress, even though programs would not start operations there until the Fall of 1995. The invitation said: "Join us in celebrating our most valuable asset – our children." On the back, it said:

> *Today, Erie House is a multi-service, non-sectarian agency, serving a predominantly Latino population. . . Erie enables families to understand the value and necessity of education and training in an increasingly technological society.*[335]

Zully Alvarado, identified earlier, when she received an award at Erie's Community Breakfast in 1994, also had a company called Producers Alley that made videos, and was hired to make one for Erie House in April, 1995. It was called "Open Doors," and first shown at the May 19 reception. It depicted a place that had been opening its doors to new Chicagoans for 125 years. Immigrants came to learn English and learn about democracy; working mothers found a safe place for their children. The doors were still open, to offer hope and enable those who walked through those doors to find and fight for solutions to social and economic problems.

The Presbytery of Chicago used this event to publicize their long-term connection with Erie in an article titled "Erie Neighborhood House Celebrates 125 Years with Presbytery" in April,1995.[336] They named key church connections like the Sawyers and Grahams of Oak Park and then Elmhurst, David Dangler of 4th Pres, Laurence Carton and Gerald Fox of Lake Forest, the McClures of Oak Park, the Gielows of Oak Park and then Glencoe, and the Quinns of Morton Grove. Six other churches were also named: Evanston, Highland Park, Riverside, Wheaton, Wilmette and Winnetka. The article also featured a photo of Erie's Teresa Jaime, who staffed Meals on Wheels, supported by church volunteers since 1958--a 37-year commitment by 1995.

The UCC Union Church of Hinsdale also had an article in their publication, "Erie House: Shining Star of Chicago's West Town."[337] The church calendar had the May 19 Grand Opening event on it and encouraged those who planned to attend to RSVP to the Armstrongs or John Jacus.

Press releases issued prior to May 19 announced three other events planned to mark the 125th anniversary. There would be a Heritage Festival on Erie Street, August 27, featuring ethnic music and dance; Milli Santiago of Channel 44 (a Spanish language station) would be the MC. The Mayor's Office of Special Events co-sponsored this event with several corporations. Erie alums were invited to come and celebrate a reunion. Then, there would be a Dedication and Ribbon-cutting ceremony at 1701, with Mayor Daley, on October 6, when the Erie Community Center was actually ready to open for business. Finally, the "Good Neighbor Awards Dinner" would take place at the Drake Hotel on November 16, 1995. Andres Bande, President of Ameritech International, had agreed to serve as dinner chair. The "Good Neighbor Award" would be presented to William Osborne, CEO of Northern Trust, and Virginia Moreno, community resident and Erie volunteer, would receive the Florence Towne Award for Community Service. Moreno was the mother of 7 and grandmother of 9, who came to Chicago from Laredo, TX, in the early 1960's. She was taking in laundry to support her family, but help from Erie House made a big difference. When she could, she started to pay it forward by volunteering at Erie, for the next 30 years. She was a translator for the clinic, became president of the Carpenter School PTA and Erie's Welfare Rights Organization, and was an active member of Santa Maria parish. Moreno said, "I help people because I saw that here at Erie House."[338]

Amidst all of this celebrating, Erie welcomed 6 new Latinx members to the Erie Board, bringing the total at that point to 13: Carmen Prieto, from the Wieboldt Foundation and daughter of Dr. Jorge Prieto, distinguished community activist and physician to immigrants; Librada Zamora, a former Erie kid, who now worked for First Chicago Corp.; Lourdes Avalos, a Day Care parent; Luis Diaz-Perez, press secretary for Cook County Clerk, David Orr; Roberto Cisneros, Jr. an attorney; and Zully Alvarado, the entrepreneur and video producer. With two Latinx in leadership roles, Ravelo and Nieves, who were both active in the larger Chicago and Latinx communities, the opportunity to find Latinx board members was evidently enhanced.

There was much to celebrate in the June, 1995 Annual Report. The co-op election day victory was highlighted along with the successful Open House Reception on May 19. The relatively new Erie Young Associates group had successfully raised $10,000 that year, through three events. Erie's Literacy Center, funded by the Secretary of State (SOS), under the leadership of Susana Ortiz, had grown from 13 volunteer tutors to 76. No doubt, this was a result of Ortiz' efforts to uphold the Erie tradition of providing a warm welcome to volunteers, as well as providing them with training to be prepared to be effective and feel successful.

And the awards kept coming. It was announced that Erie had received an Urban Leadership Award from the Lloyd Fry Foundation to establish a Technology Center at 1347, in the vacated child care space. The amount: $434,262! Ravelo recalls receiving a phone call from the Fry Foundation one afternoon, telling him the foundation had been hearing good things about Erie House. So, if he could come up with a really innovative project, they would like to give Erie a substantial sum of money. Ravelo turned to Kent Unruh, Erie's IT specialist, and together they came up with the idea for a computer center that would be open to the community. Obviously, Fry liked the idea. The Tech Center opened in 1996. YOU had secured an Outstanding Agency of the Year Award for Erie, presented by the Mayor's Office of Workforce Development, for their excellent work with the youth summer employment program. Esther Nieves was selected by the American Friends Service Committee to participate in the UN's World Conference on Women, to be held in Beijing in 1995.

On October 6, 1995, the Erie Community Center had its "ready for business" Grand Opening and Dedication ceremony. Rafael and Rupert Evans, Interim Executive Director of EFHC, welcomed guests, and Sally Lundeen, RN, PhD, was the keynote speaker. She came to work for

EFHC in 1975, when it was still "the clinic" operating out of Erie House. At the time, the clinic employed one nurse and several part-time physicians. She introduced the nurse-practitioner model, because she believed that "nursing should form the foundation of a comprehensive primary health care and education program."[339] This was a pioneering philosophy at that time that has become more widespread since then, especially as a health care model in low income communities, that are often "health care deserts," like third world countries. When she left in 1983, there were 10 full time nurse practitioner positions, EFHC had separately incorporated, and moved to its own space at Chicago and Paulina. In 1985, Lundeen accepted a teaching position at the University of Wisconsin-Milwaukee School of Nursing, and in 1987 opened the Silver Spring Community Nursing Center, where she was serving as Director when she spoke at the dedication.

One more element was added to child care and health care–art. Ellen Gates Starr of Hull House would have approved. She was the champion of the idea that settlement houses should promote art–appreciating it and creating it. It was announced that the Erie Neighborhood House Art Gallery would also open on October 6, with an exhibit by Casimiro Gonzalez, a Cuban artist, born in Havana, who migrated to Chicago in 1980. *CASIMIRO: SOMETHING MORE THAN COLOR,* a collection of the artist's paintings, would be on exhibit through December 31, 1995. This was a coup for Erie House, no doubt brought about through Ravelo's Cuban connections. Casimiro's work had been featured in the art section of the *Chicago Tribune's Exito!* edition on February, 17, 1994. In the year following the exhibit at Erie, he was commissioned to design the poster for the Chicago Latino Film Festival, in April, 1996. He has received numerous awards and commissions since then. Art has continued to decorate the walls at both the House and the Center.

The year of celebration culminated with a gala in November, at the Drake Hotel, a sophisticated downtown venue Erie had not previously pursued. They had the usual keys to success in their plan: a corporate dinner chair in Bande from Ameritech, that they hoped would draw other corporations to buy tables, and a similarly distinguished awardee, William Osborne, CEO of Northern Trust, another heavy hitter in the Chicago business community. There was appropriate media coverage, facilitated by a media consultant hired the previous summer. Greetings came in from Governor Edgar, Mayor Daley, Senators Paul Simon and Carol Mosley-Braun. Erie pre-school and after-school children performed under the direction of Salvador Lopez and Dennis Puhr. Fr. Richard Klajbor, pastor of Holy Innocents, offered the closing prayer. In the final analysis, the event brought in around $59,000; expenses were close to $28,000, with $16,000 of that going to the hotel. The net was about $31,228. It was an important event to mark 125 years, but financially, somewhat disappointing. Erie House would wait 10 years to try a gala at a downtown hotel again, for its 135th.

Life Goes On: A Lot Was Different, But Erie Continued to Prosper

Following the opening of the 1701 building, with a 400% increase in the number of children being served, and 53 new employees to introduce to Erie House values and vision, a staff retreat was held at Villa Marie on the Maryville campus in Des Plaines. There were simple matters to resolve, such as referring to 1701 as "The Center" and 1347 as "The House." But many long-term staff were sincerely concerned that such an increase in size would have a negative impact on the warm relationships Erie staff were accustomed to in their workplace. They worried that the new child care staff would remain strangers to the staff at the

House, and vice versa, and that moving administration from the House to the Center would diminish access and influence for employees at the House. Rafael and Esther did their best to offset this anxiety, but inevitably, some of these concerns manifested themselves. Since the opening of the Erie Chapel Institute building at 1347 W. Erie in 1886, for almost 130 years, the building on Erie Street had been the headquarters and heart of Erie Neighborhood House. But with the executive director and most senior administrative staff located at the Center, 1701 W. Superior superseded the House as the "main address" for ENH. Fortunately, the office of the Associate Director remained at the House, giving those employees at least one connection to "the top and the heart."

One person who could have helped build the bridge between the two locations as an employee with more than 20 years at the House, and as head of the expanded child care program, was Angel Carroll. Unfortunately, just as the transition was occurring, she took a bad fall that triggered other serious health problems. After an initial leave of absence, it became clear she would have to resign to deal with her health. Tragically, after all her work on the transition, she never got the chance to run the new program in the new space.

As Erie House did its best to settle into its new reality, good things did continue to happen. Adult Ed was reaching more and more students through its Literacy Center, a 300% increase in 1995. The New Americans grants from the state, channeled through ICIRR, continued to fund Erie citizenship classes, assisting 200 with the naturalization process. And advocacy efforts in Springfield were paying off when, in December, 1996, Governor Edgar (R) announced the allocation of another $2.4 Million for a program called Refugee and Immigrant Citizenship Initiative (RICI) to further support this work. Pathways to Success placed 70% of its students in banking jobs, and

Child Care received national accreditation through NAEYC. YOU awarded $36,000 in scholarships to TEAM grads, with 95% of them admitted to college. Erie was offering workshops to prepare parents for Local School Council elections, and Tim Bell was promoting leadership training for women at *Mujeres Latinas en Acción.*

A Director of Operations position was created to help manage Erie's growth, with an FY95 budget of $2.3 million. The revenue that supported Erie House in its 125th year was as follows. With a base allocation, plus two generous Priority Grants, United Way provided $327,907. Corporate and Foundation grants reached $756,118, and Congregations still contributed $84,458, with individuals just behind that at $76,710. Government support was at $965,642. So, at this point, private funding was the source of 53% of Erie's income. That would change in FY96, when the new child care enrollments would be added in.

In February, 1996, there was just one more event associated with the new building. This event, more or less, mirrored the one held in May, 1995. Once again, guests were invited to visit the new building, this time for the purpose of honoring those who gave generously enough to have a plaque with their name placed next to the room's name. All the pre-school rooms were named after trees and flowers, and the after-school room was called the Rainbow Room. This time the Erie House Gallery presented an exhibit called *An American Dialogue,* displaying the works of Jesus Gerardo de la Barrera, an engraver, born in Mexico City in 1954, and Benjamin Varela, born in Brooklyn in 1955, lived in Puerto Rico for 12 years, and was currently a resident of Pilsen in Chicago. He was a printmaker. There is no record of subsequent exhibits of professional artists. Mostly, the walls of Erie House today feature the art of Erie's children and youth, with a few Diego Rivera prints in between. *Quien sabe?* There may be a future Casimiro, Jesus, or Benjamin among them.

The following month, in March, 1996, the Technology Center opened at the House. The invitation to the grand opening read "We are opening doors." The opening of this door was made possible by that Urban Leadership grant of over $400,000 for a 3-year start-up, from the Lloyd A. Fry Foundation. According to the Chair of the Fry Foundation Board, Edmund A. Stephan, in their 1997 Annual Report: "We created the program to focus on needs that experienced, creative leaders of established organizations would choose to address, if only they had the resources."[340] In its 126th year when this award was made, Erie was definitely established, Ravelo and Unruh were certainly creative, and new resources were undoubtedly needed to have a Technology Center. It was a match!

The Erie Technology Center's (ETC) first director, Kent Unruh, former Mennonite Volunteer, provided the following description:

> *The ETC is a comprehensive computer laboratory dedicated to the computer and information literacy of West Town residents. Serving individuals with limited English proficiency and low educational achievement, from age 5-85, the ETC provides dynamic exposure and training in the fields of computer and information technologies.[341]*

At the time of opening, the lab had seven PCs, with a goal of 17, a laser printer, and a Windows 95 operating system. In these early days, Erie's web address was made available by piggy-backing on Loyola University's. Through the good graces of Phil Nyden, Director of Loyola's Center for Urban Research and Learning (CURL), and its Policy Research Action Group (PRAG), Erie's address read:

http://www.luc.edu/depts/sociology/pragusr/erie.

The ETC staff included Kent, as director; Marga Tokar, Project Manager and Instructor, who was fluent in Spanish; Adam Tostado, Tech Specialist and Troubleshooter, moving from intern to employee. The staff were assisted by a Mennonite Volunteer and a University of Chicago Divinity student.

The significance of having a computer lab and the internet available to its low-income, immigrant community was well-stated when Ravelo said,

> *With fewer blue-collar jobs available in Chicago, the Latino immigrants need more than a strong back and a willingness to work; they need the same technological skills as anybody else. . . **Information technology is now the third language they must learn** [342]*

Offering classes in English and Spanish, and email accounts, to about 150, ages 5 through 85, in its first year, the Fry Foundation was more than satisfied with its investment.

Per usual, amidst new beginnings, the old need, to challenge the latest wrong-minded public policy, would always rise to a place on the Erie agenda. This time, the US Senate voted to reduce job training funds by 41%, and zeroed out Title II-B that funded summer jobs for youth. The slogan for this decision might have been: "Let's keep poverty alive!" As a consequence, without the federal funding, the Mayor's Office of Employment and Training (MET) canceled the annual summer jobs for youth, a program that Erie youth counted on. So, they mobilized and collected 300 signatures to send to Congress, and Erie organized a press conference to address these cuts in April. By May, MET had restored the program. Whether federal funds were restored or not, local political leaders realized they did not want to face summer without it; neither did YOU. Keeping 250 youth, off the street, and productively engaged, was a preventive strategy that was cheap for the price.

Other funding cuts led to a difficult decision in July, 1996, when Ravelo announced that Meals on Wheels was being discontinued. It was not only funding cuts, but also the aging of the church volunteers. With so many younger women in the workforce, availability of replacement volunteers was a growing challenge. The MOW service was eventually picked up by the city's Department of Aging, but the loss to Erie House was the strong connection to the eleven churches that had carried out this work so faithfully, in person, every week, for 38 years. The staff of the Emergency Services Department, primarily Teresa Jaime, were laid off, but the food pantry would be open two days a week with the help of other staff.

Throughout the 1990s, the flow of immigrants into the US was strong. While many came from Mexico, the diversity of immigration was underscored when an organization called CAALII was formed. The initials stood for Coalition of Asian, African, and Latino Immigrants of Illinois. Members included 5 Latino organizations, two Chinese, two Korean and one each, Vietnamese, Cambodian, Laotian, and Ethiopian. Erie House was a co-founding member.

It was also during the 1990s that the issue of undocumented immigrants living in the US became a more frequently discussed "issue." A press conference was held in the Erie gym on August 20, 1996 to announce new "banners" to be posted on CTA buses proclaiming: "No human being is illegal." This was the result of a joint effort on the part of Erie, Heartland Alliance, Community Renewal Society, Centro Romero, Centro Sin Fronteras, Chinese American Service League (CASL), Korean American Resource Center, and the American Friends Service Committee. Needless to say, Erie House had strong feelings around this issue, and supported the "Justice for All" campaign organized by American Friends, calling for humane treatment of undocumented immigrants by the INS. Concerns about INS practices were prompted by their study, released in February, 1996, titled "Migrant Deaths at the Texas-Mexico Border, 1985-1994". In their press release announcing the press conference, Erie stated their position:

> *Erie does not advocate for undocumented immigration, but rather, we advocate for a humane response to the plight of those most impacted by measures which do not address the conditions and causes for migration to the USA.*[343]

Erie did not limit its advocacy for a just immigration policy to local or statewide organizations either. Tim Bell announced that his department had raised sufficient funds to take 60 adult ed students to Washington, D.C. to participate in a national immigration march. This was just the beginning of an intense decade (1995-2006) of marches and other tactics to address the immigration issue, with 911 happening in the middle of that decade, and worsening the anti-immigrant stance of many.

The theme of Erie's Summer, 1996, Newsletter was immigration. The lead article was titled "The Myths Plaguing Latin American Immigrants." [344] It set the context for the discussion of the myths, suggesting that in an atmosphere of immigrant-bashing, especially directed at immigrants from Mexico, the many contributions of immigrants to the development and success of the US are ignored. The article found that both the Republican and Democratic parties were engaged in "anti-immigrant hysteria." Claims were rampant that undocumented immigrants were taking advantage of benefits they were not even eligible for, due to their status. On the other hand, immigrants, documented or not, paid $25 billion in taxes every year, because 30% of immigrants were in the labor force. 37% of all factory workers, and 29% of all physicians in Chicago were immigrants, the article pointed out. And finally, the author advised, "Let's remember where we all came from as descendants of earlier immigrant groups, initially discriminated against, and later praised for their contributions." One must add to that memory, that the most hostile examples of anti-immigrant policies in the US have been directed against people of color and/or non-Western or non-Christian cultures. This practice was renewed with a vengeance during the administration of Donald Trump, beginning in 2016.

For Erie House and the community of West Town, 1996 was ending on a very disheartening note. Rafael Ravelo was ill, and Associate Director, Esther Nieves, was asked to serve as interim executive director while Rafael was dealing with his health. It was not looking good. He had been diagnosed with cancer, and was undergoing chemotherapy.[345] Miraculously, not sure there is another word for it, Ravelo began his recovery, a process that resulted in full restoration of his health. As it became apparent he was feeling better, what seemed reasonable to all concerned, at least at a place like Erie House, and with a beloved director like "Rafa," was the decision to create a new position just for him. They called it "Senior Advisor;" it was just part time, but included health care benefits, so important to Ravelo's continued recovery. He held that position until his retirement in 2012. (Among Erie's senior leadership, only Ross Lyman served Erie longer.) Not only did he take numerous tasks off the shoulders of succeeding directors, but his unfailing, upbeat spirit, brightened many a day at Erie House. When you spend your day with a man for whom the glass is always half full, you never go thirsty.

Chapter 7: Esther Nieves: Puerto Rican Feminist Returns to the Hood – Managing Tensions with Erie's New Neighbors (1997-2003)

Esther Nieves was a Chicago native who grew up in Humboldt Park, the daughter of a minister, and was another SSA graduate of the University of Chicago, who had received her Bachelor's degree from Mundelein College. She was a former program officer for the Field Foundation. Before that, she served as Executive Director of the Mayor's Advisory Commission on Latino Affairs under Mayor Harold Washington. Also, in the 1980s, as a graduate intern, she worked with the Jane Addams Conference on Women's Leadership. She was selected by the American Friends Service Committee to participate in the UN's World Conference on Women, held in Beijing, in 1995.

But in 1993, when she was on the Erie board, Rafael Ravelo was looking for an Associate Director, and he asked her if she was interested. She said she felt she had learned what she set out to learn by working for a foundation for about three years, and she was ready for a change. She knew Erie House was an effective organization, and a position there would give her the opportunity to work for her own community. So, she said yes, and started that job on January 1, 1994.[346] Just three years later, in January 1997, she would be moving up to executive director. While everyone was gratified to see how well Rafael was responding to treatment for his cancer, he did not feel he should continue as executive director, and resigned from that position, knowing Nieves was more than capable of taking over.

Bill Clinton (D) was still president, pushing a welfare reform policy that, while making it difficult for people to stay on welfare for long periods, failed to provide the support services, like job training, that former

Esther Nieves (Erie Neighborhood House)

recipients were going to need to make it without "public aid," as it used to be called. It was clear to CBOs like Erie, that some public "aids" would be required for a successful transition, and these were not forthcoming. In spite of an impeachment vote in the House, in 1998, he stayed in office until 2000, when he was replaced by George (the younger) Bush. On the state level, during Nieves' tenure, Illinois was governed by successive Republicans, Jim Edgar and George Ryan. Just as Esther left Erie, Democrat, Rod Blagojevich, took over. Locally, of course, Richard M. Daley was still mayor, year eight of 22. But Erie's relationship with that mayor would begin to evolve in the late 1990s.

When Esther took over, Angel Carroll, who had been at Erie for almost 25 years, was too ill to return to her position as Child Care Director. She had been involved in all of the planning for the expanded child care program in the

323

new building, and then was never able work there and see her dream come true. One of Esther's first challenges was to find a new Director for Child Care, Erie's largest and most lucrative program. One of the first assignments for the Senior Advisor, was to assist in the search. They found Sandy Schaefer, who became Child Care Director on July 1, 1997, and held that position for the next 10 years. One of her first goals was to pursue national accreditation through the National Association for the Education of the Young Child, NAEYC. She achieved that goal in 1998, and Erie was among only 5% of programs in the nation, at that time, to gain this accreditation. One of her first challenges came as early as October 1997, over a state proposal to increase Child Care fees or co-pays. Here is what the increases looked like:

	Annual Income	FY97/mo. Fee	FY98/mo Fee	Increase
Family of 4 with 2 children in daycare	$28,573	$216.65	$260	+$43.35 (or 20%
Family of 3, single parent with 2 children in day care:	$15,274	$26.00	$104	+$78 (or 300%)
Family of 2, single parent with 1 in day care:	$10,598	$1.08	$44.00	+$42.92(or 3,900%)[347]

As Schaefer explained in a *Chicago Tribune* article on October 27, 1997, the increase in fees was aimed at paying for more slots at the lower end of the income eligibility scale, even below the bottom line on the table above. And/or if people at the upper end dropped out, due to higher fees, that also made more slots available at the bottom. This policy was one attempt to accommodate those being pushed off welfare and into employment by the welfare reform policies of the Clinton administration. The upshot of this type of rationale was that it punished the working poor who had been doing better, gradually advancing in pay with some skill-building and seniority, but were still not able to afford market-rate child care. And to add insult to injury, subsidies were eliminated for parents in college or job training classes. Even if parents could squeeze out enough for their pre-schoolers, the higher cost forced them to make the decision to leave their school-age kids at home--a return to latch-key status, home alone--a giant step backwards.

These fee increases were also particularly hard on single moms with only one income to pay fees, and could result in sending them back on welfare. One goal was contradicting the other. As indicated in the table above, while $1.08/month might seem very low, a jump to $44/month is tough when your take-home pay is only $750/month. Nobody "takes home" gross income. In West Town, at that time, almost all of that might go to rent and utilities. If a single mom could find a place for only $600, utilities included, she was lucky, and then that left only $150 for food for the rest of the month plus transportation to work. $10/mo. might have been a fair increase and still be tight. So, in general, this policy would penalize both ends of the income spectrum of Erie families. Just as they might be seeing the light at the end of the tunnel of poverty, the state was creating the oncoming train. This could have been called "The Poverty Promotion Policy." Erie pre-school and after-school parents cranked out 300 letters in protest. As usual, Senator Del Valle responded. He said, "The higher fees defeat the purpose of providing subsidized day care for the working poor."[348] He and State Senator, Ricky Hendon, introduced Resolution 111 to put the fee increase on hold to have time to investigate its impact.

Whether bureaucrats and pols were simply clueless or intentionally divisive, the result was the same. A policy like this created conflict among low-income and very-low-income, mostly people of color, at least in Chicago. It got them to fight over peanuts, instead of acknowledging that the answer is to allocate a lot more funding to day care, to support the broader range of families prepared to contribute to our economy, but not at the expense of their children. Tax dollars spent there, to help more people to work, actually benefit the middle class, as it reduces the cost of payments for welfare, subsidized housing, prisons and police. It is also an investment in the next generation, reducing those same costs to support them. With generously funded day care, these children have a better chance of doing well in school, and when they are ready for college, their parents might be in a position to help them along.

Schaefer also inherited supervision of the Day Care Family Homes Network, that was approaching its 8th year. From July 1997, when Schaefer started as Child Care Director, to the Fall of 1998, the Network went from serving 42 to 70 children, and from 9 to 14 providers. Mercedes Jacome, an Ecuadoran, was the Network Coordinator.

Adult Education Grows Up to Rival Child Care in Size and Impact

Throughout the 1990s, programming for adults at Erie grew significantly. There were several factors involved. First, the amnesty that Reagan had authorized, brought many adults to Erie for citizenship preparation classes. They had come there to learn English, and perhaps to earn their GED, and found classes at Erie House much more satisfactory than those offered by CPS or the City Colleges of Chicago. So, if Erie was now offering the path to citizenship, immigrants went to the organization they already trusted.

Then, not only could they start down their pathway to citizenship at Erie House, but they also heard about the Pathways to Success (PTS) workforce development program that prepared them for jobs in the banking industry or advanced manufacturing. PTS, which had been started in the early 1990s, was continuing to do well. 19 banks were participants in Erie's employer consortium, and 23 students were enrolled for the Spring, 1997 term, as referrals rolled in from other agencies. In March, 1997, PTS hosted its Third Annual "Vocational School" Fair.[349] It represented the philosophy of PTS that:

- Traditional college education was not the only pathway to economic success;
- Adult learners needed information on the best options, best matches for them, just as their teens needed a college fair to learn the same;
- Vocational education was offered by a variety of sponsors, including many CBOs that often offered the best training at the best price.

Some of the participants in the Fair included: *American Airlines Academy, Chicago Women in Trades, Coyne Institute for electrical training, Culinary Institute of Kendall College, Greater West Town Project (Shipping & Receiving and Woodworking), Dawson Tech (printing), Robert Morris College (CMA), Humboldt Vocational Center of Wright College (CNC), Association House (Customer Service and CNA).*

So, these adults joined child care parents in swelling the ranks of grown-ups who found Erie just as valuable for them as for their children. And, at 1701, they could get child care downstairs and health care upstairs. What's not to love about that?

A second factor in the growth of adult programming at Erie had to do with leadership. No surprises here. The outline of this book revolves around the excellent leadership that carried Erie forward for 150 years. But as any executive director, from Florence Towne to Kirstin Chernawsky, will tell you, *their* leadership and accomplishments very much depend on the next level of leaders at the program level. One of those individuals was a man named Tim Bell, fluent in Spanish, who made every effort to be bicultural as well as bilingual. Hired in 1993, as Esther became Associate Director, he led the Adult Ed department through most of the 1990s, and the Erie House of Esther Nieves was still reaping the benefits when she became Executive Director. He helped convince every Mexican immigrant who came to Erie's door, that Erie House was their house. He did this, not only with high quality education programs, but also with his passion for social justice, and his commitment to activism to achieve it.

Thirdly, he had the wisdom of Jane Addams to pay attention to mother country roots and culture. As he became aware of human rights violations in Chiapas, Mexico, he engaged Erie adult students in championing their cause-- from Chicago. Erie students "adopted" 12 Mayan communities in southern Mexico. Apparently, the Mayans had long been persecuted by the Mexican government that wanted to exploit Mayan lands, rich in minerals. Literacy rates among this group of people were very low, so the Marist priests and brothers helped them to build their own schools. Erie adult ed students raised funds for school supplies by selling coffee during the day and evening adult classes.

Under Bell, citizenship classes were not just about preparing for the test, but preparing to act like citizens, i.e., they were taught voting would not become an option for them, but a responsibility. This was a guy who organized the undocumented to work on voter registration drives, from the perspective that, even if they could not vote themselves, they needed to make sure their compadres who could, did.

He also fostered the notion that Mexican immigrants should not work alone for immigrant rights, but join with others, as the Immigrant Education Conference he organized in 1995, and the Justice for Immigrants ad campaign, chronicled in Chapter 6, illustrated. For working hard on this concept, he was the recipient of an award from KACS, the Korean Agency for Community Services, viewing him and Erie House as one of their strongest allies. Bell surmised that Mexicans and Koreans could and should work together around their common interest of improving the US immigration system and fighting for immigrant rights.

During Esther's administration, in January 1997, Erie partnered with the Korean community again as they organized a National Telegram Campaign, sending 2600 telegrams to President Clinton, urging him to keep his promise to improve immigrant benefits. As co-founder and active member of CAAELII, Erie shared in the $255,000 grant they received in January 1998. A July 1998 letter to José Diaz, the Dean of Adult Learning Skills Programs at Malcolm X College, is a good example of Bell's constant advocacy to make sure that the community college that supplied Erie's ESL instructors, was responding to the needs of adult students as Erie understood them, not as the City Colleges chose to run their own programs on campus. First, he was proposing an Adult Continuing Ed program at Erie's Tech center for two nights a week. Second, he wanted to shorten ESL classes to 8 hours per week in order to be able to offer 6 levels of ESL. He explained that students had asked for this to help them transition to higher education and/or employment opportunities. Bell moved on this in 1998, but some years later, Erie lost hold of this need for multiple levels. A common complaint among immigrants was that too many organizations offering ESL, only offered Levels 1 and 2, over and over again, with no opportunities to advance. To some extent, this is the problem bridge programs were addressing in workforce development, trying to offer those advanced levels of English in the context of career prep.

As a result of Bell's effective outreach, Erie raised the funds to transform the second- floor space that had been the chapel into space for adult classes that were meeting most weekday mornings and evenings and on Saturdays as well. Nieves recalled that Erie's good friend from the days of the Co-op fight, State Senator Miguel Del Valle, helped to secure some state funding for the rehab, as did State Rep, Cynthia Soto. Del Valle would have done this because he was a good man. But also: Hey, voters are created here.

Another staff person, who supported the work Tim Bell did with adults, was Susana Ortiz. She was the Coordinator of Erie's "Literacy Center," a program funded by the Illinois Secretary of State's Office (SOS). Most people think of this office as the place where you get your driver's license. That is true. However the SOS is also responsible for overseeing libraries in the state. Since libraries are about reading, and reading is about literacy, grants came out of this office for organizations that help adults learn to read or read better. The "vision" behind this program, a nearsighted one at that, was that all of this tutoring for reading would be done with volunteers. Consequently, the grants barely included sufficient funds to hire one person to oversee this volunteer program. As is often the case, bureaucracy drastically underestimates what it takes to do the job on the ground. They certainly did not understand that volunteers do not just appear at your doorstep, and that as willing as they were, would need some training to do a good job. Yet, this one underpaid person had to recruit these volunteer tutors, train them or see to their training by others, recruit the adult learners who needed/wanted tutoring, match them with a tutor, provide space for the activity, and troubleshoot the issues that arise when either the tutor or tutee do not show up.

Fortunately, another strong tradition at Erie was recruiting volunteers and making them feel welcome. Ms. Ortiz excelled at this. In a relatively short time, she was managing over 100 volunteer tutors over the course of a year. And she did not stop with people at Erie House. She also went to schools, recruited parents there who needed the service and found volunteers to work in that setting.

Finally, adults were drawn to Erie because of its Technology Center which had opened in 1996, one of the last of Ravelo's amazing accomplishments before poor health forced him to step down. In the late 1990s, most non-profits were still weaning themselves off of typewriters in their offices. The thought of making those "word-processors," much less the internet, available to their participants, was an idea some distance down the road. But not at Erie House. You could go there to learn how to use this latest technology, get an email address, and eventually send those photos of the grandchildren back home to Mexico. This did not all happen overnight, but the door to the computer lab was open at 1347 W. Erie.

Bottom line, the Erie House of the Nieves era, had two big programs—one for children, and one for adults. Education was the Erie focus, from one end of the family to the other. Early childhood education happened at the Center, but all other education happened at the House.

It even poured across the street, when Erie rented space from the African American church there. And then there were those challenging young people in between.

TEAM Still Going Strong

In June of 1997, the TEAM mentoring program was holding its 12th annual TEAM Banquet to honor its graduating seniors. To help fund the event, there was always a TEAM booklet with ads taken by businesses, colleges and universities, and some individual supporters from the Erie

Board. A sampling of ads from 1997 include: Goose Island Brewery, Café Central, DePaul University, Hudson Boiler, Dominican University, Northeastern Illinois University (NEIU), Manufacturers Bank, The Private Bank, St. Xavier University, Whole Foods, and, of course, Northern Trust, TEAM's founding and faithful funder, and consistent provider of Erie Board members. The booklet also highlighted the stories of each of the seniors, especially where they planned to attend college, as this was the next step for 90% of them. In 1997, there were 29 seniors--26 from Wells High School, just 4 blocks from Erie House, 2 from Lane Tech, and 1 from Gordon Tech. Parents attended, beaming with pride. And Erie was proud. This event represented the immediate future of the immigrant community, the first generation of college graduates.

By 1998, under the leadership of Juan Orta and Maria Matias, recruitment of tutor/mentors was expanded beyond Northern Trust employees, to 17 new companies. There were 44 graduates that year, compared to 29 in 1997, and 23 ads filled the TEAM Banquet booklet. Some facts found in that booklet:

- TEAM's 44 graduates came from schools with 60% dropout rates;
- Nationally, only 3% of Latino high school grads attended college;
- 98% of TEAM grads were pursuing post-secondary education.[350]

So, this was the Erie House Esther Nieves had already helped develop in the three years she worked there before becoming executive director. This was how she saw the mission of Erie as she became its new leader:

At Erie Neighborhood House, we begin with the individual, then the family, providing resources and

*services that develop the whole person. But services
are not sufficient to build the community. . .We work
to provide residents with both skills and
opportunities to participate in the larger economy.
Settlement houses have a distinguished tradition of
contributing to community and economic
development. [351]*

West Town United – Filling the Community Organizing Void

One of the new additions to Erie House, related to
Erie's agenda for community and economic development,
was the founding of West Town United (WTU) in June
1997. WTU was the work of Erie's community organizer,
Erik Nordgren, and the follow-up to the Housing Co-op
fight. With a specific plan to provide affordable housing
defeated, WTU's mission was to keep challenging the
gentrification process, with the intent of creating a grassroots
power base to give local residents a voice. A grant of
$50,000 was used to fund this initiative. WTU was similar
to, but smaller than, the Northwest Community Organization
(NCO) that had closed in 1994. NCO had saved West Town
from the wrecking ball of urban renewal. That threat was
passed; now, for the working poor, it was gentrification.
WTU was a "mini" organization of organizations, with a
membership of 20 religious, ethnic, civic, business and
educational organizations and individuals who lived,
worked, or worshiped within WTU boundaries. The mission
statement follows:

*WTU's main purpose, according to its by-laws, is to
promote, safeguard, develop, and build a multi-
ethnic, mixed income, racially diverse community
through education, leadership training, organizing,
and community-based initiatives.[352]*

333

A Board of Supervisors was elected, and the first one included the following: President: Alison Meares; VP: Ric Estrada; Secretary.: Kathy Wilson; Treasurer.: Carlos Colon; Parliamentarian: Rob Gonzalez. **Institutional Members**: Holy Innocents, Santa Maria, St. Stan's, St. Mary of Nazareth Hospital, ENH, Children & Family Justice Center, East Village Youth Program, EFHC, Julia Center, Onward House, Union League of Boys & Girls Clubs, YOU(regional), Northwestern University Settlement House (NUSH), Centro Ruiz Belvis, Deborah's Place, Emerson House, Greater West Town Project, Near Northwest Civic Committee, Street Level Youth Media, Viva Family Center. **Business Members**: CABA, Chicago Ave. Discount, ICNC. An **Action Council,** composed of delegates from member organizations, set policy and determined strategies.

One strategy WTU came up with, was unique as an organizing initiative, and was chronicled in an article in *PRAGmatics, a publication of the Policy Research Action Group,* in the Spring of 1997.[353] The story of WTU's anti-gentrification strategy was called "Community Organization Resists Gentrification Through Tax Assessment Campaign in West Town Community." This article was written by a PRAG intern, Joel Elvery, and Jerry Harris, a West Town resident and member of WTU. Their narrative first laid out the gentrification scenario as middle-class professionals (Yuppies) moving into neighborhoods with desirable locations, not far from the Loop or the Lake, and with easy access to both expressways and public transit. In the 1990s this certainly applied to West Town, but also to Pilsen and Bronzeville. Realtors capitalize on this interest and prices for housing go up. As a result, taxes go up; longtime owners cannot afford to pay and rental building owners raise rents to cover the increase.

In 1997, West Town was up for reassessment with an expected jump in taxes of 30-60%! WTU was proposing a new approach to property tax assessment that allowed for income-based appeals. Let the speculators pay more, and lower income, longtime residents pay proportionately less. Side benefit: create solidarity among working class owners and low-income tenants; maintain community relationships. Art Lyons, formerly of UIC, a member of PRAG, and Director of the Center for Economic Policy Analysis (CEPA), was assisting with technical details and educational workshops for residents — a university/community collaboration. *Research showed that the average monthly rent in gentrified buildings was $856, but in smaller, long-term, owner-occupied buildings it was $414.*[354]

Cook County Assessor, Jim Houlihan, was approached by WTU and agreed to their approach. Ultimately, 130 appeals were filed; all but one got reduced assessments. However, the reductions were not as great as they could have been; more work was needed. But the idea of property tax assessments playing a role in gentrification relief was on the table. It was picked up again in 2001, by Cook County Commissioner, Roberto Maldonado, Erie's 8th District rep on the County Board. Erie House staff testified on behalf of his proposed ordinance to grant property tax relief to long-term homeowners (10 years or more) in gentrifying areas. Rafael Ravelo, who owned a 3-flat in Wicker Park, stated that he wanted to keep his rents low enough for moderate income people to stay in his building but that this was hard to do when he was facing a 52% increase in his property taxes. Maldonado's ordinance passed on a 9-7 vote.[355]

The second issue that WTU took on in the late 1990s had them partnering with the Chicago Ashland Business Association (CABA), a member of WTU. This was the chamber of commerce that represented retail interests in the Erie neighborhood, along a 4-block stretch of Chicago Avenue, between Noble (1400 W) and Wood (1800 W). In the 1600 block of Chicago Avenue sat a white terra cotta building, built in the 1920s, as a department store that became the headquarters of Goldblatt's Bros. The department store chain, which did well for many years serving low-to-moderate-income families, fell on hard times in the 1980s when they tried their hand at opening stores in the suburbs. This was not their market. In 1997, the building on Chicago Avenue was on the market. Del Ray Farms bid on it, with the plan to tear it down and build one of their grocery stores. A local group called the East Village Association (EVA), which defined their area as Division to Chicago and Ashland to Damen, protested this plan, calling for the building to receive landmark status instead, and perhaps, become residential. WTU took the position that the lower income people who still lived in the neighborhood needed an affordable place to buy groceries, and CABA wanted to maintain the face of retail on the street. In the end, a completely different plan emerged. The city decided to buy the building, put a library on the main floor, and city department offices above.

The next fight came over providing parking for the municipal employees who would occupy the building. Store owners adjacent to Goldblatt's started receiving notices that the city may take their properties. Some EVA members said this would be no loss; again, WTU and CABA objected. This time they won their point. Only one store was torn down and the city bought a parking garage nearby for employee parking. While EVA was more of a mixture of older and newer residents, and did not represent the mean-spirited attitude of the Eckhart Park Community Council that had opposed the affordable housing co-op, there was a pattern developing here that Erie would have to deal with as the neighborhood continued to gentrify.

Esther Honored

At the end of 1997, Erie shared in Esther Nieves's honor when she was named a Kellogg National Leadership Program (KNLP) Fellow. She was one of 38 selected out of

336

747 applications! In the Kellogg Foundation's press release they explained that the KNLP "encourages the formation of creative, flexible decisionmakers, prepared to take on the leadership challenges of the next century."[356] This was a 3-year, part time program that came with a grant of $42,000 for the awardee and a payment to the non-profit employer of 12.5% of the awardee's salary for release time during the fellowship. Esther's proposal, for what would be the product of her fellowship, was called "Learning and Leading: A Non-profit Women's Leadership Project." To develop this pilot project, Esther went to consult with a woman from her alma mater, Mundelein College. This was Carolyn Farrell, BVM, Director of the Ann Ida Gannon Center for Women and Leadership, located on the Loyola University campus in Rogers Park, since Mundelein, located right next door, was taken over by Loyola.

In spite of all the new beginnings with the expansion to a second facility, coming and going of key staff, FY97 had finished in the black, after two years of deficits. Revenue stood at $4,059,162, with 58.5% from public sources, and 41.5% from private sources. There were 33 Foundations/Corporate giving programs supporting Erie, 9 banks (thank you, PTS) and 13 other businesses contributing, and 35 congregations. Public funds flowed to Erie from 13 different departments of city, state, or federal government. And, Esther needed an Associate Director. That was Ricardo Estrada.

Illinois Steps Up for Immigrants and the Erie Technology Center Gains Momentum

In a January 1998 article in *Extra,* the headline read: "Edgar signs bill to help immigrants." That was Governor Jim Edgar (R) and he signed that bill at Erie House, where immigrants had found welcome for the past 128 years. He signed Senate Bill 320, providing $10 million in nutrition assistance and citizenship programs for documented immigrants living in the state. Part of the rationale for this allocation was to compensate for federal welfare reform legislation that cut *legal* immigrants off from food stamps. Bill 320 was developed by a collaboration of ICIRR, Latino Institute, MALDEF, American Jewish Committee, Jewish Federation of Metropolitan Chicago, and the SSI Coalition. Edgar's message: Immigrants are welcome in Illinois; we are not turning our backs on them. This bill created a source of grants that Erie used primarily to support its citizenship work. As noted in Chapter 6, his first bill, in 1996, created the New Americans program.

Later that year, in May 1998, Erie House became the 18th recipient of the Sara Lee Foundation "Spirit Award." The $50,000 grant that accompanied the award was earmarked to expand Erie's two-year old Technology Center. In accepting the award, Esther Nieves said:

> *In the past, Erie House taught women how to use sewing machines and typewriters. Now we use computers in much the same way – to build self-esteem, to teach job skills, and to give young people the incentive to stay in school and lead productive lives.*[357]

The existence of the Erie Tech Center led to the inclusion of Erie House in a large West Town collaboration that was called for by CPS (Chicago Public Schools) with funds from the US Department of Education, under their Technology Challenge Grant Program. What came to be called the Chicago Neighborhood Learning Network (CNLN), was based on commitment to a plan to set up a network of partner organizations in the same neighborhood that would work together to create more computer labs to improve access to technology. A consultant, named Don Samuelson, was hired by CPS to serve as the "neighborhood partnership developer." He was based at the Northwest Tower apartment building at 1170 W. Erie. This is the subsidized high-rise that was built in 1970, occupied primarily by African Americans. A number of Erie House staff and participants came from this building. They had children in Erie Day Care, teens in YOU, and Carpenter School parents knew they had Erie's support when they needed it. The West Town CNLN had the following additional partners: Holy Trinity High School, Northwestern Settlement, Carpenter School, Street Level Youth Media, Emerson House, and the Greenview/Eckhart CHA senior buildings, just two blocks north of Erie House. There was a 5-year timeline, 1997-2003. But in reality, the network did not get off the ground until 1998.

Samuelson soon became frustrated with CPS, as there was a difference of opinion as to what was expected to be done under this grant. CPS simply saw it as a means to wire a few more computer labs. Samuelson and the CNLN believed the intention should be broader–to create an educational environment for parents and children, with technology as a tool to "bridge the digital divide." That certainly defined Erie's goal for their Tech Center.

When the WTU held their annual convention in September 1998, which they called "Working Together for Diversity & Unity," the CNLN was on the agenda, along with affordable housing, the new library, job training, and the property tax campaign. WTU president, Allison Meares, sent off a letter, on WTU stationery, to CPS, noting that they had passed a resolution to press CPS to work with the West Town CNLN.

Ultimately, the project fell apart, but by way of compensation, USDOE/CPS awarded Erie House with the funds to open a second computer lab. This space was allocated for the School-Age program's use, as Tech staff had observed that adults and children work better in separate spaces when learning computer skills. Part of the problem might have been the parents' awareness that the children were generally ahead of them when it came to using computers. And, then, there was the noise.

In 2000, Byron Espinosa, a Honduran/ Guatemalan immigrant, took Kent Unruh's place as Director of the Technology Center. Also in 2000, Erie received the "Digital Stepping Stones" award, from the Tomas Rivera Policy Institute, for providing access to technology in a community-based setting. Erie Tech Center staff also came up with a unique program they called "Technology Promoters." An article in Erie's newsletter, in the summer of 2002, provides the following description:

> *The Technology Promoters program is a grassroots, capacity-building initiative designed to enable residents to create a community-based technology system, promote the use of technology, peer-to-peer, and enhance the effectiveness of community leaders and organizers using technology skills.*[358]

The way it worked was that tech students exchanged 100 hours of their instruction to volunteer 100 hours of community service. This program was certainly representative of Erie traditions and values. It underscored the importance of volunteers in expanding Erie's capacity to deliver services that were in demand but beyond the capacity of paid staff. With the Tech Promoters, more classes could be offered, and the lab could be open more hours, with someone on hand for technical assistance for users and troubleshooting with equipment. It also encouraged the idea of giving back or paying it forward, in today's parlance. And finally, as culturally sensitive as Erie's Tech staff aimed to be, some adult learners found it much less intimidating to go through trial and error with a peer than a "professional teacher." The Tech Promoter program became another Erie experiment, so popular and successful, that it was still going 20 years later.

The importance of Erie's role in developing the Tech Center was also highlighted in a digital divide study published that year that showed serious underrepresentation of Hispanics and Blacks regarding internet and computer access.[359] Ric Estrada had the opportunity to discuss the digital divide with then-Senator Barack Obama, at a meeting set up by Erie Board member and counsel, Jesse Ruiz.

It was also in 2000, that Esther visited Elmhurst Presbyterian church, and spent some time with Glen and Betty Graham, as Glen celebrated his 89th birthday. That same year, Erie received word that Mae Lyman had passed away; Ross Lyman followed her the next year on November 6, 2001. Erie staff members, Ema Lopez, who had been at Erie 23 years in 2001, and Carmen Santiago, 34 years, both remembered Ross as a "warm, caring, soft-spoken and compassionate man." A board member from the Lyman era, Eleanor Brierly, added,

> *We wouldn't have had contact with people in other cultures, as we did with him at Erie House. I learned to be more aware of how people in poorer circumstances live. Ross and Erie made me appreciate what I have, and made me want to help.*[360]

Gentrification on the Rise – Erie Continues to Dilute the Impact

When I left Erie to work for PRAG at Loyola's Center for Urban Research and Learning (CURL), at the end of 1996, I was asked to return to the Board the following year. In the summer of 1998, I was preparing to serve as president. Evangeline Del Toro and Libby Zamora, two Latinas, served as Treasurer and Assistant Treasurer. There were 28 board members at that time. Some of the more seasoned members were Chuck Armstrong (Union Church), Jack O'Kieffe (Wilmette Presbyterian), Jeff Holcomb, Dr. Ann Doege (EFHC), Carmen Prieto (Mexican, from the Wieboldt Foundation), Don Roubitchek (The Private Bank), Alicia Avila (Child Care), Sophie Oboza (a neighbor from Noble Street), Librada Zamora (First Bank, and an Erie kid), and Mike Milkie (a Wells High School teacher who would later found the Noble Network of Charter Schools). Newer members included Sy Nelson from Northern Trust (keeping that tradition going), Steve Fox (2nd generation), John Jacus (joining Armstrong from Union Church), Maria Vargas (a Puerto Rican neighbor & community activist), Juan Luis-Araiza (Dominican, from the City Clerk's staff), Richard Figueroa (Puerto Rican, from LaSalle Partners), Joe Antolin (Puerto Rican, IDHS), Matias Rico(Mexican, IBM), Maris Gonzalez-Silverstein, Stacy Thomas, and Rev. James Aydelotte(African-American). There were now 10 Latinx board members, primarily, a result of having Latinx executive directors. The budget hovered around $3.6 million, and the 1997 Christmas appeal brought in $54,000.

While the 1990 census still showed West Town to be a lower income community of color, no one thought the 2000 census would present a similar picture. As noted earlier, when Ravelo started in 1985, gentrification was already on the radar screen, and that the *Chicago Neighborhood Experiment* was aimed at getting ahead of the curve, with some off-setting measures. These were aimed at improving incomes so that some residents could afford to stay. But what started as a trend in Wicker Park in the 1980s, was rolling through the southeast corner of West Town, in "East Village" or "River West," by the end of the 1990s. As soon as you see those little signs hanging from the lamp posts with such names on them, you know that real estate interests are already bringing about--and benefiting from--escalating property values. The re-naming of neighborhoods is the baptism of gentrification. So, under Esther's leadership, Erie House was revisiting questions it started to address 10 years earlier: Stay? Go? Re-draw boundaries? Add on?

From the first round of discussion, the decision was to stay and to expand the program least vulnerable to changes in the immediate geographic area–Child Care. But at the same time, Erie acknowledged that this program would need to serve a broader area than the one that had been served by Miss Florence, Rev. Lyman, or Merri Ex. Latino families from Humboldt Park, and even Logan Square, were recruited for Erie House Pre-school. This scenario, however, did not apply to the School Age program. As time passed, the influx of young professionals, with fewer, if any, children, saw public schools in the area begin to experience declining enrollments. But there had also been some preparation in this area when Erie had added Talcott School, just west of the Center, to the program that had served only Otis and Carpenter from its earliest days of providing After-School care.

Sandy Schaefer and Dennis Puhr, School-Age director, also set about the business of making quality their best marketing tool. In 1998, they submitted proposals to the Illinois Department of Human Services (IDHS) for "Child Care Quality Enhancement" dollars. They focused on 3 areas: 1) children's programming; 2) parent education; 3) staff development and training. The request for School-Age was for $40,000/year for 3 years. At the time, they were serving 94 children. They also applied for the same amount on behalf of Day Care Family Homes, serving 84 children, 0-4 years old. This submission is an excellent example of how individual entrepreneurs had access to resources, as part of a network, that they may not have been able to acquire on their own. A third proposal was submitted on behalf of pre-school for $60,000/year, or $180,000. While the full amounts were not all approved, all three proposals were funded. Quality Enhancement dollars have been awarded to Erie ever since.

Meanwhile, another study was released in 1999, called the "ABCedarian Study."[361] The *New York Times* wrote: "Study links adult success to quality day care for kids." This was cited as the first study to track poor children from infancy to age 21. It found that *good* early childhood education provided benefits that continued to impact young adults. They were more likely to attend college and get better jobs, and their parents did better as well. While Erie House already knew this, it was always good to have "a study" that affirmed knowledge gained on the ground.

As it turned out, Adult Programming proved to be somewhat gentrification-proof as well. A convergence of several developments was responsible for this phenomenon. We have already touched on most of them. Reagan's amnesty led to a demand for citizenship classes, and more English classes to prepare for the test. Just as boundaries expanded for child care, stretching west and northwest, they ended up expanding southwest and west, for adult learners, traveling from Little Village, and the suburb of Cicero, as Latinos recognized more affordable opportunities for home ownership in this blue-collar suburb, as compared with the city. They were also willing to make the trip for a program of the quality and cultural sensitivity as the one led by Tim Bell, supplemented by access to a community-oriented Technology Center. And finally, that southwestern city/western suburban area was, virtually, an ESL/Adult ed desert in the 1990s. So, Erie provided and Erie benefited. It turned out, for adults: have ESL need, will travel. That very condition kept the House as busy as the Center in the 1990s, and led to a new direction early in the 21st century, as Erie was gradually re-defining "community-based," as more cultural and less geographic.

In March, 1999, Erie's Adult Education Department formulated this mission statement that articulates all that has been described to this point:

To offer holistic, integrated, participatory, outcomes-based educational services which promote economic justice and social equality for poor and working people in Chicago.[362]

To this end, Erie is dedicated to creating programming that:

- Celebrates student diversity and creates opportunities for students to connect across differences;
- Offers student choice and voice;
- Emphasizes the teaching of communication (literacy, language, and technology) and leadership skills, using content which centers on the histories, needs and aspirations of our diverse student body;
- Raises social and political consciousness so students may more fully exercise their rights and responsibilities as individuals, workers, citizens, family and community members;
- Builds bridges to economic self-sufficiency and advancement;
- Promotes mutual accountability among students, staff, and community.[363]

Dealing with Gentrification through More Strategic Planning

Round II of the gentrification discussion began in the context of a strategic planning activity, with a projected timeline of October 1999-June 2000. The timeline eventually spilled over to June 2002, occupying about three years of the Nieves's administration. To get the ball rolling,

Loyola University's CURL provided a strategic planning training workshop to the Board and staff Leadership Team (L-Team). The process that emerged began with Erie departments each developing their own strategic plan. A first draft of these plans was discussed at the March 2000 staff retreat, facilitated by Juana Bordas, President of Mestiza Leadership of Denver. The attendance sheet for this retreat had 96 names on it. To work with such a large group, contracting with outside facilitation services was probably wise, and Nieves made the effort to identify a culturally compatible expert.[364]

The staff plan was presented to the board at the annual board/staff retreat in June 2000. In November, the Board formed its own strategic planning committee with the intention of building on the staff plan. On May 25, 2001, in a memo to the board, Nieves reported that, to date, the strategic planning process had raised two critical issues regarding fulfillment of Erie's mission: the changing demographics of West Town and Erie's ongoing presence in that neighborhood. She argued that there were some facts already known, but insufficient data led her to propose an "Erie Research Project," to be carried out for the next year, until June 2002.

As to what was known, Nieves laid out the following. 26% of Chicago's population was Latino, a fact probably revealed by the 2000 census, and probably an undercount. From the perspective of an executive director with no small amount of political savvy, Nieves laid out an interesting scenario. With the possibility of 5 new "Latino" wards already under discussion, the interest of elected officials in Latino ethnic groups was likely to grow, and therefore, interest in organizations that knew them. By 2000, Erie had been gathering that knowledge for almost 40 years, serving both Puerto Ricans and Mexicans. She went on to say that service gaps existed on all levels–child care, adult ed, youth. At the same time, Erie's geographic base, West Town, was continuing to gentrify. Increasing property values and property taxes continued to drive the working poor out of the area. Some had moved northwest to Belmont-Cragin--some as far away as Cicero. So far, they traveled to get to Erie. In the future, should Erie move closer to them? Or can Erie stay in West Town, its home for the past 130 years, with the possibility of establishing program-focused satellites in other communities? To answer these questions and assess the impact of these demographic changes on Erie's mission, Nieves argued for more "grounded research." She also suggested that research partnerships might be established with Loyola and CNT, two organizations they had worked with before.

The foundational work for this grounded research would be a survey–of staff and participants–as to where they live, their ethnic origins, and why they come to Erie House. Other components of the research would include an environmental scan and community SWOT analysis to identify:

- Non-profits serving the community, Latino and not;
- Gaps in service;
- Stakeholders to meet and interview;
- levels of social and political capital.

At the September 2001 board meeting, Esther reported that 350 surveys of participants had been completed, in English and Spanish, with assistance from CNT. In November, data collected through those surveys was reported at a Board/Staff retreat. Chuck Armstrong opened the retreat with a brief memorial to Ross Lyman, who had just passed away. Sixteen board members were present, and members of the Leadership Team that included Tim Bell (Adult Ed), Richard Boyd (Operations), Byron Espinosa (Technology), Ric Estrada (Admin), Lisa Galicia (Development), Paul Kasper (Admin), Maria Matias (YOU),

Maria Perez (HR), Dennis Puhr (Child Care/After-School), Betty Sanchez-Azadeh (Finance), and Esther. Two panel presentations followed.[365]

Panel 1 was called "Times Have Changed: Regional Trends and Local Demographics," presenting data on the Latino community. While West Town was still in the top 20 communities in need of child care in the state, it sat near the bottom of that list. The need was far greater in Waukegan, Aurora, and Joliet, towns with growing numbers of Latino residents. Closer to Chicago, Cicero, that was 37% Latino in 1990, had become 77% Latino! In the city, the neighborhoods Erie was looking at–Belmont-Cragin (northwest side) and Brighton Park (southwest side)–were communities in need.

The second panel was called "Client Population: What Have We Learned?" presented by Rev. Clare Butterfield, of the Inter-Religious Sustainability Project at CNT, and Dr. Janet Smith, from UIC.[366] Their task was to present the data collected through the Erie participant survey. 506 participants had responded to Erie's "2001 User Survey." First, and foremost, survey respondents confirmed that West Town was being dramatically impacted by gentrification, resulting in extensive displacement of low and moderate-income people. They reported that Humboldt Park, adjacent to West Town to the west, was still somewhat affordable, but was already beginning to change as well. Other information gleaned from the surveys was that child care continued to be a critical need, but people also named adult education, job training, and citizenship classes as important services for them. Of course, these were responses of people already using these services at Erie. 51% of participants used services at the House, and 47% at the Center, indicating the balance of interest between child care services and services for adults and older children. In other words, the whole family was using the whole place. What was surprising was that 43% of participants walked to

Erie House. This would certainly pertain to school-age children and youth, but others had to be walking as well to get to 43%. 42% drove and 15% took public transportation. Finally, what came across loud and clear was the request that Erie stay put.

In the discussion that followed, it was noted that while the displacement trend was of concern, the perception that there were no more poor people in West Town was not accurate. The issue of affordable housing came up, an even more desperate need in 2002 than when Erie proposed the affordable co-op housing project in 1994, and how sad it was that the alderman, at that time, had killed it. Board member, Don Roubitchek pointed out that Bickerdike was better equipped to address the need for more affordable housing. What low income people also needed to fend off displacement was a better income, what Erie had already determined in 1990, with the *Chicago Neighborhood Experiment* report. And that hinged on education. This was Erie's strength and "we should build on that," Roubitchek argued.[367]

Roubitchek's confidence in Bickerdike's role was affirmed in the release of a study the following month, in December 2001. Clearly, Bickerdike (then in its 34th year) was as concerned about the pace of gentrification as Erie House was. So, they had been partnering with the Voorhees Center at UIC to sponsor a study of the issue. The report of their findings was written up by UIC faculty member, John Betancur, and called "Gentrification in West Town: Contested Ground." Voorhees Associate Director, Pat Wright, (a veteran of the Chicago 21 campaign) described the study as "a unique contribution to the gentrification literature, involving historic and qualitative analysis."[368] The study spanned 4 decades, 1960-2000, tracing how patterns in real estate investment, population change, and public policy converged to change West Town's profile.

One of the findings that Joy Aruguete, BRC's Executive Director, commented on was that:

Tensions are exacerbated (between the haves and have-nots) by the perception that subsidized housing negatively affects property values, a common assumption that is largely unfounded. [369]

The study found that median home prices in West Town had doubled between 1990 and 2000. During the same period, the Latino population of West Town dropped from 59% to 47%. While this was a significant change, in another way, it supported Don Roubitchek's comment that the perception that there were no more poor people and/or Latinos in West Town was overblown at that point in time. In fact, the census would reveal there were still over 126,000 Latinos living in West Town as of 2000, with an unemployment rate of 11.3%, and an underemployment rate of 87%, for those earning less than $30,000/year. As the study noted, long-term affordable rental housing comprised only 7% of the area's housing stock, another statistic Alderman Granato frequently exaggerated. Furthermore, most of that 7% had been developed by BRC, even in the face of continual opposition to their work by property associations (like the Old Wicker Park Community Council and Eckhart Park Community Council), other real estate interests, and politicians like Granato. One conclusion: the less affluent who still lived in West Town in 2000 needed both Erie House and Bickerdike, if they wanted to stay.

Finally, there was agreement that if Erie decided on opening a satellite program, that it should do so in the city, where Erie knew how politics worked, even if Erie leadership did not always agree with the politicians; the suburbs were a different animal. Jack O'Kieffe also stressed the idea that Erie needed to maintain/renew ties with the Presbytery.[370] On the one hand, the Presbytery still held title to 1347 W. Erie, a fact that had already caused complications as Erie applied for grants to maintain the building that they did not own. On the other hand, the Presbytery, and some of the more affluent congregations, like Fourth Pres, could be partners in a joint venture, if Erie decided to expand. Esther assured O'Kieffe that she was on it, visiting churches herself and inviting mission committees to visit.

Following O'Kieffe's admonishment to keep in touch with the Presbytery, Board member, Layla Suleiman, raised the question regarding increased demand for Erie's services in light of other agencies leaving West Town. Nieves acknowledged this was already happening– both the leaving and the additional demands. Indeed, before, during, and after Erie completed their strategic plan, neighboring institutions were on the move. Chicago Commons headquarters, which had been located in West Town at Taylor House, 915 N. Wolcott, since 1958, would be moving to the west end of Humboldt Park to their newly built Nia Center at 744 N. Monticello, closing Taylor House.[371] By 2001, Association House had moved off North Avenue in Wicker Park to take up residence in a shuttered hospital building at 1116 N. Kedzie Avenue, which they had acquired in 2000. It was just west of Humboldt Park and six blocks further south of where they had been since 1905. Emerson House of Chicago Commons was said to be closing, and did by June, 2002. That left Onward House, Northwestern Settlement, and Erie House to serve the eastern end of West Town, east of Western.[372]

Finally, the board discussed the Huron property as an asset that could be sold to finance the opening of programming in a new neighborhood or as seed money for a capital campaign. How this asset came to Erie House is the story that follows.

La Capilla, The Huron Property – Turning a Short-term Liability into a Long-term Asset

Before the strategic planning process began, and then running concurrent with that process, Erie House was approached by a local pastor, Rev. Abreu. He ministered to a small congregation that worshiped in a building at 1446 W. Huron that they called La Capilla, or the chapel. Most of his congregation had moved out of the neighborhood and decided it was time to sell this property and acquire a space closer to where they now lived. When the pastor came to speak with Nieves, he explained that they would prefer to sell the property to Erie House rather than to a real estate developer that would tear it down and turn it into high-end housing. Esther approached a few board members to ask for counsel on this opportunity. With Richard Figueroa's background in real estate, and other board members' experience with purchasing local properties, it was agreed this presented a good investment opportunity at a purchase price of around $300,000. Figueroa outlined several scenarios for eventual disposition, from redevelopment as affordable housing, to simply selling the property at some future date, and using the proceeds to support Erie programs. It was 1999. The deal was done, a mortgage taken, the purchase made. Rent from the 2-flat, adjacent to the chapel was collected by Erie House.

Throughout 1999, discussion ensued as to how best to use the Huron property. To evaluate an affordable housing development possibility, Erie consulted with Paul Roldán at Hispanic Housing. As that consultation was being pursued, a plan was put forward to rent the chapel space to a non-profit user. As it turned out, the YOU Collaborative became one of the tenants. The other was Erie's own Citizenship program that had grant money to spend for rent and, as always, Tim Bell needed more space. When the Huron Property Committee finally sat down with Paul

Roldán, he advised against the idea of an affordable housing development for the following reasons. First of all, he said that new construction costs in West Town were approaching Lincoln Park levels. So, to make units affordable, heavy subsidies would be required. Secondly, a zoning change would be needed, and that would likely stir up gentry opposition, a prophetic insight. Finally, Erie's target Latino population, was steadily moving out of West Town, suggesting they may not even be the ones to benefit from such a project. As a result of this advice, it was decided that the best option might be to hold it a few more years, sell the entire property at a profit, and use the proceeds to benefit the Latino community elsewhere. Meanwhile, some cosmetic improvements were made so that the proposed tenants could move in during the summer of 2000.

In November 2000, a city inspector showed up and cited Erie for "conducting business" in a residential zone. With the co-op fight still fresh in her memory, Esther went to Alderman Granato for advice on what to do. The only option he offered was to go to the Zoning Board of Appeals. Before doing that, Esther went to Erie's pro bono law firm of 50 years, Gardner Carton & Douglas, to seek their advice. They recommended that Erie use the services of Jack Guthman of Shefsky & Froelich, the leading expert in zoning matters in Chicago, and made the connection happen. Guthman said what Erie would need was a "special use variance."

It eventually came to light that the inspector's visit was the result of a complaint filed by Erie's old nemesis, the Eckhart Park Community Council, still railing against poor people of color, walking the streets of *THEIR* neighborhood. In March, Esther and Mr. Guthman went to meet with them to plead their case, but to no avail. The zoning hearing was set for April 20, 2001. Erie was not idle in the interim. As they had done many times throughout their history, they organized. Twenty letters of support were gathered from churches and other community organizations, 500 signatures were secured on petitions, and on the day of the hearing, 150 people boarded two buses for the ride downtown to pack the hearing room.[373] *¡Presente!* was Erie's "marching for advocacy slogan." It was evident that day. Between the community witness and Mr.Guthman's insider knowledge, Erie won their variance.

On April 24, Esther penned a memo of thanks to the staff for their support. She wrote:

> *Compassionate voices spoke out on our behalf and defended Erie's mission, history, and programs. . . This is not just an Erie victory, but a victory for our community. Together we spoke the truth to power and we triumphed!* [374]

Erie continued to use the Huron property for programming for another year. By the summer of 2002, the Board was ready to sell it. The plan was to list it for $650,000. Thought was also given as to how to present this decision to the community that had fought for Erie to use the space for programs. It was important to make clear that funds would be used on behalf of the Latino community, just not at this site. The scenario for keeping that promise was about to unfold.

La Villita: ¡Vamanos!

By the time the research Esther proposed as part of the strategic planning process was completed, and just as the Huron property was going on the market, another development occurred that had a major impact on Erie's decision regarding the possibility of opening a satellite program instead of moving, never a popular choice for board or staff. Back in 1999, Western Union lost its fight against a lawsuit, filed against them for over-charging in the matter of processing remittances sent to families back home by Mexicans working in the US. Erie House had joined that lawsuit.[375] When the $4.6 million settlement was announced, the judge ruled that, in light of the difficulty in finding every Mexican who had been harmed by the company, organizations serving Mexican communities could submit proposals for use of some of these funds. As organizations like Erie House pondered what to propose, the idea for a collaboration emerged--a collaboration that focused on Little Village (South Lawndale), the largest Mexican community in Chicago at that point in time.

On June 21, 2002, a meeting was convened in the offices of the Wieboldt Foundation, hosted by Carmen Prieto of the foundation, and president of the Erie Board. The purpose of the meeting was to discuss an emerging opportunity for collaboration. They were aware that Matt Piers, the attorney managing the disposition of funds from the Western Union Settlement, expressed interest in exploring the possibility of a partnership between Little Village Community Development Corp. (LVCDC) and Erie Neighborhood House, to establish a specific project to benefit Mexican families living in Little Village. At that meeting, Esther provided a history of Erie's service to immigrants. Carmen Prieto explained that Erie was in the midst of a long-range planning process. Part of that process included evaluation of possible options for Erie's expansion to a new community through delivery of one or more "portable" programs that would not require a major capital expenditure upfront. She shared that communities considered to date were: Belmont-Cragin, Cicero/Berwyn, Brighton Park/McKinley Park.

Jesus "Chuy" Garcia and Alderman Ricardo Muñoz shared general information about South Lawndale/Little Village.[376] At that time, Garcia was the executive director of LVCDC, following his time in the City Council and the State Senate. Their report noted that Little Village had

91,000 residents, and that 21.5 was the average age, with 45,000 at age nine or under. Nearly 20% of the community had a 5th grade education or less. There were some social service agencies, such as El Valor, Universidad Popular, Tepeyac, Lawndale Christian Community Church (located in North Lawndale), but they were working past their capacity to keep up with the demand. West Side Tech, a satellite of Daley College, was nearby but under-utilized. (Erie House knew this was not a new story when it came to City Colleges.) They concluded that the two areas of service most in demand were programs for youth and adult education that included ESL and citizenship and immigration services.

The meeting concluded with a decision to explore this further with Matt Piers. They met with him on July 12, 2002. Matt said Western Union funds would be available as early as September. He also liked the idea of South Lawndale as a location, accessible by areas like Brighton Park and Cicero/Berwyn. He also encouraged a partnership proposal for what he termed an "Immigrant Resource Center," that would allow him to be more generous with the release of funds. Erie went to work on program ideas and space requirements, and LVCDC took on the search for space, at least for a start-up. Piers wanted a proposal in 30 days. Once again, Erie adopted the strategy of "stay and add." Last time they focused northwest; this time it would be southwest, and would require Erie to physically open new space in a new neighborhood. A decision was made: *La Villita, vamanos.*

However, in spite of all the excitement generated by this meeting, back home at Erie House, Nieves felt compelled to do a reality check. Financially, it was not the best of times for Erie House. They had just eliminated 7.5 positions and there would be no raises for next year (FY03). Initially, just one million dollars was available from the Western Union funds–a start-up grant. If this were to become a major capital undertaking, how would it be paid for? One possibility was the sale of the Huron property. A realtor's recommendation was to list it for $625,000. If that sale were to occur, that still might not be enough. Alderman Muñoz promised to work on gaining support from Mayor Daley for the project, and thereby open the possibility of some city funding. But Esther was not persuaded that was a viable option given the city's budget constraints. Working with Chuy and LVCDC was fine, mission-wise, but she felt they were moving a little too fast. So, she recommended that Erie "get its feet wet" by offering some programs in Little Village, before any capital dollars for space were required. For the most part, the Board shared Esther's reluctance to commit to developing a third property, that would require a capital campaign, and manage a facility that was a lot farther away than the 4-block walk from the House to the Center.

On the one hand, Piers was pressing for forward motion, and wanted to know if Erie was committed or not. On the other hand, hearing Esther's concerns, he acknowledged the project was much stronger with Erie on board.[377] Furthermore, Tim Bell shared an idea with Nieves that ended up being the beginning of Erie's engagement in Little Village. In a memo dated September 5, 2002, he outlined a feasible option for a start-up project.[378] He pointed out the need for more space to enroll more students in citizenship classes. He argued that the west end of Little Village would be an ideal location. He was aware that this area was in need of services, and Erie was in need of more space for citizenship services. Since 9/11, he explained, Erie House had assisted 1,230 citizenship applicants, a 350% increase over the previous year. In the short term, the impact of the events in New York City, September 11, 2001, was generally viewed in the context of those directly affected, in and around the towers and Pentagon. In the longer term, other places, like Chicago, with large immigrant populations, felt the impact through an increased demand for services leading to citizenship, a defensive move, as yet another round of anti-immigrant sentiment surfaced.

Ultimately, Bell's proposal became the solution. Piers advanced funds to LVCDC to manage, with a longer timeframe to develop a location for a center. Meanwhile, funds could be passed through to Erie House to start adult programming. The second floor of the convent next to Epiphany Church, at the west end of Little Village, became the site for Erie to begin offering ESL and citizenship classes, and gain a foothold in their new neighborhood. Rent for the first year, as well as infrastructure improvements, were covered by a $25,000 grant from CORNET (Corporate Real Estate Network).

Certainly, the wrap-up of the 3-year strategic planning process, with the unexpected turn toward extension of Erie services into Little Village, was one of the most significant activities of 2002. Then add this to the sale of the Huron property. Gentrification was still a daunting challenge, but it was not going to chase Erie House out of West Town.

Before closing out 2002, there are a few other important highlights to touch upon. While most Erie board members have dedicated themselves to Erie House, sometimes for generations, some new people were nominated for the 2002-2003 Erie Board that should be mentioned here for their significant asset-building contribution. The first, nominated by Jesse Ruiz, was Clarisol Avila (later Duque), a Humboldt Park resident, and aide to Senator Dick Durbin for Hispanic Community Affairs. Later she became his chief-of-staff. Mark Hallett, nominated by Carmen Prieto, came from the McCormick-Tribune Foundation. He helped develop a journalism program with YOU, and was involved in the Erie Charter School start-up. John Hall, owner of Goose Island Brewery, nominated Ken Perkins, a major patron of scholarships for Erie kids. Chuck Armstrong nominated Nancy Vincent from the mission committee of his Hinsdale church. Mark Jolicouer, First Church of Oak Park, and an architect with Perkins and Will, kept that long-time church connection to Erie going, and brokered some significant pro bono architectural services from time to time.

Erie also had two important visitors in April 2002. The first was Senator Dick Durbin [379] After stopping by the Center, where a pre-schooler served him a plastic donut, he went to the House. There, Erie's Youth Options teens told their stories of being brought to the US as children, and now, due to lack of papers, were blocked from applying for financial aid to attend college. They also shared their fear of deportation when they had lived almost their entire life in the US. It was stories like this, Durbin acknowledged later, that inspired him to co-sponsor S1291 with Rep. Orrin Hatch, that came to be known as the Dream Act, or the Development, Relief and Education for Alien Minors Act. This is what the bill would do if Congress passed it:

> *Enable undocumented young people of good character to obtain legal status if they are at least 12 years old at the time of enactment, and if they have resided continuously for 5 years in the US. Youth must have earned a high school diploma before applying for this new immigration status, and must be under 21 the day they apply* [380]

Following Durbin's visit, Erie youth collected 600 signatures in support of his bill. We know now that it did not pass, nor did any successor bill. But it was Durbin who worked with President Obama years later to draft the executive order that finally gave Dreamers some hope in the form of DACA (Deferred Action for Childhood Arrivals).

Later that same month, Mayor Richard M. Daley came to Erie House, as did Sesame Street. He was invited by the *Chicago Tribune* that had chosen Erie House as the place to announce a new children's section, called "Carrusel," in their Spanish language paper, *Exito!* Esther recalled that he was very gracious, and in his remarks said that "Erie House sets the bar for excellence in non-profit service delivery." Whether Erie agreed with him all the time or not, it never hurts to get a few kudos from the mayor. She also used the opportunity to corner one of his cabinet members, Ray Vasquez. He was Commissioner of the Department of Human Services, a source of important Erie contracts for child care, as Erie's public funding was approaching 70% of its budget. He told her not to worry. "Erie has an excellent performance history."[381] That was also confirmed by the federal government that had just given Erie the highest rating for their Head Start program, which "had no findings." That means A+.

All in all, Esther summarized the event this way: "Yes, Elmo may have been present, but Erie Neighborhood House was the star of the day."[382] Communicating one's "stardom" to the public is always a priority of non-profits that are continually in search of new donors, while keeping the older ones engaged. One way to communicate one's image is in the form of a logo. The year 2002 became the time for another change. Upon completion of the House in 1936, the Erie logo became a pen and ink drawing of the "new building" on Erie Street. That remained on the letterhead until, during Rafael Ravelo's administration, a more abstract and colorful logo was adopted. This appeared in a teal color and had joyful figures dancing in front of Erie House. It was also the time when "La Casa Comunal de Erie" was added. In 2002, the logo changed from teal dancers to maroon figures holding hands to form a house. A newsletter article explained it this way:

> *Erie's new logo symbolizes the aspiration and strength of the Erie family, which is illustrated by two individuals clasping hands and reaching*

upward. In so doing, they form the very structure of our house. Alone, however, Erie House cannot be effective. As represented by the third figure, Erie extends the hand of inclusivity and opportunity to all, for only through united effort can we create a just and equitable society. Erie House is the people it serves and the partners who support our mission. You are our walls and our windows to the world, our foundation, and our future.[383]

Strategic Planning for Major Gifts

As the 20th century was coming to a close, two of Erie's long-time revenue sources were in decline–the United Way and Presbyterian Congregations. These two trends have been noted earlier in this text, and initially, Erie addressed this situation by professionalizing and expanding its Development Department staff, especially under Ravelo, to more aggressively pursue funding from foundations. While Bill Pfeiffer and Lisa Galicia were Development Directors in the 1990s, foundation funding went very well, and special multi-years grants, like the Chicago Community Trust's grant for the YOU Collaborative, and the Fry Foundation for the Technology Center, were significant achievements. But, as Erie learned over the years, both public and private grantmaking were not consistently reliable. On the public side, elections changed the leadership, and leadership shifted priorities for public spending. On the private foundation side, guidelines changed, sometimes in the middle of a multi-year grant. Some of that was based on staff or board changes; some of it was based on new demographic information and/or recognition of racially discriminatory patterns of giving, intentional or not.

In the midst of all this uncertainty, one idea that kept re-surfacing was the development of a "major gifts" program. While Erie had certainly received major gifts over its 100+ years of existence, starting with Hannah Templeton's bequest of $100,000 that financed the construction of the building at 1347 in 1935, there was no system in place to increase the frequency and the dollar amounts of these gifts. To address the goal of changing that, Erie hired Ruth Kane as a consultant to explore this possibility. She began her work toward the end of 2001, by sitting down with Erie's Senior Advisor, Rafael Ravelo, to pick his brain regarding any long-term supporters of Erie House.[384]

Appropriately, he began with Glen and Betty Graham, by far the best examples of a "major gift" donor Erie had to that point, and the middle generation of the Sawyer-Graham-Schuham dynasty of Erie supporters, described in earlier chapters. Betty's father was Dr. Sawyer. He and his wife Frances, and his sister, Anna Grace Sawyer, were all Erie supporters. It is Frances' name that appears on the plaque just outside the Sawyer rooms on the first floor of the House. Anna Grace was also a supporter of Rev. Martin Luther King and his Southern Christian Leadership Conference, as revealed in copies of her correspondence that were found in the Erie archives.[385] All three generations have supported Erie in many ways, besides cash. However, Rafael's outline of financial support, from the Grahams alone, was substantial. It included:

- $20,000 to rehab the Sawyer Rooms;
- $10,000 to landscape the empty lot Erie had acquired, next to the House;
- $10,000 to pay for an architect to work on building improvements;
- $10,000/year for 18 years for the TEAM scholarship fund = $180,000 (as of 2002);
- Periodic contributions of $2,000-3,000;
- Estimated grand total: $240,000.[386]

The Graham's daughter, Marjorie Schuham, continued in her parents' tradition, on into the 21st century. She had served as president of the Erie Woman's Auxiliary, as had her mother before her. There was no ready list of her financial contributions, but gifts came in the form of new front doors for the House when they were needed.

Jim McClure was mentioned next, also an Oak Park resident and member of First Church there. He was a neighbor of Ross Lyman when he became Executive Director in 1952. He, Lyman, Graham, Carton, and Frank Bristol, another long-time board member, were referred to by Rafael as "The Big 5" from Oak Park.[387] McClure worked for Gardner, Carton and Douglas, and was a recognized leader of the Presbytery of Chicago. He and his wife, Lynn, were both still on the board when Rafa arrived in 1985, in their 34th year. They celebrated together when they both received alumni awards from the University of Chicago in 1996. He and Lynn had both retired to Florida by that time. McClure had arranged an annual gift of $1,000 that came to Erie through the Oak Park/River Forest Foundation. McClure also served on the Investment Committee, with special attention to the McGaw fund. This was Erie's endowment account that the board established in 1944. Over the years, the account had its ups and downs, but mostly up. In 1957 it was valued at $52,000:

- In 1959, at $96,000;
- In 1983, at $75,000;
- In 2002, at $1.9 million.

With the help of Continental Bank, and then Northern Trust, one might conclude that the Investment Committee did a pretty good job over the years.

Rafael described Bob and Nancy Gielow as beautiful people with a great passion for Erie. As the son of Walter and Evangeline Gielow, who both spent a lifetime dedicated to Erie House, Bob grew up knowing Miss Florence. He revered her as someone as important as Jane Addams. He served on the board, side by side with his mother, and was also on the Endowment Committee. No dollar amounts for giving were mentioned, but one might conclude that the entire Gielow family was a "major gift."

Laurence Carton came next in Rafael's "rolodex" of significant supporters from the Oak Park Big 5. He served a term as president of the Erie Board in the late 1940s and would be described as a close friend of Florence Towne. As he was the one who brought Gardner, Carton & Douglas (GC&D) on board as Erie's pro bono law firm, how do you place a dollar amount on more than 50 years of free legal work–another major gift? Jim McClure, Mark Furlane, Noemi Flores, Jesse Ruiz, and Nick Guzman, all associated with Gardner, Carton, & Douglas, and later, Drinker, Biddle & Reath, were the firm's "gifts" to the Erie Board. Ruiz went on to serve as President of the Illinois State Board of Education, Vice-President of the Chicago Board of Education, and in 2018, was named a deputy governor by Governor J.B. Pritzker. As a graduate of the University of Chicago, he also connects to another Erie House tradition. In addition, as of 2001, Erie was receiving an annual stock gift from the Cartons valued at $15,000.[388]

Besides his connection to Erie's law firm, Nick Guzman was associated with Erie in additional ways. His sister, Maria Guzman, had worked for Erie's Youth Department before Nick joined the board, and he was destined to serve as president of the Board by 2019.

Rafael remembered David Dangler fondly as one of the "old-timers" who gave him a warm welcome when he took the job of executive director in 1985. By then, he had been on the board for 40 years and stayed 10 more. Originally from Lake Forest, he resided on the Gold Coast by the 1980s. He had been a vice-president at Northern Trust and was probably Erie's earliest contact with the bank that has itself been a long-time benefactor. There is no record of any one major gift from Dangler, but he tended to come up with $5,000 here and $10,000 there, when Erie needed it. Or, he used his connections to get it. By 2001, he was in his 80s and out of touch with Erie.

Robert Wiley had served a term as president of the Erie Board, a term as president of the Bickerdike board, and had been a volunteer with Meals on Wheels. He also organized the collection of gifts at Wilmette Presbyterian for Erie's Christmas gift drive. He has spoken of how he values Erie's commitment to the Hispanic community and speaks with great pride of the work Erie does. He believed that Erie honored its history and appreciated that Erie kept Miss Florence's picture in the lobby of the House. He always spoke with great respect for the generations of support Erie was able to secure from families like the Armstrongs, Gielows, McClures, and Jack O'Kieffe, from his own church.

John Hall was a much more recent addition to the Erie Board in 1990, but he stayed on for the next 18 years. As the owner and developer of Goose Island Brewery, he was a savvy businessman, very approachable and very generous, said Rafa. He began by donating space at his restaurant for an Erie event, donated a lot of beer for Erie's special events over the years, and eventually, much more. As an example, one year he donated the proceeds from the sale of Goose Island Christmas Ale. That donation alone totaled $37,000.[389]

With this background from Ravelo, Kane set out to meet these interesting people. By September 2002, she had set up a luncheon to be hosted by Jack O'Kieffe, and attended by the Armstrongs, McClures, and Gielows. There she told them that because Erie has a compelling story to tell, the idea for an oral history project had emerged, so that a generation of "church people" who were involved with Erie could provide a perspective to pass along to younger generations, especially from churches, to keep them engaged in supporting Erie House, hopefully, with major gifts. She did some videotaping that very day. This project expanded from there, and continued on to become linked with the Heritage Committee that took responsibility for planning Erie's 135th anniversary in 2005.[390]

Esther's Departure

Late in 2002, Esther Nieves informed the Board and Staff that this would be her last year at Erie House. Her husband had an offer for a job on the east coast, and as Esther put it, "it was his turn." But before she left, Erie received some good news on the funding front. The McCormick Tribune Foundation awarded Erie $100,000 over two years, with the likelihood of extending that to 5 years. The purpose of the grant was to "improve the quality of early childhood education through professional development": to encourage, and financially support, child care classroom teachers, to earn degrees and certifications that would enhance their expertise and their earning power over time. By increasing their self-esteem, and adding to their wallets, the goal was for them to see themselves more as professional employees on a career path than short-term "child care workers." This grant would allow Erie to take another giant step forward in ensuring the quality of an already highly-rated program.

The second piece of good news was a $360,000, 3-year award from the Marguerite Casey Foundation. The foundation had a community organizing/leadership development agenda targeting specific cities, and funding organizations they determined ready to advance their strategy. Erie House was one of 22 organizations in Chicago initially selected for funding. The fact that this was an invitation, that Erie did not apply for this grant, was an indication of the excellent reputation of this organization. As staff came to understand the foundation's values, it was understood that Erie was chosen for its excellent community-based services and long-term commitment to advocacy. But this story would unfold under Erie's next executive director.

As Erie House said good-bye to Esther in January, 2003, board and staff were grateful for her nine years as Associate and Executive Director. She had won another round of the gentrification fight with the zoning victory over the Huron property, engaged board and staff in taking the time, and doing the research, to determine where Erie was headed next. She was a thoughtful negotiator regarding the move to Little Village and kept in touch with other organizations in the community to keep Erie's spirit of collaboration alive and well. Through all of her administration she used her lively wit and political savvy to keep Erie front and center on the policy agendas that mattered. As the Commissioner of the Mayor's Office of Workforce Development, Jackie Edens, said in a farewell letter to Esther,

> *Your name has always been synonymous with social justice for the community. . .You are a person of vision.*[391]

Mayor Daley wrote:

> *Just a note to wish you well and to extend my thanks to you for all you have done for Chicago and our city's children. Erie Neighborhood House has long been a beacon of hope for countless families in need, and your tenure as executive director helped solidify Erie's position as one of Chicago's premier social service agencies.*[392]

It certainly never hurts to have the mayor refer to your organization as "a beacon of hope" and a "premier" social

service organization. Esther contributed significantly to that
perception.

Chapter Eight: Ricardo Estrada: From Undocumented Immigrant to *Crain's* List of "40 Under 40" (2003-2010)

Like Esther Nieves, Ricardo Estrada moved up to the position of Executive Director from serving as Associate Director first. Esther asked him to take that position in August of 1997, about mid-way through her first year as ED. He came to Erie after three years in various roles at a non-profit based in Pilsen, called Latino Youth. Through Latino Youth he became familiar with Erie House and met Rafael Ravelo. According to Estrada, it was Ravelo who recommended he pursue a Master's Degree at the University of Chicago, which he did through the Policy and Administration track of the SSA program (Social Service Administration). He later earned a Master's Degree in Business Administration at the University of Illinois Chicago (UIC) in 1997. His undergrad work was in psychology at Loyola University, graduating in 1989. Initially, his undergrad work was linked to his being a seminarian, as he believed he had a calling to become a Catholic priest. But after an internship experience in Bolivia, he came to believe that his calling to advance social justice would take a different path than church ministry. Nevertheless, he strives to be a spiritual person.[393] He became Executive Director, officially, in March 2003.

Estrada had been brought to the US from the state of Guanajuato, Mexico by his parents, around the age of 7, without papers, and grew up in Little Village. His path to legal permanent residency, and eventually citizenship, was linked to the citizenship of his younger sister, born in the US. Subsequent changes in immigration policy eliminated this path to citizenship. He is, undoubtedly, an outstanding example of why the US needs some form of the Dream Act, originally proposed by Senator Dick

Ricardo Estrada (Erie Neighborhood House)

Durbin of Illinois in 2002, to assist those brought to the US as children, and who Grew up as Americans, to have a pathway to citizenship. Why would the US want to forego the benefit of having this bright, career-focused young man as a citizen, contributing to American society and the welfare of his neighbors? He is an example of what the US will be missing, among the Dreamers of today, by denying them full citizenship, with every opportunity to attend college, work legally, and pay it forward.

Senator Dick Durbin answered that question in a letter he wrote to Estrada in 2004, after they had met for lunch to discuss the immigration issue. He wrote:

> *As the son of an immigrant, I believe people who have made the commitment to come to the U.S. have much to offer our country. It is in our national interest to embrace their commitment by allowing qualified immigrants to contribute to our economy and share their talents with our communities.*[394]

As of 2019, the US Congress had not yet passed any legislation that indicated they shared his belief.

As per usual, when Nieves announced she would be leaving Erie, the Board formed a Search Committee to find her replacement. While some assumed that Ric would automatically move up, the committee wanted to see who else might be out there. They received more than 25 applications, but interviewed just three, including Ric. Ultimately they came to the conclusion expressed in a letter from State Representative, Cynthia Soto, who wrote in support of Ric's application, January 17, 2003: "While I am saddened that Esther Nieves has decided to leave Erie Neighborhood House, I am comforted by the fact that an equally competent leader is waiting in the wings." [395]

Updating Context

The Political Environment

As Estrada began his time as executive director, Richard M. Daley was still mayor, in his 14th year. In the later years of his administration that aligned with the Nieves and Estrada years at Erie House, he had several opportunities for getting to know Erie House better and better. He attended press conferences at Erie's convenient location, close to downtown, and an occasional ribbon-cutting ceremony. Estrada shared that the mayor liked to hold a sort of "getting to know you" session at City Hall.[396] Shortly after becoming Director, he was invited to one of these sessions. He said they did not last long, but they achieved what Estrada perceived was Daley's goal, to make you feel important, and included in the mayor's purview. Down the road, this initial cordiality transitioned into more concrete support.

Estrada also was well-acquainted with the senior senator from Illinois, Dick Durbin. They met when Durbin visited Erie, while Ric was Associate Director, and one of Erie's youth, Maria Padilla, illustrated for the senator why there must be a path to citizenship for young adults brought to the US as children, without papers, but growing up as Americans. State Representative Cynthia Soto and State Senator Miguel Del Valle were long-time supporters of Erie House. Erie now had two, soon to be three, aldermen to deal with. The first ward aldermanic office had passed from Erie's old adversary, Jesse Granato, to a much more progressive and Erie-friendly alderman, Manny Flores. Erie was pleased with Flores' stand on neighborhood development, as he proposed to limit the construction of new multi-story apartment buildings and promote efforts to maintain the architectural character of the neighborhood.

But as maps were re-drawn, only the Center, at 1701 W. Superior was still in the 1st Ward. The House was in the 27th Ward of Alderman Walter Burnett, who also became a friend and advocate of Erie House. In her last report to the Board, Esther shared a story regarding Burnett's support for Erie. She met with him to discuss the restoration of a youth employment grant to Erie that had been cut. She described their visit as follows:

> *He picked up the phone and called Budget and Management. She heard him say, 'This grant is non-negotiable. Put the $16,000 (that Erie lost) back.' The funds were recently restored.* [397]

So, for the most part, the local political context for Erie House under Ricardo Estrada was looking pretty mellow in 2003. The one fly in the ointment was in the Governor's mansion in Springfield. Rod Blagojevich (D) was elected in 2003. To say he was not Illinois's most popular governor would be an understatement. Neither side of the aisle liked him or wanted to work with him. Non-profits found him offensive in the way he expected them to back his agenda "OR ELSE." Estrada reported that he found himself and Erie House threatened with funding cuts on a number of occasions if they did not comply with the governor's wishes. They remained only threats, and Estrada was generally confident that Erie's established reputation as a strong performer on state contracts, protected it from delivery on the threats, but observed that smaller, less well-established organizations felt intimidated. By December 2008, Blagojevich was out of the intimidation business and on his way to jail. For the rest of Estrada's time at Erie he dealt with Governor Pat Quinn (D). Founder of the Coalition for Political Honesty, Quinn was a more respectful and supportive governor.

The Immigrant Environment

As was noted in Chapter 6, Erie began serving more and more Mexican immigrants when Rafael Ravelo became director in 1985. With the table from Melvin Holli's book cited in that chapter, we saw that in 1980 there were 369,000 Mexicans in the Chicago Metro Area. By 1990 that number had grown to 547,850. It was this growth, and the effects of the 1986 so-called "amnesty" that flooded Erie House with demands for ESL and citizenship application assistance in the 90's. Not only had the Mexican population of West Town grown significantly, but Erie found that their students came from as far away as Cicero, as second-generation immigrants were starting their move to the nearby suburbs and becoming homeowners, in many cases. They came all the way to Erie House, partly because there was not much of a social service infrastructure in their new neighborhoods of choice, and, because word of mouth in the Mexican community told them of the quality and cultural sensitivity of the staff and programs of this settlement house. All of these were also good reasons for Erie to open a satellite in the west end of Little Village.

By the time Estrada became executive director in 2003, the growth of the Mexican population, in Chicago and its suburbs, was reflected in this 2000 census count:

530,000	in Chicago
256,000	in the suburbs
786,000	total in the Metro area.

In other words, from 1980 to 2000 the Mexican population in the Chicago Metro area had doubled, and represented the largest group in the overall count of 1.4 million Latinos.[398] In the city, Latinos predominated in two major clusters: 1) on the northwest side, consisting of Logan Square, Belmont-Cragin, West Town, and Humboldt Park; 2) on the southwest side, consisting of Little Village/South Lawndale, Pilsen/Lower West Side, Brighton Park, and New City/Back of the Yards. While West Town remained home to a large number of Latinos in 2000, it was also the community area that showed the greatest decline in the number of Latinos.[399] The threat of gentrification that Erie House had begun grappling with as early as the late 1980s, had moved from "down the road" to their front door. The early urban pioneers were being joined by so-called "yuppies," young white adults with professional salaries, with the goal of making money by investing in property they could "flip" and cash in on in a rapidly escalating market. The inevitable result in this type of marketplace is that lower income residents get displaced--in this case, Latinos.

In 2005, using the American Community Survey (ACS), a mid-decade report of the US Census, the Institute for Latino Studies, updated their 2004 report, setting the overall Latino population in the Metro Area at 1.6 million, of which 75% were Mexican.[400] And, for the first time, the number of Latinos living in the suburbs outnumbered those in the city. The largest of these suburban enclaves was Cicero, a suburb that bordered the southwestern boundary of the city, adjacent to South Lawndale/Little Village, and it was predominantly Mexican.

So, over a 50-year period of its history, 1950-2000, Erie House found itself working with continuously evolving service and advocacy strategies. During the Ross Lyman-Merri Ex years, Erie was working with its local civic, COPA, and the larger NCO, to fend off the wrecking ball that, in urban renewal style, aimed to wipe out the existing physical structures of the neighborhood. Then, under Ravelo, programs were initiated to create more affordable housing and add workforce development to improve the income of Latinos in the hope that they could stay in the neighborhood as rents began to rise. Erie also made the effort to reach into Humboldt Park and Logan Square, especially to promote its expanded pre-school child care program on Superior, and take advantage of that growing northwest cluster. During Nieves's administration, the search began for a possible satellite location in a neighborhood or suburb where the Latino population was on the rise. While Cicero was seriously considered, the Western Union settlement and potential partnership with LVCDC made Little Village the ultimate choice, staying in the city, but positioned next door to Cicero. And this is where Ric Estrada found himself, poised to establish an Erie House presence in Little Village. He would also add to that another move to the northwest with the development of the Erie Elementary Charter School.

The national mood, in terms of immigration, was anything but mellow. The events surrounding 9/11/2001 in New York, the assault on the twin towers, set off a wave of anti-immigrant sentiment, initially targeting Muslims, or just about anyone from the Middle East. Anyone who wore a hajib or went to a mosque to pray was subject to hate speech, and even physical threats, as an outspoken minority began to terrorize, that is, act in a similar manner to those they accused of being terrorists. Eventually, a mistrust of all immigrants turned public attention toward what was estimated to be, about 11,000,000 "undocumented" immigrants. Many Americans assumed the term "illegal" applied only to Mexican immigrants; in reality, they were not the only immigrants who made their way to America without going through the "proper" channels. There were Poles, Irish, and Asians who all fit this description.

9/11 also prompted attention to the issue of border security. And while the instigators of the 9/11 tragedy were discovered to have come to the US through Canada, this fact did not deter citizens and politicians alike, from focusing on the southwestern border instead, when it came to building walls and stepping up enforcement. The history of immigration policy in the US generally suggests a preference for discriminating against people of color, not to mention a long-term tolerance of slavery and Jim Crow. By 2006, the resentment of immigrants translated into proposed federal legislation in the form of HR 4437. This bill proposed raising penalties for illegal immigration by classifying undocumented immigrants, and anyone who assisted them, as felons. This would likely have pertained to all the settlement house workers in America, and certainly, to Erie House staff. This outrageous proposal prompted the mobilization of immigrants and their supporters and huge marches began to fill the streets in major cities across the country.

The first took place in Chicago on March 10, 2006. Why here? As Erie House could attest, as it marked its 135th anniversary in 2005, this was a city of immigrants--built by them, sustained by them, honored by their contributions to the urban economy and the arts. Any Chicagoan who knows her history would say: *We speak "immigrant" here.* Furthermore, this was the city of Saul Alinsky–community organizing is Chicago's middle name and the city had the infrastructure for empowerment to prove it. Finally, the Mexican immigrant community in particular brought along their own brand of organizing: their hometown organizations, that in 2006 moved from their connection to their past, to take a stand for their future. The estimate of 100,000 participants was the low figure; others estimated turnout as closer to 500,000. Suffice it to say the number was big enough to draw major press coverage. Over the next few months, these marches popped up all over the country, with Los Angeles being challenged to outdo Chicago in turnout.

The movement culminated on May 1, 2006, May Day or Labor Day, when workers around the world are challenged to unite. Chicago led the way again, this time with a turnout estimated to be around 700,000, with Poles, Irish, Asian, and African immigrants joining their Latino neighbors. African Americans joined in as well, being personally familiar with the fear and anger of being terrorized by your fellow citizen for more than 300 years. It was called by some "The Great American Boycott," as Mexican workers, in particular, were encouraged to boycott their jobs, keep their children home from school, and not to spend one dime in the American economy that day, to dramatize what "a day without immigrants" would be like for the rest of Americans who depend on them for so many services. Their slogan was not lost on politicians everywhere. "Today we march–tomorrow we vote." For as much as the louder voices talked about undocumented people who could not vote, in the Chicago Metro Area, by

2004, two thirds of Latinos were citizens, i.e., potential voters.[401]

Hundreds of Erie participants and the staff who served them, marched. They proudly carried the Erie banner frequently described in this text that said, simply: Erie Neighborhood House--¡PRESENTE! It was a good choice. It represented the collective witness of being present to and present for successive generations of immigrants who arrived long before, and just before, these families who traveled across a southern border instead of across an ocean.

The good news was that HR 4437 did not pass, and when states passed similar laws, they were eventually declared unconstitutional. The bad news was, the strategy that emerged was massive deportation. At least 300,000 were deported during the first few years following the marches, during the final days of President Bush, and throughout the Obama presidency. The strategy was intimidating enough to suppress further demonstrations on the scale of those of 2006. Some form of the Dream Act and comprehensive immigration reform stayed on the legislative agenda in Washington, but as of 2019, never got the votes to pass both houses.

Meanwhile, Chicago declared itself to be a "sanctuary city." This means local law enforcement was instructed not to cooperate with ICE in any of their efforts to pursue undocumented immigrants in Chicago. By the time of the big marches, Mayor Richard M. Daley was, unequivocally, on the side of immigrants. On more than one occasion, one could witness the mayor as he would get worked up, and red in the face, when addressing the issue of immigration. He would lean over the podium, point at the audience, and loudly proclaim: "You're an immigrant," then thumb pointed at himself, "I'm an immigrant," and with a broad sweep of his arm, "We're ALL immigrants." Enough said, in case you were not sure where the mayor stood on the issue.

With all of this as a backdrop, the scene is set to look more closely at how Erie Neighborhood House was prospering in this milieu, under the leadership of Ricardo Estrada.

Erie House takes Root in Little Village – A Partnership Begins

While discussion of the concept of an Erie presence in Little Village (LV) began on Esther Nieves's watch, implementation mostly took shape when Estrada was executive director. As discussion continued, and steps were taken to acquire and develop new space for the Little Village Immigrant Resource Center (LVIRC), Erie began, as Esther had recommended, with programming that did not immediately require a new building. Per Adult Program Director, Tim Bell's suggestion, Erie began in LV by offering ESL and citizenship classes in the space they rented on the second floor of the Epiphany convent at 4225 W. 25th Street. The first floor was occupied by Instituto del Progreso Latino (IDPL), headquartered in Pilsen. In her last report to the Board, January 28, 2003, Nieves explained that a 2-tier approach had been agreed upon with LVCDC (Little Village Community Development Corp.) and Matt Piers, who was overseeing disposition of the Western Union Settlement funds. Erie would begin services in a satellite location, while there would be a gradual exploration for property and a capital campaign to develop it for the LVIRC. LVCDC would be the fiscal agent and take the lead on the property search. Ric Estrada would be Erie's lead staff on this project. Little Village updates would now be on all subsequent Erie Board meeting agendas.

When Ric took over as ED in March, 2003, one of his first announcements was that $600,000 had been allocated from the Western Union settlement to LVCDC to get the ball rolling on the LVIRC project. The plan to purchase a building was still in the future, and a project timeline would be drafted and submitted to the Board soon. Meanwhile, he informed the Board that the Huron property was under contract. Also, as the tax-exempt status for the property was finally approved, Erie could expect a tax refund of about $25,000.

Programs and Press Coverage

During Ric's tenure, all Erie programs continued to provide quality services and adapt to the changing times and the ongoing need for advocacy. Erie House generally found itself seeking more funding, fighting funding cuts, challenging changes in guidelines that negatively impacted their participants, or proposing policies that would better serve them, and fighting for their implementation. Advocacy was generally done in collaboration with others, an Erie tradition, and a representative from Erie could be found on many councils and organizational boards, some of which Erie helped start. Sandy Schaefer assumed a lead role with the Day Care Action Council and the Coalition of Site-administered Child Care Centers. Bell was involved with various ICCB councils for adult education, and organizations like ICIRR (Illinois Coalition for Immigrant and Refugee Rights) and CAAELI (Coalition of Asian, African, European and Latino Immigrants). Byron Espinosa was on the board of CTCNet, a coalition of community-based technology centers. Since Erie was among the first to open a technology center in 1995, the idea had caught on at other settlements and social service organizations throughout the city, making Chicago home to one of the nation's most extensive networks of community-based tech centers. Evidence of this claim came in the latter half of 2003, when Erie was named as one of the 10 organizations participating in a national program run by IBM, called *Traducelo Ahora (Translate Now!);* 6 of the 10 participants were from Chicago.[402] Besides Erie, they included: Aspira, Association House, Central States-SER/Jobs for Progress, Instituto del Progreso Latino, and Spanish Coalition for Jobs (later, NLEI). There was also a Mayor's Council of Technology Advisors, and Ric served there.

Strong program directors like Sandy Schaefer for Child Care, Tim Bell for Adult Programs, and Byron Espinosa for Tech Services, made Estrada's life easier, as he could count on them to keep Erie's name and reputation for excellence in the forefront of the social services world, in Chicago and in Springfield, even nationally. Erie staff were invited to serve on panels and speak at conferences at all of these levels. Furthermore, both their excellence and their advocacy drew the attention of the press.

Consistent coverage, often praise, by the media, is important on several fronts. On the one hand, funders, both public and private like to see recognition of their wise decision to invest in such an organization, and on the other hand, such recognition can serve as a shield to protect the organization when they are threatened with harm, as in the case of Governor Blagojevich, or when their front-and-center presence in rallies and marches irritates the powers that be. The message that takes shape is that, if you go after Erie House, there may be consequences you do not want to experience. You will be viewed as "the bad guy/gal," picking on this stellar organization. Savvy program directors understood this, and Erie's very capable Development & Communications Department, led by Lisa Galicia, and then, Ami Novoryta, understood it as well. The board was also kept informed about all of this, receiving copies of news clippings and reports about advocacy activities. There was never a suggestion that the Board should determine what kind of advocacy activities staff should or should not undertake, not a hint of interference, whether individual members always agreed with the strategy or not. They wisely adhered to the principle of "if it's not broke, don't fix it." This was true from the days of NCO under Ross Lyman, through the tense adversarial moments of the co-op fight under Ravelo, and the major immigration marches that emerged in 2006, under Estrada.

Some examples of coverage shared at the March 2003, board meeting[403] on the side of praise included: a *Tribune* article that praised Erie's After-School program, a *Catalyst* article that praised TEAM, and an article in a publication of the Presbyterian Church USA,[404] that chronicled Erie House's community-based efforts on behalf of the working poor since 1870. In light of the successful advocacy to roll back citizenship application fee increases instituted by Homeland Security, the *Tribune* covered a press conference at Erie where Senator Del Valle and Erie's Citizenship Coordinator, Leticia Torres, encouraged people to start applying once again. While applications had lagged in the Fall of 2002, in just the first two months of 2003, Erie had doubled their Fall numbers.

The Board heard that Sandy Schaefer presented a report on Day Care Homes Online (DCHO) at a conference. Erie had been staffing a network of women running day care programs at their homes, mostly for children 0-3, for a number of years. Sandy and the Erie Development staff secured funds for the network that would provide computers for these female entrepreneurs, who now needed to "go online" to track and report service data so that they could get paid for the work they did for families eligible for subsidies. Erie experimented with how to deliver their training. At first, they were invited to attend a class at the Erie Tech Center. This milieu, with a professional instructor, proved to be too intimidating. Erie then assigned Tech Promoters as instructors, who went to a provider's home and worked with a small group of three or four. The level of attention possible in a small group, in a familiar environment, with an immigrant instructor that had to learn "all this tech stuff" in the recent past, fit the bill. With this approach, Day Care

Homes were online in a short time. The irony, of course, was that the teacher in the classroom, Byron Espinosa, was himself, an immigrant from Honduras/Guatemala. But Erie did not argue with these participants. If the first design for service did not work, they tried another.

This respect for the input of their participants was a hallmark of Erie's success with immigrant groups through the ages. It also reflected their growing understanding of the "popular education" approach to learning that was frequently utilized in Latin America. At the risk of oversimplifying, this approach basically believed that, with a certain level of support and training, ordinary people, with limited formal education, could effectively teach other ordinary people of their own background. It is also rooted in the belief that, organizing generally disenfranchised people to have a voice in their own personal growth, goes hand in hand with basic education, and recognizes the value of what a community already knows from lived experience. Techniques used are always appropriate for the group, are participative, and promote communal decision-making. Popular education was initially developed by the Brazilian educator, Paolo Freire. Erie's Adult Programs staff studied this model, in the early 2000s, utilizing materials and trainers from The Institute of Popular Education of Southern California (IDEPSCA), and "Cantera," a Popular Education and Communication Center.

The Parent-to-Parent (PTP) program, funded in the early 2000s, had a similar approach. PTP involved Erie staff in organizing parents to offer ESL and GED classes at local schools, another example of Erie's willingness to take services out the front door and down the street, if that was what was needed. These classes might be in the morning, to serve stay-at-home moms, or in the evenings to serve working parents. By March of 2003, these programs involved 25-30 parents at each of the following schools: Talcott, Chase, Yates, Otis and Mitchell. While Otis and

Talcott were schools that Erie was already connected with through After-School programming, the other three reflect Erie's stretch to communities to the west and northwest of what had once been Erie's much smaller catchment area. In 2004, CPS gave Erie a grant of $1800 to work with PTP participants to encourage and guide them to submit applications to run for their Local School Council seats, when CPS recognized that 60% of LSC seats had no candidates for upcoming elections. Since PTP was as much about leadership development as ESL, this was a wise investment. It paid off. Eventually, 25 community members were mobilized by PTP to run for LSC seats; 20 were elected.

Erie was also an early advocate of STEM (Science, Technology, Engineering, Math) programming, even if that acronym was not always used. In 2003, on Saturday mornings, NASA offered a science program to YOU participants and a group of students at Wells High School, the local public high school that Erie worked closely with for many years. There were 21 youth at Erie House, and 20 at Wells, that completed the program. Besides having science classes, Erie began to evaluate the need for some mentors for the TEAM program that would be well prepared to tutor students who were struggling with math. While Northern Trust Bank continued to provide a majority of mentors for the TEAM program they had supported since its inception in 1984, the realization dawned that bankers don't use math-- they use arithmetic in their daily work. For tutors in algebra, geometry, and calculus, it seemed wise to recruit a few engineers. The first few that responded to the call opened the door to many more, as their companies recognized that this was also an opportunity to plant the seed with young Latinx to consider engineering as a career. In order to aspire to a career, youth need to know about it. Too often, if they don't see it on TV, it does not exist. Doctors, lawyers, and police filled the small screen, but not too many engineers. In addition to math tutors, TEAM now had a new group of professionals for job shadowing. Before long, Erie graduates were enrolling in engineering programs at college. It was a small number, but larger than zero. When the first engineering graduate returned to Erie House as the keynote speaker at TEAM's annual high school graduation celebration, the message was clear. I look like you, I grew up in the same neighborhood, I was an Erie kid; you could do what I did. It was a powerful message.

In the early 2000s, as in most of Erie's years, advocacy went hand in hand with programs and services. Staff and participants did this work together. Some of the best teachable moments, for adults and youth alike, were trips to Springfield or city hall, but the state capital was the most frequent destination. It is about a four-hour bus ride, requiring participants to be at Erie by 6:00 am to board the bus and arrive in Springfield in time to meet with their representatives and senators during prime business hours, and to be on hand around noon to join other groups for a larger rally on the front steps of the capitol building. On the return trip from one of these visits, an Erie staff member asked participants what most impressed them about this experience. One of the women raised her hand and said, after visiting with Representatives Cynthia Soto and Maria Hernandez, and Senator Iris Martinez, that she had not realized how many Latinas were elected to represent her community--*las mujeres en acción* was an eye-opening realization.

In May of 2003, two important bills that Erie and other CBOs were pushing for, got passed. HB0060 assured undocumented high school grads the right to pay the in-state rate for college tuition. HB0294 updated the income eligibility guidelines for state government subsidized programs from the 1997 level to 2003, and more importantly, made it the law that this number be updated *every* year. A busload of Erie participants had been there to "educate" their legislators on the merits of these bills.

As Estrada reported to the board, he accompanied seven Erie participants to Springfield for Community Technology Day on May 14, 2003. There they met with Rep. Connie Howard, the chair of the House Computer Technology Committee, and talked with staff at the Department of Commerce and Economic Opportunity (DCEO), urging them to release Digital Divide Elimination funds, one of the key funding sources for Erie's Community Technology Center. While there, they stopped in to see Rep. Cynthia Soto to get an update on the $100,000 dollars she had promised to earmark to fund building repairs and improvements for Erie. She assured them the funds were forthcoming.

That same month, Ric also announced to the board the sad news that Glen Graham (1911-2003) had passed away on May 6, 2003. He was a beloved former board member and Life Trustee, and a generous supporter of Erie House for many years. Between 1984 and 2003, he had provided $435,000 for TEAM scholarships. Rafael Ravelo and Esther Nieves joined Ric and the McClures, Armstrongs, and O'Kieffes in paying their respects at the funeral. On June 11, 2003, as Erie celebrated the 18th Annual Graduation and TEAM Scholarship Banquet, the event was dedicated to the memory of Glen Graham with these words:

> *No tribute could be more fitting than celebrating our TEAM graduates and mentors this evening, who honor Glen Graham's memory through lives of noble service, the pursuit of excellence, and the promise of young leadership.*[405]

The MC for the banquet was Betsy Perez, a 1993 TEAM graduate, a mentor since 2002, and at that time, employed by Erie as Assistant Director of HR. It was the first year for the

Jaime Esparza Future Leader Award, named after a friend of Ric Estrada, who had died rushing into a burning building in an attempt to rescue his father. The winner of the award was Oswaldo Alvarez, who would graduate from the University of Wisconsin, and then return to Erie to work in Community Literacy, and eventually, be promoted to Director of Workforce Development. Both Perez and Alvarez were examples of another Erie House tradition–returning to Erie House to work after college–paying it forward, valuing attachment.

There were 17 TEAM graduates in 2003. By this time, the high schools represented had moved far beyond Wells High School alone. Besides the 3 from Wells, they came from Steinmetz, Kelvyn Park, Noble Street Charter, Holy Trinity, Schurz, Morton, and Foreman. They would be attending: U-W, Madison, Beloit College, University of Illinois at Champaign, Northeastern Illinois, DeVry, DePaul, Colorado School of Mines, Eastern Illinois, Morton College, Columbia College, Malcolm X and Wright Community Colleges of Chicago. Two were entering military service; 16 were Latinos and one was white/non-Latino.

By the middle of his first year as executive director, Estrada informed the board that long-time Development Director, Lisa Galicia, had been promoted to Deputy Director, formerly called "Associate" Director, when Ric held that position. At the same time, Ami Novoryta became Development Manager, with the primary responsibility for writing grant proposals. Sadly, Erie bid farewell to Adult Programs Director, Tim Bell, with Erie for 10 years, who was taking a position with the Day Labor Coalition under the auspices of St. Pius Church in Pilsen. He was replaced by Joanna Borowiec, with Lora Oswald named Assistant Director. Dennis Puhr, Director of After-School, was also leaving to take a position as a teacher in Berwyn, a western suburb with a growing Latino population. He was replaced by Amy Kinney, and Jesus Rodriguez was named the new

Citizenship Coordinator. Former Admin, Paul Kasper, was now Director of Operations, and had the pleasure of overseeing the installation of new front doors at the House, a gift of Schuham Building & Supply Company. That would be a gift of the Sawyer/Graham/Schuham family. When Borowiec decided to take a position with then-Congressman Rahm Emanuel, at the end of 2003, she was replaced early in 2004 by John Taylor, who came to Erie from Chicago Commons.   When it comes to staffing, among the settlements of Chicago, it's a village. Also, in 2004, Roxana Vergara became Development Director.

Major staff changes are usually serious hits. On the other hand, the good news was that, while many agencies were struggling due to cuts in funding from United Way and SOS (Secretary of State community literacy grants), Erie's UW grant went up, and SOS stayed the same. The ICCB awarded Adult Ed an increase of $51,116, based on the program's excellent performance. This performance-based funding opportunity had been the result of earlier advocacy by both Tim Bell and Joanna Borowiec.   Performance and reputation do pay the bills. $327,000 of the foundation goal of $517,000 for an FY04 budget of $5.3 million was already committed.   The value of the endowment stood at $1.8 million. And finally, the allocation for LVIRC from the Western Union settlement was increased to $750,000 instead of $600,000.[406] Budget challenges for FY04 included a 19% increase in health insurance, followed by a whopping 406% increase in unemployment insurance due to numerous lay-offs the previous year.

Checking in with Child Care

In 2003, Erie's pre-school program went through its first NAEYC re-accreditation process. It did so well, accreditation was extended for 5 years, until 2008. With this endorsement in hand, Erie applied for what the state called

Illinois Quality Counts (IQC). IQC proposed a tiered reimbursement system whereas, the higher the tier of quality a program achieves, the higher the financial reimbursement per child, based on the correlated assumption that the higher the quality of a program, the more it costs. Both licensed child care centers and licensed Day Care Homes were eligible to apply. Unfortunately, not all state-funded programs were based on that assumption. Recognition of what one would think was a logical assumption was actually a giant step forward in funding practice. Too often government funding guidelines have little to do with what programs actually cost. Instead, funding is based on an underestimate, or the failure to update poverty guidelines, as noted above. It also happens that, due to inadequate allocations by legislatures, the bureaucracy just does not have the funds required to cover actual costs.

Aiming for the stars was an Erie tradition. In this case, "stars" were actually used to report levels of evaluation, as each star awarded to an organization was associated with an increased level of funding, ranging from one * at 5% to 4 **** at 20%. The stars were associated with four areas of evaluation: 1) Learning environment; 2) Regulatory compliance; 3)Program design and management; 4) Staff qualifications and training. To illustrate how this worked, a center with a 4-star rating and 15 subsidized children, would earn $18,401; a center with a 4-star rating and 150 subsidized children, would receive $184,000. That was Erie, plus they earned $122,000 for After-school. Erie also worked with the members of their Day Care Family Homes Network, helping them to each earn 4 stars. In a kind of "big sister" role to network members, Erie encouraged them to serve more subsidized children and helped to increase their earnings as women entrepreneurs. As of 2018, Erie Pre-school was still at the 4-star level.

Early in 2004, Erie's Child Care department launched yet another reach for the stars with the opening of the Sunshine Room. This was to be a therapeutic classroom designed to address the socio-emotional development of pre-school children with special needs. Generally, these were children that exhibited disruptive behavior in their classrooms, to the extent that they were often dropped from child care programs. In fact, Erie noted in its proposal that 42% of programs in Illinois had asked families of disruptive children to withdraw from their program.[407] Initially, eight children were selected who spent half of each day in a space where they would receive special developmental support, and the other half in their regular classroom. A special ed teacher worked in the Sunshine Room, assisted by social work interns from various universities, and psychology externs from the Chicago School of Professional Psychology (CSPP). The Sunshine program benefited greatly from the fact that Erie House was fortunate in two areas. First, Dr. Elizabeth Yelen, with a PhD in psychology, was a full-time staff member of the Child Care department, and therefore, had the credentials to supervise graduate interns. Second, Dr. John Benitez of CSPP, lent his support as a consultant and supervisor of his externs. Benitez also joined the Erie Board in 2004, not only as a welcome professional addition, but also as a neighbor. He lived just around the corner from Erie on Noble. Another Board member, Mark Joliceour, contributed his pro bono architectural services in the design of the space. In December, 2004, Erie received a grant of $125,000 for the Sunshine Initiative from the Illinois Children's Healthcare Foundation of Hinsdale, Illinois. The primary funder, however, was CPS who had encouraged the development of such a classroom.

While Erie was busy qualifying for the highest ratings for their child care programs, and thinking about the Sunshine Initiative, on November 6, 2003, Mayor Daley visited Erie again for the purpose of a press conference. This was actually a press conference organized by Mujeres Latinas en Acción, an organization that Erie often worked with, who had asked to use Erie space for this event. Clearly, Erie's proximity to downtown Chicago made it a convenient and popular location for press conferences pertaining to the work of CBOs. Even though Erie House was not on the agenda for this press conference, when Mayor Daley stepped to the podium, he included praise for Erie House in his opening remarks. (2nd visit, 2nd kudo from the mayor). Congresspersons Luis Gutierrez and Jan Schakowsky were present. A note should be made here of the ardent support for immigrants always demonstrated by Congresswoman Schakowsky of the far north side of the city and lakefront suburb of Evanston.

To close out 2003, people associated with ENH were enjoying recognition at the University of Chicago 2003 Alumni Assembly. Not only Estrada, but two former ENH executive directors were U of C alums--Rafael Ravelo and Esther Nieves. They were honored at the 2003 Assembly. Esther Nieves (MA, 1987) received the Public Service Citation "for creative citizenship and exemplary leadership in service that has benefited society and reflected credit on the university." James McClure, Jr. (AB, 1942, JD, 1949), a dedicated ENH board member, a lawyer with Erie's counsel, Gardner, Carton & Douglas, former Oak Park Village President, and chair of the board of McCormick Theological Seminary, was awarded the Alumni Service Medal. The award recognized McClure with this far too limited citation: "to honor a lifetime of achievement in service to the university" (and a whole lot of other organizations). In reviewing this list of Jim McClure's achievements, one can understand why Eleanor Brierly, a fellow board member was led to comment, "Jim McClure was a leader in everything he's ever done. . . You could go on for a year with what Jim has done."[408] Also, in the 2000s, two more Erie staff would earn their MAs at this university: Cristina Garcia and Oswaldo Alvarez.

2004: Steady as She Goes – But Let's Explore New Possibilities

As the Erie board met for the first time in 2004, they learned that the financial situation of the organization was very positive. The value of the endowment stood at $1.9 million, and endowment interest had not been tapped to cover cash flow for an entire year. With extra effort on the part of board members, the Holiday Appeal revenue was way up, bringing in $72,330, as compared with the previous year of only $48,800. As the Development staff reported that they were already at 109% of the FY04 goal for foundation and corporate giving, it seemed likely Erie could achieve its budgeted revenue of $5.3 million. At this point, board member, Mark Hallett, who worked for the McCormick Foundation, commented, that from a foundation perspective, "It is a credit to Erie to have such a positive financial situation. Working toward a balanced budget shows a commitment to planned excellence."[409] At this same meeting, Ric recommended that Erie join NCLR (National Council of La Raza). As a Latino-serving agency, it made sense to join with others to collaborate on national policy that affects the Latino community.[410]

When Ric shared with them that Erie turned down a fairly large grant from the Quantum YouthNet program, one might assume that Erie did so because they did not "need" the money. That was not the case. YouthNet had been reorganized with new guidelines that Erie believed did not fit with their mission. This was not the first time that Erie made such a decision, and this type of decision is one of the keys to success and longevity for non-profit organizations. Taking on inappropriate contracts, beyond an organization's mission and/or capabilities, generally leads to trouble. Too often, their failure to perform under these circumstances results in a loss of future funding and the beginning of doubt regarding their reliability on the part of other funders. This also pertains to the importance of negotiating for the appropriate goals outlined in the grant, and getting as close to actual cost, rather than committing to a project that is full of unreasonable expectations with an inadequate rate of reimbursement. Of course, this is easier said than done. An organization's ability to say no and/or negotiate is generally based on their prior levels of performance, and the extent to which the funding agency needs that organization's "numbers" in order to make them look good to another entity, higher up the ladder.

This turned out to be that kind of situation. Youth Director, Maria Matias, had done such a good job with Erie's YouthNet contract under the old guidelines, that the Youth Services program director from the City Department of Human Services (CDHS) called Ric, requesting a meeting to discuss reconsideration of Erie's decision. Ric agreed to the meeting, but the decision did not change. He commented:

> *While the nature of the non-profit sector leads many organizations to chase dollars, Erie has turned away hundreds of thousands of dollars when we have felt that accepting the funds would compromise our philosophy and approach to service delivery.*[411]

Meanwhile, YOU was happy to receive an increase in its CDBG grant, up from $45,000 to $62,000.

It was also in early 2004, that Erie formed a Charter School Exploration Committee, later re-named the Charter School Task Force (CSTF). By this time, charter schools were emerging as the educational topic of the day, a topic that was controversial. In Erie's case, they were very familiar with one of the most successful charter school promoters in the city, the Noble Network of Charter Schools (NNCS), co-founded by Michael Milkie. He and Tonya Hernandez started the Noble Network in 1999, with support from Ron Manderscheid, Executive Director of Northwestern University Settlement House (NUSH). Noble Charter High School was the first to be opened. It was located on NUSH property at the corner of Noble (1400 west) and Augusta (1000 north), in the heart of West Town, and about 4 blocks from Erie House. The next two were even closer to Erie. Rauner College Prep was located in the old Santa Maria School building on Ohio Street, just behind Erie, and Golder College Prep was located in the old Holy Innocents School, less than two blocks from ENH. By 2017, the Noble Network was running 16 high schools and one middle school. Their student population was 98% people of color and 89% low income, with an overall college acceptance rate of 90%. The School Quality Rating Policy (SQRP) of the Chicago Public Schools had NNCS schools occupying 10 of the top 15 high school slots in the system.[412] Understandably, many of Erie's TEAM participants are also students at one of the three high schools nearby, based on excellence and proximity, and conversely, students from those schools were often Erie kids and TEAM participants. Together, NNCS and Erie House/TEAM make an extraordinary educational resource for the community's youth.

So, what could be controversial about excellence? First, not all charter schools are excellent. Second, advocates for low-income families argue that charter schools draw the "best" students away from regular public schools, making it even more difficult for those schools to survive or get better. They see them as a distraction, preventing more parents from working hard to improve the traditional public schools. And finally, the Chicago Teachers Union dislikes the idea that charters have the option of hiring non-union teachers. Erie House was aware of all this, and that they may come under criticism from some of their usual allies by considering an Erie charter school start-up. Nevertheless, in discussion with child care staff, and some parents, there was frustration in exposing pre-schoolers from a nationally accredited educational program, designed to make them exceptionally prepared to start school, only to find that the school fell far short of what was needed to pick up where pre-school left off. Thus, Estrada and some board members began to seriously consider starting an elementary charter school that Erie kids could count on for a continuation of the excellence they were used to.

As Estrada explained on the video prepared for Erie's 135th anniversary, Erie could safely continue down the successful and comfortable path of their current programs, or they could, as in the tradition of their forefathers and foremothers, take the risk that was often required to go the extra mile to meet the needs of their community, and try something new.

In his report to the board in March 2004, Estrada described the work of the Charter School Task Force, which included ENH board members, Troy Harden, Mark Hallett, and Ken Perkins, and consultants, Mike Milkie, Ruth Kane, and Linda Ponce De Leon. He shared what they had learned in their research to date on charter schools. The important factors for the success of a charter school underscored what numerous studies had already revealed. *An excellent leader/principal is key.* Then, add to this an institutional culture that honors and respects people, allows teachers to implement their craft without bureaucratic intervention, allows teachers to have a say in professional development, and expects excellence. Since this pretty much describes Erie's Pre-School program, and overall practice for 135 years, it re-enforced the belief that Erie Neighborhood House was in an ideal position to design and operate an elementary school along those lines. Ric wrapped up his remarks by adding, "I am convinced that the greatest risk is not doing anything to provide our children with the high-quality education they deserve."[413]

So, in the first year of his administration, March 2003-March 2004, two of the major accomplishments of his tenure were under way. Erie was established in Little Village, and mapping out with its partner, LVCDC, the plans for the Little Village Immigrant Resource Center. And, the exploration stage of a major undertaking, such as starting a school, was under way. As it was poised to celebrate its 135th year in the business of advancing social justice for the immigrants of Chicago, its choice of a theme was: *A Legacy of Excellence; A Future of Promise.* Neither is possible if you just stand still. So, *¡Vamanos!*

With the deadline of October 1, 2004 for new charter school proposals, a special board meeting was scheduled for June 29, 2004 to discuss how Erie should proceed. President-elect, Librada Zamora-Killian chaired the meeting attended by 13 other board members, mostly Erie veterans. Ric reviewed the nature of charter schools and why there was a need for them in Chicago. He reminded the board that Erie would have the guidance of charter school experts, and proposed a budget that compared with other charter schools in the Midwest. On the recommendation of attorney and board member, Jesse Ruiz, the board voted to form a separate corporation for the charter school. The motion was made by John Hall and seconded by Jack O'Kieffe. It then authorized that a loan of $100,000 from Erie's reserve account be made to the new corporation as a start-up fund. That done, Zamora-Killian moved, and Sy Nelson seconded, the authorization for ENH to pursue the creation of a charter school. Both motions passed. As Ric observed in one of his reports,

> *Erie is a special place, not just because it has lasted 135 years and has great programs, but especially, because of the unwavering commitment of board members who help staff make decisions that empower the community.*[414]

By the time of the September 2004 board meeting, Ric reported that Erie had received a $20,000 planning grant from ISBE to support preparation of their charter application. Linda Ponce de Leon (MEd from Harvard) was developing the curriculum and was the lead candidate for principal. Assistance was also coming from the Erikson Institute and National Louis University. Support for the application, he said, has been forthcoming from Mayor Daley and Alderman Flores, and a letter of intent to use the vacant St. Mark's school building at 2510 W. Cortez was also in hand. The city's DHS Commissioner, Mary Ellen Caron, told the CEO of CPS, Arne Duncan, that she had no doubt Erie would operate a charter school at the same level of excellence as its Pre-school program. Finally, again typical in Erie's history, a former "Erie kid," who lived just down the block from the House stepped up to help. Agustin Gomez-Leal, now of Wallin/Gomez Architects Ltd., would be providing his design services for retrofitting the old school building to meet the needs of the new charter.

On November 15, 2004, at a public hearing on charter schools, Eliud Medina, Director of the Near Northwest Neighborhood Network, spoke on behalf of Erie's application to demonstrate local community support, to offset some of that potential criticism of charters mentioned above. An excerpt from his testimony follows:

> *Despite the divide and conquer tactics you have heard in the media by opponents of charter schools, you must realize that Erie House . . . will do everything in its power to partner with the local public schools, so that together, they can increase achievement for all children–it is what Erie does. . .I believe that if the past is the best indicator of the future, that Erie House has demonstrated that they have the resources, experience, commitment, and will to succeed. They have planned what many in*

the community believe is an integrated, value-driven approach that will produce the results Erie seeks, and provide important models for other Chicago schools.[415]

A final decision on Erie's application would be announced in December 2004. If it was positive, the Erie Elementary Charter School would open in September 2005. It was, and it did.

Leaders, Learners, Partners, Friends

That was the theme of Erie's 2004 Annual Report.

Some of the examples of the stories presented in the report are worth repeating here. One was the story of Angel Martinez, who had enrolled in the Tech Promoter program in 2002. Since then, he had begun teaching computer classes. His full-time day job? Parking lot attendant. Another was an Erie Parent Council member, Gladys Guerra, who addressed Congresswomen Nancy Pelosi and Jan Schakowsky, and Congressman Danny Davis during a press conference in Erie's Templeton Hall, to advocate for a child care tax credit benefiting working-poor families. YOU participant, Isaac Castro, was featured, as a young man who came to check out Erie's computer center and found YOU. He ended up serving as president of Erie's Youth Council and spent four years in TEAM with his mentor from Northern Trust. Following a stint with the US Marines after high school, he returned to Erie to become an employee in the Tech Services Department, following the Erie Kid model of "succeed-and-return." Partners included Jumpstart, a program of DePaul University that provided student volunteers to work in child care classrooms. Another partnership involved police from the 13th District who worked with Erie teens on an improv show called "Hey, Officer Robles." Clearly, this was not the Officer Krumpke of West Side Story. Someone who had evolved as a good friend was Alderman Walter Burnett, pictured in the report with Jesus Gomez, an ESL student that Burnett tutored, while learning a little Spanish in the bargain. Erie's African American alderman loved to greet with *"Buenos dias"* on his "official" visits.

Governor Blagojevich announced his "Pre-school for All" initiative in 2004, with quality standards that Erie House could have written for him. But, when Erie staff heard the official presentation of how it would work, they re-named it "Pre-school for a few more, some of the time." The additional state investment of $90 million was welcome, but it would not be available until 2005. IDHS (the Illinois Dept. of Human Services) which had been formed by Governor Edgar in 1997, also organized the state's Child Care Development Advisory Council in 2004, to serve as a link between IDHS and the community. Erie, and other agencies it considered allies, like CASL (Chinese American Service League), Casa Central, Centers for New Horizons, and the Carole Robertson Center in North Lawndale, were all members.

The ongoing challenge of continuing to provide quality pre-school service, especially center-based, all-day care, that allowed parents to work, was how to fund it, as demand continued to grow. To make quality care possible, Erie House developed a blended funding approach: Head Start + state/city + parent co-pays + any private money they could apply for. One of the effects of the welfare-to-work policies of the Clinton administration in the 90s was that between FY95 and FY 01, the number of children needing child care while their parents worked rose from 65,000 to 198,000, a 300% increase. The government's answer: reduce demand v. making the effort to respond to it. They did this by making it more difficult for working-poor families to be eligible for subsidized child care, by lowering income eligibility. Thus, the effect of this policy was to make parents work for lower wages so they could stay poor and qualify, or go out and shop for private care. Same result. Bottom line: children were the losers, and their future contribution to American society was jeopardized. For Erie families, their "neighbor" would fight this result every step of the way.

There were also proposed changes for funding Adult Education in August 2004, coming from key state funder, the Illinois Community College Board (ICCB), that would negatively impact community-based providers in order to favor community colleges. This was yet another phase of a long-term battle between the two types of providers. Time and time again, CBOs had outshone Chicago's community colleges' performance in completion rates and customer satisfaction. Earlier they had won access to extra dollars based on performance. So, when a new funding formula was announced in 2004, one of Erie House's community partners, Greater West Town Project, did an analysis and provided testimony titled "Unfair Dual Adult Ed Funding Systems Put CBOs at Grave Disadvantage: Problems & Possible Solutions." Their executive director, Bill Leavy, presented the following analysis:

> **Main conclusion**: New funding formula will favor community colleges that can choose which funding stream is most advantageous to their institutions, and thereby, putting CBO providers at an unfair disadvantage. For example:
> **Formula not linked to real cost of instruction.** Funding is tied to enrollment v. actual *cost of instruction*, which probably has more to do with quality. Thus, it favors community colleges with rewards for filling seats v. actual hours and quality of instruction offered.

Formula assigns false relative costs assigned to differing types of instruction. With the outcome being that "vocational" adult ed will lose over 50% of its current relative value. Under the old formula, funding was based on acknowledged higher cost of providing a vocational context v. simple HS credit. In other words, the higher cost of this value-added approach is ignored.

Formula allows short-term, high-turnover programs to win big $$. For the first time in State history, reimbursement for instructional services will be based primarily on body count of enrollments, rather than long-term practice of reimbursing only on the amount of instruction provided. In Chicago, for instance, a provider can get $111 per body in a seat, but only $13 per body for 15 hours of instruction, compared to current reimbursement level of $80 for that same 15 hours. Big bucks for high enrollments in spite of short tenure (dropouts).

Formula's unfair hidden matching funds requirements inflate funded services count, deflate reported costs. Task Force claims they removed the matching requirement, but in reality, CBOs will still need matching funds to keep their unit cost competitive, especially with the CCC that dips into a wide range of funding to reduce their "cost", thus making them appear more cost-effective than CBOs.

Possible solutions:

Solution 1: One Unified System. A uniform funding system for all eligible institutions based on the *known range of unit costs* of instruction. i.e. no built-in advantages for community colleges

Solution 2: Two separate systems – One for CBOs and one for Community Colleges. One for CBOs and one for tax-supported schools. CBOs maintain a proportional share of funding, based on their current share.[416]

Erie's Director of Adult Ed, John Taylor, also provided testimony. He highlighted two points: 1) **CBOs "in-kind" contribution**; 2) **Smaller is better**. He illustrated the first point as follows. ENH currently offers 9 adult ed classes, but Malcolm X College, that only provides instructors, gets all the credit and all the money, while Erie does the recruiting, provides the space and cost of utilities, child care, and free parking. Yet Erie is reimbursed for none of this. And, there are many more "off-site" programs that CBOs provide with high enrollment, attendance, and quality, compared to instruction being offered on CCC campuses. *ICCB needs to re-visit their funding formula in light of this distorted situation.*

As to the second point, he said, *the two demographic groups that populate adult ed,* are early high school leavers and immigrants; *both thrive in smaller settings.* Thus, the more personal, culturally sensitive environment provided by CBOs leads to greater success. But the Funding Task Force was emphasizing quantity over quality, contradicting current educational philosophy. In conclusion, Erie favored Leavy's Solution # 2: separate funding for CBOs and community colleges, with CBO funding remaining at the current level. Furthermore, Erie House continued to argue that funding should correlate with outcomes, defined as completion of classes attempted, not just number of bodies in the seats the first week of the term. While CBOs consistently showed retention and completion rates of 70-80%, the rate at City Colleges, for more than 20 years, hovered around 7%. That dismal figure came from their own annual report. If you extended completion time to 6 years, it went to 13%. The needle did not move on those numbers until Cheryl Hyman became Chancellor of the CCC in 2011.

While John Taylor was on hand to testify about Adult program funding, all was not well on the home front. There had been two directors of Adult Programs since Tim Bell left. Borowiec barely stayed long enough to know what needed to be done. John Taylor took the position in February of 2004, and at the end of his first year, an analysis was done regarding data collection to measure program outcomes. The conclusion was that the department was in disarray, with no consistency in program objectives, structure, data collection, or management. The programs of this department included:

- *Parent-to-Parent* -- an off-site program that happened at a variety of school sites;
- *GED* – students enroll but don't finish; mixing moms and teen high school dropouts, not working;
- *Citizenship* – should Erie add legal services for applicants?
- Literacy/SOS – high numbers of students and tutors, but what are the outcomes? impact? Is it quantity v. quality?
- *ESL* – seemingly owned and operated by Malcolm X community college, a step back from the days when Tim Bell insisted on competent teachers and even had Erie hiring some of their own. And, as John Taylor had testified in Springfield, Erie did all the work recruiting and supporting retention without compensation, and without access to data on completers, that was retained by the college.

The final overall question raised in the report was whether John Taylor was right for the job. The observation was made that managing programs that were running smoothly, versus restructuring programs to ensure success, required two different skill sets. The latter would be required, and it was not Mr. Taylor's strong suit.

In conclusion, some short-term recommendations, for the six months remaining in FY05, were made:

- Start focusing on the strongest programs that are immediately re-fundable;
- Then, evaluate what can be salvaged from the weakest programs, or determine if they need to start from scratch;
- Map out viable and measurable goals for each program;
- Establish a timeline for the tasks to be undertaken.

The following year, Assistant Director, Lora Oswald, took John's place, the third director in two years, since Tim Bell left in August 2003. As she made her first report to the board, she noted that growth was not the problem. Since the first ESL class in Little Village of 15 students, in the Fall of 2004, the program had grown to seven ESL classes serving 90 students, with two more planned for January, bringing the total to 136 students since inception. Reorganization to improve funding and continued emphasis on community accountability would be the hallmarks of her tenure.

Preparing to Celebrate 135 Years

While Erie was moving forward on two very significant new initiatives in 2003-2004, Erie Board members were planning for Erie's 135th anniversary in 2005. The task of developing the concept and content was definitely managed by board members. The logistics of the event, as usual, were handled by the staff and event planners. One of Erie's most dedicated board members, Jack O'Kieffe (Wilmette Presbyterian), became chair of the Heritage Committee. Rev. Richard Poethig, a Presbyterian church historian, served as an invaluable consultant. He had been Director of the Institute on the Church in Urban Industrial Society in Chicago, and a teacher at McCormick Theological Seminary, located at Halsted and Fullerton, before the property was taken over by DePaul University in the late 20th century.

Dr. Patricia Mooney-Melvin, director of the Public History program at Loyola University, was approached about the possibility of getting some graduate students to work with Erie House to provide background research that could enhance the anniversary celebration.[417] She shared that she herself was an admirer of the settlement movement and thought it could be a good theme for one of her classes to work on. The result was two-fold. First, she identified a graduate student, Catherine Maybrey, who made the Erie history project her internship, followed by Rebecca Banks, who did the same. Secondly, Mooney-Melvin's class adopted the Erie House story as their class theme for the Fall of 2003, and set out to produce papers and poster presentations on various topics pertinent to Erie history.[418] Maybrey contacted Professor Chris Manning, who also committed his class to doing some Erie oral histories. In all, 28 oral history interviews were done, mostly in October 2003. Among those who came to the House to be interviewed were participants in what was called the Erie Annual Reunion. Hosted by two former Erie kids, Tony and Marion DeVincent, at their farm in Coloma, Michigan, it brought together people who came to Erie in the 1930s, 40s, and 50s. The reunions began in 1989 and were in their 14th year in 2003, when the preparation was under way for Erie's 135th.[419]

While much of this material was not directly put to use for the anniversary celebration, the entire process raised awareness of the importance of historical context when an organization lasts 135 years. Board and staff learned many things they had not known before; patterns of success took shape. Ruth Kane outlined themes she believed were developing from this work, themes that would still apply as Erie planned to celebrate their 150th anniversary:

- There continues to be a partnership at Erie of religion, faith and social work;
- The strength of ENH, past and present, is the ability and commitment to adapt programs to meet the needs of the "neighbors" being served;
- Erie continues to provide programs that are unique and successful;
- Erie House remains a "winner" with local and national tributes, major grant support, recognition in the media, from politicians, and other community leaders;
- The leadership of ENH – executive directors, staff, board and volunteers – exhibit exceptional vision and dedication to meeting the needs of the community.[420]

But the overriding message of this work, especially the interviews, was the affection and respect people had for this place called Erie House. Whether they had been a participant or a volunteer, so many said that Erie House had been a major force in their lives, contributing to who they had become as humans, what careers they pursued, and what they were able to pay forward. As Mrs. Herrera put it on the video developed to be shown at the anniversary dinner: "For my family, Erie House is our second house, our second home."

She echoed the sentiment of Rev. Alan Searles, from his interview. Rev. Searles was Miss Towne's nephew, and, as noted in an earlier chapter, was adopted by Rev. George Searles when Florence's sister died. He said:

*Erie became a second home for so many who were
poor or new to the country. I have learned
compassion that Erie House and Florence instilled
into my life. . .it directed me to the ministry. Part of
the legacy. . .is the success of our lives. It sounds
like the Erie House of 2003 is the Erie House that I
knew. Miss Florence doesn't die; she is still
there.*[421]

Mary York, an Armenian immigrant, was born in
1929. A few other Armenian immigrants have appeared in
Erie history, indicating that there were other immigrant
clusters, besides Poles and Italians, that lived in the Erie
neighborhood, that simply received less attention, as a
smaller proportion of the whole. She started going to Erie
House in 1939, at the age of 10. For a while, her family lived
at 1341 W. Erie, where the playlot is today. She was a
member of the Erie Chapel congregation and shared these
memories in her interview.

*We always saw Florence with a smile. We
wondered how she could smile, since everyone
came to her with their problems. . .*[422]

She was obviously present, and part of the story that had
been written about in *Time* magazine in 1948, as she
recalled,

*Doug Cedarleaf was young, in his mid-twenties
when he came to Erie House as a boys' worker. He
then became pastor. He was young, dynamic,
ahead of his time. When a black family moved
nearby, and their windows were broken, he held a
solidarity march to their home after church.*[423]

Finally, she reminisced about helping out with Meals on Wheels:

> *We prepared dinners for the elderly. We learned to serve. We learned practical things like how to make gravy without lumps. We were poor in wealth, but so rich in the opportunities that came to us through Erie House. We absorbed it all like sponges. . . The most important thing we learned was about giving. This is our legacy. . .to help.*[424]

Erie opened its 135th anniversary year, on the fantastic news that the Holiday Appeal of December 2004, had brought in an "astounding" $100,900 from 251 donors, compared to $80,000 the previous year. The other piece of December good news was the approval of Erie's charter application, which meant that, in its 135th year of service, it would, once again, launch something new and challenging, as it did on its 120th, when the Erie Community Center opened on Superior. The plan was to open the school doors in September 2005, with Kindergarten and first grade. Then, one grade would be added each year, through 5th grade. At that point, the school would be evaluated for charter renewal. When, not if, it was approved, it would add the last three grades and be a K-8 school. Linda Ponce de Leon would be at the door, as principal, to greet the Erie Elementary Charter School's first pupils; Ric Estrada would be the President and CEO. As Estrada said to the board, "Our goal for the new year is to settle in to our new skin, in two new neighborhoods–East Humboldt Park and Little Village."

As the Heritage Committee continued its work in 2005, the focus shifted to preparing a video on Erie's history to be shown at the 135th gala/dinner, and that could be used for future opportunities to promote the work of Erie House. The research and oral histories that had been done to that point gave direction as to who might be featured. When it was finally put together, the video included the McClures, Daisy Genova Braucher and Mary Burns, who had been active with the Erie Clinic, Bob Wiley, Mrs. Herrera, Rafael Ravelo, Ric Estrada, and myself, recalling Erie's connection with NCO and Bickerdike.

Attention then turned to finding a producer. Ruth Kane wrote to Jan Thompson at Southern Illinois University about developing this documentary for Erie's 135th. Thompson's production company was called *Food for Thought,* and she had produced several award-winning documentaries for PBS. As of 2005, she had won two Emmys. She accepted and was joined by Carole Cartwright. As the production team, they promised that, in highlighting Erie's key accomplishments, they would aim to make the video "evergreen," so it would be useful for other purposes beyond the 135th gala. The final cost for the production was $19,477.

With that task under way, the committee began to brainstorm on how best to involve the Presbyterian churches and their congregants in this historical celebration. It was decided to invite pastors to a "preview," in June 2005, before the gala in November. Rev. Poethig assisted in organizing this event, to be held at Elmhurst Presbyterian Church, home church of the Grahams. It was decided that Jack O'Kieffe, outstanding Presbyterian that he was, should emcee, with Ric as the main speaker. The agenda included a timeline titled "ENH--History in the making." Needless to say, the important role of the Presbyterian church throughout Erie's history was highlighted. The program was well-received and well-attended by about 300 people from Presbyterian churches throughout the metro area.

At the June 2005 board meeting, Ami Novoryta gave an update on the Gala. The Co-Chairs were Joe Scoby of UBS and Ron Rivera, Defensive Coordinator for the Chicago Bears. The Honorary Council for the Gala represented all the major elected officials of the time, as well as Robert Reynolds, Executive Director of the Presbytery of Chicago, and Paul Roldán, Founder and Executive Director of Hispanic Housing. UBS secured the services of Event Planner, Pat Hurley, who assured Erie they would raise $200,000. At that point, about $63,000 was already in hand; by early September it would be up to $93,000. The special awards were proposed as follows: Community Leader Award, Mike Milkie, the Distinguished Grantor Award, McCormick Tribune Foundation, and Northern Trust would receive the Corporate Partner Award.

Ric reported that finally, on June 1, 2005, the IFF sent the Quit Claim deed to the Condo Association, and Erie Neighborhood House and Erie Family Health Center now owned 1701 W. Superior free and clear. ENH ownership pertained to the 1st and 2nd floors and the side yard. EFHC had floors three and four. Moreover, FY05 ended with a surplus of $51,000, while returning $77,000 to the endowment fund. There were still open bills from late payments to Child Care, but Erie no longer borrowed from the reserve account to cover those. Instead, it borrowed from the account set up with the proceeds from the sale of the Huron Property. Private revenue for FY05 totaled $1,455,596, up 27% from the previous year, with $111,000 earmarked for the school. The FY06 budget was set at $6,637,885, and the endowment reached the $2,000,000 mark.

As FY06 began in September 2005, Erie was invited by the Marguerite Casey Foundation to apply for another 3-year grant of $360,000. This renewal did not look good at first, but the Leadership Team brainstormed on how to present the best perspective on Erie's advocacy work. Erie presented that plus their two newest projects: the satellite operation and plans for the Immigrant Resource Center in Little Village, and the opening of the Erie Charter School. At the Casey national convening in Albuquerque, the pitch made by Ric and Ami Novoryta was successful.

Ric also introduced three new board members to replace Prieto, Duque, and Suleiman-Gonzalez. Of particular interest was Noemi Flores, *another attorney from Gardner, Carton & Douglas, a Harvard grad, and a former Erie kid.* She shared with the board that her father took citizenship classes at Erie and her younger sister was in Erie's Child Care program. Since age 7, she herself participated in After-School, and TEAM, winning a TEAM scholarship. She concluded her story with this insightful comment: **"If funders were interested in seeing the results of the Erie experience, 29 years later, here's what they get."**[425] Joining Flores was John De Carrier, a returning board member, and one of the few Latino owner-operators of McDonald's restaurants in Chicago. Jane Hunt was the third nominee, from Fourth Presbyterian Church.

Reporting on the opening of the school, EECS Principal, Linda Ponce de Leon reflected:

> *After 4 years of thought, 3 years of dreaming, 2 years of planning, and one year of blood, sweat, and tears, the big day came and went without a glitch. I tell everyone who congratulates me that it took about 300 people to make this happen, from the day Steve Fox first edited my presentation to the board, asking to proceed, to this past weekend with Ken Perkins and Nancy Vincent on hand to wash windows and stamp books, it was a complex, all-hands-on-deck process.*[426]

In other words, it opened in the Erie tradition.

During that same September, which is Hispanic Heritage Month, Citibank honored four individuals who had made significant contributions to the Hispanic community. Ric Estrada was informed that he was one of the four for 2005. He was in good company, as prior recipients included

Raul Raymundo of the Resurrection Project, Carmen Velasquez, founder of the Alivio Medical Center, and Congressman Luis Gutierrez.

At the November 2005, board meeting, just a few weeks before the Gala, Novoryta reported that revenue was at $180,543, with expenses at $ 80,000. Attendees at the tables would be encouraged to donate to the TEAM Scholarship Fund. Ric thanked board members for their tremendous effort in setting the Gala on the path to success. And speaking of success, Ric cited a study done by the Donors Forum and IFF, analyzing the financial health of non-profits, 2001-2003. At that time, 65% of non-profits had year-end deficits. Erie, on the other hand, had not had a year-end deficit for over a decade, since at least 1995. And during that time, Erie expanded child care, took on another building, opened a satellite in Little Village, and a charter School in East Humboldt Park. Hull House, unfortunately, reported a $3.8 million deficit, no doubt a foreshadowing of their demise in 2012.

2006: What's Next?

2006 began with the good news that the Gala revenue exceeded the $200,000 that event planner, Pat Hurley, had forecast, at $238,000. With expenses of $114,000, the profit was $124,000, with $42,000 going to the TEAM scholarship fund. Just before the gala, a donor announced a $40,000 match. Since Erie earned it, those funds brought the total infusion for scholarships to $82,000.

With all of the new and exciting ventures happening in 2004 and 2005, it is important to remember that, ticking along in the background was Erie's hallmark program–Early Childhood Education. If you reflect on the fact that Erie had been doing early childhood education since the day it opened its Kindergarten program in 1893, its 100th anniversary came and went without candles or a cake, marking its 112th year as the agency celebrated its 135th anniversary. Not only was its quality recognized with national accreditation by NAEYC, but it received kudos all the time from the mayor and just about every bureaucrat that had oversight of government contracts that funded this program. And finally, hardly less important, was the fact that its generous contracts helped make Erie financially strong. With that in mind, it is worth putting this program into the important context it deserves, as was laid out in an article in *The Wall Street Journal,* dated January 11, 2006, and entitled "Catch 'Em Young," by James H. Heckman, an economist, pertaining to the value of investing in early childhood education.[427]

Heckman is described as a Nobel laureate in economics in 2000 and a professor at the University of Chicago. His thesis: ***"It is a rare public policy initiative that promotes fairness and social justice and, at the same time, promotes productivity in the economy and society at large. Investing in disadvantaged young children is such a policy."*** He argues that such an investment is based on economic efficiency, often a more compelling argument than the equity case, partly because the gains can be quantified and they are large, as high as a 15-17% ROI. Why this high rate of return? He itemizes the benefits of early interventions for disadvantaged children as:

- Promotes schooling;
- Raises the quality of the workforce;
- Enhances the productivity of schools;
- Reduces crime, teenage pregnancy, and welfare dependency (In 2006, the estimated cost of crime: $1.3 trillion per year, or $4,818 per capita!);
- Provides early remediation for impoverished environments that becomes progressively more costly the later it is attempted.[428]

He concludes that "Families are the major source of inequality in American social and economic life." He asserts that relatively more US children are born into disadvantaged environments compared to 40 years ago (one generation). Children born to single parent families went from less than 5% in 1968 to more than 22% in 2000. Few of those families are headed by well-educated mothers. One might conclude that all of these are good arguments, for the combination of quality pre-school and workforce development for parents, and settlement houses that provide for both--settlement houses that serve those "*families* that are the major source of inequality in American social and economic life."

With the charter school open, and the gala over, in March of 2006, Erie returned its attention to Little Village. The beauty of having the luxury of a "Senior Advisor" was that while Ric was busy with the charter school and the 135th anniversary, Rafael Ravelo was serving as liaison to the emerging partnership in Little Village. So, he provided the board with an update on the project that was the beneficiary of the Western Union settlement, the establishment of the Little Village Immigrant Resource Center (LVIRC). Ravelo reminded the board that since Erie started offering various adult education classes in 2004, then added a computer lab and tech classes, the demand for these services had been huge, with often 100 on a waiting list. He pointed out that Erie had already outgrown the convent space they rented.

Ric then interjected that the next step was for Erie and LVCDC to acquire a building, and that one was recently identified in the 2700 block of South Kildare. With more space, he pointed out, Erie could bring all of its services to LV. As a neighborhood with more children under the age of 9 than any other community area, there were unmet needs for serving children as well as adults. As this would, potentially, be Erie's third project in 11 years that involved another building, it was understandable that board members had feasibility questions. First of all, they wanted to know more about LVCDC and their leader. At that time, it was Jesus "Chuy" Garcia.[429] Ric spoke favorably of LVCDC's executive, known to him and his Senior Director of Programs, as a good man, former alderman and state senator. It was believed this would be a good partnership.

As a next step, both Sy Nelson and John Hall, experienced men of business, stated the need for a proposal with a 3-5-year plan that included projected revenue and expenses. Ric agreed that it would be forthcoming. The Board then authorized Ric to continue to research and analyze this project and return with a full proposal.

Ric expressed his pleasure at the excellent fiscal status of Erie for the coming year, noting that Erie was one of very few organizations that can say it is at 100% of its private revenue goal this early in the fiscal year. He commented that when asked by a program officer from the Prince Charitable Trust, how Erie is in such a better place than her other grantees, Ric responded that it was a combination of:

- Erie's great programs;
- The great relationship between Erie staff and board;
- The legacy & reputation the organization has earned through the years; and
- As long as Erie continues to provide the quality of services it has until now, in spite of gentrification, Erie will survive, because people will travel to get these services.[430]

He then notified the board that he was happy to report he had hired Maureen Hellwig (me) as Senior Director of Programs and Quality Assurance. He said he thought I fit the position perfectly, not only due to my commitment to the community, but to my experience as an educator, community organizer, researcher, and Board member. He concluded with "Glad I convinced her to come back home." I responded that this opportunity was a great gift to me and that I was honored to become an Erie staff member once again.

Ken Perkins, chair of the EECS board, reported that the school had been visited by Patty Hoersche, senior specialist from the Erikson Institute. She made the following observation:

> *This school is right up there with the best schools I have ever observed. The environment makes literacy accessible. From the hallway walls to the classrooms, to their houses, students are encouraged to read. There is so much evidence of relational trust–students, teachers, and parents. . . drawing all the students to learn to read.*[431]

On that note, it was understandable Juan Andrade had invited EECS principal, Linda Ponce de Leon, to address the US Hispanic Leadership Institute on "The State of Latino Education in Illinois."

Los Mexicanos Estan Aqui – The Mexicans are Here

As was noted earlier in this book, by the time Ric took over at Erie House in 2003, Mexican immigrants and Mexican-Americans represented more than three quarters of a million residents of the Chicago Metro area. About two thirds of that number were still in the city, while a significant one third had moved to the suburbs. Apparently, the Chicago Council on Foreign Relations (CCFR) (later the Chicago Council on Global Affairs) thought it was time to give some attention to this reality, possibly influenced by the fact that Ric Estrada had joined their ranks. Consequently, in 2006, they formed a Mexican-American Task Force and set about the task of developing some recommendations to support the success of this large group of residents, based on an understanding that their success would impact the success of the Chicago metropolitan area in the 21st century.

A review of their prescriptive recommendations might have been taken from an Erie House brochure on services offered to the immigrant community, as the task force placed emphasis on:

- The importance of early childhood education and readiness for school, with literacy being a key factor;
- Setting a goal for every child to be bilingual and college ready by the time they finished high school;
- Supporting after-school programs that keep children engaged after the traditional school day ends;
- Establishing higher standards for the professional development of teachers;
- Making sure parents understand and are involved in supporting their children's education;
- Engaging the business community in mentoring programs for high school students;
- Helping students navigate the college application process & increasing scholarships;
- Expanding availability of quality ESL programs for adults in partnership with the CCC;
- Creating pathways to careers;
- Getting Mexican-owned businesses involved in supporting schools and students. [432]

On most of these points, Erie House could say "check."

The *Chicago Tribune* commented on the Task Force report, prepared by Beatriz Ponce De Leon, in an article by Oscar Avila, entitled "City's future tied to Mexicans."[433] Avila commented that the authors of the report noted the urgency of the issues they highlighted, given that 1 out of 6 area residents were of Mexican descent, and that the Mexican community was expected to double by 2030. The argument continued that the best-case scenario would involve helping Mexicans to help Chicago become a global center and expand the local economy. The worst-case scenario: Allow Mexicans to lag behind in education and income to become a drain on the region and a segregated underclass. The article even went on to say that what was needed were "welcoming centers" like the settlement houses of the 19th and 20th centuries. At which point, Erie House, Onward House, Association House, Christopher House, Marillac House. Chicago Commons, Gads Hill, Northwestern Settlement, Ada S. McKinley, Marillac House/DePaul settlement, and Casa Central could have all stood up and waved: "Yo, over here. In the 21st century, some of us are still here!" And with its focus on Little Village, with the densest Mexican population in the region, Erie House was, as usual, ahead of the curve.

To make sure the Board was well-informed about the potential next step of acquiring a facility in Little Village, the May 2006 board meeting was called to order early, so that, following a brief business meeting, they could have a tour of Little Village and visit the site of the building being considered for purchase. Before the tour, Ric reviewed the steps in the process since the Erie/LVCDC partnership proposal for a Little Village Immigrant Resource Center (LVIRC) in LV met the approval of Matt Piers, the attorney overseeing disbursement of Western Union settlement funds. He awarded this collaborative initiative $750,000, the largest settlement grant in the country, early in 2004. He approved a two-step approach that began with Erie House starting to offer services in LV in rented space, to be followed by the acquisition or construction of a facility for the LVIRC that would take time to find and raise funds to complete. Ric explained that Erie had outgrown the second floor of the Epiphany convent almost immediately but had been a bit "distracted" with starting a new school and assuming ownership of 1701, not to mention celebrating its 135th anniversary. Meanwhile, LVCDC had found a building, a former cookie factory, that they proposed would be jointly owned by the two organizations.

Before the Board visit that evening, LVCDC had made an offer on the building, believing they had to move ahead in light of other competitive bids. Their offer of $284,000 was accepted. However, they assured Erie House that LVCDC was prepared to make the purchase themselves if Erie did not want to buy in. Ric told the board that, given Erie would be providing all of the services in the building, he felt it would make more sense for Erie to have a stake in the property rather than paying rent. It would also be an appreciating asset. He called for the formation of a committee to review the appraisal and the structural and environmental assessments. Following the visit of the Epiphany site and the cookie factory, the Erie delegation would join staff and board members for dinner at Mi Tierra, where, then 22nd ward alderman, Ricardo Muñoz, would join them.

Before boarding the bus, Board members had some questions, as any responsible board should. Would taking on this project have any negative impact on Erie's new charter school? The response was NO, as the school already had a good financial base and would not need a new building for at least another two years. Nancy Vincent added, that while the school was a great project, Erie needed to help other communities as well. Following on Nancy's comment, Ric made the point that it was getting harder and harder to raise funds for adult and youth programming in West Town. The MacArthur Foundation, for example, had taken West Town off their priority list, but LV was definitely on it. Sy Nelson, banker and frequent Erie Board Treasurer, raised the concern about impact on Erie finances. What was the estimate for Erie's share of rehab costs? Answer: about

150K. The Board then voted to form the Little Village Building Committee.

Chuy Garcia joined the Erie Group on their tour. At the first stop, Adult Programs Director, Lora Oswald, provided a tour of the Epiphany site and introduced the staff there. The second stop was the cookie factory that was then being used to store equipment. It was a 2-story building, sitting on a double lot. It had an attached garage, but no basement, but Garcia suggested adding a third story might be possible.

Special Projects Are Exciting, but the Day-to-Day Programs Pay the Bills

While plans for the LVIRC were being renewed in Little Village, the Program Report to the board provided some stats that had not been updated for a while. In **Adult Programs,** there was particularly good news to report regarding the SOS. This Secretary of State- funded literacy program had met its goals in all 7 categories and exceeded them in 5. There were 255 participants who came for tutoring, mostly in English, but also math, being served by 167 volunteer tutors. The SOS program was now being offered in Little Village as well. Enrollment in ESL was at 281, with 75% of those students from Little Village. 47 people were enrolled in English GED and 27 in Spanish GED.

In **Child Care**, the After-School program added 30 additional slots at the charter school, bringing their enrollment to 70; the House added 10 more slots to bring their total to 90. Erie Day Care Family Homes were serving 115 children. And in pre-school the fight continued over the government's goal to reduce family eligibility by 20%, mainly cutting off those families that had been with Erie long enough to reap the benefits that were intended, to be less poor. But they were not yet rich enough to afford private care. They were out, unless they were willing to get poorer again. With a waiting list of 140, Erie would survive the loss of some families; the issue was the survival of the families.

In **YOU,** 22 youth participated in NetGain, a 10-week technology-based apprenticeship funded by After School Matters. They learned to manipulate graphics, create their own writing, and then use that material to create their own web pages. In June, 14 seniors were honored at the annual TEAM celebration. YOU staff were also considering expanding TEAM to include 8th graders, to help them better prepare for the transition to high school, and in choosing among the increased number of options for their high school education.

Tech Services, active with CTCNet in advocating for an increase in the state-funded Digital Divide grants program, was celebrating success. Erie received a grant of $45,000; but more importantly, DCEO increased the annual allocation for this program from $1 million to $8 million! And, now in its 10th year, the Tech Promoters program would be graduating 60 students in June 2006, one of the largest classes to date. In the previous year, 2005, 1,172 adults and 491 youth and children visited the Erie computer labs. The house had two labs with 34 work stations, plus the YOU MAC lab with 10 work stations; the Center had a lab with 14 work stations and LV had 12, for a total of 60 PCs and 10 MACs available to the community.

Candidates were being interviewed for the **Advocacy and Leadership Development** Coordinator for the initiative funded by the Marguerite Casey Foundation. But Casey or not, in March 2006, Erie was marching, as 300 Erie participants from West Town and Little Village joined one of the largest immigrant marches Chicago or the nation had ever seen. The rationale for the marches was explained above, but, restated here, they were triggered by the proposed HR4437 that identified all undocumented immigrants and anyone who helped them as felons.

On a less exciting plane, Erie was also embarking on an initiative to create a database that would support an intake and tracking system to capture program outcomes, to enable that "quality assurance" that was tacked on to the Senior Director of Programs job description. Counting the "number served," was no longer sufficient; funders wanted to know how their lives improved after they were served. What did they learn? What certificate did they get? How did their income improve? Etc. As misery loves company, Erie partnered with Chicago Commons and Albany Park Community Center to figure out how to do this. This collaboration added more partners as the struggle to get this right affected all social service agencies.

At the June 2006 annual meeting, Sy Nelson was approved as the next board president, and Celena Roldán was introduced as the new Director of Child Care. After 10 very productive years, Sandy Schaefer left Erie House, recommending Celena as her successor. She had been the social worker in the Child Care program for the previous 5 years, giving Sandy ample opportunity to know and mentor her.

Director of Finance, Betty Sanchez-Azadeh, reported that the coming year financial situation looked promising enough that Erie should not have to use its line of credit or tap into the endowment fund. Always good news. The additional after-school slots would probably yield about an $800,000 increase in revenue, bringing the projected FY07 budget to $7.4 million. Compare this with the FY95 budget of $2.3 million, just before the Center opened to a much expanded child care program. In a little over 10 years, the budget had tripled. From this perspective, one could understand the caution in the voices of the Board, as the Little Village project presented another giant leap up the finance and facility responsibility ladder.

When Ric had explained Erie's early achievement of its annual private fund-raising goal, he mentioned that Erie was well-known. Based on Ami Novoryta's report, ENH and EECS had been featured in the news 29 times since the beginning of the year, in both English and Spanish media. Not only was Erie House mentioned as serving the Puerto Rican community, on the occasion of media recalling the so-called Division Street riots 40 years earlier, but the *Chicago Journal* featured an article on May 11, 2006, with the sub-heading: "Latino-focused Erie House hosts citizenship workshop for Ukrainians." Ironically, there was a little foreshadowing here. By 2019, Erie would be serving enough Ukrainian pre-schoolers to fill two classrooms!

In the summer of 2006, the latest version of an Erie House newsletter, this time called "Erie InSight," featured a photo of Veronica Duque and her two daughters, Maria and Alissa. When Alissa started college, she worked part time as receptionist at the House. When she finished college, she joined the Erie Child Care staff--another Erie kid makes good and returns to serve the next generation. And, there were photos from the 135th: Second generation board member, Steve Fox; David Tolen who came to Erie for ESL and ended up joining the Erie board; Elizabeth Herrera, with her TEAM mentor, James Reavy, of Northern Trust.

Beatriz Lazala, an Erie pre-school teacher shared the story of her struggle, as a single mom of two, to earn her bachelor's degree and Type 04 teaching certificate, while continuing to work at Erie. She shared how this was possible due to a grant to Erie House of $215,000 from the McCormick Tribune Foundation to support professional development of early childhood teachers. But, not only did Beatriz earn her degree, but along with former Child Care Director, Sandy Schaefer, they challenged Roosevelt University's stringent internship/student teaching requirements to include any NAEYC-accredited child care program as a site for student teachers in the early childhood education field. This made it possible to continue working at Erie and use it as her internship/student teaching experience, instead of having to quit her job and go to another site. Allowing your work to work for you--that is an approach the academic world needed to learn from a working mom.

There was also an article about one of Erie's Mennonite volunteers, Brian Paff, who went from a volunteer in Child Care in 2004, to a full-time classroom teacher in 2005. Celena Roldán said that "Brian is nurturing, kind, and bilingual, making him a good fit for the two-year old classroom."[434] As Brian came to volunteer at Erie in 2004, he was following what had become another tradition, both for Erie House and the Mennonite Volunteer Service. MVS started in 1944 and it is the oldest continuing voluntary service program in Mennonite circles. Kent Unruh, the man who founded the Erie Community Technology Center, was Erie's first MVS volunteer in 1994. There continued to be one or two MVSers every year after that, for the next 20 years. And Brian, who eventually became Erie's Director of Marketing and Communications, was not the only one who stayed on to become a staff person. The relationship between Erie House and MVS was so strong, that when a new MVS National Director was hired, a visit to Erie House was part of his or her orientation.

In an article about the Erie Elementary Charter School, having completed its first school year, with Kindergarten and first grade, Principal De Leon described the school environment as a "culture of literacy with a commitment to high achievement." She listed the school's "partners" as Erie House, Erikson Institute, the Chicago School of Professional Psychology, the Chicago Children's Museum and DePaul University. As every charter school must raise some private dollars, EECS funders in Year One included Sara Lee, the Walton Family Foundation, the Renaissance School Fund, and McCormick Tribune Foundation. Average daily attendance was at 93%, student/teacher ratio was 10:1, due to an assistant teacher in every classroom, and parent participation was at 90%.[435]

Finally, the Operations Department was asked to share what it takes to maintain the buildings at 1347 W. Erie and 1701 W. Superior. Here is what they said:

- 75 gallons of floor wax
- 200 gallons of paint
- 1200 light bulbs
- 3,950 buckets of water to mop floors
- 9,984 rolls of paper towel
- 19,000 rolls of toilet paper
- 22,600 plastic garbage bags

Never think any non-profit runs any programs without back-up from a well-oiled maintenance machine.

Back to Little Village

Board President, Sy Nelson, convened a special board meeting in August 2006, to discuss the closing on the Kildare property that was being acquired as the future home of the LVIRC. Prior to the closing scheduled for September 5, Board approval was required. Ric provided a packet of materials that included:

- A letter from Matt Piers, confirming that purchase of the Kildare property met the guidelines of the WU settlement, and therefore, the $750,000, minus the advance of $50,000 given to ENH and LVCDC earlier, would be forwarded to LVCDC as fiscal agent for the project;
- Budget for the LVIRC project, with a total development cost of $1,596,763, with the rehab portion estimated at $798,382;

425

- Draft of a Board Resolution to be voted on to approve the project;
- Draft of a proposed fundraising plan, as $1,596,763 - $700,000 from WU = $896,763 TBR.[436]

Board member and architect, Mark Jolicoeur, reported that he had toured the building and noted it was a solid 1901 building. The plan would be to retain the shell and do extensive interior renovation, including new electric and heating systems. He added that he sees the purchase of this building as an opportunity rather than a risk, and that the estimated cost of renovation was realistic. Getting permits for the work would be facilitated by Alderman Muñoz, who already supported the plan. While LVCDC would be the initial title holder, a 3rd entity, perhaps an LLC, would be formed to reflect joint ownership with LVCDC. Programs would not move in until 2008, so plenty of time to work out that move. With funder interest in LV already established, the effort to raise the capital funds seemed doable.

The resolution was put on the table for a vote. It authorized Sy Nelson, Ric Estrada, Mark Jolicoeur, and Richard Figueroa to serve as "authorized individuals" to execute further instruments, excluding any loan documents, with an understanding that a collaboration agreement would be brought to the board for approval when it was drafted. The resolution passed unanimously.

The discussion continued at the September 2006, board meeting. LV alderman, Ricardo Muñoz, spoke to the board, once again assuring them of his support and how much the Little Village community needed the services Erie was bringing to their adults. He looked forward to having youth services as well. Since becoming alderman in 1993, he saw to the building of 5 schools in the ward, including Little Village High School. As a supporter of education, as THE critical service, he was anxious to have that supplemented with the kind of quality youth services Erie was known for.

Other News in 2006

Ami Novoryta reminded the board that the second annual gala was coming up in November. With AT&T as a sponsor, and significant involvement by Microsoft that past year, the focus of the event would be Technology Services. Erie's United Way Venture grant for FY07 had increased and United Way funding for YOU was restored at $156,000 over three years. Rhea Yap, a new Development Associate, had been hired.

Program highlights were dominated by a report from Erie's new Child Care Director, Celena. She began with an announcement that Erie's 19 Day Care Family Homes were finally approved to receive State Pre-K dollars, something Celena's predecessor had been working on for three years. She also reported on some results from the funding the McCormick Tribune Foundation had been providing for professional development of Child Care staff. So far, she said, staff had completed five Associate Degrees, two Bachelor's degrees, two Master's degrees, and three Illinois Director's Credentials Certificates. In other words, about one third of the instructional staff earned a new/higher academic credential.

She also reported on what was learned through a recent evaluation of the program. For example, the turnover rate among the Child Care staff was 10%, compared with the national average of 40%. Six classrooms received average scores of 5 or above, based on a 7-point evaluation scale. As to work environment, staff rated ENH with an average score of 8 out of a possible 10. Bottom line, not only did Child Care have a happy, committed staff, Celena explained, but the higher the rating level, the more funding Erie was eligible to receive to maintain their quality.

The Board was advised that Cristina Garcia had been promoted from admin assistant to Citizenship Coordinator, and she would be working on her MSW at the University of Chicago, in the SSA program. TEAM grad, Angelica Herrera, would take her place as admin assistant.

Ric noted in his report that Joe Scoby, 2005 Gala Chair, was featured in *Crain's* "Who's Who" section, and listed ENH as his main civic involvement, positive publicity you cannot buy. He also noted that Erie and EECS were profiled in a report of the Chicago Council on Global Affairs titled "A Shared Future: The Economic Engagement of Greater Chicago and its Mexican Community," by Beatriz Ponce De León. They were mentioned as places that promote a "culture of literacy."

The report was also covered in an article in the *Daily Herald,* September 16, 2006, "Economy's fate rests on immigrants, study says." Reporter, Tara Malone, highlighted some findings of the report. She said that the report concluded that immigrant workers, store owners, and shoppers represent the region's economic engine, a refreshing contrast to the negative argument that immigrants are a drain on the economy. But it also concluded that if Mexican workers remain on the fringes, with low pay and limited education, the financial standing of Chicago and suburbs could stumble. The report does not get into documented or undocumented, but simply points out that 4 of every 10 immigrants in the region are Mexican, representing 16% of the region's population, which was expected to double in 30 years. The report recommended that the region:

- Invest in skills training coupled with on-the-job English classes,
- Encourage entrepreneurship training,
- Create financial literacy programs,
- Boost home ownership, and

- Expand bilingual education in schools to speed up the learning of English by immigrant children.[437]

The Fall 2006, issue of *Erie InSight* highlighted Erie's citizenship work, as funded by the New Americans Initiative (NAI) and administered by ICIRR. During 2005-06, 232 immigrants became citizens through Erie House, 284 more, through the NAI Northwest Collaborative led by Erie. There were photos of Erie participants marching for immigrant rights during the huge Chicago March that took place the previous May 1. There was also an article about long-time board member, John Hall, president and founder of Chicago's Goose Island Brewing Company. Hall recalled that he first became acquainted with Erie House when Goose Island hosted an Erie fundraiser back in 1988. By 1990, he had joined the board, drawn, as he put it, to the character and high motivation of people connected with Erie. He had seen three expansions in his 16 years: Erie Community Center, the charter school, and now, Little Village. His hope was that Erie maintain the same spirit as it expanded, and added, "So far, so good."[438]

At the final board meeting of 2006, Mark Hallett reported that the EECS enrollment was at 125, and about 17% of the children were African American. Sara Lee donated $50,000 for a library, and the school received a Renaissance grant of $50,000.

Erie counsel, Noemi Flores, was working on a proposed entity that would reflect joint ownership of the Kildare property in Little Village. She also announced that Gardner, Carton & Douglas, Erie's legal counsel for 58 years, was merging with Drinker, Biddle and Reath. She could not say at that point how this might affect her/their relationship with Erie. As it turned out, Drinker Biddle basically took over where GCD left off, as Erie's counsel.

Ric noted that he had met with US Senator Barack Obama to voice Erie's displeasure with his vote to extend the border wall. When he met with Miguel Del Valle, then City Clerk, Ric encouraged him to continue as an advocate for education. In a meeting with former Erie Board member, Jesse Ruiz, who had become a key figure in state education policy, he was assured that Erie remained a recognized leader in education.

Reassurances from the policy wonks are always welcome. However, an article that appeared in the *Chicago Sun-Times* on December 20, 2006, illustrated Erie's favorite way to affirm the quality of its work--a good story about a participant. The article, "Sharing the wisdom–Once unable to read, immigrant now teaches others," tells the story of Jackie Ortiz.[439] She came to the US from Zacatecas, Mexico, in 2000, with only a third-grade education, unable to read or write, even in Spanish. She worked as a seamstress to support her four children. Eventually, she found her way to an Erie ESL class in Little Village, where she met Erie staff member, Elva Serna. Elva encouraged her to not only continue with her English studies but to also sign up for a Tech Promoters class. Ms. Ortiz recalled what Elva told her. "It does not matter what level of education you have; all that matters is how much you want to learn." Ortiz successfully completed the program and, that December, when the second class of Tech promoters in Little Village graduated, Ortiz commented: "This is the first time someone I taught will receive a diploma." She not only wanted to learn, she came to realize she wanted to share the gift and teach. And Erie made her believe she could. By March of 2007, Ortiz was organizing a computer class at Telpochcalli School. She got the school to commit a classroom, got nine computers donated, and 16 parents were enrolled. English + technology + leadership = success. That has been the Erie curriculum for adult education since the days of Tim Bell.

Lastly, senior staff had been making the rounds to visit Erie's 5 most supportive churches: Wilmette, Lake Forest, Elmhurst, and Oak Park Presbyterian, and Union

Church of Hinsdale (UCC). At Wilmette, the pastor presented Ravelo and Ponce de León with a check for $20,000.

Director of Development, Ami Novoryta, reported that the 2006 gala revenue was $247,000, up about $9,000 from the previous year, and, expenses were less, generating a net gain of almost $163,000. This was read as an indicator that the good result in 2005 was not due solely to Erie's benchmark 135th year, but rather, that Erie may have finally found a formula for an annual fundraiser worth repeating. And, so it was, for the next 15 years and counting.

Charter High Schools and Bridge Programs Take Erie Down New Pathways

Charter, Charter, Everywhere a Charter

In spite of all the demographic changes in West Town, as it became more middle class and less diverse, it became clear that Erie House was, indeed, still thriving at 1347 W. Erie. As a result, space for programming, even in Erie's 137th year, and its 110th year at the same address, was becoming a problem.[440] Granted, most adult education was now happening in Little Village. On the other hand, a new local demand was emerging. With the success of the Noble Street Charter High School, housed at Northwestern Settlement, this charter school network kept going. In 2006, Rauner High School opened, utilizing the former Santa Maria Addolorata grade school building on Ohio, just behind Erie House. In the Fall of 2007, Golder High was set to open at the former Holy Innocents school on Superior, just two blocks from Erie. Some of the youth who attended or would attend these schools were already linked to Erie House, but many others were not. Still others who might have lost a connection at Erie because of traveling outside the

431

neighborhood for high school, now found it easier to stay local and stay connected.

Then, in addition to this now, very dense high school attendance area, Youth Options Unlimited (YOU) was adding Monday night TEAM for eighth graders. Partly due to the addition of these charter schools, and partly due to other changes at CPS, choosing the right magnet school, academy, charter school or other special application school for secondary education, had become almost as complex as choosing and applying for college. Parents and students, as was customary, turned to Erie House for guidance. And just as the argument was made for the benefit of the early intervention that pre-school represented, YOU staff had come to realize that the right choice of high school was an early intervention that could affect a child's eventual success in getting into and succeeding in college. And, whatever guidance these children received in preparing for the high school experience could be the intervention needed to prevent them from dropping out. Dropout statistics pointed to the first two years of high school as the critical choice years for dropping out or staying in. So, while mornings were busy at the Center as those toddlers and pre-schoolers were being dropped off at the Child Care department, afternoons and evenings were the busy times at the House.

Amidst all of these changes, there were staff changes as well. After nine years, Maria Matias left Erie House, ironically, to take a position with the Noble Network. Rebecca Estrada became the YOU Director, Maria Guzman, Assistant Director, and Joshua Fulcher was hired to be the TEAM Coordinator. Eventually, Fulcher became YOU Director, and was still there in 2019, with a new title and broader responsibilities that included overseeing the School Age program. His department also had a new name: "Extended Learning Programs," focused on expanding what was learned in grade school and high school with the learning experiences Erie provided after school.

Building Bridges

In addition to an expanded YOU, Erie's Literacy program, referred to as SOS, because of its funding from the Secretary of State, continued to draw adults to the House. This program continued to prosper due to the warmth, dedication, and unlimited energy of Susana Ortiz, noted over and over in this text, who, by 2019, had been on the job at Erie for more than 20 years. The one-on-one tutoring this program offered helped adults who, either could not fit regular classroom sessions into their schedule, or who were particularly interested in having the opportunity to practice conversational English, in addition to attending classes. Tutors at the House also assisted adult students preparing for their citizenship test. Tutoring at the House was like a "pop-up event." One could open any door, at any time of the day, and witness a tutor working with a student. They also needed space(s).

Soon, this challenge would be further complicated by the addition of a new, or actually, renewed program at Erie. It was not yet under way in 2007, but an idea for reviving Pathways to Success was under discussion as Lora Oswald, Director of Adult Programs, and Susan Bernhart, the GED instructor (and former Mennonite Volunteer), commiserated over the low completion numbers for the GED program. Susan was tweaking the curriculum and researching other programs, but no magic bullet was emerging. The primary purpose people come to Erie House, or anywhere else, to learn English, is so they can get a job, or a better job with a living wage. The frustration staff were experiencing and witnessing was two-pronged. On the one hand, a high school diploma would probably get a person a better job than one they could get without it; on the other hand, it took a very long time to earn one. During the long haul, no matter the desire for completion, life had a way of interfering. Hours changed for the part time job, a full-time job opportunity emerged that offered more money, if not yet a living wage. Child care evaporated, children just needed more attention, or rent increases forced moves away from needed services. All of these circumstances can and did interfere with GED completion, no matter how good the program was.

Reviving And revamping Pathways to Success

Dissatisfaction with outcomes in the GED program, finding them below par for Erie standards, led to brainstorming for alternatives. Out of this process, emerged an idea that came to be known as a "bridge program." This concept could actually be traced back to the 1990s when Erie House named their workforce program "Pathways to Success." Whether it is called a bridge or a pathway, the point was that low- income people, immigrants or African Americans, or any other low-income group, needed guidance, not just to "get a job," but to get on a path to a "career." Help was needed, both to visualize a realistic career goal, possibly one that did not require a 4-year degree, and then, to understand the steps required to get there. As always, education and training were keys to success. But the form that education should take as part of the first steps on the pathway, were not the same for everyone. While Erie was helping their children to ultimately be ready for college, this was not an immediately realistic goal for their parents, especially for those in their middle age with limited formal education. On the other hand, the better the earning power of their parents, the more likely they could support their child's college plans. Too often, YOU staff reported that one of their high school grads, who was ready and willing to go to college, had to postpone it, either because their families depended on the additional income they were bringing home, or because their families could offer no financial support for tuition, much less room and board. And only a few win those all-expenses-paid scholarships.

The Pathways program of the 1990s had led to a training program Erie offered to get adults on a path to a career in financial services, starting with entry-level teller jobs or work in the back-office processing checks, etc. At that time, banks complained they had difficulty finding people for these jobs, and if individuals came to apply with a rudimentary understanding of what banks do, along with competency in arithmetic, they would be thrilled to hire them, especially if they were bilingual. If they did well, many banks would even offer tuition support to pursue a degree. With computers and adding machines, this was a program Erie could do in-house.

But, even with the swing in the economy toward the service sector, Chicago maintained a healthy manufacturing base. Erie was not in a position to offer skills training in this area but made the effort to link participants with the training programs that other CBOs had developed. In the 1990s, that was Greater West Town Project that offered Shipping & Receiving and Woodworking; Jane Addams Resource Corp. (JARC), originally out of Hull House, that offered skill preparation for careers in the metalworking sector; or Ric Gudell's Chicago Manufacturing Institute out of Chicago Commons. It was Gudell that taught JARC and Greater West Town everything they needed to know about careers in manufacturing and how to prepare the educationally disadvantaged to get them. The Senior Director of Programs had listened and learned as well.

By 2007, banking was so restructured it did not offer the options it did 10 years earlier. But manufacturing was still there, as were the CBO programs just described, and a new career path was emerging called CNC, Computerized Numerical Control. Technology was having its impact on manufacturing as in every other sector. The larger companies at the top end of the supply chain, like the automotive industry, that depended on many smaller companies like those in the Chicago region for various

435

components, were demanding that their suppliers had CNC in place. Hence, there was an explosion in demand for anyone with CNC training.

This time, Erie House took the bridge program idea and connected it with CNC skills training. Here was an opportunity to get Erie adult learners on a career path that was well-paid, even at the entry level, and did not require a high school diploma or GED. And math skills were even more important than English, coupled with some basic computer skills. It was not gender specific; either a man or a woman could be a CNC operator.

Erie had math teachers and computers; what remained was to add an introduction to CNC. With the gift of a bilingual adult ed instructor, eager to learn something new himself, Erie crafted its first CNC bridge program, and David Swanson found himself on a new career path as a bridge program instructor. He already was good at math and knew his way around computers. He then set out to learn all he could about CNC and what was feasible to include in an Erie House classroom. Soon, Erie was ordering micrometers and calipers and David was generating Erie's own CNC Bridge curriculum, and scheduling time in Erie's Technology Center where students could try out sample CAD-CAM computer programs. What a bridge curriculum did was to continue teaching English and math, while putting them in the context of a career path. "Contextual learning" was the key. Adults were more willing to continue their English or math studies if they could see a direct connection to a new and/or better job at the same time. Pathways to Success was re-born.

Along with converting an adult ed instructor to a CNC Bridge instructor, an opportunity was emerging with another Erie kid who had finished college at the University of Wisconsin-Madison and come back to work at Erie. He was a TEAM grad who credited that program with his application and admission to an out-of-state school, that was still an uncommon experience for many immigrant youth. His name was Oswaldo Alvarez, and he was working for Susana in SOS. He was also not averse to taking a lower paying job than his college degree might have warranted if it meant he could be of service to his community. He had obviously paid attention to the values he learned at Erie, in addition to how to fill out a successful FAFSA application.[441]

When Herbert Moreno replaced Lora Oswald mid-year, he embraced the bridge program concept and agreed that Alvarez might be ready for a new challenge, and an increase in pay. So, he was offered the job of Pathways to Success Coordinator and jumped at the opportunity. From his first day on the job, his enthusiasm prepared him for an aggressive recruitment effort. He did not wait for people to figure out Erie had hung out a new shingle; he went out to all the places he could think of to find them. From unemployment offices to laundromats, he sold this new opportunity. Enrollment blossomed. Next, he came to understand that finding the right CNC advanced skills training program would be a challenge. JARC was the first option that emerged, as they were aware of the demand for CNC as well. A collaboration was developed with them.

Next, he looked into what the City Colleges of Chicago (CCC) had to offer. In Erie's experience, working with the City Colleges of Chicago around the education of immigrants had always been a slippery slope. This dated back to Tim Bell's efforts to work with Malcom X College that provided Erie with adult ed instructors in the 1980s and 90s. In the opinion and experience of many CBOs, the network of seven community college campuses in Chicago, had never measured up to other community colleges around the country, or even in downstate Illinois, in meeting the needs of adult learners, especially those seeking quality vocational education. On many levels, that disappointment was part of the motivation for setting up their own programs.

When the CCC announced they were considering opening a vocational satellite of Wright College in Humboldt Park in the early 1980s, then-State Senator Miguel Del Valle, set out to make sure this satellite would focus on *vocational* education. He argued there were plenty of non-profits in his district that did a superior job in teaching ESL and ABE. What was needed was a place with the resources to install labs and equipment that non-profits could not afford to do, and then add to that infrastructure a commitment to offer the type of instruction that connected people to career paths that were relevant to the late 20th century, and on into the 21st.

The Humboldt Park Vocational Education Center (HPEVC) opened in 1989 and set off down a bumpy road. The initial leadership had not received or did not understand Del Valle's message, and fell back on offering remedial adult education. Eventually, with Del Valle's help and the engagement of the community, a new Dean was hired. Her name was Madeline Roman, a woman of the community, who set out to turn HPEVC around to what it was supposed to be. When Roman and Alvarez connected, they put each other on a "pathway to success." Oswaldo sold her on CNC, she sold Wright College, and Erie's first experience with an effective partnership with any institution connected with the CCC was born. It worked so well that Ms. Roman got into the habit of calling Erie House first to find out how many students they might be sending to HPVEC. After that call, she knew how many more she needed to enroll; Erie had already done part of her work for her. She understood and appreciated that, as other CCC administrators did not. This was partly due to the fact that she was not an academic, but an advocate for her community. Working at a "college" was not her *raison d'etre*; working for her community was.

HPVEC set up a creditable CNC program, and Erie House sent them bridge program graduates. But Oswaldo did not stop there. He found another CNC training program in Skokie, called Symbol. It was not a non-profit, and it was not community-based, but it was run by people with years of experience in the manufacturing sector and an excellent program. Could this work for Erie PTS graduates? Erie and Symbol worked together to figure it out. Erie helped their participants access grants from the city that subsidized the cost of training, making it possible to pay tuition at Symbol. But who wanted to go all the way to Skokie? Once the first completer reported on his experience there, and described the great job he got, more Erie students were determined to go to Symbol themselves, and, car pools were organized. Because, as it turned out, Symbol, like the best CBOs in the field, not only trained you, they found you your first CNC job. That was gold and worth the commute.

But realistically, Symbol was not going to work for everyone, and HPEVC did not offer job placement services, so Erie stepped up to that challenge and Jesus Rodriguez, who had been working in the Citizenship program at Erie, was recruited to learn how to be a job developer. He enrolled in the training program for this role that was offered by the Chicago Jobs Council (CJC) and started visiting companies to find out what they needed and suggest that Erie might be able to help them out. He was often given a tour of the factory, as the harried owner would point at a worker with gray hair and complain that he would soon retire. That story repeated itself until the owner would look at Jesus, sigh, and say something like, relatively speaking, in another 10 minutes I am going to be in *deep* ---- unless you can send me some younger, well-prepared workers.

Recalling the Origins of the Chicago Jobs Council

A word about the Chicago Jobs Council is in order here. It was founded in 1981, with 18 member organizations, mostly non-profits, working to help Chicagoans out of poverty through worthwhile employment. Early histories are often forgotten at the expense of losing lessons learned that could inform later generations of what has worked and what has not, and why. Of course, new ideas and solutions to problems are always needed, but often, the better solutions are deeply rooted in the past and just need to be dusted off and updated. CJC was one of those good ideas that has lasted and prospered for 38 years.

Ann Seng, even before becoming Director of the Chicago Council on Urban Affairs, along with her partner in many endeavors, Anne Markowitch, were both former School Sisters of St. Francis.[442] They organized something called the Jane Addams Conference, that coincided with the fight for women's rights in the latter part of the 20th century. This was the fight that led to the formation of NOW and the call for the Equal Rights Amendment (ERA). Out of concerns for equal pay for equal work came the concern about access to jobs for the poor--jobs they had to get first, in order to be paid--before they could call for equal pay. As "the Anns" were affectionately known, were advocates of better public policy as the basis for better programs, they saw the need for a group that would work with community-based organizations, their advocacy preference, to collaborate on behalf of better workforce development policy that would benefit the disadvantaged workforce. And CJC was born. To get it started, they called on a bright, young African American woman by the name of Toni Preckwinkle, to be the first director. Today, she is the President of the Cook County Board and Chair of the Cook County Democratic party. The Anns had an eye for talent.

Before returning to Erie's workforce development story, it might also be worth noting a pattern here. All of these very successful and groundbreaking policies and organizations had the same roots. Ann Seng spent many years working for the Hull House Association.[443] Bill Leavy, who founded Greater West Town Project, started his focus on workforce development when he worked at Association House. The Jane Addams Resource Corp. started at the Jane

Addams Center of the Hull House Association, and everyone learned from Ric Gudell, who started down the block from Erie House at the Emerson House, a Chicago Commons agency. The pattern should be obvious: settlement houses birthed some of the best ideas and organizations in the workforce development field--something they should be credited with, along-side their contribution of Kindergartens and early childhood education.

Once the CNC program was under way, as good as it was, not everyone wanted to work in a factory. Just as the demand for CNC workers was large, the demand for bilingual staff in the allied health care careers was also growing. Nurses were certainly in demand, but that was a longer career path. So, Erie explored shorter term options. Both Certified Nursing Assistants (CNAs), and Certified Medical Assistants (CMAs), came into view. When Oswaldo inquired whether HPEVC offered these courses, it turned out the CMA training was available at the Wright campus only. Once again, Madeline Roman got to work and soon that program was available at HPVEC.

The Erie Institute for Social Justice (EISJ)

Another program for adults that began in FY07, was a program to develop leaders in advocacy among both Erie staff and participants, called the Erie Institute for Social Justice (EISJ). This was funded by the Marguerite Casey Foundation. As a grantee that always supported community organizing, but also did not claim this as their sole mission, Erie House struggled to some extent to continue to fit the Casey guidelines. This was the latest attempt to demonstrate proactive programming in this area, and be in sync with the Casey national agenda called "Equal Voices for America Campaign." Amy Klein started the program. Then, in the Fall of 2007, Edgar Ramirez was hired to take her place. Ramirez had been another intern at Erie, from the SSA program at the University of Chicago. Now he was back as an employee. Here is another example of the pattern that had Erie kids, MVS volunteers, and interns, sticking around and/or coming back to work at Erie.

The Institute next offered their program in Little Village at the new high school. In 2008, Edgar was hired by LVCDC. From there, he went on to become Executive Director of Chicago Commons. Erie appreciated his time with them and was proud to play whatever small part in preparing him for such an important role in the settlement house movement. Possibly that was the most important contribution of the EISJ, which did not continue for very long.

Losses in 2007

The first loss was the announcement from Linda Ponce de Leon that she would be leaving her position as EECS principal to move back to California. Board members expressed their profound disappointment. They were very grateful for all that Linda did to get the charter school up and running but had hoped she would stay on for more than two years. The search was on for a replacement and Dr. Jane Montes was hired.

The second "loss" would not have been described that way in 2007, but all was not right in Little Village. Progress on the Little Village Immigrant Resource Center was behind schedule. Erie's legal counsel was drawing up a partnership agreement, but it was a process that dragged on into 2008. At the March 2007, Board meeting, Ric reported that the following arrangement had been made. "We now have a $300,000 CD, earning 5.75% interest, and $89,000 in a money market account that also earns interest but is more liquid." However, nothing more was said about the pending partnership agreement. Meanwhile, LVCDC had a new executive director; Jorge Cestou had replaced Jesus Garcia.

As to other LV developments, the City Zoning Board approved the LVIRC project on June 14, 2007. Then, another opportunity emerged when a residential property adjacent to the cookie factory came up for sale. The Board authorized Ric to join with LVCDC in purchasing this property if that became feasible, at a price not to exceed $235,000. The sale did not happen then, but the property was acquired later at a bargain price. Merri Ex, a former Erie ED, was hired as a consultant to assist with the Capital Campaign, to work closely with Erie's new Development Director, Alex Montgomery, in raising the balance of funds Erie would need for its share of the costs to get the cookie factory ready to open in 2009 as the Immigrant Resource Center. Ami Novoryta's departure was another loss, as Ric ranked her as one of the best Development Director's Erie ever had. She left to pursue her Master's degree at Harvard's Kennedy School of Government. Erie always felt honored when one of their own, participant or staff, left a special place to go to a special place.

The final loss for 2007 was the passing of Nancy Gielow, wife of Bob Gielow, both longtime Erie supporters and Life Trustees.

Awards & Recognition

Ric reported on recent awards and recognition for Erie House. In Nov. 2007, Erie received the Bank of America Neighborhood Builder Award, which included a $200,000 grant and leadership development opportunities for staff. The bank also took full page ads in *La Raza* and the *Chicago Tribune* to announce the award. Both the Chicago School of Professional Psychology and the Erikson Institute had published articles about their work at Erie. Each touted Erie's work as exemplary, he said.

Ric informed the Board that he had been notified that he was selected as one of 59 fellows for the 2008 Marshall

Memorial Fellowship. The German Marshall Fund of the US offers its fellows the opportunity to travel to Europe for a cultural exchange between European and American leaders. He said,

> *I am excited and humbled by this honor. I feel extremely fortunate to be at Erie at this time; it is because Erie is so strong that I am able to go. Any number of my ED colleagues, even if selected, could not leave their organizations to take advantage of the opportunity. I am blessed.*[444]

He reported that, during his month-long absence, Senior Director of Programs, Maureen Hellwig, would assume day-to-day responsibilities and serve as interim director. Senior Advisor, Rafael Ravelo, would serve as interim liaison for EECS.

Blessings and Challenges Persist in 2008 and 2009

Blessings came mostly from Erie's continuing good reputation, and that of its executive director. On both of those levels, recognition for the quality of their work came from funders and the media, with support from those with political power on all levels except the governor's mansion, at least through 2008. In 2009, Governor Quinn was on board. And Erie created its own good will on the part of politicos who knew they would always find Erie at their door, advocating for what was right, what was needed in policies and legislation, and explaining what was wrong. Watching the crowds that rallied in Springfield, Erie tee-shirts were always visible. Pols learned there was no use hiding, although that was sometimes tried. Generally, it was best to listen or prepare to take the heat, eventually-- heat that was dialed up by participating in advocacy coalitions like ICIRR, CAAELII, Alternative Schools Network, Day Care Action Council, and Chicago Jobs Council.

Nationally, Erie was an active member of NCLR (National Council of La Raza, now, Unidos US), and was participating in the Equal Voices for America's Families campaign being promoted by the Marguerite Casey Foundation (MCF). With multiple, renewable 3-year grants of $360,000, MCF was, by far, one of Erie's largest private funders. Equal Voices was on Erie's agenda, leading up to the 2008 presidential election.

In terms of new programming, health education and promotion of healthier living came to Erie House during these years, through the initial leadership of Dr. Patricia Novick, a minister, counselor, and spiritual guide for Erie staff toward the end of the first decade of the 20th century. While this programming did not receive the same fanfare as starting a new school or opening an immigrant resource center, the impact was significant and long-lasting.

And while the machinations of crafting the LVIRC partnership ground on, the people of Little Village, the Mexican immigrant community, could not have been happier with Erie's services there. The demand was constant and larger than the space available, almost immediately, and all the time.

On the other hand, challenges arose with both of Erie's signature accomplishments under Estrada, LVIRC and the charter school. Added to that was trouble with one of Erie's most reliable sources of public dollars–State Pre-K funds–mostly due to a decision at CPS.

In the face of all of these developments, Erie thrived and survived. The old adage applied: "No guts, no glory." Guts can be messy, but they clean up, if you have the right crew and right tools on hand. With that introduction, here is what transpired during Ric's last two years at the helm.

Erie Elementary Charter School (EECS) Prospers and Struggles

In its first years, Erie House and Erie Elementary Charter School were joined at the hip. Ric was the Executive Director of ENH and the CEO of EECS. Several Erie Board members took on the responsibility of serving on both boards, and Erie board member, Ken Perkins, became the first chair of the EECS board. A report on the EECS became a regular agenda item at all Erie House Board meetings. Erie House's Finance and HR departments managed payroll and benefits for the school's staff, and the Development Department raised funds for the school to ensure they would meet the private revenue charters needed to supplement the funding they received from the Chicago Public Schools. This type of support was in Erie's DNA. They had provided it for the early days of the Erie Family Health Center and Bickerdike.

With Linda Ponce de Leon as principal, who had been intimately involved in the shaping of the school's philosophy, hiring the right staff, and creating the "culture of literacy" as a primary focus, the EECS was off to an excellent start. As Ken Perkins noted, following Erie's annual gala fundraiser, the EECS principal and board members were well-represented at the dinner, "demonstrating both the school's appreciation of Erie House and our feeling of unity."[445] Adding to that unity, was the fact that Erie House ran the charter's After-School program, at the school, and it too, was growing steadily. The search for a larger building than the old St. Mark's school was already under way.

Another search, one that the EECS board had not anticipated, was the search to find a replacement for Linda Ponce de Leon at the end of the school's second year. As noted earlier, they hired Dr. Jane Montes for the 2007-2008 school year. However, that did not work out as hoped, and the search re-opened for the following year. With the help of the Erikson Institute, they found Dr. Eleanor Nicholson, a former principal of two prestigious schools, The Latin School and the University of Chicago Lab School. She was hired with the understanding that she would work for the charter for one year, with Velia Soto, an EECS teacher, assuming the role of Vice-Principal and benefiting from Nicholson's mentorship. This would give the school's board more time to look for a principal for the longer term--or have time to assess whether or not Soto could step into that position. Nicholson stayed on a second year, to facilitate the application for renewal of the charter. After that, Velia Soto became the EECS principal.

In March of 2008, Ken Perkins shared the "great anticipation" as EECS third graders were preparing to take the ISAT, the first standardized test the school would participate in. Enrollment was at 162, and a lottery was being used to draw some students from the waiting list. When the scores were finally released, the anticipation was rewarded. EECS students did very well, scoring in the 67.6 percentile in literacy and 88.2 percentile in math. What was not going as well as planned was meeting the school's biliteracy goal. This was reported to the Erie Board by Nancy Vincent, the new Chair of the EECS Board, in January of 2009. She pledged that efforts were under way to change that, with some help from DePaul University.

As 4th grade was added, enrollment moved up to 210, with 20-21 students in each room, and a ratio of 10:1, as each room had a lead teacher and an assistant teacher. The IFF (Illinois Facilities Fund) was brought in to assist in the search for an appropriate space. Part of the reason the EECS was running out of space earlier than anticipated was the fact that the After-School program was growing right along with enrollment. Rooms they had been able to use when the school first opened were now taken up by the additional grades and special programs the school added to complement its regular curriculum. In the interim, a building across from the school, what came to be known as the Annex, served as the new quarters for the After-School program. The continued growth of After-School at the charter was also important to Erie House, as gentrification in West Town was decimating the enrollment at Erie's partner schools there, causing under-enrollment at the House. And, under-enrollment means loss of funding.

As the 2008-09 school year was coming to a close, Valery Shepard, Director of Erie's School-Age Program, was looking for a new site director for the program at the school. She was also preparing with her staff for what would be an awkward move out of the Annex, and back into the school basement. The school was now claiming the annex for the 5th grade that would be added for the 2009-2010 school year. For the last 2 years of EECS in the St. Mark's building, space was a source of constant irritation between the staff of the school and the staff of the After-School program, in spite of the fact that most parents would have said that both programs are what made the school so appealing to working families. And it was appealing. Nancy Vincent reported that they had 84 applicants for 30 slots in Kindergarten for the 2009-10 school year, and there was a waiting list for every grade. She also noted that 4th Pres, her church when she moved back to the city, had donated books and cash for the school library. And the Presbyterians keep on giving.

State Rep Cynthia Soto also kept on giving. At the September 2009 ENH board meeting, Mark Hallett, VP of the EECS Board, reported that she had secured a $12 million dollar grant for the acquisition and development of a new site for the EECS, guaranteeing it would be in her district. As the story goes, Soto had gotten wind of a large state grant that was being set aside for a new network of charter schools to be hosted by UNO, a Pilsen organization under the wing of then Alderman Danny Solis. She is said to have met with

House Speaker/Power Broker, Mike Madigan, and insisted on comparable consideration for THE charter school in HER district. She was no freshman legislator at this point, and thanks to her *hutzpa*, EECS benefited. Ultimately, these funds were applied to the acquisition and development of the former St. Fidelis School at Wabansia and Hirsch, a little further northwest, but still in east Humboldt Park, and still in Soto's district. Not only was this building acquired, but a new wing was constructed as well, and special space was set aside for After-School in the building.

This story will continue in the next chapter, but as Estrada said in an interview pertaining to his years of Erie leadership, he came to wish that the school had not been set up as a separate corporation from Erie House. As the school grew into its own, it discontinued its dependence on Erie House for management assistance. New EECS board members came and went and, in Ric's opinion, that feeling of "unity" Ken Perkins had spoken of in the early years of the school dissipated. Clearly the school could manage on its own, and it was a relief for Erie staff to no longer share that burden. But sadly, over time, the spirit, values, and tradition of Erie House were not as deeply shared either. This situation was revisited in 2019, as Ric Estrada was asked by the new EECS Board president to re-engage, which he did.

The Little Village Immigrant Resource Center (LVIRC): Year Five and Still Counting

Having acquired the vacant cookie factory building on South Kildare in 2007, the Erie board had authorized Ric to move forward with the purchase of the adjacent residential property if a reasonable opportunity presented itself. When the LVCDC board proposed buying the property outright, Ric argued that Erie's position was to use Western Union funds only for a down payment for the property and take out a mortgage for the balance so as to keep more cash liquid. While the argument over how to proceed went back and forth, the opportunity to buy for around $200,000 improved greatly. Due to a foreclosure situation, the partnership was able to acquire the property for just over $50,000.

However, "the partnership" was only a word at this point. From the beginning of the LVIRC project, when the $750,000 grant from the Western Union settlement was released in 2004, Erie agreed that LVCDC would serve as the fiscal agent while Erie began what was called tier one of the project, the provision of services in the rented space in the Epiphany convent. Then documents would be drafted, creating a new partnership entity that would legally make Erie and LVCDC partners, and co-owners of the property and the bank account that held the balance of the settlement funds. Unfortunately, the completion of this paperwork task dragged on.

No doubt, in the first two years, Erie was distracted with the start-up of the charter school. After that, it is unclear what was holding up the partnership document. Nevertheless, Ric and the Erie Board moved forward with plans to launch a capital campaign to raise their share of the funds that would be needed to rehab the cookie factory. With the advice of Merri Ex, consultant on the Capital Campaign, a goal of $4 million was set, and the formation of a Capital Campaign Committee was under way. Erie already had $400,000 in hand from the Chicago Community Trust and NCLR and planned to make LVIRC the theme of the annual dinner in the Fall of 2008. Alex Montgomery assured the Erie Board that a separate cost center was established to keep income and expenses for the LVIRC project separate from other Erie accounts. With the assistance of Mark Jolicoeur, Perkins & Will had agreed to provide architectural service at 25% of actual cost. Erie even secured the services of volunteers from PepsiCo who spent a day emptying the building of the contents that filled 5 dumpsters. Erie was poised to move forward on tier two of LVIRC.

In March of 2008, Ric reported that Drinker Biddle had completed the partnership agreement, and arrangements were being made to present it to the LVCDC Board. In May, Herbert Moreno, who had become Director of Adult Programs, gave the following history of expenditures in Little Village since the base allocation of $750,000 in 2004:

- 2004: Erie and LVCDC each got $25,000 to begin programming and planning for LVIRC;
- 2005: From the $700K that remained, $9,192 was spent on programs, leaving $690,807;
- 2006: an additional $54,479 came from the settlement, bringing balance to 745,287;
- 2006: purchase of Kildare property at $285,000 = 460,287;
- 2006: program expenditures of 76,010 = 384,276;
- 2007: Program expenditures of 52,780 = 331,497;
- 2007: Interest earned, 14,225 = balance of 345,721.[446]

The opportunity to buy the residential property for $50,000 came after this report.

Plans for the design of the facility were already under way. Six classrooms were envisioned, a community tech center with 25 workstations, a legal services and other offices, and a multi-purpose room for community events. Besides the ever-popular ESL classes, there would be SOS tutoring, tech classes, citizenship services, and leadership training through Tech Promoters and community organizing. Ric told the board that on May 14, 2008, he was going with LVCDC to transfer the fund balance to a joint account at Chase Bank. Then he and Merri Ex would be making a presentation on the Capital Campaign planning to the LVCDC Board.

But it was not until November 2008, that Anna Singh, of Drinker Biddle, was presenting the Joint Venture document to the Erie Board. Two years had already passed since the purchase of the Kildare property and four years since the allocation of the Western Union settlement funds. The Joint Venture Agreement laid out the plan to create a new non-profit entity that would be known as the Little Village Community Center (LVCC). The title for the Kildare property would be transferred to this new entity, as well as the fund balance. The goal was then set to get sign-off from both parties before the end of calendar year 2008, and that this would be a key item on the January 2009 board agenda. The final chapter of this saga was still to be written and appears in the succeeding chapter.

Child Care Funding Formula Changes Hit Erie Hard

Child Care contracts had long been the largest and most consistent source of funding for Erie House. This was due, in large part, to the quality of the program, and foresight involved in expanding it greatly with the opening of the Erie Community Center at 1701 Superior in 1995. NAEYC accreditation followed, Head Start reviews were without findings, Quality Counts dollars were at the highest level, and all in all, blended funding was working to provide working parents with all-day care. It was a well-oiled machine, with compliments offered by the mayor of the city at regular intervals.

Unfortunately, as Ric complained to the Board in December 2007, the city department that managed Child Care contracts was anything but a well-oiled machine. In commenting on a *Crain's* article that reported charities were caught in a squeeze as surging demand for services outstripped their funding growth, he observed that in the case of child care, it was not demand that was so stressful but the inefficiencies of the city's approach to "managing"

452

accountability. He bemoaned the fact that redundant reporting, lost documents on the part of city staff, and, therefore, unpaid vouchers, almost always in at least 6 figures in Erie's case, were the real source of stress.

He then followed that venting with the good news that Erie remained in a good place financially due to the tremendous support of the board, growth in private funding, great staff, and hard-working volunteers. The November 2007, the gala had grossed over $300,000 and the Holiday Appeal netted over $86,000. Added to that, Erie had received $200,000 in connection with their Bank of America award. That money, Ric told the Board, was being put into a separate account as a "rainy day" fund. By June 2008, the FY09 budget was projected at $8,274,914, the largest ever. As he marked his 11th year at Erie there were no rainy days in sight.

By the time of the November 2008 board meeting, the rain had come. There was a boatload of trouble with State Pre-K funding that came through CPS (Chicago Public Schools) to Erie. When that contract came out at the end of summer, Erie discovered that the method of funding providers had changed. Without any prior notice, CPS had switched from a cost reimbursement to a "flat-fee" approach, deciding to pay all providers $4,000 per child. They said this was based on a "fairness concept" of everyone getting paid the same. In reality, there was nothing fair about it, since programs were not equal in what they provided and what they cost. Erie had submitted its Child Care budget of $915,690, the actual cost of providing nationally accredited child care with the extra bells and whistles of a full-time psychologist, social worker, and a therapeutic classroom. Under the new system, at $4,000 per child, Erie would only be paid $664,000, creating a shortfall of $251,690 in regular child care, and a shortfall of $132,436 for the Sunshine therapeutic classroom, for a total shortfall of $384,126, or 42%. Ric assured the board that Erie would challenge this change every conceivable way. He noted that no personnel cuts would be made without serious deliberation, but also promised that "we are willing to make painful cuts to assure long-term sustainability and success."[447] He provided a copy of the letter he had sent to Dr. Barbara Bowman, the head of Early Education Services at CPS. These were the highlights:

- For 10 years we have had a good working relationship;
- This flat fee plan will reduce the service we can provide to at-risk Latino and African American families that we serve;
- Erie's actual cost for 0-3 care is $5,417/child, and for 3-5, including the therapeutic classroom that CPS encouraged us to start, is $6,242/child;
- If you insist on the flat rate approach, a detriment to our community, then Erie requests an add-on of $164,000 to cover the cost of the Sunshine Room, and re-consideration of the rate for other child care contracts;
- An investment in these children now, will save even higher expenditures for mental health services in the future.[448]

In May 2009, Ric reported to the Board that he had been able to secure $200,000 for the Sunshine Room, with some funds coming from the city's Department of Family Support Services (DFSS) and the state Department of Human Services. This would help offset the FY09 projected deficit and keep the Sunshine Room open a little longer, just through the end of FY09, which still finished with a $55,000 deficit. The Sunshine Room would not continue in FY10. The good news out of all this was that the flat fee rate for 0-3 contracts was raised from $4,000 to $6,000 per child. Perhaps Dr. Bowman read Erie's letter after all.

What Was Upbeat about 2008-2010?
EECS Moves Forward

First of all, while the Erie Elementary Charter School was thrust into a search for new leadership, as their star principal departed prematurely, and they struggled to find a new building that would accommodate their growth, their charter application was renewed. Velia Soto moved from assistant principal to principal, and they finally found a new space, the vacant St. Fidelis school building, that the $12 million Rep. Soto secured would help pay for. EECS was prospering.

Little Village

While Erie struggled with the changes in Child Care funding, programming in LV was moving right along. In true Erie House fashion, adult students there organized a Student Council to offer feedback on the curriculum. They wanted it to include topics such as the legacy of Dr. Martin Luther King, and other American and Latin American leaders. They also wanted workshops on nutrition and environmental issues. They expressed concern about health issues like obesity and diabetes that they felt were all too prevalent in the Mexican community. As such, they were right in sync with Erie's emerging health focus in West Town.

Erie Health Promoters Launched

Indeed, health had started to emerge as an area that needed attention, first, for the staff, but eventually, for participants as well. This began with a staff retreat facilitated by Patricia Novick in 2006 that led to the development of Health Promoters among Erie staff. This is not to suggest that Erie House never addressed health issues before. They already had a dental clinic in the 1939 and a health clinic in the 1950's, that successfully evolved into the independently owned and operated Erie Family Health Center, that was headquartered at the Erie Community Center on Superior. But this approach was less about the medical treatment of health problems and more about promoting good heath to avoid illness. It was right in line with Erie's strengths: education and community engagement as a preventive strategy. This goes back to the days of Miss Florence, when she would argue that, while she appreciated the development of a Juvenile Court, her preference was that "her boys" never need to go there in the first place.

The Health Promoters phase of what eventually evolved into a program department at Erie, still active 10 years later, was also based on a popular education approach. Each group of health promoters Erie trained would then take on the responsibility of training another group at another organization. It was hoped that the "pass-it-on" model would accelerate good health outcomes across the Latino community. At Erie House, health education became a component of the School-Age curriculum first, adopting the name "Super-H" for happy, healthy kids. Wisely, if children made Super-H a choice program, their parents had to sign up for an evening, 8-week session on nutrition themselves. The goal was to avoid arguments between parent and child as to why mom should buy wheat bread instead of white--to educate the whole family at the same time. At first, this evoked some grumbling and resistance during the pre-interview and registration period. But, when Dr. Novick did post-participation interviews with parents, all she heard was how much fun they had, how much they learned, and how great it was to have an opportunity to spend time with other adults in a learning situation. Based on this success, work was begun on Super-H-itos, for the "little ones" in Child Care.

Learning English, Becoming Citizens, Protecting Dreamers

Needless to say, immigration issues were still on the table in 2008 and would be a topic for debate leading up to the presidential election in November. Right at the end of 2007, on December 6, Erie wrote a letter to the editor in response to an editorial that had appeared in the *Sun-Times*, on November 30, that said, "Immigrants should learn English," implying that they resisted doing this. Erie described the high demand for ESL classes in Little Village, with 100 on the waiting list, to make the case that Mexican immigrants, like others before them, want to learn. What was needed was more funding to meet the demand.

In January2008, ICIRR Executive Director, Josh Hoyt, was reminding NAI (New Americans Initiative) grantees that, while members had successfully assisted over 30,000 immigrants to become citizens since the program's inception, there was more work to be done. Remembering their pledge when they marched in 2006, "First we march; then we vote," there was a wave of applications for citizenship in 2008 as part of the rush to be able to vote for president later that year. And adding to the excitement, a Chicagoan was running for president, and a person of color besides. Erie folks acclaimed: How cool was that? Erie did its part, leading the northwest side collaborative of NAI organizations in the citizenship and voter registration campaigns throughout 2008.

The following year, in May of 2009, another immigration issue drew Erie's attention. A former YOU participant, and student at UIC, received a deportation notice. His plight drew Dreamers out of the shadows to stand up in defense of youth, like themselves, who grew up American but lacked legal status. There were rallies and press conferences, university professors from across the country signed a petition declaring their outrage at the vulnerability of so many students in their classrooms who could become important, educated contributors to US society (like Ric Estrada) instead of being sent away. Congresswoman, Jan Schakowsky (D) even looked into how one proposes a "personal bill" in Congress that she would use to block this young man's deportation. Finally, all the protests had the desired effect, and the deportation order was deferred. Many believe that this story re-energized the fight to protect Dreamers. While no such bill passed Congress, before Obama left office, he issued the executive order that created DACA (Deferred Action for Childhood Arrivals) that offered some protection to Dreamers.

TEAM Marks its 25th Anniversary

The following month, in June, 2009, Erie's TEAM mentorship program, marked its 25th anniversary. By the time of TEAM's 35th year in 2019, a youth who was 14 in 1984, when TEAM started, could conceivably have a 14-year old of their own in the program that year. It seems reasonable to conclude that there was a formula for success embedded in the TEAM strategy. Support to finish high school, guidance for gaining college admission, and a professional adult to talk with, who is not your parent--these were all components of TEAM. Perhaps, most importantly, TEAM was a safe place to identify with and embrace values that were not always popular among teen peers. Here, the pressure was on to grow up and take responsibility for your life--to aspire versus going with the flow of life in the hood. Moreover, since the very first days of scholarship funds from the Graham family, Erie kept fund-raising for that purpose. TEAM scholarships were not large in terms of dollars, but they were huge in terms of the respect they represented for the accomplishments youth on the margins were not expected to achieve.

STEM Focus in Youth Department

What started as a science program for middle school, first offered at Erie by Columbia College in 2006, evolved into a full-blown STEM focus. Besides TEAM, the Columbia College science program was also popular with YOU participants, and Erie House was popular with Columbia College. The NASA program of 2003 provided the foundation for an ongoing STEM focus in YOU, including the addition of more engineers as TEAM mentors. Next to the budding scientists stood the dancers, under the direction of Nilda Ruiz-Pauley. Art and science were comfortable companions in YOU. And, the promotion of good health, both an art and a science, was being fostered as youth health promoters were being trained.

Pathways to Success Succeeds

While TEAM participants were readying themselves for college, their parents were preparing for careers that might make it easier for them to finish college, or a younger sibling to start. The Pathways to Success bridge programs in manufacturing and health care were prospering under the leadership of Oswaldo Alvarez and guidance of Herbert Moreno. Many statistics could be cited, but one good story is often worth a thousand statistics. Basilla Vargas was a single mother of four who came to Erie for help in getting the kind of wage she needed to support a family of five. The minimum wage was not that. When she took the TABE test, the standard tool to measure adult literacy and math skills, she tested at the 2nd grade level. This was usually not sufficient to enter a bridge class, but the staff had the feeling that her commitment to learn was so strong she could handle the challenge. In 12 weeks of bridge classes, plus after-class tutoring, she tested at the 6th grade level. When she completed the bridge class, she was admitted to CNC training at JARC. When she finished that, she was hired by Rolex at $17.10/hour, far above the usual, and decent, entry level wage for CNC operators of $12.00/hour.

Of course, not every PTS student was a Basilla, but many were, and the adoption of the bridge program as a key component of workforce development for educationally disadvantaged and/or non-English-speaking adults spread, even to the City Colleges of Chicago. But the most effective bridge programs, as was the case with ESL and ABE, remained at the CBO level. As many workforce development professionals would argue, it was the job of the community colleges to develop high quality skills training, evident in the success of Humboldt Park Vocational Education Center of Wright College. CBOs would take care of remedial adult ed and bridge programs. The argument over roles has been ongoing.

A final upbeat note for Erie House at the end of 2009, was a trip to Mexico, supported by a grant from the MacArthur Foundation, and in conjunction with the work of the May Foundation, involved in economic development work in the state of Guanajuato. The trip was educational in purpose, offering longer-term Erie board members and senior staff, the opportunity to understand the two-pronged conflict on the part of Mexicans who made the decision to emigrate to the US, with or without papers. On the one hand, by witnessing the beauty of Mexico, both physical and cultural, an understanding dawns that many would rather not leave if they could survive financially by staying home. On the other hand, visiting with communities of squatters who were living in shacks and hauling water up a hill from a delivery truck underscored the compulsion to seek something better. This journey concluded with sharing in the local celebrations of *El Dia de los Muertos*, the Day of the Dead, as it was observed in small towns in the state of Morelia. *Catrinas* and *calaveras* were encountered everywhere, and all the beautiful altars were decorated with an abundance of marigolds. As a result of that shared experience, a special bond developed between senior staff and board members who journeyed together.

The Transition

As the decade turned into 2010, in Ric Estrada's 12th year at Erie and 7th year as executive director, he made the decision to leave Erie House. He had been offered a position as Deputy Director of the city's Department of Human Services and believed this was the right opportunity to make a transition. He recommended the board consider offering the position to Celena Roldán, Erie's Director of Child Care since 2006. He explained to the Board that he had identified her three years earlier as a leader with the potential to succeed him as executive director and he had been mentoring her for that position. After some consultation with senior staff, the board followed his recommendation and promoted Celena to that position as only the 7th executive director in 140 years, and the second Puerto Rican.

In his final report to the board in January 2010, titled "Transition," he provided a kind of "State of the Organization" overview, and then laid out the type of leader a place like Erie House needs. Significantly, he devoted an entire page to the concept of effective leadership for a non-profit organization. It was the most thoughtful transition reflection on record of any of Erie's prior executive directors.

Budget & Finance

Ric began with Budget & Finances, noting that Erie's budget had grown by nearly 100% since he was named executive director in 2003. He also noted that then Erie had two facilities and now it had four—two in West Town, one in East Humboldt Park, and one in Little Village. In the light of this growth, he did not believe the finance department had been given sufficient resources to effectively manage all that had been put on their shoulders. So, he was glad to know that FMA, management consultant that the Wallace Foundation grant was paying for and that they recommended, would be helping to sort this out. Their first recommendation, to hire an accounting manager, was in progress. Next would be the installation of new accounting software that should also help.

Fiscally, Erie continued to be strong, but it was always moment-to-moment, year-to-year, in the non-profit world. Public funding for child care, for example, had been problematic lately. But, in general, he argued we are well-respected on both the city and state level. Even when cuts come down, Erie is in a better position than most to survive and rebound. We have learned how to challenge public funding policies, but still maintain our public support, because our programs are that good, and because we invested the time to cultivate the respect of the elected officials and bureaucrats even when we were telling them they were wrong.

In the realm of private funding, we are very strong, but foundations are fickle. We continued to do well, again because we performed, but also because I made it a priority to know and establish a good relationship with all the key foundation leaders. Our Development staff writes good proposals, about great programs, but we would not be successful if we operated on the naïve belief that good work should be enough. We have great individuals that support us, but there is lots of room for growth in this area.

Programs

He repeated his sense that Erie programs were strong, but Erie has to figure out how to answer the question "how do you know?" more effectively. Our Leadership

Team has understood this and are committed to adopting tracking and evaluation procedures that help us to answer that question, hopefully with the help of the proposed ETO software.

Our Peers

This is worth quoting verbatim:

> *Most small, mid-size and Latino-serving nonprofits view Erie as a leader in the field. They really do envy our leadership team, our systems, legacy, reputation, and our governance model. . .Other organizations are bigger and some are more politically connected, but Erie is considered to be a place where quality happens. Whether that is an illusion or reality, it is our reputation.*[449]

The Leader

Estrada prefaced this section by stating that he would not want the reader to think that he possessed all the qualities he has outlined for the leader Erie needs, but that these qualities are ones he aspired to, and so should Erie's next leader. He placed the greatest emphasis on "being authentic." To be authentic, he explained,

> *The leader must be able to relate to the impoverished parents of a suffering child, and later, to leaders of the civic committee of the Commercial Club, and be equally authentic [in each case] . . . All the technical elements of the job can be learned much more easily.*[450]

Some of those technical elements included experience in program development, fiscal management, people management and human resources, donor and funding trends, public policy trends and analysis, awareness of politics, neighborhood and inter-ethnic politics, governance, facility management, collaboration, and team management. Added to these, he said that Erie's next leader must also be an able public speaker, negotiator, team-builder, tactician, strategic thinker, goal-setter, networker, and fundraiser. With so much to do, this individual must have the ability to self-regulate, delegate, and keep and attract the best talent we can afford.

The good news is we have that person in house, he said. Because I understood the importance of a succession plan, I hired and promoted with the idea that one of these colleagues would be able to replace me. That colleague is Celena. "I cannot recommend her more highly, and have no doubt she can follow the example of servant leadership set forth by Florence Towne, Rafael Ravelo, and so many others." [451] With that sterling recommendation before them, the board did not hesitate to name Celena the next executive director of Erie House.

Chapter Nine: Celena Roldán: From Social Worker to Child Care Director to Executive Director (2010-2015)

Celena was born in the Hyde Park neighborhood on Chicago's south side, but the family moved to the near west suburb of Oak Park when she was five. So, that is where she grew up. Certainly, she had no idea that she was growing up in a suburb with so many ties to her future place of employment, Erie Neighborhood House. She was not the daughter of immigrants, but second stage Puerto Rican migrants, whose parents initially left the island to settle in New York. While, like Rita Moreno of *West Side Story,* the first generation liked being in America, the next generation was not so sure they liked being in New York, and headed west, for Chicago. Both of Celena's parents were what came to be called New Yoricans. Both were born in New York, met and married there, and found professional success in the Chicago metropolitan area where they raised their family.

Her father, Hipolito (Paul) Roldan, was involved in the founding of the non-profit Hispanic Housing Development Corp. in Chicago in 1975 and was still serving as the President and CEO in 2019. Hispanic Housing was founded to develop affordable housing in Latino neighborhoods, just eight years after Erie House helped start Bickerdike Redevelopment Corp. in 1967, also with an affordable housing agenda. However, Hispanic Housing operated citywide, while Bickerdike remained committed to West Town, Humboldt Park, and Logan Square.

Her mother, Ida, earned her doctorate in clinical social work and eventually opened her own clinical practice. She actually did some work at Wells High School as the student population was becoming more Puerto Rican, as that community migrated to West Town

Celena Roldan (Erie Neighborhood House)

and Humboldt Park from neighborhoods further east, like Lakeview and Lincoln Park. Wells was another Erie House connection, the source for many teen participants who went to Erie House after school, to use the gym or join TEAM, when that program started in 1984.

Celena followed in her mother's footsteps and earned her undergrad and graduate degrees in social work at the University of Wisconsin in Madison. She started her professional career in East Humboldt Park at a social service agency called Casa Central. Founded in 1954, it does not share the long history of the settlement house movement, but it does provide some of the same services, and grew to be one of the largest Latino-serving, social service organizations in Chicago. She took a position there as a social worker in their child care program, her first step on her career path for almost the next 20 years. In 2001, that path led to Erie Neighborhood House, where she was also hired as a social worker in Erie's Child Care program.[452]

The Political Context

As is evident throughout this text, Erie House lives in the real world, and the politics of that world may either help or hinder Erie's work. Moreover, Erie was never one to passively wait for the hammer to fall, or to lay prostrate as a victim. Call it education, advocacy or straight-out lobbying, Erie was always active, making a place for itself at the policy and/or legislative table. Many times, it was invited there based on its excellent reputation; other times it simply insinuated a space.

During her administration at Erie, Celena would have to cope with significant changes in the political landscape. Barack Obama, America's first African American president was mid-way through his first term in office. Pat Quinn had succeeded Rod Blagojevich as governor when the latter was sent to jail for unethical conduct at the end of 2008. Quinn earned the gratitude of social service agencies when he raised the income tax rate in 2010 to cover a major state budget gap, but he lost the governor's race to Republican, Bruce Rauner, in 2014. Rauner failed to endear himself to Celena and other executive directors of non-profits when he refused to approve a state budget for two years. And last but not least, the mayor who had become an Erie House cheerleader, Richard M. Daley, left office after 22 years, and Rahm Emanuel took his seat on the 5th floor at City Hall in 2011. He had earlier served as a Congressman from a Chicago district, and returned to Chicago from serving as President

Obama's chief of staff. So, a new president, a new governor, and a new mayor--a definite change in political context for Celena to work out.

When Celena first arrived at Erie House, Sandy Schaefer was still the very capable Director of the Child Care Department. As Sandy left Erie in June of 2006, she recommended Celena as her successor. Some staff raised the issue that she did not have a degree in early childhood education, but most senior staff figured Sandy knew what she was doing. And then Celena went out and got her Master's in Early Childhood at National Louis University. Enough said.[453]

The First Two Years – 2010-2011

Trial by Fire: Celena's First Year as Executive Director

As was often the case at Erie, during Celena's first year as executive director, there was good news and bad news. The good news included addition of a new program for Little Village, funded by the state's Department of Children & Family Services (DCFS), which came to be called Proyecto Cuidate (The Take Care Project). The purpose of this new program fit well with Erie values, as it was preventive, providing services that would help families to stay well and stay together, preventing children from going into the state system. It began with a contract for $83,000 for the last four months of FY10 and required hiring a full-time social worker. Sandy De Leon, a University of Chicago/SSA student who had been an intern at the House, fit the bill and took the job. The intern-to-employee pattern continues.

In the Citizenship Department, the New Americans Initiative (NAI), administered by ICIRR (Illinois Coalition for Immigrant & Refugee Rights), was now in its fifth year. While helping legal permanent residents to become citizens was still part of the work, a major focus for 2010 was to improve Latino participation in the 2010 census. At the time of the previous census in 2000, the participation rate for Latinos in the Erie service area had been around 43%. Since census data is used to determine eligibility for a wide range of government subsidies for both Erie participants and programs, this was a priority. ICIRR used NAI dollars to provide their member organizations with what were called Census Fellows. This was the same concept they used to facilitate voter registration, only they were called Democracy Fellows. It was an effective concept that provided an extra pair of hands to address the priority of the moment, usually for a 6-month period. It also proved effective in meeting the objective. As a result of the efforts of Erie's Census Fellow, Latino participation in the 2010 census went from 43 to 53%.

As "Eliminate the Digital Divide" funding from the state became scarce, the Technology Department at Erie was folded into Adult Programs, partly to save the cost of a program director position. It also became necessary to start charging a fee of $25 for computer classes. Tech students themselves had agreed that this was affordable to most Erie participants and remained well below the market rate for such quality classes in the for-profit world. The fact that the technology program at Erie had always underscored the importance of taking responsibility and giving back to your community, the mission of the Tech Promoters program, made the idea of assuming some responsibility for its own future a given. Besides the addition of class tuition, the Tech Promoters set about additional fundraising, and on February 10, 2010, presented their new executive director with their amazing gift of $10,000.[454]

The following month, YOU participants, through their Youth Council, took on another form of giving back. This was an outcome of the trip to Mexico by Senior staff and board members. The Youth Council was shown pictures and told the story of how the village of Tamaula, a squatter settlement that had no running water, would benefit greatly if they had cisterns next to their dwellings to capture rain water. Each cistern cost $300. The May Foundation, that had helped organize the Erie trip to Mexico, was partnering with a foundation in Mexico to raise money for the cistern project. The Youth Council decided to join the effort. They hoped to raise at least $600 to pay for two cisterns. The youth called their fundraiser "Water for Water." On March 22 and 24, 2010, with photos of their neighbors in Tamaula all over the lobby at the House, they sold cups of flavored water to their TEAM mentors and fellow students. They met their goal, raising $635 for two cisterns.[455]

When an Erie Advisory Board member and fellow sojourner on the Mexico trip heard of their efforts, he set out to match what the students had raised. This initiative yielded sufficient funds to buy 10 more cisterns. The youth had understood the call to "Love thy neighbor;" what they learned was, when you do, you may inspire others to do the same. Furthermore, this is a concrete illustration of Erie's preventive approach and their capacity to instill values. These kids could have been on the street selling drugs; instead, they were at Erie House selling water for water

Clearly, there was a lot of good news during Celena's first six months on the job. Unfortunately, finances were not part of the good news. There were several factors that converged, creating the necessity for serious cutbacks at the end of FY10. This included the elimination of 12.5 positions, what Celena herself described as "some of the most significant reductions and restructuring in the history of Erie House.[456] She related to the board how program directors were revising job descriptions, collapsing two positions into one, re-doing their organizational charts, and committing to do more with less in order to maintain the high quality synonymous with Erie House.

470

A close examination of the various factors that led to the need for drastic action sheds light on the vulnerability of non-profits that depend heavily on government funding, and the reasons why Erie House has the capacity to recover. The problems being spawned by public funding had begun when Estrada was director. Recall that CPS initiated their flat fee payment plan that created an enormous shortfall in child care payments for the 3-to-5 contract and maintenance of Erie's therapeutic Sunshine classroom. Ric did manage to get some supplementary funding, but in reality, it only put off the inevitable, and FY09 still ended with a large deficit. By the end of FY10, it became clear that the Sunshine Room could not be sustained. While it appears that CPS may have read Ric's letter, and eventually raised the per child amount to $6,000 for 3-5 contracts, it was too little too late for the Sunshine Room. Further challenges emerged when CPS announced in September 2010, that 3-5 contracts would only be for 10 months, parallel with the school year. This decision illustrates the misunderstanding that child care is only about the children. It is not. While early childhood education is one of the benefits of child care/pre-school, the other is an economic one. It allows both parents, or a single parent, to work and support their family, and they don't get two months off in the summer. Their ability to work year-round saves the taxpayer the cost of paying for multiple welfare benefits that non-workers require, and it is often what makes it possible for their children to use that pre-school educational benefit to be in a position, academically and financially, to advance to college. The center-based, non-profit child care programs that understood this banded together to protest this proposal. Eventually, they won their case, but damage is done during these prolonged advocacy battles.

Besides these funding issues with CPS, the more stringent income guidelines to be eligible for child care at Erie House or any other place, played havoc with full enrollment. In the past, Erie had always had a robust waiting list and never had to do much marketing; that was changing too. It was time to go out into the highways and hedges and find more pre-schoolers. While all of this was happening, a new director of Child Care was in charge, but not a new person to the program. When Celena stepped up to executive director, Louis Falk, who had worked in Erie's child care program for more than 25 years, stepped into the position she had vacated. Needless to say, his program familiarity was a plus, but there are still losses during times of transition.

Besides these losses in public funding, private funding had also fallen short of expectations. With changes in foundation guidelines, some grants were lost that resulted in a 5% shortfall in reaching Erie's foundation fundraising goal. This loss was compounded by the fact that the 2010 Annual Dinner fell short of its goals as well. The dinner grossed $247,187 versus the target amount of $300,000, partly due to the fact that the "ask on the night of" only yielded $17,149 versus the usual $40,000. This was all in spite of record attendance of 430 and attendance by Mayor Daley.

Then, adding to this, as of September 2010, the state still owed Erie House money from FY10 that they did not anticipate paying until December 2010, 6 months after it was due. This was putting a tremendous strain on Erie's reserve account and line of credit to meet payroll. As Celena gratefully noted, "Imagine how this is affecting agencies that have neither."[457] What must be added to the fact that Erie had such financial back-up, was the wisdom and support of a Board of Directors that carefully monitored the organization's expenses and did not hesitate to support the difficult decisions that necessitated those 12.5 layoffs.

As Celena reflected during her interview for this book,

*Board Members at Erie House were some of our
most committed and invested volunteers. They are
just as responsible for the successes and community
impact of Erie as the executive directors. So many
of them not only attended board meetings, but they
were actively involved in supporting the programs
of Erie House, whether that was through
volunteering as TEAM mentors, or reading in one
of our pre-school classrooms. . . The board
members were guides, advocates, and coaches, as I
encountered the challenges, had successes, and
developed as a leader in and outside of Erie
House.[458]*

Picking Up the Pieces in Little Village

At the May, 2010 board meeting, Celena reported to
the Board that a termination agreement had been signed by
ENH and ENLACE (formerly LVCDC) to end the
partnership formed to develop the Little Village Immigrant
Resource Center (LVIRC) and acquire the properties on
Kildare. As part of that agreement, ENH became sole owner
of the cookie factory and the adjacent residential property.

There was no doubt in Celena's mind, or that of
senior staff, for that matter, that Erie House belonged in
Little Village. Since first launching programs there in 2004,
the steady and constantly growing demand for services and
the warm welcome extended to Erie on the part of LV
residents, made that fact evident. In addition, the further
gentrification of West Town had removed it from many
funders' priority lists, while Little Village was high on those
same lists. At the same time, the second floor of Epiphany
convent had long ago become inadequate for Erie's effort to
respond to community needs and demands. Since it would
be some time before the Kildare properties could be

rehabbed and ready for programming, it seemed reasonable to seek some alternative space in the interim.

As Director of Adult Programs, the kind of programs provided in LV in 2010, Herbert Moreno set out to find new space, assisted by the Senior Director of Programs. A promising option was found in a building known as the Atlantic Mall, at the corner of 26th and Pulaski. There was already one non-profit in that building, Central States SER, and there was plenty of vacant space to join them. Early conversations with the landlord indicated he would be glad to have a tenant like Erie House move in. So, courtesy of Mark Jolicoeur and the architects at Perkins & Will, who helped Erie House numerous times over the years, their pro-bono work on a basic design for the space began. Funds to update the property, create signage, and purchase furniture were at least partially in hand from a grant that had come from the Chicago Community Trust for $50,000 for work in LV. The hoped-for move-in date was set for March 2011.

Meanwhile, in August of 2010, a committee of board and staff members met to discuss Erie's options regarding future use of the Kildare properties. Options discussed included:

- Hold the property, incurring insurance and minimal maintenance costs until funds are raised to develop it, in keeping with the promise to open LVIRC;
- Demolish the buildings;
- Sell the property as is;
- Develop the Atlantic Mall space as THE LVIRC, instead of using the Kildare properties.

The discussion shifted the focus of the Board Facilities Committee to the fourth option. ENH was looking at 2300 sq. ft. on the third floor of the Mall building. What was envisioned in that space was a computer lab, a classroom that would hold 25, a demo kitchen that would serve Erie's Little

Village health and wellness program, space for Proyecto Cuidate to have an office and counseling space, and a lobby area with space for a receptionist.

Celena pointed out that the estimate, at that point, to turn the Kildare properties into habitable space, was at least $2.5 million. As had been discussed all along, to move forward on that project would require a major capital campaign. On the other hand, the estimate for bringing the Mall space up to speed was around $300,000, and Erie had $150,000 in hand. Would it make sense to spend that kind of money just for an interim location? Should Erie, instead, develop the Mall space as the final LVIRC site, in fulfillment of Erie's commitment, and do something else with the Kildare properties?

The "something else" had already surfaced, as Celena put one more idea on the table. She related the fact that the Latino Policy Forum (LPF), under the leadership of Sylvia Puente, had pressed the state to commit $45 million to develop child care centers in Latino communities throughout Illinois; of that, $9 million was earmarked for Chicago. Celena would know this, both because Erie was a member of the LPF, and, as a former Child Care Director, she kept her finger on the pulse of developments in that field, in Chicago and in Springfield. And so, she posed the question: Should Erie consider the Kildare property as a candidate for a Child Care Center? With Little Village high on the needs list for more child care services, Erie's success with other programming in LV since 2004, Erie's excellent reputation for high quality child care programming, and ownership of property in the community, she expressed her belief that a proposal from Erie would be quite competitive.

Before leaving discussion of capital development, Celena also brought up the need for improvements at the House, which was immediately linked to the question that was off-and -on the table since the mid-1990s: Was that location demographically sustainable? This question was connected to the gentrification of West Town that had only become more pervasive by 2010. However, there were other circumstances that might offset the demographic concern. First, what continued to remain true was the location that was so convenient to downtown that elected officials and the media liked to stage press conferences and other events there, contributed to Erie's visibility. Second, the location of three Noble Network charter high schools within 4 blocks of Erie House, joining the public school (Wells), and the Catholic school (Holy Trinity), meant that demand for youth services had grown exponentially, with a waiting list for TEAM, in particular. Thus, restructuring of and adding to YOU space would mean Erie could serve more youth. Thirdly, Erie had long benefited from the fact that adults would travel for the quality program they need, which at the moment, was Erie's Bridge to Employment program, Pathways to Success. With both TEAM and PTS, Erie's "brand" at the House was strong. And while not entirely clear yet, After-School enrollment was going to bounce back with the addition of transport service.

Following that August 2010 meeting, an application had to be filed with the city Zoning Board for a special use permit for the development of the Mall space. That came through by January 2011, and the new move-in date became August 2011 rather than March 2011. At the Erie board meeting on March 28, 2011, the space question in Little Village was still under discussion, reviewed once again were the facts that the convent space was inadequate, the Mall space could provide some relief, and the Kildare properties still had to be dealt with.

By May of 2011, Erie's lease at Epiphany had expired, and the space at the Mall was developing as *the* strategy to address the problem. Mark Jolicoeur spoke to this, suggesting Erie ask Drinker Biddle to review the draft of the Atlantic Mall lease. Once that was done and approved, construction could begin, taking about 2-4 months, with a partial move-in by October 2011. The construction budget was estimated at $195,000 and had been kept down due to the diligence of Perkins & Will in securing a lot of donated material. As Mark understood, funds had already been raised from several sources to cover the amount he quoted. But the deal was not done yet.

The following month, in June 2011, a brief business meeting of the board was held prior to the Board/Staff annual meeting. Besides the FY12 budget, the only other item up for discussion was Little Village. Apparently, Mike Rodriguez, ENLACE's new executive director, reached out to Celena and said ENLACE was interested in buying back the Kildare properties, offering $100,000. The board said that was too low and countered with $300,000 to test the waters. Meanwhile, the city (DFSS) asked Erie to think about infant care at the Kildare sight or somewhere else in LV, suggesting Erie House see if Erie Family Health Center might be interested in another joint venture, like the one that resulted in the development of 1701 W. Superior. Board discussion followed.

Jolicoeur pointed out that infant care space is very expensive to develop. Steve Fox felt that if the city thought this was important, they should step up with some money, as the state had done, offering up to $5 million per project in their Child Care Center RFP. Dan Hartnett was not in favor of developing the Kildare property, period. He favored continued planning for the Mall space and raising capital funds for the House. As he put it, "The House is really our cornerstone."[459]

In September, the Facilities Committee reported that they had received a draft lease from the Mall landlord. Based on this document and a series of meetings with him, they said they were not comfortable moving forward with the project there and were taking it off the table. But, knowing the inadequacy of the convent space, they started looking at other commercial space available on 26th Street.

Then discussion moved on to whether Erie wanted to apply for the state money to do infant care in LV. The general consensus was that besides construction cost, Finance needed to run some operational numbers. If there was no indication that such a program would pay for itself, Erie should not do it. What also remained on the table was how to provide space for the adult programs struggling with tight quarters at Epiphany. It turned out that the answer to that did not lay on 26th Street but back at Epiphany. In the Fall of 2011, Instituto del Progreso Latino, which had occupied the first floor of the convent since Erie moved in on the second, announced they were moving out. So, Erie signed a new lease that would allow occupation of the first floor and the basement, providing much needed relief to their overcrowding problem. It was a one-year lease for 2012 that evolved into occupancy for seven more years and counting.

With LV Adult Programs taken care of at Epiphany for the time being, Celena and the committee returned to consideration of applying for the state funds to develop infant care at the Kildare property. They decided to go for it. Celena described the early draft concept. It would include: three infant rooms, serving 0-15 mos.; three Toddler rooms, serving 15-24 mos.; three 2-year-old rooms, serving 2-3 year-olds. Infant care rooms have just eight children per room. And Betty assured the Board that the revenue numbers would work to cover the costs. Unfortunately, this concept never got off the drawing board, as Erie was not awarded a grant.

To say that the entire Little Village situation was complex would have been an understatement. No doubt, having an active and informed Facilities Committee to work with Celena throughout what was now a 7-year deliberation process, was linked to her gratitude to board members underscored above. The Facilities Committee would continue dealing with all of this during the rest of Celena's time as ED. However, Adult Programs Director, Herbert

Moreno would not. He was leaving Erie to work on his Master's Degree in public health, and perhaps his own, after dealing with what was a very stressful time.

Erie Elementary Charter School – Seeing it through its Expansion Phase

The second major Erie House endeavor, that carried over from the Estrada administration to the Roldán administration, was the Erie Elementary Charter School (EECS) that Ric and some of his board members had championed his very first year as executive director. It opened in the Fall of 2005 at the former St. Mark School. When Celena took over in January 2010, the charter had begun the new school year in September 2009, as a K-6 school with 299 students. The EECS board had just concluded a long search for a larger facility to accommodate the 7th and 8th grades that would be added next and were in the process of purchasing the former St. Fidelis School at 1405 N. Washtenaw. While the Archdiocese had driven a hard bargain on the rental of St. Mark's, they were eager to sell St. Fidelis to the EECS. As the Erie House Board had learned in September, funding for the new building had been made a lot easier when Erie's State Representative, Cynthia Soto, had secured a $12 million earmark of state funds for the much-needed new location. Two players familiar to Erie House were also at the table–Northern Trust Bank and the Illinois Facilities Fund (IFF). All of this support would not have been as likely without the Erie Neighborhood House name associated with this project, from the initial application for the charter to the securing of the $12M in state funds from a state rep whose grandchild attended Erie House. It was a powerful brand.

So, as Celena moved into the executive director's office, what role would Erie House continue to play in regard to the school? First of all, that role would differ from Ric's.

He had served as Erie House executive and CEO of the EECS at the same time. This would not be the case for Celena. She had an *ex officio* role on the EECS board, but Ric stayed on as CEO. Then, in May of 2010, Celena informed the ENH Board that Alex Montgomery would be leaving her position as Director of Development to become Director of Operations for the school, to provide business management and fundraising support for the expanding venture. Fortunately, the very capable Rhea Yap stepped up to become the new ENH Director of Development, then in her fourth year at Erie. Nevertheless, while this transition was described as beneficial to both agencies, and that Celena and Alex were committed to staying connected to continue to foster this partnership, ENH had just donated an experienced fundraiser to EECS. It had also donated several ENH board members: Troy Harden, Ken Perkins, Nancy Vincent, and Mark Hallett. While Hallett and Vincent continued to do double duty on both boards for a while, and Hallett was especially helpful with a McCormick Foundation-funded YOU project, eventually, the double duty wore thin and they limited their membership to the EECS Board. And last but not least, the Erie Child Care social worker would be spending three days a week at the charter, since they had lost their own psychologist due to CPS cuts. The argument was that ENH could spare her because Dr. Yelen had so many interns helping out at the Center. Meanwhile Ric Estrada and the EECS attorney (from Drinker Biddle, of course) continued to negotiate the purchase of St. Fidelis.

So, when the EECS board voted to ask Erie House to continue to support the school by managing their back-office operations for 2011, some questions and some eyebrows were raised. There were those who felt that so much of Erie House's time, energy, and resources had gone into the school already, this had led to neglect of Erie facilities (including the LVIRC), staff, and some fundraising. Celena herself articulated her experience with fundraising and board development messaging as getting more complicated. She said that she found her role as "salesperson" for both entities confusing to the outside world. If funders were donating to ENH, did that not include the school, and vice versa: if they gave money to the school, was that not giving to Erie Neighborhood House, as they viewed the EECS as a program of the settlement house. It felt like the relationship was competitive versus collaborative. Finally, in light of the severe budget and staff cuts ENH had made in June of 2010, that affected ENH capacity for FY11, the board was clear that the MOU with the charter needed a thorough review before committing to any further service. Minimally, the price for this service probably needed to go up.

At the March 2011 ENH Board meeting, Alex Montgomery reported that the IFF had come up with more money, and that New Market Tax Credits were bringing down the cost. They just needed to get the balance of $8.5 million from Soto's earmark released to close the deal on the purchase and hoped that Erie House would keep pushing its political advocates to get that money released. While Celena and Erie participants were in Springfield fending off budget cuts to child care and other Erie programs, this was added to the list. One of those advocates was former alderman, Billy Ocasio, who helped get the release of the funds that Spring. ENH and EECS came to an agreement over a reduced package of services at a price both could live with. At the November 2011 Board meeting, Montgomery reported that EECS was now planning to build a new wing at the 1405 Washtenaw site.

If You Are Not on the Bus, You Will be Under It

From the days of Ross Lyman and NCO to the days of Celena, Erie House was committed to advocacy, both as a matter of survival and as a tenet of settlement house work.

The concept of empowerment of participants to have a voice on behalf of good policy, and in opposition to bad, was written into Erie's mission statement. It was everyone's job, from Child Care moms to the executive director. Renting a bus to carry staff and participants to Springfield to "educate" state legislators was an annual event at least, generally toward the end of the session in the Spring. There they joined many other non-profits, proudly wearing their Erie House tee shirts that made it clear to legislators and the governor that Erie was ¡PRESENTE! But, many times during the course of a year, Celena made the trip to the state capital on Erie's behalf by herself.

The state tended to be the target more than the city. This was definitely due to the fact that the state was the source of many streams of revenue for Erie House programs, with the city or CPS only functioning in a pass-through capacity. Erie's representation in Springfield was supportive. From the days of Sen. Miguel Del Valle to Sen. William Delgado, through Rep. Cynthia Soto's earmarks for the House and the charter, Erie was well-supported. However, in the matter of day-to-day funding, so to speak, it was a constant battle with the larger legislature, led by Speaker Mike Madigan, and eventually with Governor Bruce Rauner. The constant postponement of funding the state's pension obligation, coupled with Rauner's decision to take the state budget hostage to force the legislature to adopt his "reforms," began to erode the state's capacity to fund anything, much less, social services, too often a low priority vulnerable to cuts.

Furthermore, on the city level, since Alderman Granato left office in 2003, every subsequent alderman was a staunch supporter of Erie House, and Mayor Daley had become a fan. When Rahm Emanuel was elected mayor, Celena was invited to serve on his education transition team. On the federal level, advocacy for comprehensive immigration reform was always on Erie's agenda. But, in that fight, US Senator Dick Durbin and Erie House were of one mind, and Erie's US Representative, Congressman Luis Gutierrez, was the recognized champion of immigrants in the House. Getting everyone else on the side of immigrants was their constant frustration that Erie House shared. Even at the federal level, when asked, Senator Durbin came up with an earmark for $250,000 in 2010 that provided support for Erie's Child Care supportive services--Dr. Yelen and her crew of interns.

In addition to "being in the face of" elected officials, Erie was committed to encouraging their participants to be engaged in selecting those faces in the first place. It was important to not only be on the bus, but also, to be in the voting booth. From the days of Tim Bell in the 1990s, citizenship was not about the swearing-in ceremony, but about participation. At Erie House, even the undocumented were engaged, encouraged to knock on the doors of the documented Latinos who were citizens, to get out the vote. They also got on the bus on December 14, 2010, to attend a mayoral candidates forum at UIC that was organized to specifically promote a social justice agenda to the candidates. There were 2,000 in attendance, and Erie participants were assigned leadership roles. Candidate Emanuel did not show up, a pattern that almost cost him his second term.

In November 2010, Celena was off to Springfield for the so-called "veto session" to support passage of Governor Quinn's proposed 1% income tax rate hike. As one of the few states that had a flat income tax, the current rate was not bringing in adequate revenue. Since elected officials generally do not want to be associated with increases in taxes, pressure had to be applied. With considerable reluctance, Madigan got it through, but only with a three-year sunset provision.

As her first year was coming to a close, Celena shared with the board one of her freshman year lessons. Throughout the election season and the veto session she said:

> *I was reminded how much politics truly does impact Erie House and the work we do. But, more so, I realized that Erie Neighborhood House has such a distinguished reputation with the city and state that we are also sought out by politicians looking to align themselves with a community-based organization that they know is doing good work and represents the community.*[460]

In that same report she gave evidence of this lesson. CPS had backed down from their proposal to only fund the 3-5 pre-school contracts for 10 months. She noted that this policy affected 14,000 families in Chicago and that ENH should be proud of its leadership role in effecting this reversal. It also saved Erie from a loss of at least $50,000.

However, the fight with CPS was not over yet. Erie and the other center-based child care programs would now have to address a new, punitive CPS policy as they rolled out new penalties for "non-compliance." In this new scenario, if one 0-3 classroom was over-enrolled by one child, CPS would reduce Erie's rate/child from $6,000 to $4,000 for all four 0-3 classrooms. No need for a bus to go across town to CPS, but the concept was the same. Advocacy was required.

Next, Celena was on a mission to educate the State Comptroller, Susana Mendoza, in regard to the extreme delays in paying for child care vouchers. Her point to the comptroller was that even with Erie's access to a reserve account and line of credit, there was a limit to these options. If the state did not make some payments on FY 10 soon, even Erie would be missing payroll; other agencies were already beyond that point. Payments were finally forthcoming.

While she was educating the State Comptroller, Erie was engaging in another area of advocacy at a meeting with new Chancellor of City Colleges of Chicago (CCC), Cheryl Hyman, and board chair, James Cabrera. Erie's battle with the City Colleges over quality and collaboration had been going on almost as long as the War of the Roses (32 years). But in 2011, Erie joined with 12 other organizations to advise the new leadership of the CCC where improvements were needed for the two populations served by the CCC: 1) younger students headed to 4-year universities; and 2) adults seeking to gain skills that would lead to careers with decent wages. The Chancellor praised Erie's input and invited participation in her "Reinvention Task Force"--a promising sign of change. While it turned out to be not as promising as was hoped for, it did signal an acknowledgment of the valuable input CBOs could provide, and a foundation was laid for improving skills training programs at the CCC.

Besides going to visit elected or appointed officials, they also visited Erie House, as noted several times in this narrative. Early in 2011, the new president of the Cook County Board, Toni Preckwinkle, *called and asked* to visit Erie House. *Reputation, reputation, reputation.* While Erie and other city-based organizations tended not to pay much attention to county elected officials, this one deserved more attention. She was smart, she was progressive, and, eventually, she would rise to Chair of the Cook County Democratic Party. But there was much more excitement around another visitor--not an elected official, but an appointed one. Courtesy of former Erie Board President, Joe Antolin, supreme court justice Sonia Sotomayor was planning to visit Erie House. Not only was she a progressive appointee of President Obama, but she was also Puerto Rican. What a role model for Erie families! Sotomayor and Antolin had gone to high school together back in New York, Erie's ED was Puerto Rican, and Joe knew firsthand that if Sotomayor wanted an experience with children at a non-profit organization, Erie would fit the bill. *Connections, connections, connections.* Sotomayor came, talked to parents, read to the children, and impressed everyone with her genuine warmth.

While Erie was entertaining distinguished visitors in early 2011, Celena was in Springfield twice in three weeks to fight cuts to child care funding. She met with the governor's chief of staff and testified before the State Senate, arguing for restoration of Early Childhood Block Grants to FY09 levels, i.e., putting back about $34 million for early childhood education in Illinois. Working with Erie's non-profit colleagues, their efforts were successful. Funding was restored to previous levels. What this all added up to, she explained to the board, was that FY11 would end without a deficit, digging out from a very deep hole the previous year. In fact, by the time the fiscal year ended Erie had a surplus of about $179,000. The Board instructions were to pay back 100K to the reserve account, put back the $70,000 that was routinely taken from the interest earned on the endowment, and then roll over the remaining $9,000 to FY12. In other words, you have to get on the bus.

Programs and Fundraising, 2010-2011

Other developments were beginning to add up to a balanced budget for FY 12 as well. These were on the private side of fundraising. Even though it is true, as Ric Estrada once commented, that foundations can be fickle, as they are continually changing their guidelines, non-profits cannot live without them. For all the reasons just outlined above, Erie struggled to maintain private dollars as 30-40% of their budget. This is possible because, while the executive director is away, and trips to Springfield have to be organized, staff and participants do what they always do-- staff, lead, and participate in great programs. The Marguerite Casey Foundation awarded Erie an unprecedented fourth three-year grant, this time for $75,000/year. The first such award was announced in late 2002.

On the other hand, some public funds came to Erie that they did not have to fight for. The Chicago Housing Authority awarded Erie a contract for $782,000 to open offices in West Town and Little Village to inform the Latino community about the housing benefits available to them through the CHA. Erie named this program "Buen Hogar" (Good Home). For its excellent performance in workforce development, the joint county/city workforce department awarded Erie $250,000 over two years.

To keep things in perspective, besides the fact that good programs attract good money, Erie also had some very creative staff, and they paid attention to what was relevant in the moment, not simply doing the exact same thing over and over. There were many examples of this over the years, and throughout all of Erie's departments. Child Care had created the Sunshine room and an extraordinary support program headed up by Dr. Yelen. How many child care support services are run by a PhD--one who stayed at Erie House for more than 20 years? Erie was among the first to have a computer lab and teach IT skills. The Workforce Development Department had such an effective bridge program it was copied by others and helped participants get careers, not just jobs. PTS received a grant of $30,000 from the Fry Foundation, $10,000 more than requested, as Program Officer, Sharon Bush, was that impressed with Erie's program in workforce development.

YOU was excelling in two areas--STEM and *Visionaries*--above and beyond its 25+ years providing TEAM. When, in 2009, Columbia College no longer had the funding to continue their program at Erie, the YOU staff and a Mennonite Volunteer, Katie Vander Heide, took over. The STEM focus was also fostered by the engagement of engineers as mentors and math tutors in the TEAM program. Even parents were engaged in the Fall of 2010, as youth and parents participated in "Noche de Ciencia," hosted by the Society of Hispanic Engineers and their two partner campuses, UIC and IIT. To say that this investment in STEM paid off was literally true, when, in 2011, NCLR/Unidos US awarded Erie $60,000 for STEM programming. Erie only asked for $50,000. This grant funded Saturday morning workshops which often involved visits to engineering firms so students could get a picture of this type of working environment.

Visionaries was staffed by YOU's very creative Digital Media Coordinator, Riza Falk. The opportunity to do creative things in digital media was fostered by Comcast. On August 31, 2010, the new Comcast Youth Digital Media Lab was unveiled, and the company presented Erie with a check for $20,000 to support Visionaries. This significant financial support from Comcast was fostered by providing the company with volunteer opportunities, or Comcast Cares Days, that began in 2008. The volunteers were so impressed with Erie that they invited Erie to apply for funding.

Visionaries funding also came from After School Matters (ASM) that funded 18 technology "apprenticeships" for the summer of 2010. The apprentices were learning photography skills and making documentary films. Writing skills were developed as they had to provide scripts for their films. In the Fall, Visionaries turned their attention to developing journalism skills, and 15 participants visited a newspaper and the studio of Erie's photographer neighbor, across the street from the House. This was in the building that went from synagogue-to Baptist church-to live/work studios. All of these experiences led to the publication of a Visionaries "news magazine" in 2011 called *Visionaries 411,* with articles written by youth about topics like immigration, using that digital media hardware and software that Comcast provided. Also, in 2011, ENH Board member, Mark Hallett, took note of these efforts and facilitated a grant from the McCormick Foundation that supported a partnership between Visionaries and the Loyola University School of Journalism. The partnership's goal was to engage in the writing and creation of a magazine called *My Chicago, Your Chicago.*

At the end of this productive period, in November 2011, YOU Director, Rebecca Estrada, left Erie to become Director of El Hogar del Niño. Joshua Fulcher, who had been working with YOU since 2007, was promoted to Director, and he hired Maria Muñoz to succeed him as Academic Coordinator for TEAM and other educational endeavors. Erie's culture of promoting from within was, once again, a smart decision. Eight years later, Josh was still leading YOU. During his tenure, YOU would be rewarded with expanded and upgraded space for their excellent programming.

Two other events contributed to improved private revenue for FY11. The annual Holiday Appeal that took place in December 2010, was back up to its more traditional yield at $43,983. After raising only $28,990 in December of 2009, the decision to move the Annual Dinner from Fall to Spring was carried out and, obviously, paid off. While the Holiday Appeal had recovered, that first dinner in the Spring of 2010 was disappointing, with revenue at $247,987 in light of a goal of $300,000. A big part of that lower number was a much lower intake on the night of at only $17,000, when $40,000 was the norm. Celena and Rhea put their heads together and came up with the idea of a "paddle raise," referred to as a "Dutch Auction." Instead of just asking people to slip their donation into an envelope left on the tables, the paddle raise was a much more active approach. The key is to start out with a pre-arranged, substantial "bid" to get people into the spirit of thinking generously. Erie's long-time supporter and board member, John Hall, of Goose Island Brewing Co., provided that kick-off bid. That night, "the ask" returned to its traditional giving target, just over $40,000. The paddle raise strategy became a permanent part of the annual dinner, with its yield steadily increasing each year after 2011.

One last strategy that strengthened Erie's earning capacity was its diligent effort, over a few years, to implement a data collection system to document the outcomes of Erie programs, appropriately called "Efforts to Outcomes" or ETO for short. "Senior Director of Programs and Quality Assurance" was actually the full title that was generally referred to as simply Senior Director of Programs. As early as 2006, Ric Estrada noted that Erie had to start preparing itself to not just answer the question: How many? But also, So what? In other words, how much better off were Erie's participants when they signed up for Erie's programs? If Erie was offering education, what percentage of students made educational gains that could be measured? If helping people get jobs, how many got them and what were they earning that indicated they were financially better off? When pre-schoolers were tested, how many met the standards expected for entering kindergarten? Etc. etc.

As Erie often did, in 2011, it joined a collaborative with five other organizations led by another settlement, Christopher House, to work together on the adoption of this 21st century approach to measuring results. By 2013, it was running in all departments. Erie was ready for those harder questions.[461]

2012-2013: Funding Children's Programs: What Miss Florence Never Had to Deal With

With much of the focus for Celena's first two years facing outward--dealing with Little Village and the Erie Elementary Charter School--Celena told the ENH Board in January 2012, that it was time to look inward for a while. As the last strategic plan had outlived its timeframe, it was time to launch another strategic planning process. This time Erie availed itself of the services of the Executive Service Corps.

(ESC) to guide the process, which they aimed to complete by May. She and Rhea would also be focusing on the Gala, also scheduled for May, in anticipation of using it to mark the 27th anniversary of the TEAM banquet that celebrates graduation of its seniors in June 2012.

However, there is no such thing as just working on an inward focus because the outside world keeps impacting Erie's plans and programs. This was certainly true of Erie's children's programs. Child Care would spend these two years in State administrative hell, playing havoc with their revenue stream and Celena's peace of mind. And After-School was right there with Pre-school, struggling to deal with enrollment and revenue losses. As a former Director of Child Care, Celena was probably affected by this more than others might be. She recalled that as she was walking down the hall at the Center one day, looking depressed, Rafael Ravelo, still in his role of Senior Advisor, approached her and encouraged her not to worry so much. He said, "Remember, the angels watch over Erie House."[462] She said that shortly thereafter, she received a letter notifying her that Erie was to receive $140,000 from the estate of G. Hudson Wirth. No one currently associated with Erie House knew who he was, but somewhere along the way in his life he had come to understand who Erie was and remembered when he wrote his will.

The Wirth legacy was a boost to Erie's morale and coffers, but the income eligibility cap in child care still impacted families, causing them to lose their care and Erie to lose revenue. This affected both Pre-school and After-School programs, but it tended to harm After-School more. These were often more mature families, perhaps second generation, that were in the US long enough to be making more money than the younger pre-school families. It was not enough money to pay for private care, as discussed in earlier chapters, often leading to school age children being left at home alone after school. Then, at the same time that

491

income eligibility was being lowered, co-pays were going up. The School Age program lost out again. If families had children in both programs, they would choose to make the co-pay for their youngest children, who could not be left home alone and take their children out of After-School care. If these challenges were not enough, Mayor Emanuel made things worse when he extended the school day. When that was implemented at the charter, After-School enrollment declined there as well, as the program time was shortened. Furthermore, the school added some other after school activities that competed with what Erie House was offering. At the House, these were just the further complications added to the loss of children due to gentrification and the closing of one of its key feeder schools, Carpenter. After five years of struggling with enrollment decline, it became apparent that a new strategy was needed. Otis and Talcott, Erie's stalwart after-school partners, were just not enough. Erie would have to start recruiting from schools that served the same populations of Latino and African American children, but that were farther away than walking distance. The After-School program would have to go into the transport business and drive children to the program. That process began with Hope School, south of Erie on Ashland Avenue, in 2013.

The After-School got some extra help from Barb and Dan Hartnett from Union Church of Hinsdale. As a board member, Dan had been hearing about the struggles in enrollment and funding. So, he and his wife invited Val Shepard, Director of After-School, to speak at their church (the ever-faithful Union Church of Hinsdale). Following her presentation, the church presented her with a check for $5,000, and a member who chose to remain anonymous, put up another $10,000 to be matched, and it was. It should also be noted that Barb was known as "volunteer extraordinaire" in Child Care, showing up there on a weekly basis to read to the pre-schoolers or do whatever else was helpful. The

Hartnetts were an example of what was much more common in the past--church members coming to Erie to volunteer and get involved with the Erie neighbors, as well as inviting Erie to their church to tell their story in person. They were successors of people like the Armstrongs and Nancy Vincent, from the same church, and originally recruited by Chuck Armstrong.

In the Pre-school program, income eligibility hurt in another way. While more families were approved, those that were not still had their children in the program on the assumption that Erie staff had accurately gaged their eligibility. Erie was not reimbursed for those children when Illinois Action for Children (IAFC) notified Erie that *their* information determined a family ineligible. Dealing with IAFC instead of DFSS was an adjustment in itself, but it was made more difficult when Erie did not have access to the same data bases, like social security and public aid, to make their determination of eligibility. So, Celena talked with IAFC Director, Maria Whelan, an old advocacy buddy, to arrange for more training for the Erie intake staff. It helped.

Then, out of the blue, on March 19, 2012, DFSS informed Erie House that they would no longer have an oversight or funding relationship with the city. Instead they would be funded through IAFC, that had, in reality, become a state agency. The immediate issue that emerged was that IAFC did not pay for administrative costs, which would cost Erie about $125,000 per year. It also meant that Erie would not be paid for administering the $2 million contract they managed for the Network of Day Care Home Providers. Erie shared this surprise shift with Christopher House, Chicago Commons and the YMCA. The city's only explanation was they figured these four large and competent agencies *could handle it*. Nothing like being punished for your good deeds.

The relationship with IAFC did not work out and led Celena to pursue another path. Through her efforts, State Senator, John Cullerton, President of the Senate, helped Erie secure a state-administered child care contract in 2013. This was good news, Celena explained, because: 1) we no longer have to struggle with IAFC over eligibility processing; 2) we return to reimbursement for our administrative costs. This increased Child Care revenue by approximately $150-200,000. But before that happened, in November of 2012, after 22 years, Erie had bid a sad farewell to the network of Day Care Family Home providers. Just as had been predicted, Erie could not afford to maintain this relationship under IAFC without the reimbursement for administrative costs. A dinner was organized to say goodbye, and many of the providers rose to say how much the relationship with Erie had meant to them, so grateful for that support. Given the switch to a state-administered contract, less than a year later, the question needed to be raised if this decision was premature.

Erie House Hires a Lobbyist

For years, non-profits avoided using the phrase "to lobby" for fear they would lose their 501c3 tax exempt status. In speaking with elected officials about policies or legislation, they would say they were "advocating" for funding, or "educating" politicians regarding the rightness or wrongness of their proposals. From the non-profit's point of view, they were interpreting on behalf of their low-income, immigrant or African American population what would serve them best. As Celena noted above, some pols even sought out the advice of the organizations they respected the most. But more often than not, Erie House and their non-profit colleagues had to track them down, testify before their committees, or show up at their offices with a hundred or so folks, to get their point across.

By 2012, Erie House, for one, and not the only one, decided it was time to put someone with special skills in charge of the euphemisms, and hire an l-o-b-b-y-i-s-t. In discussing this with the Board, Celena assured them that the companies who did this work, representing non-profits, understood the rules pertaining to "lobbying/advocating." After many good questions from board members, concerned Erie would get in trouble with the IRS, or that the return on investment (ROI) might not be worth it, there was agreement to interview some of these companies and bring back a recommendation to the Board. At the March 2012 meeting, the lobbyist interview committee that consisted of John Van Pelt, Mark Jolicoeur, John De Carrier, and Celena, reported their experience with interviews to the board, who then authorized Celena to spend $60,000 to hire a lobbyist. They hired All-Circo who sent John Kelly to represent them at the May Board meeting. The message he got from the board was to focus on securing capital dollars in Springfield.

At the September 2012 board meeting, Celena introduced Michael Houlihan, who had been assigned by All-Circo to serve as the ENH lobbyist. By this time, he had already secured a capital grant of $500,000 for Erie that was sponsored by Sen. John Cullerton. This first connection led to another when, as noted in the Child Care saga just told, Cullerton was the one who secured the state administered contract for Erie the following year. There were no further questions from the board in regard to ROI. Clearly, Houlihan had been able to go right to the top of the leadership to get the job done. That was impressive. Erie continued to cultivate the relationship with Cullerton, inviting him to visit the House, and honoring him as an awardee at their Gala.

Advocacy Work Continues

Lobbyist or not, it would still be in the job description of Erie participants to engage in advocacy. In the Health Department, under the direction of Michael Guarrine, and ably assisted by Micaella Vero, the Parent

Council became the advocacy arm of Erie House. Following the loss of 10 families in the School-Age program due to income eligibility guidelines, and with word of more cuts in funding proposed for the state budget, the Council organized a public meeting to address these issues early in 2012. Over 200 people gathered in the Erie gym to voice their opposition to what was going on in state policy to State Reps, Cynthia Soto and Toni Berrios, a representative from the governor's office, Erie's two aldermen, Proco Joe Moreno (1st Ward) and Walter Burnett (27th), and Maria Whelan from IAFC. The Latino Policy Forum provided an excellent Power Point illustrating their research on how Latino communities were underserved when it came to child care. There was no immediate response from state officials as to what they would do, but, once again, Erie gave voice to the community. And then they got back on the bus.

As Child Care Director, Louis Falk, reported to the board, parents had a little fun with their advocacy in Springfield that year. They decorated toy blocks with kids' pictures and left them as reminders to the legislators they visited that Child Care is critical to keep parents working, and therefore it is also critical to the economy of the state. Sarah Rios, a member of the Parent Council, accompanied Michael to Springfield twice that Spring to personally testify as to why subsidized child care was so important and how the income cap eligibility guidelines had disqualified her from participating in the Child Care program at Erie House. She presented the following case to the ISBE Child Care Funding Committee. She was forced to function as a single mother with three young girls, ages 3-5, since her husband had been deported the previous summer. She had her hands full raising her children on her own and working full time for a construction company. Yet, she made time to serve on the Head Start Parent Council, became a Health Promoter, and joined the agency-wide Erie Parent Council. She was articulate and did not miss a beat when speaking about the impact of lower-and-lower income eligibility guidelines on her family taking away her child care. She made it known that Erie had become her second family--her safety net--and she would do whatever it took to keep Erie House in the lives of her children, while keeping the job she needed to feed them. Her testimony made abstract guidelines real. A member of the committee who worked for IDHS (Illinois Department of Family Services) was so moved, she approached Sarah after her testimony and helped her to get her reinstated. Sarah experienced firsthand the value of speaking up and the support of her "second family" in preparing her and escorting her to that opportunity. At the same time she understood that the fight would continue for all the other Erie families who had lost their care.

Another issue Erie House advocated for was "Drivers Licenses for All." Because Illinois law required a person applying for a driver's license to provide a social security number, it was estimated that 250,000 Illinois immigrant motorists could not get licenses but still needed to drive to support their families. Without a license, they were also uninsured. ICIRR had put this issue on the table, and Erie joined with fellow ICIRR members to push for the removal of the SSN requirement. SB957 passed the Illinois legislature in December 2012, changing that requirement.

In April 2013, advocacy efforts would move from Springfield to Washington, D.C., when the "Border Security, Economic Opportunity, and Immigration Modernization Act of 2013" was introduced in Congress. Celena explained to the board, that while this had been a long time in coming, "the bill was less than inclusive, and certainly not comprehensive."[463] What was missing? Issues related to e-verify, family reunification petitions, special work status, a fast track for Dreamers to attain citizenship had not been included. There was work to be done, and amendments were already developing. She announced that Erie was in discussion with key political leaders, like

Gutierrez and Durbin, and was planning to host a panel on immigration reform on May 30, 2013. Erie also hosted an event at the request of Congressman Luis Gutierrez, who brought Republican House Leader, Paul Ryan, to the stage in Templeton Hall to "discuss" immigration reform in front of an audience of immigrants. Ryan was cordial but did not budge. However, the event was a plus for Erie insofar as the event was picked up by CNN and the *New York Times,* and there was the Erie logo displayed on the podium.

Later in the year, Erie hosted a joint press conference with Senator Durbin and Congresswoman Jan Schakowsky and a group called Illinois Women for Comprehensive Immigration Reform. Some 5th graders from EECS were there, writing letters to parents that had been deported.

That Fall, Erie folk were back on the bus, headed out to the western suburbs to rally in front of the office of another Republican congressman, Peter Roskam, to "encourage" him to change his negative position on immigration. Roskam did not budge either. However, he subsequently got budged when he lost his re-election bid. In October, Erie marched with many others, in Chicago and around the country, to continue to press for comprehensive immigration reform. On November 6, 2013, Celena participated in an act of civil disobedience, joining 142 faith, labor, and elected officials, documented and undocumented immigration rights leaders, who sat down in the intersection of Congress (now, Ida B. Wells Parkway) and Clark, just outside Chicago's INS office, and blocked traffic until they were arrested. It was an outpouring of frustration over the fact that 2 million deportations had happened since Obama took office, leaving over 3 million children without one or both parents. She shared this reflection with the board:

> *We know that these actions may not get us a vote but that is not necessarily the point. There has never been a time in our history where we have*

been as close as we have been to finally making the immigrant community a fully respected and included part of our economy and social structure. Even if we lose the vote we need to continue to make the message of our immigrant families heard. The time is now and we may not see this opportunity again for a very long time. I truly appreciate the unconditional support of our board on this issue, as it is the basis of what we do and who we are at Erie House.[464]

Capital Spending Decisions

No doubt the largest capital project Erie had been involved with, since the purchase and rehab of 1701 W. Superior, was enabling the charter school to purchase the old St. Fidelis school building, rehab it, and build an addition, mostly courtesy of the $12 million secured for Erie House by State Rep Cynthia Soto. The money actually went to the school, not to Erie House, but as Erie's lobbyist pointed out, he had to explain that to the folks in Springfield when he was there asking for, what appeared to them, as *more* capital dollars for Erie House. And Rep Soto was assisting with an important Erie House project in addition to wanting a share of charter school money spent in her district.

Actually, throughout its history, the leadership of Erie House, board and staff, did not shy away from spending money to build and maintain the physical space needed to carry out their mission. From the first facility constructed at 1347 W. Erie in 1886, as the new home for the Noble Street Mission/Erie Chapel, to the construction of the yellow brick building called Erie Neighborhood House in the midst of the Depression, in 1935, to the acquisition of a vacant factory on Superior Street in 1995 to expand child care services, Erie invests capital dollars. When it was time to consider extending Erie's mission to serve immigrants in another location, they committed to creating the physical space for the Little Village Immigrant Resource Center and started planning a capital campaign to make that happen. They were prepared to invest the Western Union capital dollars they shared with LVCDC to buy the cookie factory on Kildare. When the Epiphany convent became the LVIRC, the Kildare property was considered for development as a child care center in response to the state's RFP to build one.

When the board learned that Erie did not get the capital grant to develop a child care center on the Kildare site, the Facilities Committee concluded that the Kildare properties were no longer of strategic value and would be put up for sale, even though the appraised value was "disappointing." The Board asked Celena about Erie's future in LV. She stated it was unlikely Erie would leave. Demand for service was so high and never seemed to slack off. Just recently, Tribune Charities gave Erie a grant to start a children's literacy program in LV. Parents enrolled in Erie's adult education program there had been asking for years that Erie do some programming with their children. So, she explained, this new grant would facilitate a response to that request. The "Little Village READS" program was born and partnered with local schools to promote early intervention with 1st through 3rd graders who needed extra support to read better. Rachel Serra was assigned to recruit and supervise volunteer tutors who would work with the children after school.

Besides the demand for services, based on demographics, funders were giving preference to LV over West Town. Finally, Celena shared that ENH senior staff felt an ethical obligation to be in LV to fulfill Erie's LVIRC promise, even if "a new center" was not developed. It was nine years since the Western Union allocation in 2003. Erie had been serving Mexican immigrants in LV all that time, Celena pointed out, and should continue to do so. Little

Village had become an integral part of the mission of Erie House.

While waiting for a response, the board Facilities Committee pondered what to do with the $500K just secured. Given Dan Hartnett's earlier comment about the House being Erie's cornerstone, he felt strongly that it should be invested there. Celena suggested that new first-floor bathrooms were a definite priority. With only minor updates since 1935, these 75-year old facilities were woefully inadequate. Both staff and participants would endorse this investment. But, before getting too far down the road on planning for this, the question was raised about investing in a property that Erie House did not actually own. The Presbytery of Chicago still held the deed to this building, making it available for programming for the community for 75+ years, at no cost, but also with no written lease. This was not the first time that Erie's lack of ownership had presented a problem when it came to capital investment of public dollars. Esther Nieves had to maneuver these muddy waters 10 years earlier. The Board decided it was time to stop trying to work around this situation and directed the Facilities Committee to go to the Presbytery to sort this out, hoping to secure the deed. If that did not happen, then minimally, to get some sort of lease in writing. In the short term, to avoid further delay in making improvements at the House, a written "lease" was secured, giving Erie the authority to move forward with the proposed improvements at the House. The deed was eventually transferred to Erie House prior to its 150th anniversary in 2020.

While meetings were being set up with the Presbytery, Mark Jolicoeur came over to look at the situation at the House that Erie's faithful friends at Perkins & Will would once again be engaged in as a pro bono project. In discussion with the Senior Director of Programs, it was pointed out that the location of the maintenance department was taking up valuable space next to the YOU area. If they could be moved, YOU could use that extra space to serve teens from those five high schools so close by. One option was to remove the stage from Towne Hall, occupied by the After-School program that was smaller than it used to be. If a stage were needed, there was another one in Templeton Hall on the second floor. Jolicoeur agreed that this idea had possibilities. Discussion then moved on to the possibility of adding an elevator to the building. While the House had been grandfathered in as ADA-compliant, as pertained to its first floor, and in consideration of the age of the building, an elevator would add access to the upper floors. A possible location was identified that would require an external addition at the back of the building, but the price tag would be high. The lease came through from the Presbytery, and by the summer of 2014, the bathrooms were modernized and expanded, and the maintenance area was relocated so that YOU would have more space; the elevator was left out. A full-fledged celebration and pronouncement over new bathrooms did not seem appropriate, but the staff was, privately, jumping for joy.

There was cause for more joy when, Erie's lobbyist secured a promise of another capital grant from the state in 2013, this time for $1,000,000. But, in order to claim this money, Erie would have to provide an address to indicate where the capital improvements were to be made. This amount of money had the board, once again, turning toward the idea of some kind of building in Little Village. The Kildare properties were still on the market when they discussed this in September of 2013. The asking price had started at $249,999, but was now down to $174,999. If there was no longer any intent to use the cookie factory, but build something new instead, there was no doubt that much more than the state grant would be required and a capital campaign would be needed to raise the balance. As Chair of the Board Finance Committee, Steve Fox raised the question of feasibility. Could Erie raise a sufficient amount? A very preliminary estimate was that about $10 million would be needed. To get an answer to this question, the board decided to hire the Alford Group and use the Wirth legacy to cover the cost.

Back in West Town, the design work on the EECS addition was complete. The addition, which would be built on the space created by demolition of the vacant convent, would include: a new lobby, an elevator connected to both buildings, a parent resource room, computer lab, library, gym, and a rooftop playground. Furthermore, the EECS had been able to purchase the adjacent city-owned lot for $1.00 (thanks to the Community 21 Adjacent Neighbor Acquisition proposal that had been adopted by the City Council years earlier). With assistance from KaBoom, a wonderful playlot was being developed there.

In her Director of Operations role for EECS, Alex Montgomery also provided the following profile of the student body. Enrollment was at 415, with 50% coming from the surrounding neighborhood. 85% received free or reduced lunches and 14% had special ed needs. Proudly, she reported that CPS had named EECS a Level 1/Excellent school. While all the new construction was exciting, this was, in fact, the whole point of Erie House starting a new school in the first place--so that her neighbors' children could excel in a high-quality educational environment.

With capital spending an ongoing challenge, raising money for operating expenses had to move forward at the same time. That task was facilitated by a successful Holiday Appeal at the end of 2012 that brought in $44,000, supplemented by John Hall's generous donation of the proceeds from the sale of Goose Island's Christmas Ale, bringing in $37,000. The holiday spirit, no pun intended, was ever present in the 550 gifts for Erie families, delivered to Erie by its faithful church partners. In the Spring of 2013, Erie celebrated the most successful Gala to date. With

Workforce Development as the theme, gross revenue was $353,000, with the paddle raise bringing in a record $67,000, 50% more than usual. José Ramos, Manufacturing Bridge grad, with a good job in CNC, stole the show with his story of how one good job, instead of three part time jobs, made it possible for him to be present for important family events that he had been missing. Added to this was a great video message from a happy employer of one of Erie's CNC grads. This was an outcome story.

Another tenet of non-profit fundraising is that one must be visible for people to be inspired to give. In the first half of 2013, Erie was visible in one form of media or another, 29 times. When Erie met Melissa Ballate of Blue Daring, through their CHA contract, she was hired to update Erie's Web site. After that, traffic increased by 500%.

Program Ebbs and Flows

As should be evident from this narrative, hardly a year goes by without some outstanding accomplishment that continues to underscore Erie's reputation for excellence. Conversely, most years also had some significant challenge, sometimes life-threatening in terms of the continued existence of the organization, or at least some important program. What Erie House, and the other settlement houses of Chicago, all over 100 years old, demonstrated was the ability to do what the Jerome Kern song advised. "Pick yourself up, dust yourself off, and start all over again."

One of the disasters of 2012 was the failure to be funded by the ICCB for adult education and citizenship classes. The level of support generally provided from this source was over $500,000, and Erie had counted on this funding for many years. So, what happened? There was a convergence of two factors. Erie had a new Director of Adult Programs who was submitting her first ICCB proposal and, as her supervisor, the Senior Director of Programs, should have reviewed it more carefully. All the essentials were there, and in the past, because of the quality of Erie's performance, winning additional performance-based federal dollars year after year, re-funding by the state was hardly an issue. However, that year, ICCB hired an outside consultant to review proposals and they decided that prior performance would not be considered as criteria for being funded. Approval rested solely on the quality of the proposal, which in Erie's case, they deemed inadequate and Erie was not awarded any funds. Losing half a million dollars was a blow. It was also a shock to other CBOs who were aware of Erie's reputation among ICCB grantees. So, Erie did what Erie had to do. The director who had submitted the proposal was replaced by Cristina Garcia, an Erie employee who had been steadily promoted to positions of greater responsibility over her previous seven years at Erie. The department was reorganized, bringing Workforce Development, that was well-funded, back under its wing and shifting some other funding around to cover ESL and citizenship classes. Garcia called upon the hard-working ESL instructors to do more with less, which they did. Furthermore, Erie's years of collaboration also came to the rescue, as the Chinese Mutual Aid Association invited Erie House to be an ESL subcontractor and passed through ICCB funds for that work. Erie and Adult Ed survived.

Citizenship was bringing in new funds. Due to the BIA certification it had secured, it was doing more fee-for-service legal work, which helped to subsidize its classes and workshops. Viviana Mendez, Erie's immigration attorney, became full time. And, following Obama's executive order of June 2012 that created DACA (Deferred Action for Childhood Arrivals), the Citizenship staff were assisting youth with their DACA applications. Given the fact that applying for DACA meant that youth were acknowledging their undocumented status, legal review was part of that assistance to make sure it was safe for each youth to apply. Funding to support this work was forthcoming from a number of sources. In 2013, ICIRR rewarded Erie for its good work with a larger NAI grant. Citizenship workshops were still drawing about 100 people per quarter, with over 100 enrolled to prepare for their naturalization. Erie's DACA applicants numbered more than 200 by 2013, and that flow was ongoing. Finally, with DOMA (Defense of Marriage Act) declared unconstitutional, Erie was assisting same sex couples to apply for residency.

Over in Youth Options Unlimited (YOU), approved DACA status meant increased numbers of students were eligible for scholarships. 2012 proved to be an exciting year in that area, as one young lady won a full ride scholarship to Northwestern University, one of the top five most expensive universities in the country. A young man was going to Oberlin College for free with a $120,000 scholarship. The following year, YOU Director, Joshua Fulcher, proudly announced that Erie had six Posse scholarship finalists. The Posse Foundation is a non-profit organization that identifies, recruits, and trains student leaders from high schools to form multicultural teams of 10 called "posses." Each Posse scholar is awarded a full scholarship to a top tier college or university.

STEM workshops were continuing, and a TEAM mentor, who worked for a company called Radius, a Design and Development firm, hosted a workshop at their offices, demonstrating for the students the process of creating and designing many types of products. This activity was followed by a project that involved students in designing robotic cars.

Riza Falk was preparing to launch the first year of Visionaries programming the McCormick Foundation's News Literacy grant by attending workshops at the Medill

School of Journalism at Northwestern. When it rolled out in 2013, it was a smash hit, with the participants and its funders. Erie hired four high school and college interns who wrote the curriculum for teaching "news literacy" to youth, and then taught it themselves. The McCormick Foundation was so impressed, they invited the youth team to present at one of their conferences. Their reputation was such that Mike Hannon at the Alternative Schools Network (ASN) reached out and asked them to train ASN teachers how to teach news literacy. In the Fall of 2013, they took their show on the road, so to speak, as they adapted it to teach news literacy in Spanish as well as English to adult students in Little Village. Their approach was to guide the adults in comparing news reporting in Mexico with that of the US, and to identify the biases in both. The adult students loved it. Next step for Visionaries? How about starting an online business to sell Visionaries art through Etsy? *Porque no?*

[Check out www.fourstarcreations.etsy.com.]

Health and Leadership (H&L) was awarded a two-year grant of $205,000 by the Kellogg Foundation to engage Association House and Northwestern University Settlement House in adopting the health promoters idea. Erie arranged for the recruits from these two agencies to join with Erie's to attend a training provided by COFI (Community Organizing for Family Issues) that had moved to offices just a few blocks from Erie House. COFI Director, Ellen Schumer, had worked with Erie House earlier in her career, and was recommended to the Health and Leadership staff. The COFI training was crafted to balance self-esteem, organizing, and health education. The participants loved it. In 2013, H & L received a grant of $200,000 from Johnson & Johnson that was accompanied by a doctoral student intern from Johns

Hopkins University, who joined two students from UIC and a Mennonite Volunteer in the cramped H&L office on the third floor of the House. Camaraderie was unavoidable and the program prospered.

2014-2015: *The Capital Campaign Gets Wheels*

By March of 2014, the Alford Group had done 20 interviews in their process of determining the feasibility of a successful capital campaign. They promised a final report for the next board meeting in May and outlined areas to be addressed in that report that were gleaned from the interviews. They confirmed that there was an abundance of respect for ENH –quality of programs, leadership, history and legacy. They identified some prospects at the top level of giving, mostly individuals at the executive level of corporations that would consider a donation from their own funds rather than from the company. At this point, they suggested a target of $20 million, but by May, they were only recommending a target of $7-10 million. Jim Fitzpatrick said that the Finance Committee was not comfortable committing to the proposed 12-18-month Advancement Phase, and only approved the first four months at $45,000. In September 2014, they would evaluate a continuation for an additional 6-12 months at $75,000-105,000. When September came, the board voted to approve the launch of a capital campaign. With no bids for purchasing the Kildare properties, Mark Jolicoeur had suggested demolition as an option and proposed a plan to use capital campaign funds to build a new building on the vacant land available. Sy Nelson agreed that option made sense since, he noted, Erie had been looking for a building in LV for a decade with no luck. The programs offered would be infant, toddler, and pre-school, with the goal of recruiting from Cicero and Berwyn as well as LV.

The goal of the next phase was to gather sufficient pledges to secure a construction loan, and get Perkins & Will started on design work. With the $1 million pledge from the state, and $1.4 million of private pledges already in hand, another $2.2 million would be sufficient. Once that goal was met, the campaign would go public to raise the rest. A Board Capital Campaign Committee was formed. If this plan moved forward, an estimated completion date was projected for 2017. Meanwhile, Erie negotiated an extension on the Epiphany lease through December 2016, with a 3% per year increase. Improvements at the House were on budget and on time. A ribbon-cutting ceremony was planned for June of 2014, with Senator Cullerton invited to attend.

The following year, in March of 2015, the capital campaign had a name, "Raise a Village," and a logo. Perkins & Will's design had been approved, the Kildare properties were set for demolition, and Senior Director of Operations, Mike McGlinn, and board member, Dan Hartnett, were meeting with the IFF (Illinois Facilities Fund) to discuss financing. Chase Bank was identified as the likely source for the construction loan and $2 million in New Market Tax Credits were pending. This project was the theme of the 2015 Annual Gala. All the pieces seemed to be falling into place. But, in June of 2015, pledges only totaled $2,671,750, and, nine months earlier, the Alford Group had projected $4.6 million as the needed base before going public. This was the 500-pound gorilla in the room. Moreover, the state's promise of $1,000,000 was caught up in Governor Rauner's state budget "freeze." As a result, this whole project was frozen.

Development Department Takes on New Responsibilities

As part of her strategic plan as Senior Director of Development, Kirstin Chernawsky suggested a stronger focus on board development. She advocated for increasing the number so as to accommodate more corporate-type members, especially in light of the proposed capital campaign. Furthermore, the board was losing some key people with capacity to either donate themselves or inspire others to do so. Ken Perkins and Nancy Vincent chose to serve on just one board, and that was EECS. Chuck Armstrong's son had informed Erie that due to his worsening dementia, Chuck had to step down. Chuck had given 50+ years in service to Erie House on the Board of Directors, having succeeded his father, Harry, who also had a long board tenure. Both father and son had served as board president. Chuck was probably the last member of the board who had known Miss Florence, as he was listed as a guest at a 1948 board meeting, three years before Florence Towne died; he had worked with every executive director, from Lyman to Roldán. And then, Jack O'Kieffe announced he was retiring from the board "to make room for the younger generation." He had served for more than 30 years, since the days of Merri Ex. The officers for FY15, that would have to carry on without these four heavy hitters, included: John DeCarrier as president, Patricia Perez as Vice-president, Fitzpatrick as Treasurer, and Van Pelt as Secretary. By today's standards, they would be considered veterans, all having been around for more than five years. The first nominee under Chernawsky's plan was Laura Duda from Exelon. Throughout the remainder of Celena's time at Erie, she and Kirstin worked on the addition of new members to the Board. During this period, Paul Gassel and Craig Castelli (who lived in the neighborhood) also joined the board.

Chernawsky also followed through on her plan to hire a government grants specialist. For years, program directors bore the burden of soliciting public funds and then managing those contracts in partnership with the Finance office. First, it seemed that it was a lot to ask of program directors while they were also responsible for the day-to-day running of programs. Second, considering that public funds made up about 70% of Erie's budget, did this practice make Erie vulnerable, as in the case of the lost ICCB grant? Third, senior leadership suspected that money was being left on the table, certainly at the federal level, without someone on the staff responsible for going after it. So, this was good news, a good plan.

Probably the best news for the new SDD and her department was the revenue from the Gala in March, 2015. Erie topped its previous record, just set the year before, raising $434,900 (17% over 2013), with a blockbuster paddle raise of $95,175. Sarah Rios shared the story told above, and the paddles popped up. Mayor Rahm Emanuel had ended up as one of the honorees that year, but he should have been honored to be in the company of Sarah Rios, who spoke to honor her neighbor, Erie House. Once again, private fundraising was the bridge over public funding troubled waters, that were about to rise to hurricane strength.

State Finances Enter Troubled Waters; Erie Struggles to Keep Afloat

During Celena 's last two years at the helm, Erie House, and all the rest of the non-profit, social service agencies in Illinois, had to navigate strategically--or drown during a time of extremely difficult state budget challenges. The situation began at the end of 2014, when the tax rate increase that Governor Pat Quinn had convinced the legislature to approve was approaching its sunset date. Finance Director, Leslie Okamura, told the Board that, on the one hand, IDHS was paying promptly under Erie's new direct contract for child care; on the other hand, the rest of the state's departments that administered Erie's other grants were holding their breath and their money until they knew if the sun was going to set or not. If it did, it would be a dark day all around, with the state starting 2015 with an estimated $2.5 billion dollar deficit. Everyone would take a hit, but experience suggested that human services would bear the brunt of the hit. This was all the more unfortunate when the 2015 budget reflected some allocations that Erie had been fighting for. The line items for early childhood education and job training had increased. Those victories were short-lived.

Speaker Madigan and Senate President Cullerton both said they supported the extension of the increased tax rate and were working to encourage the legislature to approve it. They did not. With Madigan's well-known, ironclad control of the House, there were those who did not believe he actually had been doing all he could to prevent this outcome. Nor had he and other legislative leaders done what they should have to responsibly manage appropriate payments into the state pension fund all along,--failed decisions that had now come home to roost.

As was noted earlier in this chapter, Illinois elected Rauner governor, who took the state budget hostage for two years in his effort get rid of Madigan by imposing term limits on legislators. Madigan did not lose this fight, but the residents of Illinois, and the non-profit organizations that served them, were the losers, while politics took precedence over the responsibility to govern.

So, how did Erie respond? Seeing the writing on the wall, one strategy that Celena deployed was to instruct the child care staff to load up on Head Start-eligible children. This was federal funding outside of Rauner and Madigan's purview. Of course, the Head Start income cap always made it a difficult recruitment target, but the full court press was on and resulted in shifting the Child Care enrollment to 2/3 Head Start-eligible. Finance Director, Okamura, was pressing the IAFC for the 125K they still owed Erie and got them to pay at least $65,000. When Celena sought advice from the lobbyist, he just said to prepare to lean hard on your line of credit, which the ENH board raised to $1.5 million in 2015. In addition, the drawdown from the endowment was increased from the usual $70-75,000, to $125,000. This was unprecedented but necessary. Senior staff took furlough days, Program Directors tightened their program belts, and some programs were restructured to reduce costs. One of those mergers involved bringing YOU and School-Age programs together, with YOU Director, Joshua Fulcher, in charge of what came to be called the Expanded Learning Department. School Age Program Director, Valery Shepard, became assistant director for a short time, and then chose to retire.

Besides the work to raise capital dollars, Erie also contracted with the Executive Service Corps (ESC) to explore the feasibility of Erie starting a "social enterprise." The idea of running a small business was to generate revenue that was not subject to the politics of public funding or the ever-shifting guidelines of foundations. This idea had been percolating for years in the non-profit world, and there were several examples of successful endeavors. One of the most successful and longest running examples was Homeboys Industries in Los Angeles. It was founded by Fr. Greg Boyle in the 1990s and employed former gang members successfully for 20 years. Locally, the North Lawndale Employment Network, under the leadership of Brenda Palms-Barber, founded Sweet Beginnings in 2008, a bee-keeping, honey-producing business that hired ex-offenders. The story of Homeboys running into financial difficulties in 2010 was a cautionary tale. They had launched a capital campaign to buy a building, but, according to Fr. Boyle, failed to include operating expenses to support the programming that would occupy the building. Whether the Alford Group or Erie House, or both, knew this story, they included those operational start-up costs in their capital campaign planning.

When the ESC made their initial presentation to the Board in September 2014, Sy Nelson asked for some examples of the kind of enterprise Erie might consider. Kirstin responded with the possibilities of privatized child care, or a possible expansion of Visionaries' Etsy Store, "Four Star Creations." At that point, no one was left on the board who would have remembered Erie's earlier "social enterprise." It was called the thrift shop, and in Erie's early days, the revenue from this enterprise was always reported as one of Erie's revenue streams, as well as an example of how church volunteers were helping their neighbors in need of clothing at rock bottom prices. This enterprise had been the special domain of Erie's Woman's Auxiliary. They opened it in 1958, and as late as 1975, it was adding $12,000 to Erie's annual budget. It closed in 1992 after 34 years due to an increase in rent that Erie could not justify paying. The lesson here being, if you wait long enough, old ideas become new again, and probably, get a new name.

Quality and Consistency = Money in the Bank

As the Capital Campaign planning and Social Enterprise exploration proceeded, Erie continued to raise money the usual way--by working hard, running old programs better, and experimenting with new ideas. But the stalwart recipe was program quality + staff dedication, with a pinch of belt-tightening.

After an unprecedented 12 straight years of funding in six figures, the Marguerite Casey Foundation announced that 2015 would be the last year, but MCF left a parting gift of $75,000. Development would have to hustle to make up the difference. But other funding was in hand from prior years of success. For example, Health and Leadership was spending down its two 6-figure grants from the Kellogg Foundation and Johnson & Johnson.

ICIRR was so pleased with Erie's leadership of the NAI Northwest Collaborative, they increased Erie's grant in 2014 and added PASO (Proyecto de Acción de los Suburbios) to the group to assist the growing number of immigrants living in suburbs, such as Melrose Park, Stone Park, and Northlake. But in 2015, in the face of uncertain NAI funding, the Citizenship program decided not to schedule any workshops and to focus instead on their below-market-rate, fee-for-service, legal assistance for immigrants. By the end of the year, revenue from fees was up by $43,000. The suburban members of PASO were so thrilled with those newly accessible legal services, they gave Erie House an award.

After three years of successful outreach to the Latino community for CHA, Buen Hogar was poised to receive another CHA contract at the end of 2014. Instead the CHA extended their current contract to May of 2015, and then, to February of 2016. During this extension period, Buen Hogar received an award of $98,000 from an unusual source, the office of the Illinois Attorney General. Could this have been Erie's lobbyist at work?

Workforce Development had a new director, Julian Lazalde, and the Chicago Cook Workforce Partnership, with federal WIA (Workforce Investment Act) dollars to spend, increased Erie's allocation from $90,000 to $108,000. The program hosted a visit from

Eric Lugo, then at the Chase Bank Foundation, that was considering a grant for Pathways to Success. A grant was forthcoming, requiring a focus on OJT (on-the-job training). The Allied Health Care Career Network, organized and led by Erie House, was funded by grants from the Fry Foundation and Boeing. When Lazalde moved on, David Swanson, a workforce veteran by this time, took his place as Director. Pathways to Success also added a third bridge program in IT, sending their completers off to HPEVC for A+ certification training. Finally, at the invitation of the Puerto Rican Cultural Center and Community as a Campus, Swanson offered a class at the new "Parent University" housed at Clemente High School.

YOU was celebrating the 30th anniversary of TEAM in June 2014, and Visionaries was celebrating the first anniversary of the opening of its Etsy Store. STEM programming was engaged in a new venture with the Chicago Public Libraries through After-School Matters. As a consistent grantee of ASM, YOU participants were chosen to be part of the pilot for a new STEM-focused program called *Iridescent* that used a website called *Curiosity Machine.* Through another ASM science initiative, younger children got to work with youth and with their parents to build a sailboat and test it in a youth-built "mini-pond."They also built "an earthquake/tornado-resistant building they tested in "mini-gale force winds." This was followed by a STEM program led by an astronomy professor from Columbia College who worked with youth on understanding our sky, space, and the solar system and their importance in history. Youth were guided in building "nanotoriums," which are portable, electric displays of constellations. In the module following that, youth were building different musical instruments, and learning about frequency and the math behind sound. Scientists of the future were born every minute at Erie

House. And this was verified when YOU followed up with their grads in college in 2015 and discovered that 53% had chosen STEM majors.

Based on a follow-up study, YOU was able to document that 68.4 % of their former participants were on track to finish college in 4 years, a much less common occurrence among 21st century college students. No doubt, this outcome was fostered by the scholarship support that YOU had connected them to through the POSSE program, first mentioned in 2012. In 2014, YOU had a POSSE winner, for the second year in a row. Eddie Martinez would head off to Trinity College in Connecticut with a 4-year free ride.[465]

Side-by-side with science, Riza Falk had the Visionaries launch year two of their Etsy Store with a new product. It was a "Lotteria" set of cards that featured Chicago-based characters, with a special focus on activists in Chicago history. (The lotteria is described as "Spanish bingo.")

Besides enrolling more Head Start children than usual, to have more federal dollars to offset the reductions and delays in state payments, Child Care enrollment also received a boost from referrals that came from Onward House, when they closed their West Town site in August 2014, and moved to Belmont-Cragin. At the same time, in the Wicker Park neighborhood of West Town, North Avenue Day Nursery was closing their doors after 125 years. Gentrification and the state budget crisis were definite factors, but so was their model. They offered only Pre-school and After-School care. Celena, who had consulted with the Nursery director in an attempt to help, pointed out that Erie had been more successful in coping with gentrification because of more diversified programming and funding. Again, Erie benefited from referrals as they closed out their program in 2014. Along with referrals, Erie House received a gift of $750,000 from the Nursery.

Last but not least, almost two years to the day that Erie bid farewell to the network of Day Care Family Home providers, in November 2012, the city (DFSS) asked Erie to consider working with this type of provider again. At the time, Erie had discontinued support for the network because CPS had pulled its supplemental funding that paid for administration of the network, and because the Early Head Start (EHS) rate per child was so low. Under the new contract proposed by DFSS, Erie would be paid $170,000 to provide oversight for 16 homes, with an EHS rate of $8,000-9,000 per child. It is likely that Erie House was offered this opportunity based on their expert credentials. In 1990, they had been a pioneer in recognizing the value of a support network for independent providers—support that increased their success rate significantly. Their network oversight had gone on for more than 20 years when funding was withdrawn in 2012. For Erie, it was good to be back in a role they never wanted to step away from in the first place.

Also, after five years of struggling with enrollment, the After-School program got approved for an increase in subsidized slots, getting up to 99 at the House, + 5 private slots. In a sense, they did what Pre-school did 15 years earlier: reconfigure the service area and add whatever tools you need to make that work. They added a van to the tool box and went out to schools that did not have after-school care. In many cases, the children they recruited there had been Erie kids in pre-school who entered kindergarten in the neighborhoods where they lived, away from Erie. Many parents were glad to have their children in Erie's care once again. A few years later, the principal at the Erie charter school learned this lesson the hard way. Apparently, without consulting parents, he abruptly cancelled the ENH agreement to provide After-

School care. This angered many parents who held Erie House in great esteem and could not imagine what the principal was thinking. It would seem that he lacked an understanding of this historical relationship between the school and the House. Perhaps for this and other reasons the EECS Board let him go shortly thereafter. By then the After-School program had moved to a nearby CPS school, José De Diego Academy, and some EECS families followed. Attachment is a powerful emotion.

But in 2015, as Bruce Rauner took office, Erie House and the non-profit sector that depended on so many state contracts, could not imagine how bad things were going to get. For the next two years, the governor and the legislature would be engaged in a knock-down-drag-out fight that left the state without a budget, and the inability in too many cases to honor their contracts and pay their bills. A casualty of this situation was the capital campaign to build in Little Village. Part of the funding for that was a $1 million allocation from the state that provided a good baseline for private donors to match. But when those funds were frozen, private donors were reluctant to proceed without it. The Capital Campaign was put on hold, assuming that status would be short-lived. But as what was hoped would only be a month or two stretched into two years, the energy to resume had expired. Demolition of the residential property was carried out, but the cookie factory remained, symbolic of a dream deferred.

Staff Turnover Puts Erie on Edge

Frequent staff turnover was not a characteristic of Erie Neighborhood House. The first two executive directors each stayed for more than 20 years. Ravelo was ED for 12 years, and then stayed on as Senior Advisor for another 15. Nieves, Estrada, and Roldán, if you combine their time in a previous role with their time as ED, each stayed at least 10 years or more. Their HR Director, Maria Perez had reached her 30-year mark, and so would Louis Falk, in Child Care, before he retired in 2018. Dr. Yelen was well past 20 years, as was Susana Ortiz. Ema Peña rounded out 40 years. These were the extraordinary examples, but when Erie celebrated staff anniversaries each year, there were often a half dozen marking 10 years or more.[466]

So, Board members like David Tolen expressed concern when he heard that Sandy De Leon was leaving Erie not so long after being promoted from Director of Proyecto Cuidate to Director of Adult Programs. She was, in fact, the fourth Director of AP in less than three years since Tim Bell left, at the end of 10 years, in 2003. Celena attributed the turnover to the loss of the ICCB funding in 2012. That was certainly a destabilizing factor, but it could also be attributed to the fact that running AP was a little bit like herding cats. It consisted of several programs that came in and out of the department, including ESL, Community Literacy, Technology, Workforce Development, Citizenship and Immigration Services, Proyecto Cuidate, and Buen Hogar. Indeed, all of these programs did serve adults, but on so many different levels, and at two different locations. Maria Ugarte-Ramos was hired to replace Sandy as AP Director, but by September 2015, she was replaced by Cristina De la Rosa, while she continued to manage Buen Hogar.

Other turnover during this 2014-15 period included, Workforce Director, Julian Lazalde, who left for a position at the Latino Policy Forum after less than a year at Erie. Jane Lombardi replaced Megan Granados as Citizenship Coordinator, and Evelyn Rodriguez left Buen Hogar for a position in Alderman Moreno's office. Susana Ortiz, Coordinator of Community Literacy, was the only AP veteran employee left standing in an admin position.

As a response to all of this turnover, Celena offered the following:

> *Erie House has documented its ability to develop great leaders. Several have left to go on to run other great nonprofits, work in the Mayor's office or into philanthropy. Some stay and serve and are going on their 20th year of service with Erie. I learned at Erie House that you should invest and support people to be their best selves and their best leader, even if it means they end up leaving. If they do, it just means that Erie can say they had a part in their leadership development and what they are now doing to change the world.[467]*

As it became clear that Celena was thinking of moving on, possibly in 2015 or 2016, it was agreed it would not be wise for the Executive Director and the Senior Director of Programs to leave at the same time. So, discussion of a succession plan got under way.[468] This plan was based on the idea that the search for candidates should focus on someone with the qualities that could make them a candidate for executive director when Celena left. Ric had worked with programs when he succeeded Esther, and Celena came out of program experience to succeed Ric. The conclusion was that this position might again be the source of the next executive director.

The Search Committee offered two options for final interviews by the executive. Rebecca Estrada was chosen. She was known to Erie House for her competent role as TEAM Coordinator and YOU director, and she had administrative experience as Director of El Hogar del Niño. Rebecca held the SDP position for three years and moved on. Furthermore, the planned departure in the SDP position was followed by the unplanned departure of Betty Sanchez-Azadeh, the long-time Senior Director of Operations. There was not a new SDO until early 2015. That long a break in senior leadership is never good for an organization, and it did not reflect the type of succession planning Erie had been accustomed to. In the end, Erie persevered, managed changes it was not accustomed to dealing with, and continued the important work of helping its neighbors. Ultimately, the new executive director would come from within, but rather than from the program side, the source was the Development Department.

The Return of the Executive Order as Comprehensive Immigration Reform (CIR) is Deferred Again

It had been 27 years since the Immigration Reform and Control Act of 1986 was signed into law by President Ronald Reagan. There had been nothing since then, until the Senate passed the Border Security, Economic Opportunity, and Immigration Modernization Act (S.744) in June of 2013. However, it died in the 113th Congress when the House never even considered it. Thus, in 2014, the best CIR advocates could hope for was what was referred to by the Obama administration as "Administrative Relief" (AR). It was, more or less, a follow-on to DACA. This would also be an Executive Order, the president's strategy for dealing with an unresponsive Congress. The general ideas surfaced earlier, but the announcement was put off until after the elections in the Fall of 2014. The announcement outlined two components of Administrative Relief:

1. Deferred Action for Parents of Americans (DAPA) impacted undocumented parents of natural born citizens who have resided in the US since before January 1,

2010, and at the time of their DAPA request, have no criminal record.

a) DAPA was only a temporary protection from deportation, and does not provide a path to citizenship.
b) The application fee was $465, and application process opens May 19, 2015.
c) Employment authorization was for just 3 years.

2. DACA was expanded.

a) Removed the age cap requiring an individual to be under 31 as of June 15, 2012.
b) Start date for continuous residence period was advanced from June 15, 2007 to January 1, 2010.
c) DACA coverage now lasted for 3 years instead of 2. Applications opened Feb. 18, 2015.

On December 2, 2014, Celena reported to the Board the excitement surrounding the new executive order and what could potentially provide work authorization for up to 5,000,000 undocumented immigrants. Erie staff were preparing to share this news with Erie participants and the larger community, and to assist them with the application process once that was formalized. Specifically, she said,

> *All of us should pause to celebrate and acknowledge the importance of this moment and this announcement. Erie House was founded 145 years ago on the premise of assisting and empowering the immigrant community. Now after all of these years, we are once again being asked to assist and empower a whole new wave of parents and families that will need our help. This is our*

*mission and what we were created to do. . . All of
you as board members also had a part in this
historic advocacy victory as well because you
support Erie House and our work.* [469]

Erie house had figured out how to cope and survive, and
Finance Director Okamura pronounced that Erie was
doing OK. There had been losses, absolutely. And as
always, they impacted the community just as much, if not
more, than Erie House. But in its 145th year, it did it again-
-it survived, and it maintained its quality. Celena felt it
was time to move on, as she had planned, and be confident
that Erie would live to see its 150th year in 2020. During
her time at Erie, she had followed in Estrada's footsteps,
becoming a Leadership Greater Chicago Fellow, a
German Marshall Fund Fellow, and Erie House was
named Midwest Affiliate of the Year by Unidos US.

While the Board did conduct a search for her
replacement, she recommended passing the baton to her
Senior Director of Development, Kirstin Chernawsky. As
she described her recommendation to the Board, because
it was their decision to make, she said she believed that
the ongoing nightmare with public funding was moving
more and more non-profits to place greater emphasis on
private fundraising. She believed that Kirstin had the
heart to serve, had the political and corporate connections,
could make the six-figure ask, and could make the difficult
decisions to ensure Erie would make it for another 150
years.

Celena bid farewell to the Board at their February
2016 meeting. She shared in her interview that leaving
Erie House was one of the hardest things she had ever
done. "Erie helped me raise my son, and as a single
mother, it is something I will be forever grateful for."[470]
But her last hurrah for Erie was running the paddle raise
at the March 2016 gala. By this time, Erie had added the

projection of a thermometer on the hanging screens in the ballroom so the guests could see the red stripe go up as the bids came in. As she faced the audience to call for more bids, her back was to the screen, but she recalled that she did not have to turn around when the audience response indicated something exciting had happened. The red stripe had gone over $100,000. It was a thrilling moment for everyone and a great way for her to say *Hasta la Vista,* never *Adios.* Erie House never lets go.

Chapter Ten: Legacy of Excellence; Future of Promise

This final chapter, begins with a quote from Lonnie Bunch, historian and 14th Secretary of the Smithsonian Institution in Washington, D.C. He said, "History tells you as much about tomorrow as about yesterday."[471] As Mr. Bunch suggests, people should be studying the history of Erie Neighborhood House so that the Erie House of today, and anyone who cares about the future, knows what to do tomorrow. In other words, what lessons can be learned from this story that might direct, even inspire, forward movement with the mission, the sustaining vision, that takes an organization through 150 years? Such milestones should be celebrated, but also reflected upon. The occasion calls for recognition of this achievement; that is the primary purpose of this book and this final chapter--to highlight the wisdom in the Erie legacy of excellence, to sustain that future of promise, meeting challenges no more insurmountable than they were in the past.

The Immediate Future

As Kirstin Chernawsky succeeded Celena in 2016, providing a "historical perspective" at the time of this writing does not seem wise, while her leadership is still in forward motion. But what can be observed are the changes in the political context as Erie House was approaching its 150th year. On the national level, Erie House would face a major challenge in its work with immigrants as Donald Trump won the presidency late in Chernawsky's first year of 2016. The details of his anti-immigrant policies do not need to be repeated here. Throughout its history, since 1870, Erie

Kirstin Chernawsky (Erie Neighborhood House)

witnessed many waves of anti-immigrant policies, generally directed at non-European people of color, and rolled up its sleeves to provide support and defense for its neighbors impacted by these policies. But suffice it to say Kirstin recognized the need to change what had been a *program* of Citizenship & Immigrant Services on the Erie organizational chart into a *full department*, to address the tsunami of anti-immigrant, anti-refugee, white nationalist rhetoric threaded throughout the policies of Donald Trump. In launching its "deportation and removal defense initiative," Erie declared, once again: *¡PRESENTE!*

While Erie House remains non-partisan, experience has taught its leadership to run the social justice test on candidates in order to plan for new opportunities or to brace for negative impact. In this regard, Kirstin and Erie House could hope for a better scenario on the state and local levels, with the election of J.B. Pritzker as governor in 2018, and Lori Lightfoot as mayor in 2019. While most immigrant and refugee regulatory policies are federal, both of these officials have affirmed the commitment of Illinois and Chicago to be a sanctuary state and city. Hopefully, that will make state public funding for the services Erie provides more accessible, at least in principle. Unfortunately, both the state and city budgets were in deep holes dug by a long line of their predecessors. This reality underscores the point made in Celena's succession plan that private fundraising would remain a key to Erie's survival, and part of the rationale for her recommendation for a successor, such as Kirstin Chernawsky, who had demonstrated significant skills in this area. Kirstin herself followed the Erie Executive Director path as a Leadership Greater Chicago Fellow and in making *Crain's* "40 under 40" list. She was named Executive Director of the Year by the Executive Service Corps.

Besides serving immigrants and standing with them to challenge immigration policies that often need challenging, Erie has been well-known and well-respected for working with children. Since they opened their kindergarten in 1893, before kindergarten was offered through the public schools, Erie specialized in the pre-school years. When World War II drew many mothers into the workplace while their husbands fought overseas, the economic dimension of all-day care began to evolve. Over time, the demand for such care continued to grow, influencing Erie's decision in 1994 to take on a major organizational expansion to accommodate a much larger program, moving from serving 40 pre-schoolers to 185. Previous chapters traced the yin and yang of government support for this service, as more and more studies underscored the importance of these earliest years in the development of the child. Most policy-makers embrace these findings, but that has not meant that they accept the math that documents the actual cost of a high-quality program, or prioritize funding for this work at the top of their list. Or, as in the case of former mayor, Rahm Emanuel, they fail to understand the value of center-based child care at community-based organizations that can provide so much more than a classroom and an instructor.

Erie House has always had a high-quality program. That is a fact, and it is undisputed--by accrediting bodies, by funders, and by their peers in the field. Nevertheless, the maintenance of that quality has been under siege for the last 10 years. If crafting clear and fair immigration policy is complex, child care is right along-side it. In what might be called the golden age of child care around the time that Erie expanded in 1995, they would put together their budget, outlining actual costs, send the bill to the various city, state and federal agencies, and await their reimbursement. The funding agencies began to play havoc with quality in 2009, when they announced they were simply establishing a flat rate per child and said every agency would be paid the same. But programs were not the same. They were happy to tell Erie that they admired their Cadillac service, but they were only going to pay for a Chevy. On top of this move to pay less for more, a decision was made to do less. This would be accomplished by establishing income eligibility caps that cut off the working poor, that with the help of center-based child care, were becoming less poor, and without it, would go back to being poorer again. This also made it harder and harder for organizations like Erie to find children with working parents that could only have the poorest paying jobs to qualify--and dare not try to do better.

This scenario is now becoming further complicated by two new policies. First, the long fight to raise the minimum wage, a fight that Erie House fully supported, will, however, make the eligibility for affordable child care even more challenging, unless the income eligibility caps are adjusted accordingly. The good news is you are making more money, a more equitable wage; the bad news is you are going to have to quit your job if you can't find child care you can afford, because you just exceeded the income eligibility cap. At the proposed minimum wage of $15/hour, a worker's gross pay would be $31,200 per year. Of course, you can only spend net pay, generally about 75% of gross, after FICA and other taxes, and a possible deduction for the company health insurance. That leaves about $23,400 to spend. The housing expense guideline suggests a family should pay around 30% of their income on housing, rent and utilities. In that case, the housing allowance would be $7020/year, or $585/month. Good luck finding a decent place to live at that price in Chicago. By the time food and clothing are factored in, there is not a lot left to even pay for a Chevy's-worth of child care.

The second policy came as Mayor Emanuel was leaving office. His "parting gift" was to call for "Universal Pre-Kindergarten," or UPK, to be offered to all 4-year-olds at public schools. The good news for parents is that this will be free; the bad news is that it pulls the rug out from under center-based child care programs offered in the non-profit sector. Even Head Start, the lowest income-support program, requires providers to charge a sliding scale fee. As it was evolving, "no cost" service at CPS trumps "low cost" service at non-profit centers.

But it also means that the poor, once again, will have to settle for less. Waving a wand and saying "Presto!" you are now a provider of pre-school, may not result in what parents hope for. This program will be opening in schools that already lack the kind of "wrap-around" services like nurses and social workers—an issue in the 2019 Chicago Teachers Union contract negotiations. What might also be lacking is the expertise of "cultural sensitivity" that community-based centers have always demonstrated. Among many components that are lacking in the UPK plan, this one is especially critical. As Erie has always argued, effective education has never been simply about a classroom and an instructor. Immigrants have voted with their feet for years, opting for services at community centers versus public institutions because they do better when they are encouraged to not just gain knowledge, but also the respect and self-esteem that goes hand in hand with the books and the homework. If experienced providers, like Erie House, with a full-time psychologist and social worker, as well as a steady stream of graduate interns and other volunteers, were invited to bring their program into the school buildings, many of which are half empty, families and schools would both benefit. A good example of this approach is in evidence in the case of Erie's After-School program that moved into Jose De Diego Academy in 2018.

Needless to say, Erie House and their colleagues in the field have hit the advocacy trail to do their best to rescue the investment, made over 100 years, that evolved into a formula for how to deliver pre-school care in the Hallmark tradition: "When you care enough to send/do the very best. . ." That story is for a book on the next 150 years.[472]

Historical Foundations for the Longer Term

So, what does one look for, in Erie's history, that might indicate how many tomorrows Erie House is likely to see? As this chapter reviews key findings from this story, some of them simply underscore why Erie House is good. Examples of this goodness might include: a nationally accredited pre-school program, the 35-year old TEAM youth mentorship program, and all of the fine organizations Erie helped to develop and then spin off, such as Erie Family Health, Bickerdike, and the charter school. Part of the presupposition regarding a likely future is, of course, based on how good you have been so far. However, being good is not enough. Hull House was good, but it still closed its doors in 2012, and they are not the only ones. The question is: What are the characteristics of an organization that enables it to prevail when circumstances change, which they always do, when political environments become hostile, which they often do, and when leadership turns over, which is bound to happen? How does an organization grow older with wisdom, and yet stay evergreen? The answers to these questions found, in the Erie House story, should be indicators to funders, policy-makers, and even participants, that the Erie House model--the settlement house model--is worth their investment of money, and attention to their example. Erie has moved forward into its 3rd century of service--born in the 19th, lived through the 20th, and making it through the first 20 years of the 21st. The stories in this book suggest that Erie House could adopt as its slogan a quote from a frequently aired TV commercial, "We know a thing or two, because we have seen a thing or two." A logical conclusion: Pay attention.

The next few pages have utilized the "Values," posted on Erie's current web site, to correspond with an historic tradition that showed itself through the prior narrative, as an illustration of another way to communicate Bunch's message.

Promote education and wellness for families and individuals

A Holistic Approach with Educational Objectives

To begin with, the basic approach to programming at Erie is holistic. Erie House does not just offer child care, it is not a youth program, and it does not offer only adult education. Its services address the entire family. This is important for several reasons. First, a family is like a body: an integral unit with interconnecting parts. Children are the heart--a high priority in that unit. Parents care about their children's safety and their education, both of which affect their future. So, an agency that provides these for their children draws a parent's attention. But, as Jane Addams made clear, the settlement house was not just for children, but also for their parents and other adults. Over the years, Erie has found that it is rare when only one member of a family is enrolled in one program. The wrap-around service approach contributes to the overall success of the family and to the organization that provides it. So often, when one program is struggling with funding or enrollment, another one is thriving; a win in one area offsets a loss in another.

The child that comes to Erie House as a 2 or 3-year old, participates in After-School programming that continues all day during the summer, and then goes through high school with support from TEAM, and the opportunity to participate in STEM and/or Visionaries, has, in fact, been co-parented by Erie House. They have grown up in a milieu of service, of paying it forward. It is no wonder that many of them come back to Erie as employees, or TEAM mentors, or place *their* children in Erie's early childhood program. For 150 years, Erie has developed the capacity for multi-generational impact and created multiple pathways to success. This was not just a good name for Erie's workforce development program, but actually a description of its lifelong mission.

Even for those who first encountered Erie House as adults, they recognized this was a special place. Again, the wrap-around approach to adult education and citizenship has underscored one more time: that a classroom and an instructor were never enough. The availability of free tutoring and/or computer classes to supplement an ESL classroom experience, or get help with the math you needed for CNC class, has been there. Wrapping around that has been Erie's cultural sensitivity. Not only has Erie literally spoken their language, but every generation of immigrants has been able to celebrate their ethnic heritage, from the St. Joseph Table to the *ofrendas* for *El Dia de Los Muertos*. Whatever adults came to Erie House for, knowing their child was being taken care of in the next room, while they were striving for the skills to make that child's life a little more secure, was just one more reason why the immigrant communities of the last 150 years called it their second home.

With the family as the focus, promoting education and health became primary objectives. Erie concluded that education was the most important resource they could provide to assist families down that pathway to success, to climbing out of the cellar of poverty. Erie begins with early childhood education, continues through youth and adult education, with the understanding that education is linked closely with empowerment. This does not mean that Erie has shied away from "casework" when it was needed, but the focus on education has meant that teachers at Erie far outnumber social workers. Every department at Erie "teaches," whether the staff in that unit are formally called teachers or not. Erie is not officially a "school," but it is a laboratory that encourages experimentation in every way to help their neighbors to learn.

Early on, the corollary to education was health. Erie opened its first dental clinic in 1939. In honor of the occasion, Erie participants composed "The Dentist's Song," cited on page 58, but worth repeating part of it here:

For children who can't afford to pay
To have dental care, and so we say...
Our children can have this dental chair, and expert
care, because you share.
Our thanks to you. [the volunteer dentists]

Less than 20 years later, Erie opened its health care clinic with Dr. Snyder, and then the medical students from Northwestern. They became eager, not only for the opportunity to practice medicine on behalf of the poor, but also, grateful for the environment of a place like Erie House, already grounded in the community for more than 75 years, that had earned the trust of their neighbors who became trusting patients.

With a home and financial support for its first 30 years, the clinic was able to move forward as a separately incorporated entity that grew into the Erie Family Health Center, a metropolitan-wide, first-rate health service for the poor. What better gift could Erie give toward the health of its neighbors, in the community-sense of that word?

But medical services are only part of the health care equation. Prevention of poor health, through education, and example, took Erie back to Miss Florence's firm belief that prevention was of the utmost importance. Dr. Patricia Novick began with the Erie staff in 2006. If staff were not educated regarding their own health, how could they "sell" it to participants. Beginning with Super-H, aimed at healthy children, staff immediately took into account that this had to be a family approach, and parents were also engaged. As is often the case, the engagement itself turned out to be a mental health benefit, in the process of promoting physical health.

Amplify the voice of our community; Advocate for social change

The Bus is Out Front

Erie's adult education has always been more than programs to increase a participant's cognitive skills. Citizenship classes have never been only preparation for the test, but always a call to act like a citizen--to vote and to advocate for what you, your family, and your community need. Adult learning at Erie House is about finding your voice and your dignity. It may begin by speaking up with feedback on curriculum, through a student council, and move to knocking on doors in a GOTV campaign, whether documented or not. It might be by becoming a Tech Promoter and gaining the confidence to teach others the computer skills you have now mastered--in their own language, and from the perspective of one who had started where they are. It certainly involves getting on the bus, seeing what your state capital looks like, and insisting your elected officials hear what you have to say. Just because they have more education than you, does not always mean they are smart--in the sense of street-smart, neighborhood-smart, immigrant-smart.

Foster a spirit of service and inclusion

A Place to Come, An Open Door

Erie House, and settlement houses in general, have provided a welcome refuge for immigrants in a country with a history of welcoming them on one hand for their

536

contribution to the economy's bottom line, and then maligning their very persona on the other hand. When you are talked about as a "drain" on society that should be sent back to where you came from, or be prevented from coming here in the first place, it is essential to have a place to go that provides a respite from the harassment and embraces you as a person of value, "foreign" culture and all--a place that actually does speak your language, a place where the lady with the lamp is just outside the door, and that door is wide open. Erie participants have been quoted in this text, over and over, describing Erie as "a place to come to" or "my second home." Erie itself personifies the name of its housing services program; it is truly *"Buen Hogar,"* a good home, a warm hearth.

While Erie was making immigrants feel at home, the same hospitality was extended to volunteers. Many times over, volunteers commented on how welcome they felt when coming to Erie House. This has been another hallmark of Erie's success, while also contributing to the fulfillment of one of the goals of settlement house work, which is to facilitate an experience of reciprocity. Or, as Francis of Assisi put it, "It is in giving that we receive." One thing in particular that Jane Addams hoped they would receive was an understanding of and empathy for, the working poor, of people who were different, but NOT ALIEN. Not only did volunteers feel welcome, but they felt blessed, when they acknowledged how often they felt they got back even more than they gave. "Education through permeation," was the recommendation that came from Toynbee Hall in the earliest days of the settlement movement. Whether they were Presbyterian church volunteers, Mennonite Volunteers, or Northwestern University medical students, the value of reciprocity was acknowledged.

But before everyone gets too comfortable, basking in the warmth of reciprocity, genuine inclusion has not been endorsed by everyone in America. Far from it. So, it is time to get back on the bus, to take up the Erie banner and march, to go on record in a public way, that we, the immigrants of today and yesterday, are *¡PRESENTE!* Erie House can proudly say:

> *We have marched for civil rights with Rev. Cedarleaf, we have defended our neighborhood from the wrecking ball through COPA and NCO, we have fought to save our country from wasting the amazing potential of our Dreamers, who have grown up as Americans.* Join us.

Maintain strong community presence and partnerships

"If we don't hang together, we shall surely all hang separately." - Benjamin Franklin

And when Erie could not do it all, they created, or helped to create, other institutions to share the load: Erie Family Health Center, The Northwest Community Organization, Bickerdike Redevelopment Corp., West Town United, the Erie Elementary Charter School. Add to that some unique programs that served the community for decades, like the Thrift Shop, Meals on Wheels, and TEAM. Erie could also adopt the slogan: *Built to last.* The school is only 15 years old, but Bickerdike turned 50 in 2017, and Erie Family Health Center is past the 60-year mark. Meals on Wheels ended after "just" 37 years; TEAM celebrated its 35th anniversary and is still going strong. And, of course, Early Childhood Education/Day Care/Pre-school/Head Start, whatever you call it, Erie has been doing that for more than 125 years.

Throughout its history Erie has collaborated, coalesced, made sure Erie and their neighbors had a place at the table, that they "have their shot," as Alexander

Hamilton put it, via Lin-Manuel Miranda, who captured the immigrant experience so well in *My Shot.* "*I gotta holler just to be heard,*" and wisely added, "*With every word I drop knowledge.*" Erie recognizes that ordinary folks know what they need, and, when encouraged to speak, pols and bureaucrats need to listen. From Jane Addams, to Florence Towne, to Kirstin Chernawsky, this is what organizations serving in the settlement tradition do, whether they call themselves a settlement house or not. And when the neighbors are at work and cannot be present themselves, Erie speaks for them, as a "translator," not only from Spanish (or Italian or Ukrainian) to English, but also making known important community priorities to policy staff who make mistakes in isolation, when they only talk to one another. It does not always work, but its reputation has often preceded it: When Erie speaks, smart people listen.

And Erie also listens to its colleagues who have come to the table on behalf of *their* participants. And when there is no table, they join with others to set one. There have been so many "umbrella" organizations over the years that Erie House helped create or joined through their executive director, another staff leader, a board member, or one of their own participants. Just to name a few: Chicago Federation of Settlements, the Welfare Council, COPA, NCO, NCLR (now Unidos US), Latinos United, the Latino Policy Forum, the Illinois Coalition for Immigrant & Refugee Rights (ICIRR), the Coalition for African, Asian, European, and Latino Immigrants of Illinois (CAAELII), Equal Voices for America Campaign of the Marguerite Casey Foundation, Illinois Action for Children, the Coalition of Center-based Child Care Providers, the Chicago Jobs Council and the Allied Health Care Career Network. Just to name a few.

The Presbyterian Church and Erie Neighborhood House: 150 and Counting

Perhaps the longest-lasting partnership has been between Erie Neighborhood House and the Presbyterian Church. The Presbytery of Chicago, through its Mission Extension Board, has had the vision and understanding of the social gospel. When Holland Presbyterian Church was struggling, they did not walk away. Third Presbyterian Church stepped up and took the Noble Street Mission under its wing. When the Mission needed to evolve, the Erie Chapel Institute was incorporated. When new leadership was needed, Dr. Clyde Smith reached out to Rev. George Searles to take the risk for an opportunity to work with "people worthy of his time and commitment."[473] From there, the lay members of the church took on the responsibility of supporting Erie Neighborhood House, both financially and with great love. Hannah Templeton of Third Pres provided the funds to make the construction of the new building at 1347 W. Erie possible in 1935. Then it became the responsibility of board members like Walter Gielow and N. Ray Miller, to get it built—and to continue building, in the broadest sense of that word.

While Gielow and Miller were exchanging correspondence about who to give the carpentry contract to, the women of the church formed the Erie Woman's Auxiliary in 1924, and continued to meet monthly, at Erie House, for the next 70+ years. They raised funds and they raised volunteers and they founded "social enterprises." In 1964, their annual Sunshine Luncheon drew 200 women, representing over 30 Presbyterian churches throughout the metropolitan area. Together, these lay men and women put the wheels under the meals, showed up with their boxes on Tag Day, sorted clothes in the Thrift Shop, delivered gifts at Christmas, started a scholarship fund for youth to go to college, and painted a room or two. They showed up on Demonstration Night and applauded the children as they sang, danced, and staged plays. Then they created an endowment in the 1940s, the McGaw fund, as back-up for rainy days, a shelter Erie House has turned to many times. In the 1950s it was valued at around $52,000; in the 21st century it has been valued at over $2 million.

Often leading the way among their fellow congregants was First Church of Oak Park. Whether Rev. Ward was giving feedback to Miss Florence on her book, or Jim McClure of Gardner, Carton & Douglas (now Drinker, Biddle & Reath) was assisting with a legal matter, or Mark Jolicoeur of Perkins & Will was doing pro bono design work on an Erie project, or the women of First Church were holding their annual tea, and dropping checks in the basket by the door on their way out, First Church of Oak Park has been ¡Presente!

While Saul Alinsky went to the Catholic Church to start NCO in West Town, Protestant churches did not hesitate to join in, and the neighborhood houses of the Presbyterian church were leaders among them. Those Presbyterian clergy, some in leadership positions at the Presbytery who met Saul Alinsky, recognized the social gospel being preached by a Jew, and recognized the modern-day version of the kind of people Jesus hung out with in the person of poor, immigrant Catholics. They understood the point made by Fr. Richard Rohr, years later, as he argued that there is a problem with religion and/or Christianity, if it makes us feel "separate and competitive," instead of deeply connected. Dogma was not the issue; taking care of your neighbor was, whatever it took.[474]

In terms of the future, data suggests that church affiliation is not what it once was, in any denomination. Among the younger adult representatives of a smaller membership today, the daughters and granddaughters of

Erie Woman's Auxiliary are now frequently in the workplace, with less time to volunteer or attend meetings in West Town. How to engage the fourth generation, after the three prior generations have supported Erie, is a question Erie is attempting to sort out. The leadership at the Presbytery is still engaged, and when they turned over the deed to the building at 1347 W. Erie expressed their wish to continue this relationship that has been in place since Holland Presbyterian opened its doors on December 4, 1870. What form this will take remains to be seen.

Savvy and Caring Leaders

Characteristics described so far are true, due at least, to two key elements present at every stage of Erie's history: dedicated and savvy leadership, both in the form of executive directors and its board of directors. As to the executive directors, their extraordinary contributions influenced the decision to highlight each administration as a separate chapter in this book. Their time at Erie has never been just a "job." Their dedication represents a vocational call, even a ministry--not necessarily in the religious sense, but definitely in a spiritual one. Only one of Erie's executive directors was an ordained minister, but the first definition of "minister" is "servant." That description has fit them all, and most had the opportunity for an apprenticeship in servant leadership, in the position they held at Erie before becoming executive director. All, except Florence Towne and Merri Ex, have groomed their successor. Promoting from within has been another lesson that every organization should do its best to implement.

Every one of them has stepped up and taken the risk to lead, and leadership does involve risk. If you are doing the job right, you find yourself in someone's face on a regular basis. Often this is about money; even more often, it is about government policies and/or legislation.

Every one of them has followed the community organizing mantra: *Lead, follow, or get out of the way.* Erie executive directors have often led the way, sometimes yielded the lead to colleagues, and sometimes stepped out of the way to allow the community to speak for itself. This is the servant leadership praised in Isaiah 42:1-4.

Standing right behind these good executive directors, has been the Erie Board of Directors.[475] Of course, faces have changed, but the spirit seems to get passed on regardless. They do not micro-manage, but they keep their finger on the pulse of management. Treasurers and Finance Chairs know what they are talking about when they make their reports. They raise red flags, they establish review dates when funding is unsure, they applaud program quality, and they raise money. Whether it has been shaking a box on Tag Day, running a booth for Mayfair, writing to friends and family for the Holiday Appeal, or writing checks themselves, they have been beyond generous. Whether they "approve of marching" or not, they do not question Erie's commitment to advocacy. For much of Erie's history, the majority of board members came from Presbyterian churches or were descendants of church people. Gradually, that has been changing, with both the addition of program participants, and other non-Presbyterian folks. Maintaining a board with the same spirit of commitment will be one of those assets that ensures Erie's future.

The Ongoing Funding Challenge

With a budget in the $9-10 million range, raising that amount of money year after year continues to be both an art and a science. Directors of Development are there to help, but often it is the ED that has to make the sales pitch. For the most part, Erie has received support from numerous foundations. Just about every major foundation in Chicago has given to Erie House, sometimes with grants in six figures. The Chicago Community Trust (CCT) and the Wieboldt Foundation were among the earliest donors, starting in the 1940s before writing proposals to foundations was even a significant component of Erie's fundraising strategy. The McCormick Foundation, The Northern Trust Bank, and Tribune Charities have also been long-time funders. The MacArthur Foundation, the Lloyd A. Fry Foundation, Woods Charitable Fund, Prince Charitable Trust, Sara Lee, Boeing, Goose Island Brewing Co., Chase Bank, Bank of America, have all been donors. Outside of Chicago grants have come from the Kellogg Foundation, Johnson & Johnson, the Marguerite Casey Foundation, and NCLR/Unidos US. More recently, as engineers were recruited to serve as TEAM mentors, financial support has come from several engineering firms, with Woodward being the most prominent. There have been many others that have been unintentionally omitted here.

It is also important to note, that some funding opportunities were intentionally omitted, so to speak. Besides raising funds, the success of Erie House and other non-profits lies in knowing when to say NO. The temptation to take whatever money is on the table has led to the ruin of more than one organization. If the funding calls for work outside the mission, or beyond an organization's expertise, experience recommends it be left on the table. Erie has generally made good decisions in this area. Its future success will depend on continuing to make that call.

Also, on the private side, but in a different context, Erie House has been the beneficiary of United Way, since it was still called the Community Fund. There was a period of decline in general operating grants, a drop of about $100,000 between FY93 and FY99. But that was actually offset by United Way's new concept, called Priority Grants. These were grants that followed the manner of foundation-giving. They were awarded to a specific category of program, such as Child Care, Workforce Development, etc. Erie was awarded several of those grants that were often quite generous. United Way is still a significant funder, but with the movement of many companies out of the city, the state, or even the country, there are fewer and fewer employees to donate through payroll deductions, the source of UW's funding.

Erie House has also been successful in securing public dollars, mostly on the state and city level, and some of that money involves federal dollars that are passed through local governing bodies, like Head Start. The Erie budget is full of government department acronyms, such as CCW, CPS, DFSS, DCFS, IDHS, DCEO, ISBE and ICCB. Without spelling them out, at one time or another, one of these public entities sent money to Erie House. The largest amounts were always for Child Care. The 21st century challenges with child care/pre-school funding were chronicled earlier, a potential threat to Erie's revenue stream down the road.

Besides changing foundation guidelines and the vagaries of politics that affect government funding, the other issue that might have been a threat to Erie funding was the gentrification of West Town. Beginning with Rafael Ravelo in 1985, Executive Directors and board members have worried about the changes in neighborhood demographics that have taken Erie's home base community off of funding priority lists. The questions of "move or stay" have been on and off the agenda for years. Onward House left West Town for Belmont-Cragin, Association House moved to Humboldt Park. Chicago Commons closed Emerson House and Taylor House and is now headquartered on the south side. It maintains one facility near Erie House in West Humboldt Park.

To date, Erie House has maintained its "motherhouse" at 1347 W. Erie, and its child care facility at 1701 W. Superior--both locations that have been within a half mile of their beginnings in 1870. However, beginning with the opening of the Erie Community Center in 1995, Erie began to re-define "Neighbor." It was no longer just the person who lived next door or down the block. The expanded child care program marketed itself to Humboldt Park and Logan Square as well as West Town. Then, in 2004, Erie House arrived in Little Village, not with a building, but with plenty of services the Mexican immigrant community there was hungry for, and Little Village was on every funder's list. They became Erie's new neighbors and will continue to be for the foreseeable future. With the outstanding reputation that YOU has maintained with its TEAM mentoring program, and with the addition of three Noble Network high schools within a half mile, YOU has been able to put its space expansion of 2009 at the House to good use, staying on and thriving in West Town. With these strategic adjustments, Erie has been able to maintain its place in West Town and still be eligible for funding to serve low-income immigrants.

So, to paraphrase Ravelo's observation back in the early 1990s, when the Chicago Neighborhood Experiment report was published, we cannot stop gentrification, but we can influence its effects, and we must plan for the future before it is upon us. So far, Erie House has followed that advice, and managed the impact of gentrification successfully. By inviting new neighbors to benefit from its quality programs, it has managed to stay *and* move.

In Conclusion

"Staying" and "moving" are actually two good concepts to wrap up the essence of Erie House. It has had the staying power for 150 years, for all the reasons above, and for those same reasons, has been able to stay at its address on Erie Street since 1886. But in Erie's case, staying has not been a static affair. Their scope of service, their outreach to those in need, has gone far beyond Erie Street. On the one hand, they have stayed with their family orientation which has fit the needs of every immigrant group that has come to their door, while at the same time, making those changes that diversity and changing times required.

Reflection on this process brings to mind Aretha Franklin's iconic song: R-E-S-P-E-C-T. That is what Erie has earned for its dedication to quality and the R-E-S-P-E-C-T it has demonstrated for its neighbors. R-E-S-I-L-I-E-N-C-E does not lend itself so well to becoming a song lyric, but it stands in importance next to respect. Some might say that resilience is synonymous with 150 years. But like so many other resources for survival, resilience has to be earned--worked for. As Merri Ex said to the *Reader* reporter in 1980, ". . .nothing miraculous, just hard work and enthusiasm."[476]

Enthusiasm may not head the list of how to be successful, but it should. People have kept coming to Erie House over the years for the quality of their programming, for the respect that empowers them, and along the way, get caught up in the enthusiasm for service that has infected generations of participants and volunteers. Moving forward is important; having the pleasure of paying it forward is invaluable.

The Open Door, A Place to Come to, Our Second Home--these are all reflections of a deep attachment to a place--and an experience. In her biography of Juliette

Kinzie, a founding mother of Chicago, Ann Durkin Keating writes:

> *Many Chicagoans in subsequent generations share her [Kinzie's] loss of place as their neighborhoods also evolved beyond recognition. But the idea of a neighborhood, grounded not in individuals or the market but in families and households working together, endures to the present.*[477]

That grounding is reflected in Erie's 2019 Vision Statement, that describes Erie as "A home with no borders." Following the mass shooting in El Paso in 2019, a *Wall Street Journal* reporter reflected on the notion of "attachment," and put forth the argument that the increasing frequency of such horrific events in the US, are due to an alienation of individuals who have lost places, or a sense of attachment. Families break up, churches decline, settlement houses have closed. It is worth thinking about, and part of why it is important to celebrate 150 years of attachment, as Erie House has continued to be a neighbor among neighbors, and followed "Our Creed", spelled out in 1951:

> *We believe all men are our brothers*
> *And within our neighborhood*
> *That which separates us from each other*
> *Also cuts us off from God.*
> *Here at Erie all are equal*
> *Striving for a common good. . .*
> *As we gladly share with others*
> *So, we find ourselves made whole.*

Amen. May the fostering of wholeness continue for another 150 years.

Photos Throughout the History of Erie Neighborhood House

*This selection of photos is courtesy
of Erie Neighborhood House,
Maureen Hellwig, Bickerdike, and
the Chicago History Museum.*

The sign that was posted on the wall of the Erie Chapel Institute building that served as the early version of Erie Neighborhood House from 1886 to 1936.

Sunday Services took place in the Templeton Memorial Chapel from 1936 until 1968. During the week, it often served as a meeting place for groups like the Erie Woman's Auxiliary, that prompted Miss Florence to remark: "We pray and spill coffee in the same space."

Rev. Doug Cedarleaf at the pulpit from which he urged his members, in 1945, to accompany him and Miss Florence as they escorted their new African American neighbors back to their home on Throop Street.

The Strong family, whose home and whose lives had been threatened by local racists, pictured here, surrounded by their new friends at Erie Neighborhood House. The words "Neighbor" and "Democracy" are evident on the signs carried by Erie marchers that day.

Rev. Cedarleaf leads his congregation in song, as the words "neighbor" and "Democracy" are evident on the signs carried by Erie marchers that day.

Here is Miss Rose with her Kindergarten class, acknowledging that she, herself, had attended kindergarten at Erie 15 years earlier—the beginning of a continuous pattern of an "Erie kid" returning as an employee years later.

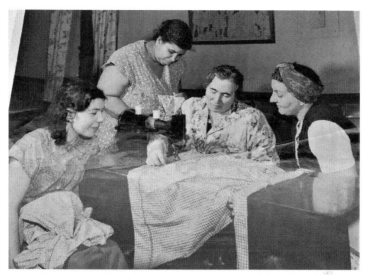

Mrs. Mary Savino, known as "Mom" to everyone at Erie, (seated here to offer a sewing lesson) crossed the street in 1928, and entered the place she would volunteer, work, and eventually live for the next 50 years. With a little help from Miss Towne, she would be named "Mother of the Year" in 1949 by the State Street Council.

Seated on the left is Dr. Snyder, co-founder of the Erie Clinic, with Rev. Ben Richardson & Rev. Lyman to the right of the nurse. From its beginning at Erie in 1957, the clinic grew into the Erie Family Health Center with 13 locations in the Chicagoland area in 2019.

Sister Antonelda (Sister Marian Dahlke), a School Sister of St. Francis, was principal of Santa Maria Addolorata school, and the first nun to serve on the Erie Board. Here she is addressing a community meeting, probably sponsored by NCO or COPA, where she and her sisters were also active in the 1960s and 70s.

Assembled at this groundbreaking are key players that founded Bickerdike Redevelopment Corp. in 1967 that successfully built affordable homes and apartments for low-and-moderate-income residents in West Town for the next 50 years. From left to right is Fr. Pajak, pastor of Holy Innocents, Juan Sierra & Jack Irving from COPA, and on the far right is Ross Lyman of Erie House.

Bickerdike began by building single-family homes, like this one in the 1400 block of Erie Street, with mortgages subsidized under the federal Section 235 program.

To address the demand for more affordable rental units, Bickerdike started building units like these, located in the Erie service area at Noble & Huron in the 1970s, under the federal Section 8 program.

These Erie pre-schoolers could be building the city of tomorrow. At Erie's Child Care Center they were given the tools to make that possible—the building blocks of imagination and encouragement.

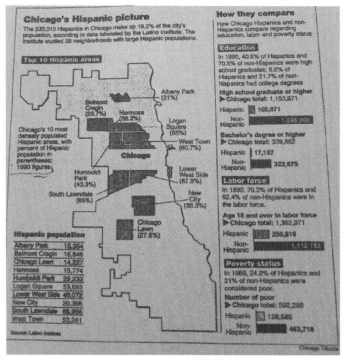

Erie studied these 1990 statistics on Latinos in Chicago. Only South Lawndale (Little Village) and Logan Square had more than West Town.

When Erie was approached by the Lloyd A. Fry Foundation in 1995 to come up with a really innovative idea, and thus, win a very large grant, Erie's Technology Center opened to the community, providing them the opportunity to learn a "third language"—IT.

In 2004, at the invitation of that community, and with support from a Western Union grant funded by a court settlement, Erie opened its door in Little Village at 4225 W. 25th Street to serve its burgeoning Mexican immigrant community.

John Hall, founder of the Goose Island Beer Company, and supporter and benefactor during his 30 years on the Erie Board, would be honored with the "Lifetime of Legacy Award" at Erie's 150th anniversary dinner.

In August, 2019, the 1300 block of Erie Street, the home of ENH since 1886, got one of Chicago's Honorary Street Signs.

Here they are, the men and women who led Erie House from 1977 to 2015. L to R: Ricardo Estrada, Merri Ex, Celena Roldan, Rafael Ravelo, and Esther Nieves.

Erie Youth participants of 2019, the fifth generation of young immigrants who found an open door and a second home at Erie House.

NOTES

[1] The idea of a "heyday" of the settlement movement is presented by Allen Davis, *Spearheads for Reform: The Social Settlement Movement and the Progressive Movement, 1890-1914.* Rutgers University Press, 1985.

[2] See www.eriefamilyhealth.org

[3] See www.bickerdike.org

[4] Moreover, starting with Miss Towne's successor, Rev. Ross Lyman, and continuing to the present day, I have known and worked with every director, as a volunteer and/or employee, giving me a unique perspective for relating this story that has been waiting to be told.

[5] Interview with Mary York, October, 2003

[6] For those unfamiliar with Alinsky, a Chicagoan by birth and temperament, he is best known as "The Father of Community Organizing." He outlined his beliefs in the importance of a community organizing strategy in his book, *Reveille for Radicals,* first published in 1946, and many times thereafter. He advocated that strategy primarily to engage ordinary people in fighting for their rights, to defend their local communities against both private and public agendas to destroy them, or at least reshape them in their own interests. After his success in a Chicago neighborhood, called Back-of-the-Yards, he went on to establish the Industrial Areas Foundation to raise funds, to promote community organizing and train organizers to work in many other cities.

[7] Chicago is divided into 77 community areas. West Town is Area # 24, and each community area number corresponds to the same census tract numbers.

[8] Humboldt Park is both a community area (#23) and an actual park. It was developed as part of what came to be known as the "boulevard park system" in Chicago. The concept was approved by the Illinois state legislature in 1869. It consists of 26 miles of parks connected by boulevards, from the north to south sides of the city. That portion of the system that included Humboldt Park was designed by William Le Baron Jenney, an architect, considered to be the "Father of the American Skyscraper." The main body of the park lies between California (2800 west) and Kedzie (3200 West) and North Avenue (1600 north) and Division (1200 north) and is linked by boulevards to Garfield and Douglas Parks to the south.

[9] Andreas, Alfred T. *History of Chicago: From the Earliest Times to the Present, Vol. 3, 1872-1885.*

[10] *Encyclopedia of Chicago.* Edited by James R. Grossman, Ann Durkin Keating, and Janice Reiff, and developed by The Newberry

Library with the cooperation of The Chicago Historical Society. University of Chicago Press, 2004, p. 1002.

[11] Ibid. p. 250-251.

[12] Erie Neighborhood House Archives, Chicago History Museum (CHM), hereafter referred to by box number and file number. This note is from CHM Box 4, File #1.

[13] Third Pres 100th Anniversary booklet, CHM Box 14, File 31.

[14] CHM Box 4, File #1.

[15] Lovoll, Odd, *Encyclopedia of Chicago*, pp.579-580

[16] Tjoelker, Elizabeth. "A Neighbor Among Neighbors: Erie Neighborhood House and the Presbyterian Church of Chicago, 1870-1990." Unpublished Master's Project, Loyola University Chicago, 2004, p. 7.

[17] Ibid.

[18] Ibid.

[19] See Chicago Ancestors site/Newberry Library. www.chicagoancestors.org

[20] Ibid.

[21] Holli, Melvin and Peter d'A. Jones, Editors. Grand Rapids, Michigan: William B. Eerdmans Publishing Company, 995, p. 93.

[22] Ibid.

[23] Nelson, Bruce. *Beyond the Martyrs: A Social History of Chicago's Anarchists, 1870-1900. New Brunswick, NJ, 1988, p. 333.*

[24] As late as 1922, four years after World War I had ended, my own third generation German father was warned by my grandmother never to speak German, only English. And, as he shared later in life, he missed out on the opportunity to be bilingual.

[25] CHM Box 4, File #1.

[26] CHM Box 13, File #6

[27] *Chicago,* poem by Carl Sandberg

[28] Holli, p. 230

[29] Candeloro, Dominic. *Italians in America.* Images of America Series. Arcadia Publishing. 1999, P.23.

[30] Pacyga, Dominic, *Encyclopedia of Chicago,* p.622

[31] Kantowicz, Edward, Holli, p.174.

[32] Victoria Granacki. *Chicago's Polish Downtown.* Images of America Series. Arcadia Publishing, 2004, p.6.

[33] *Pacyga, Encyclopedia of Chicago, p. 624.*

[34] Holli, p. 176.

[35] Encyclopedia of Chicago, p. 624

[36] Holli, p.179.

[37] Kantowicz, in Holli, p, 177, cites the work of Jacob Horak, "Assimilation of Czechs in Chicago" (PhD diss., University of

Chicago, 1924), pp. 74-75; and the work of Victor Greene, *For God and Country, pp.54-56.*

[38] Holli, p. 178. Source: Polish Museum.

[39] CHM Box 13, File # 6.

[40] In addition, the author had access to unpublished research done by Elizabeth Tjoelker, conducted as a graduate student at Loyola University Chicago, in 2004.

[41] Davis, Allen F. *Spearheads for Reform: The Social Settlement Movement and the Progressive Movement, 1890-1914.* Rutgers University Press, 1985, p.13.

[42] Stockwell, Clinton. "Standing on the Shoulders of Giants: The Protestant Legacy of Urban Social Justice in Chicago" *PRAGmatics,* February, 1999, p. 6.

[43] Ibid.

[44] Addams, Jane. *Twenty Years at Hull-House,* 1909. Signet Classics edition, 1961. Reprinted 2009, pp. 52-56.

[45] Ibid., p.54.

[46] Stebner, Eleanor J. *The Women of Hull House: A Study in Spirituality, Vocation, and Friendship.* New York: State University of New York Press, 1997, p. 44.

[47] "Religion in the Settlements," *National Conference of Charities and Corrections Proceedings, 153.*

[48] Ibid.

[49] Marty, Martin. *Modern American Religion, Volume 1: The Irony of It All, 1893–1919, 76.*

[50] Cited by Stebner, p. 30.

[51] G.K. Chesterton, *Irish Impressions.*

[52] *Twenty Years at Hull House*, p. 83.

[53] *CHM Box 13, File # 6.*

[54] Ibid.

[55] *Twenty Years at Hull House,* p. 59.

[56] Ibid., p.73

[57] Ibid., p. 67

[58] Ibid., p. 70

[59] This statement was personally heard by the author on many occasions, as Ann Seng was one of her mentors, an early and important one.

[60] Davis, *Spearheads,* 20

[61] Stebner, p. 75

[62] Ibid., p. 3

[63] Ibid., p. 40

[64] Addams, "Social Settlements in Illinois," *An Illinois Reader,* ed., Clyde C. Walton. De Kalb: Northern Illinois University Press, 1970, 332.

[65] CHM Box 13, File #6

[66] CHM Box 4, File #1

[67] Today, a bank, with a small strip mall behind it, occupies the space that was originally La Roc's.

[68] CHM Box 9, File #

[69] CHM Box 12, File #7

[70] See Ganz, Cheryl R. and Margaret Strobel, editors. *Pots of Promise: Mexicans and Pottery at Hull House, 1920-1940.* Chicago and Urbana: University of Illinois Press, 2004.

[71] CHM Box 12, File #7

[72] CHM Box 4, File #1

[73] Ibid.

[74] CHM Box 12, File #4

[75] Ibid.

[76] Poethig, Richard. "Toward Worldwide Industrial Mission: The Presbyterian Story, 1945-1975." *American Presbyterians,* Vol. 73, #1, Spring, 1995, p. 35

[77] Towne, Florence H. *Neighbors.* Chicago: Published by the Board of Directors of Erie Neighborhood House, 1940, p. 25

[78] Thomas had been a "silent partner" at Marshall Field's.

[79] CHM Box 1, File #2

[80] Ibid.

[81] Ibid.

[82] Ibid.

[83] CHM Box 13, File # 6

[84] CHM Box 1, File #4

[85] Ibid.

[86] CHM Box 11, File #9

[87] His plaque still hangs, somewhat obscurely, in the outer vestibule that precedes the lobby.

[88] CHM Box 1, File #7

[89] CHM Box 13, File #7

[90] CHM Box 1, File #7

[91] Vol. 17, pp. 33-34

[92] CHM Box 2, File #1

[93] Ibid.

[94] CHM Box 1, File #3

[95] CHM Box 13, File #1

[96] CHM Box 12, File #3

[97] CHM Box 14, File #1

[98] Ibid.

[99] CHM Box 12, File #3

[100] Marion De Vincent, Interview in 2003

[101] CHM Box 11, File # 2

[102] CHM Box 4, File #1

[103] Ganz, Cheryl R. and Margaret Strobel, editors. *Pots of Promise: Mexicans and Pottery at Hull House, 1920-1940.* Chicago and Urbana: University of Illinois Press, 2004.

[104] CHM Box 4, File # 1

[105] CHM Box 3, File #3

[106] Towne, Florence H. *Sheep of the Outer Fold.* Chicago: Fleming H. Revell Company, 1929.

[107] Towne, Florence H. *Neighbors.* Chicago: Published by the Board of Directors of Erie Neighborhood House, 1940.

[108] Ibid.

[109] Forward to Florence Towne's *Neighbors*

[110] Ibid., 14-19

[111] Ibid., 60-66

[112] Ibid., 60

[113] CHM Box 11, File #3

[114] CHM Box 13, File #6

[115] CHM Box 2, File #3

[116] CHM Box 3, File #3

[117] Ibid.

[118] In citing documents from historical periods, the word "Negro" was the common parlance. It is used strictly in that historical context. Otherwise, in all but this historical context, it is replaced with the more respectful and politically correct "African American."

[119] Kurt Peterson, *Forum, Dialoging with the Covenant Quarterly*, no date, but after 2003, http://forum.covquarterly.com. Found in CHM Box 2, File #6.

[120] CHM Box 3, File #3

[121] Ibid.

[122] "With Dismal Regularity," *Time,* March 5, 1945, 54, in CHM Box 2, File #6.

[123] Peterson, *Forum, Dialoging with the Covenant Quarterly.*

[124] CHM Box 13, File #6

[125] CHM Box 13, File # 6

[126] Ibid.

[127] CHM Box 13, File # 8

[128] Gielow memorial Service, CHM Box 3, File #3

[129] CHM Box 13, File #1

[130] CHM Box 3, File #4

[131] CHM Box 4, File # 6

[132] "Gardner Carton set to merge," by Ameet Sachdev, *Chicago Tribune,* November 14, 2006

[133] CHM Box 3, File #4

[134] CHM Box 2, File #6

[135] CHM Box 2, File # 2

[136] Ibid.

[137] CHM Box 13, File #21

[138] CHM Box 2, File #5

[139] CHM Box 12, File # 7

[140] CHM Box 2, File # 5

[141] Ibid.

[142] As Senior Director of Programs, and a long-time associate of Erie, I was often called upon to give a tour with a little history thrown in. We would generally start in front of the portrait of Miss Towne that hangs over the fireplace in the lobby of 1347 W. Erie. I recall thinking that this was the first Japanese person I was aware of that had stopped by with an interest in Erie House.

[143] CHM Box 2, File # 4

[144] Ibid.

[145] Ibid.

[146] CHM Box 11, File #2

[147] Ibid.

[148] CHM Box 3, File # 5

[149] Ibid.

[150] At the time of this writing, in 2019, all but Emerson House still exist, but not all in the same location.

[151] CHM Box 4, File # 4

[152] From years of working at Erie House, I met a number of people who just stopped by to share an Erie connection that had either made a difference in their lives or that of someone else in their family.

[153] CHM Box 2, File #5

[154] Ibid.

[155] Ibid.

[156] Jim Wallis. *America's Original Sin: Racism, White Privilege, and the Bridge to a New America.* Grand Rapids, Michigan: Brazos Press, 2016.

[157] For an in-depth look at how federal, state, and local government partnered with the private sector in promoting segregation see Richard Rothstein's *The Color of Law.*

[158] See *American Pharoah* by Cohen & Taylor.

[159] Pérez, Gina M. *The Near Northwest Side Story: Migration, Displacement, and Puerto Rican Families.* Berkeley: University of California Press, 2004.

[160] Luis Gutierrez with Doug Scofield. *Still Dreaming: My Journey from the Barrio to Capitol Hill.* New York: W. W. Norton & Company, 2013.

[161] Perez, 11.

[162] CHM Box 2, File #6

[163] CHM Box 5, File # 2

[164] Ibid.

[165] Ibid.

[166] CHM Box 12, File # 3

[167] CHM Box 7, File # 1

[168] *CHM Box 8, File # 8*

[169] Ibid.

[170] Ibid.

[171] Ibid.

[172] Ibid.

[173] A copy of this issue, dated March 1, 1959, can be found in CHM Box 4, File # 1.

[174] Ibid.

[175] Ibid.

[176] CHM Box 4, File # 1

[177] Ibid.

[178] Ibid.

[179] Ibid.

[180] Ibid.

[181] CHM Box 13, File # 5

[182] E-Box 2, File # 1. "E-Boxes" refer to those boxes of Erie papers not yet archived at the Chicago History Museum, as of December 31, 2019.

[183] Ibid.

[184] Ibid.

[185] Ibid.

[186] CHM Box 8, File #8

[187] Some funds also came from the Chicago Federation of Settlements annual United Settlement Appeal.

[188] Harrington, 5-7; 38-39. Found in CHM Box 14, File #1.

[189] Most of the churches in this story, referred to as Protestant, were Presbyterian. However, Union Church of Hinsdale and Glenview Community Church belonged to the United Church of Christ. The UCC came into existence in the 1950's as a result of the merger of two denominational strains: the Evangelical and Reformed Church & Congregational Christian Churches.

[190] Horwitt, Sanford D. *Let Them Call Me Rebel.* New York: Vintage Books, Division of Random House, Inc., 1993.

[191] Ibid, 269

[192] Ibid., 321

[193] Ibid., 333

[194] Ibid., 361

[195] Ibid., 366

[196] English Standard Version

[197] Horwitt, 384.

[198] Ibid., 386

[199] Most of the description of NCO here is based on my own, first-hand knowledge of NCO, as I came to know it and work with it, from 1968-1978, supplemented by the NCO files archived at the Chicago History Museum.

[200] Summary based on personal observation and participation

[201] In the early 1970s, I chaired the NCO Education Committee, which, in turn, organized the Campaign for a new Tuley High School. The new school was built at the corner of Western (2400 west) and Division (1200 north) and was named after Roberto Clemente, the Puerto Rican baseball player who lost his life on December 31, 1972, in a plane crash, bringing emergency relief to victims of an earthquake in Nicaragua. The old Tuley building, at 1313 N. Claremont, became the Jose De Diego Academy, a K-8 school.

[202] Janiak Obituary, *Chicago Tribune,* December 22, 2000.

[203] Jane Jacobs. *The Death and Life of Great American Cities.* New York: Vintage Books, A Division of Random House, 1992. (First published in 1961), 171.

[204] See Adam Cohen & Elizabeth Taylor. *American Pharaoh.* Boston: Little, Brown & Co., 2000.

[205] See Rothstein, *The Color of Law.*

[206] I heard, first-hand, the story told by Fr. Frank Cantieri, pastor of what was then Annunciation parish in West Town. Since the rectory looked like other Victorian buildings on the block, Cantieri opened the door one day to a realtor making a block-buster call. The real irony was that Fr. Cantieri was the chair of the NCO Real Estate Practices Committee that was picketing real estate offices known for block-busting.

[207] 50 years later, the Noble Square Co-op has prospered. Over the years, while some questioned if the lone high-rise was a "project," a reference to public housing, the townhomes were seldom thought of in those terms. Supporters of "community-based planning" would argue that it would be a different story if 3 high-rises and no townhomes had been the final plan.

[208] Much of the material for this story from the early days of NCO, and the steps that led up to the creation of Bickerdike are taken from an unpublished paper, "Bickerdike, The Early Years: Building the Base, 1966-1974," by Bruce Gottschall, an eyewitness and participant.

[209] Gottschall paper.

[210] CHM Box 8, File #12

[211] Ibid.

[212] "Erie-Eckhart Project First NCO Rehab Plan." *Northwest Community Observer,* February 21, 1965. Found in CHM Box 8, File #9.

[213] CHM Box 8, File #12.

[214] Ibid.

[215] E-Box 2, File #9

[216] Gottschall's paper on origins of Bickerdike.

[217] CHM Box 12, File # 7

[218] CHM Box 13, File # 17

[219] Rothstein, Chapter 4.

[220] NCO Box 60, File #8. NCO boxes are also archived at the Chicago History Museum.

[221] Reference is to book by Cardinal Leon Joseph Suenens. *The Nun in the World: Religious and the Apostolate.* Newman Press, 1963.

[222] Interview with Annette Ferriano Wood, 5/22/ 2019

[223] Terese Brown Sanchez interview, 5/18/2019

[224] The Y used to be located on the southwest corner of Division and Ashland

[225] Phone interview, 5/22/2019.

[226] As Sister Maureen, I became chair of the NCO Education Committee, eventually served on the NCO board, and co-chaired the "Campaign for A New Tuley High School" that resulted in the construction of Roberto Clemente High School at Division and Western in the 1970s.

[227] *Chicago Presbyterian,* December, 1968, p. 1

[228] Interview with Merri Ex, 3/6/2019

[229] Interview Angela Carroll, 6/8/2019

[230] CHM Box 14, File # 1

[231] E-Box 1. File #3

[232] Ibid.

[233] By 2020, having served in that role for about 40 years, she has attained significant influence on behalf of her constituents, and is considered a close associate of Speaker of the House, Nancy Pelosi.

[234] Interview with Merri Ex, 10/2/2018

[235] Ibid.

[236] Ibid.

[237] See William Grimshaw, *Bitter Fruit: Black Politics and the Chicago Machine, 1931-1991.* Chicago: The University of Chicago Press, 1992.

[238] Interview, 10/2/2018

[239] I had also gotten involved with the planning process, working with Ms. Kaptur and the community leaders who participated on her committee – a group of Poles, Puerto Ricans, Mexicans, and Fr. Hillenbrand. It had been a great opportunity for a newly minted planner to work with a more experienced one on behalf of the neighborhood she had come to know and love. And in the field of planning, the concept of a neighborhood planner was just being discussed and promoted in the literature. While it was touted as a good idea, there were seldom the resources at that level to hire one. The Community 21 leaders of NCO made the commitment to secure those resources. Hillenbrand had gotten to know me from Community 21 committee work, and as a parishioner of St. Boniface. He cast the deciding vote to hire me.

[240] "Erie's Neighborhood: West Town in the 1980s," a 4-page report found in CHM Box 13, File #6.

[241] CHM Box 12, File # 6

[242] Interview with Merri Ex, 10/2/2018.

[243] CHM Box 7, File # 6

[244] Ibid.

[245] Ibid.

[246] Ibid.

[247] Bob Daily, "The House on Erie Street," *Reader,* February 22, 1980

[248] Ibid.

[249] Special edition of BPI magazine, 1980.

[250] Hank De Zutter, "A Cold Christmas in West Town: God help us every one." *Reader,* December 19, 1980

[251] CHM Box 12, File #8

[252] Ibid.

[253] CHM Box 12, File #8.

[254] CHM Box 14, File #4

[255] Ibid.

[256] Cited in CHM Box 13, File # 6

[257] E-Box 5, File #2

[258] Ibid.

[259] Interview, 10/2/2018

[260] Jirasek, Rita Arias and Carlos Tortolero. *Mexican Chicago, 51.*

[261] Ganz, Cheryl R. and Margaret Strobel, editors. *Pots of Promise: Mexicans and Pottery at Hull House, 1920-1940.* Chicago and Urbana: University of Illinois Press, 2004.

262 Arredondo & Vaillant, 532-534

263 See Arias-Jirasek and Tortolero, in *Mexican Chicago.*

264 Holli, p. 347

265 Holli, p. 353

266 De Jesus said this when he was Executive Director of Latinos United in Chicago, 1991-2001. In 2019, he was Director of Special Housing Initiatives at Northeastern Illinois University.

267 Interview with Rafael Ravelo, 2/26/2018

268 CHM Box 6, File #1

269 Ibid.

270 CHM Box 13, File # 6

271 Ibid.

272 CHM Box 8, File # 13

273 Kyle, *"Los Preciosos"*

275 E-Box 3, File # 16

276 It eventually moved to Lincoln Square, into the old Hild Library on Lincoln Avenue

277 CHM Box 12, File #8

278 E-Box 2, File # 8

279 CHM Box 12, File # 8

280 CHM Box 4, File #11

281 Ibid.

282 CHM Box 3, File #8

283 CHM Box 14, File #2

284 Ibid.

285 CHM Box 3, File # 8

286 CHM Box 6, File #13

287 Ibid.

288 Ibid.

289 E-Box 1, File #4

290 CHM Box 12, File # 8

291 *Chicago Neighborhood Experiment* (CNE) Report, p. 7

292 CNE Report

293 CHM Box 12, File #8

294 *Chicago Neighborhood Experiment Report*

295 Ibid.

296 CHM Box 14, File #2

297 Ibid.

298 John McCarron, *Chicago Tribune,* Sept. 5, 1990

299 Ibid.

300 CHM Box 4, File # 1

[301] When he approached me about the job, he explained that he wanted someone he could trust to follow through on goals for improved employment opportunities and affordable housing options, during the year he would be away on his fellowship. I began on a part time basis as I was finishing up my dissertation, and moved on to full time in 1993.

[302] CHM Box 7, File #9

[303] When I accepted the job at Erie as the new Director of Community Economic Development (CED), I was transitioning from seven years of work at CNT, and was already familiar with the CMHN, as well as CNT's Tenant Ownership Project (TOP).

[304] Freedberg, Michael and Gail Schecter. "The Tenant Ownership Project: Preserving Affordable Housing through Alternative Ownership Strategies for Low-income Families," December, 1991.

[305] I lived on Chestnut Street at that time, just west of the expressway, and happened to be home that day. I heard and felt the explosions.

[306] It was based on a concept paper I had developed while working for them, naming the idea "Adjacent Neighbor Acquisition" (ANA), and ideas I had laid out in a project I had done with Art Lyons at UIC, even earlier, that we called "The Vacant Lot: Obstacle or Opportunity."

[307] Both known to me from my time at CNT.

[308] CHM Box 13, File # 19

[309] E-Box 3, File # 15

[310] Ibid.

[311] CHM Box 12, File # 8

[312] This information was included in the EFHC's own capital campaign brochure, "Commitment to Care", found in CHM Box 8, File #8

[313] CHM Box 12, File #8

[314] Ibid.

[315] E-Box 4, File #18

[316] Figures gathered from various files in the CHM boxes

[317] CHM Box 12, File #8

[318] Ibid.

[319] CHM Box 12, File #1

[320] CHM Box 8, File # 6

[321] CHM Box 7, File # 11

[322] CHM Box 7, File # 10

[323] Ibid.

[324] Ibid.

[325] I had worked in many campaigns for independent candidates over the years, and these were the rubrics.

[326] Garza, Melita Maria. "Erie vote: Blueprint for a fight," *Chicago Tribune,* January 23, 1995, CHM Box 14, File #3.

[327] Neal, Steve. *Commentary, Chicago Tribune,* January 23, 1995. CHM Box 14, File #3.

[328] CHM Box 7, File #10

[329] Garza, March 17, 1995.

[330] CHM Box 14, File #3

[331] Ibid.

[332] CHM Box 12, File #11

[333] Ravelo Interview

[334] Credit cards were invented in 1950, but became more widespread in 1958, when the Visa card became available. So, Erie, like many non-profits, was playing catch-up.

[335] CHM Box 11, File # 10

[336] CHM Box 14, File #3

[337] CHM Box 4, File #1

[338] CHM Box 12, File #10

[339] CHM Box 11, File #10

[340] CHM Box 14, File #3

[341] CHM Box 9, File # 3

[342] CHM Box 14, File # 3

[343] CHM Box 6, File # 15

[344] CHM Box 9, File #3

[345] So, it was with a heavy heart, on many levels, that I was leaving Erie House to take a position as Coordinator of the Policy Research Action Group (PRAG) at Loyola University Chicago's Center for Urban Research and Learning (CURL) in January, 1997.

[346] Interview with Nieves, 6/28/19

[347] CHM Box 12, File #11

[348] CHM Box 14, File # 1

[349] I believe this was a unique event in Chicago at the time.

[350] CHM Box 9, File #2

[351] E-Box 1, File #1

[352] CHM Box 14, File # 3

[353] When I left Erie House at the end of 1996, it was to start a new job as the Coordinator of PRAG, the Policy Research Action Group, an organization set up to foster university/community partnerships. As a former employee of Erie House, I did what I could to make one or more of those partnerships included Erie. *PRAGmatics* was a publication of PRAG.

[354] CHM Box 14, File #3

[355] E-Box 4, File #10

[356] E-Box 1, File #1

[357] CHM Box 14, File # 5

[358] CHM Box 12, File # 8

---

[359] E-Box 2, File # 9

[360] Ibid.

[361] E-Box 4, File # 41

[362] E-Box 4, File #4

[363] Ibid.

[364] Of the 96 names on the list, I knew or had worked with 32; 6 of them still worked at Erie in 2018.

[365] E-Box 4, File # 3

[366] Ibid.

[367] Ibid.

[368] Betancur, "Gentrification in West Town: Contested Ground."

[369] E-Box 4, File # 3

[370] Ibid.

[371] This was the third time Commons had moved their headquarters. A fourth move would locate the HQ on the south side, at 515 E. 50th Street, in 2012.

[372] In 2014, Onward House sold its property at Leavitt and Ohio and moved to Belmont-Cragin

[373] E-Box 4, File #3

[374] E-Box 1, File # 1

[375] E-Box 5, File #16

[376] E-Box 4, File #3

[377] He may have had additional insight on Erie's history, and potential value-added, given he was married to Maria de Los Angeles Torres, herself a Pedro Pan child and friend of former executive director, Rafael Ravelo.

[378] E-Box 4, File #4

[379] E-Box 5, File #16

[380] CHM Box 12, File # 8

[381] E-Box 5, File # 16

[382] Ibid.

[383] CHM Box 12, File # 7

[384] E-Box 5, File #16

[385] E-Box 2, File # 1

[386] These figures were gathered from a variety of sources in the Erie archives.

[387] E-Box 2, File #1

[388] E-Box 2, File #10

[389] Beginning in 2010, board minutes are saved as electronic files. The Christmas ale donation is cited in the minutes from Erie's board meeting, January 22, 2013.

[390] I served on that committee and also worked to bring resources from Loyola University, where I was working at the time, into the project. More on that in Chapter 8.

[391] E-Box 5, File # 17

[392] Ibid.

[393] Interview with Estrada, August, 2019

[394] E-Box 5, File # 19

[395] E-Box 5, File # 17b

[396] Reported in an interview 7/30/2019

[397] E-Box 5, File # 9

[398] Paral, Ready, et al. *Latino Demographic Growth in Metro Chicago,* Institute for Latino Studies, University of Notre Dame, December, 2004

[399] Ibid., 20

[400] Ready, Brown-Gort, *The State of Latino Chicago: This is Home Now,* Institute for Latino Studies, University of Notre Dame, 2005

[401] Ready et. al.

[402] E-Box 5, File #17

[403] E-Box 5, File # 17

[404] *Church & Society,* January-February, 2003, 56-61

[405] CHM Box 9, File # 2

[406] E-Box 5, File # 17

[407] E-Box 4, File # 27

[408] E-Box 2, File # 9

[409] E-Box 4, File #4

[410] Years later, NCLR changes their name to "Unidos."

[411] E-Box 5, File # 21

[412] From NNCS literature

[413] Ibid.

[414] E-Box 4, File #4

[415] E-Box 5, File # 23

[416] E-Box 4, File #25

[417] As a member of the Heritage Committee, and serving on the faculty of Loyola University, I was in a position to tap resources at Loyola to assist in fleshing out Erie's history.

[418] A list of 10 research papers that Dr. Mooney-Melvin's US Local History class produced, can be found in the appendix. [See pp. 600-608 in Text doc]

[419] A list of interviewees appears in the appendix. [see p. 424 in Text doc.]

[420] E-Box 2, File # 9

[421] Ibid.

[422] Ibid.

[423] Ibid.

[424] Ibid.

[425] E-Box 5, File #27

[426] Ibid.

[427] E-Box 4, File # 28

[428] Ibid.

[429] Garcia had served as an alderman during the Harold Washington administration. Later he secured a seat as a State Senator in the Illinois legislature. In 2010 he was elected to the Cook County Board from the 7th District, and in 2018 he won a seat in the US House, replacing retiring Representative Luis Gutierrez.

[430] E-Box 5, File # 30

[431] Ibid.

[432] Report authored by Beatriz Ponce de León. Quoted in E-Box 4, File # 29

[433] Avila, Oscar. "City's future tied to Mexicans." *Chicago Tribune,* September 13, 2006.

[434] E-Box 1, File # 1

[435] Ibid.

[436] E-Box 5, File #33

[437] Ponce de León, Beatriz. *A Shared Future: The Economic Engagement of Greater Chicago and Its Mexican Community.*

[438] E-Box 1, File #1

[439] E-Box 5, File #36

[440] Having grown up with Star Trek, I often found myself sitting at my desk, muttering "Space – the final frontier."

[441] By 2019, Alvarez was serving as Director of the 2020 Census for the State of Illinois

[442] Ann Seng, my own mentor, had her hand in this, as she had in many other good things that helped poor people, people of color, and women in Chicago do better. She was the one who had partnered with Rafael Ravelo and Erie House in the 1980s to conceptualize the ideas contained in "The Chicago Experiment" report. And, the School Sisters of St. Francis was the order of sisters that partnered with Erie House in the days of Ross Lyman and NCO.

[443] She recruited and trained me, as I worked for the Hull House Association twice, at their Uptown Center before moving on two terms at Erie House.

[444] E-Box 5, File #42

[445] Ibid.

[446] E-Box 5, File #44

[447] E-Box 5, File #47

[448] As was laid out in an article in *The Wall Street Journal,* dated January 11, 2006, and entitled "Catch 'Em Young," by James H. Heckman, cited on p. 294 in this text

[449] "Transition," Ric Estrada's final report to the Erie board, January, 2010.

[450] Ibid.

[451] E-Box 5, File #52

[452] I was working at Loyola University then, and doing my second tour of duty on the Erie House Board. I had been around long enough to know who her dad was, and was impressed that Erie had hired someone from a distinguished Chicago Puerto Rican family. Later, I would serve alternately as her boss and her employee.

[453] We developed a good working relationship, and she paid me the highest of compliments when she said she did not think anyone could measure up to Sandy as a supervisor, but I had passed the bar. Even after she became executive director in 2010, she would sometimes smile and greet me in the hall with "Hi, boss." While that was said with humor, it also reflects a characteristic one wants to see – a settlement house leader should be a "servant leader," with a recognition of those who work for you as neither above nor below, but on the team, regardless of their title.

[454] E-Box 5, File # 52

[455] Ibid.

[456] Executive Director's report to the board, September, 2010, Erie electronic files

[457] Ibid.

[458] Interview, September 7, 2019

[459] Board Minutes, May 23, 2011, Erie electronic files.

[460] From Executive Director Report to the Board, November 22,2010, E-Box 5, File #52

[461] No doubt the software has changed by now, but the goal remains the same.

[462] This comment and others like it were all part of the Ravelo "legend."

[463] May 23,2013 board report

[464] Notes from ENH Board Meeting, September 24, 2013, from Erie digital files.

[465] Board Notes, Erie digital files.

[466] Then there were those who came, went, and came back, like me, who worked at Erie for a total of 15 years, but in two different decades. Herbert Moreno did the same.

[467] Interview, 9/13/19

[468] 2014 was the year that I retired, in my 9th year of my second round of employment at Erie House.

[469] ENH Board Notes, Erie digital files.

[470] Interview with Celena Roldan, September 7,2019

[471] Appearance on WTTW's *Chicago Tonight,* June 20, 2019

[472] With its strong foundation and wisdom of many years, my money is on them to figure this out. As I used to say to my staff as they faced a difficult challenge: "Fingers crossed; candles lit." (Older Catholics will understand the reference to lighting vigil lights as a practice to complement the prayer of petition.)

[473] CHM Box 4, File #1

[474] Rohr, *The Universal Christ*, p. 16

[475] I have observed, sat next to, and worked for an Erie Board over a 50-year period.

[476] CHM Box 14, File #2

[477] Keating, *Juliette Kinzie,* 204.

SELECTED BIBLIOGRAPHY

Addams, Jane. "Social Settlements in Illinois," *An Illinois Reader,* ed., Clyde C. Walton. De Kalb: Northern Illinois University Press, 1970.

Addams, Jane. *Twenty Years at Hull-House,* 1909. Signet Classics edition, 1961. Reprinted 2009.

Andreas, Alfred T. *History of Chicago, Volume 3, 1872-1875.*

"Area Home Values Climb." *Chicago Sun-Times,* August 4, 1991.

Arredondo, Gabriela & Derek Vaillant. *Mexicans. Encyclopedia of Chicago, 532-534.*

Avila, Oscar. "City's future tied to Mexicans." *Chicago Tribune,* September 13,2006.

Betancur, John. "Gentrification in West Town: Contested Ground." UIC, December, 2001.

Bowen, Louise DeKoven. *Growing Up with a City.* Originally published: New York: Macmillan, 1926. Reprinted in 2002 by University of Illinois Press: Chicago and Urbana, with introduction by Maureen Flanagan.

Boyle, Brian. *Chicago.* New York: Thomas Dunne Books, St. Martin's Press, 2016.

Brehm, Bob. "Keeping the Jobs in House." *Shelterforce,* October 2, 2014.

Candeloro, Dominic. *Italians in America.* Images of America Series. Chicago: Arcadia Publishing. 1999.

Carson, Mina. *Settlement Folk: Social Thought and the American Settlement Movement, 1885-1930.* Chicago: University of Chicago Press, 1990.

"Classes pose hurdle for new immigrants." *The Chicago Reporter,* January, 1990.

Cohen, Adam & Elizabeth Taylor. *American Pharaoh.* Boston: Little, Brown & Company, 2001.

Cook, Frederick F. *Bygone Days in Chicago.* Chicago: A.C. McClurg & Co., 1910.

Daily, Bob. "The House on Erie Street," *Reader,* February 22, 1980.

Davis, Allen F. *American Heroine: The Life and Legend of Jane Addams.* 1973

Davis, Allen F. *Spearheads for Reform: The Social Settlement Movement and the Progressive Movement, 1890-1914.* Rutgers University Press, 1985.

Deegan, Mary Jo. *Jane Addams and the Men of the Chicago School, 1892-1918.* New Brunswick: Transaction Publishers, 1988.

Detzer, Karl. "Why Chicago Feted Mrs. Savino," *Readers Digest,* October, 1949.

De Zutter, Hank. "A Cold Christmas in West Town: God help us every one." *Reader,* December 19, 1980.

Dietrich, Jean. "Meals on Wheels Brings Cheer to the Needy" *Chicago Sun-Times,* March 11, 1962.

Encyclopedia of Chicago. Edited by James R. Grossman, Ann Durkin Keating, and Janice Reiff, and developed by The

Newberry Library with the cooperation of The Chicago Historical Society. University of Chicago Press, 2004.

Erie Neighborhood House Archives, Chicago History Museum (CHM), 14 boxes.

Erie Neighborhood House Archives, temporarily at 1701 W. Superior, E-Boxes, 6 boxes.

"Erie Neighborhood House Cleans Up Dirty Alleys." *Chicago Daily News,* March 4, 1939.

Fitzpatrick, Rita. "Erie House – the Story of a Great Venture." *Chicago Tribune,* November 10, 1945.

Fix, Michael, Demetrios Papademetrious, Betsy Cooper. *Leaving Too Much to Chance: A Roundtable on Immigrant Integration Policy.* Migration Policy Institute, 2005.

Freedberg, Michael and Gail Schecter. "The Tenant Ownership Project: Preserving Affordable Housing through Alternative Ownership Strategies for Low-income Families," December, 1991.

Ganz, Cheryl R. and Margaret Strobel, editors. *Pots of Promise: Mexicans and Pottery at Hull House, 1920-1940.* Chicago and Urbana: University of Illinois Press, 2004.

Garza, Melita Maria. "Erie vote: Blueprint for a fight," *Chicago Tribune,* January 23, 1995.

Gonzáles, Mirza L. *Cubans, Encyclopedia of Chicago, 222-223.*

Gottschall, Bruce. "Bickerdike, The Early Years: Building the Base, 1966-1974. An unpublished paper prepared for Bickerdike Redevelopment Corp. on the occasion of their 50th anniversary in 2017.

Granacki, Victoria. *Chicago's Polish Downtown.* Images of America Series. Chicago: Arcadia Publishing, 2004.

Grimshaw, William. *Bitter Fruit: Black Politics and the Chicago Machine, 1931-1991*. Chicago: The University of Chicago Press, 1992.

Gutiérrez, Luis with Doug Scofield. *Still Dreaming: My Journey from the Barrio to Capitol Hill*. New York: W. W. Norton & Company, 2013.

Harrington, Janette. "Antidote for Delinquency." *Presbyterian Life*, May 15, 1962.

Hayes, Frank L. "Erie House Head on the Job for 25 Years," *Chicago Daily News*, February 12, 1951.

Holli, Melvin and Peter d'A. Jones, Editors. *Ethnic Chicago*. Grand Rapids, Michigan: William B. Eerdmans Publishing Company, 1995.

Horwitt, Sanford D. *Let Them Call Me Rebel*. New York: Vintage Books, Division of Random House, Inc., 1993.

Informal History of Northwestern University Settlement Association, 1891-1991

Jacobs, Jane. *The Death and Life of Great American Cities*. New York: Vintage Books, A Division of Random House, 1992. (First published in 1961)

Jirasek, Rita Arias and Carlos Tortolero. *Mexican Chicago*. Images of America Series. Chicago: Arcadia Publishing, 2001.

Keating, Ann Durkin. *The World of Juliette Kinzie: Chicago before the Fire*. Chicago: The University of Chicago Press, 2019.

Kunze, Carr. "Mutual Housing Associations: Expanding Housing Cooperative Potentials," *Cooperative Housing Journal*, December 14, 1990.

Malone, Tara. "Economy's fate rests on immigrants, study says." *Daily Herald,* September 16,2006.

Mehta, Chirag, Nik Theodore, Iliana Mora, and Jennifer Wade. *Chicago's Undocumented Immigrants: An Analysis of Wages, Working Conditions, and Economic Contributions.* UIC/CUED, Feb. 2002.

McCarron, John. "For 120 years, Erie House has soothed the unsettled." *Chicago Tribune,* Sept. 5, 1990.

Northwest Community Organization (NCO) Archives, Chicago History Museum.

Neal, Steve. *Commentary, Chicago Tribune,* January 23, 1995.

Nelli, Humbert S. *The Italians in Chicago, 1880-1930.* New York: Oxford University Press, 1970.

Nelson, Bruce. *Beyond the Martyrs: A Social History of Chicago's Anarchists, 1870-1900.* New Brunswick, NJ, 1988.

Pacyga, Dominic. *Poles, Encyclopedia of Chicago, 623-626.*

Pacyga, Dominic. *Polish Immigrants and Industrial Chicago.* Chicago: University of Chicago Press, 1994.

Paral, Rob, et al. *Economic Growth & Immigration: Bridging the Demographic Divide.* Immigration Policy Center. November, 2005.

Paral, Rob and Timothy Ready. *The Economic Progress of US and Foreign-Born Mexicans in Metro Chicago: Indications from the United States Census.* Institute for Latino Studies, University of Notre Dame, May, 2005.

Pérez, Gina M. *The Near Northwest Side Story: Migration, Displacement, and Puerto Rican Families.* Berkeley: University of California Press, 2004.

Peterson, Kurt. *Forum, Dialoging with the Covenant Quarterly.* No date, but after 2003. See http://forum.covquarterly.com.

Poethig, Richard. "Toward Worldwide Industrial Mission: The Presbyterian Story, 1945-1975." *American Presbyterians,* Vol. 73, #1, Spring, 1995.

Ponce de León, Beatriz. *A Shared Future: The Economic Engagement of Greater Chicago and Its Mexican Community.* A Report of an Independent Task Force, co-chaired by Douglas Doetsch, Clare Muñana, & Alejandro Silva, and sponsored by The Chicago Council on Global Affairs, 2006.

Ramirez, Leonard G. *Chicanas of 18th Street.* Chicago and Urbana: University of Illinois Press, 2011.

Randle, Wilma. "Lots of eyes on day-care expansion try," *Chicago Tribune*, February 10, 1993.

Ready, Timothy Ready, & Allert Brown-Gort, *The State of Latino Chicago: This is Home Now,* Institute for Latino Studies, University of Notre Dame, 2005.

Rohr, Richard. *The Universal Christ.* New York: Convergent Books, 2019.

Rothstein, Richard. *The Color of Law.* New York: Liveright Publishing Corp., A Division of W.W. Norton & Company, 2017.

Sachdev, Ameet. "Gardner Carton set to merge," *Chicago Tribune,* November 14, 2006.

Stebner, Eleanor J. *The Women of Hull House: A Study in Spirituality, Vocation, and Friendship.* New York: State University of New York Press, 1997.

Stockwell, Clinton. "Standing on the Shoulders of Giants: The Protestant Legacy of Urban Social Justice in Chicago." *PRAGmatics, Vol 1, No. 3, Fall, 1998.*

Suenens, Cardinal Leon Joseph. *The Nun in the World: Religious and the Apostolate.* Newman Press, 1963.

Supple, James. "Erie House – It's Neighborliness in Action," *Chicago Sun-Times,* March 8, 1950.

Tjoelker, Elizabeth. "A Neighbor Among Neighbors: Erie Neighborhood House and the Presbyterian Church of Chicago, 1870-1990." Unpublished Master's Project, Loyola University Chicago, 2004.

Towne, Florence H. *Neighbors.* Chicago: Published by the Board of Directors of Erie Neighborhood House, 1940.

Towne, Florence H. *Sheep of the Outer Fold.* Chicago: Fleming H. Revell Company, 1929.

Uribe, Laurina and Kate Pravera. *A Community Inventory: The Southeast Section of West Town, a report of the Chicago Neighborhood Experiment.* Published by Erie Neighborhood House & The Chicago Council of Urban Affairs, March, 1990.

Vecoli, Rudolph F. *Italians, Encyclopedia of Chicago, 429-430.*

Wallis, Jim. *America's Original Sin: Racism, White Privilege, and the Bridge to a New America.* Grand Rapids, Michigan: Brazos Press, 2016.

Author Maureen Hellwig

Maureen Hellwig is a lifelong Chicagoan. She is a fan of her hometown, with so much to offer, but also a student of its history and critic of its flaws. She is the great-great-granddaughter of Irish and German immigrants, and her mom and dad grew up on the same block. While she is quite a few generations removed from her origins, she has kept her roots in mind while working with more recent immigrants during her time spent as both a volunteer and an employee at Erie Neighborhood House. It was that rich experience that inspired her to write this history, as this settlement house celebrates its